Political Oppositions in Industrialising Asia

In the light of sweeping social and economic transformations across Asia, some political commentators have predicted that the expansion of civil society and the rapid development of liberal democracy will necessarily follow. But the scenarios may be more complex. This book reveals the diversity of political oppositions in Asia, including analyses of the nature of the social movements and organisations outside institutional party politics which are contesting the exercise of state power.

Studies range from Garry Rodan's analysis of non-governmental organisations and the formal opponents of the PAP in Singapore to He Baogang's scrutiny of Chinese dissidents based outside the People's Republic of China. All take up the challenge of looking at political opposition in the light of the new social phenomenon of the rising middle class or 'New Rich' of Asia.

Rodan's hard-hitting analysis of the problems of current political theorising in relation to Asia sets the case studies firmly in the midst of the latest debates about democratisation. *Political Oppositions in Industrialising Asia* shatters complacent assumptions about the progress of liberal democracy.

Garry Rodan is Senior Research Fellow at the Asia Research Centre, Murdoch University.

The New Rich in Asia Series

Edited by David S.G. Goodman and Richard Robison

Who are the new rich of Asia? This new series from the Asia Research Centre at Murdoch University will examine questions of political and social development by analysing the phenomenon of the rising middle class in East and Southeast Asia. The first book, *The New Rich in Asia*, sets the scene for later studies which will include work on political opposition and on sex and power in Asia. Edited by David S. G. Goodman, Director of the Institute for International Studies, University of Technology, Sydney, and Richard Robison, Director of the Asia Research Centre, Murdoch University, this series brings together experts from the region and beyond.

The New Rich in Asia
Mobile phones, McDonalds and middle-class revolution
Edited by Richard Robison and David S.G. Goodman

Political Oppositions in Industrialising Asia

Edited by Garry Rodan

London and New York

This book is a project of the Asia Research Centre, Murdoch University, Western Australia

First published 1996
by Routledge

2 Park Square, Milton Park. Abingdon, Oxon, OX14 4RN

711 Third Avenue, New York, NY 10017

*Routledge is an imprint of the Taylor & Francis Group,
an informa business*

Typeset in Times by
Ponting-Green Publishing Services, Chesham, Bucks

British Library Cataloguing in Publication Data
A catalogue record for this book is available from the
British Library.

Library of Congress Cataloguing in Publication Data
Rodan, Garry, 1955-
    Political oppositions in industrialising Asia / Garry Rodan.
        p. cm. – (New rich in Asia)
    ISBN 0-415-14864-2. - ISBN 0-415-14865-0 (pbk.)
        1. Opposition (Political science)-Asia.   2. Political
    participation-Asia.   3. Industrialization-Political
    aspects-Asia.   4. Asia-Politics and government-1945-
    1. Title.   II. Series.
    JQ36.R63   1996
    324'.095-dc20   96-3329
                                                         CIP

ISBN 0-415-14864-2 (hbk)
ISBN 0-415-14865-0 (pbk)

CONTENTS

Illustrations

Contributors

Edward Aspinall is a Ph.D. candidate in the Department of Political and Social Change at the Research School of Pacific and Asian Studies, Australian National University, Canberra. He has published work on contemporary politics in Indonesia in the journal *Indonesia*.

Anita Chan is an Australian Research Centre Fellow at the Contemporary China and Korea Centre of the Australian National University, Canberra. She is co-editor of *The China Journal* (formerly the *Australian Journal of Chinese Affairs*) and editor of the translation journal *Chinese Sociology and Anthropology*, as well as author of *Children of Mao* (University of Washington Press) and joint author of *Chen Village Under Mao and Deng* (University of California Press) and a book in Chinese, *Symbolism and Undercurrents: the 1989 Mass Movement*. Her current research focuses on changing industrial relations in the People's Republic of China.

James Cotton is professor of political science at the University of Tasmania, Hobart. He is editor of *Politics in the New Korea State* (St Martin's Press, 1995) and *Korea Under Roh Tae-woo* (Allen & Unwin, 1993), and author of *Asian Frontier Nationalism* (Manchester University Press, 1989). He has held positions at the Australian National University, the National University of Singapore, the University of Newcastle upon Tyne, and the University of Western Australia.

Bronwen Dalton was, at the time of writing this volume, Assistant Director of the National Korean Studies Centre. She has also lectured in Korean politics at Swinburne University of Technology and in Korean language at the University of Melbourne. Currently she is a D.Phil. candidate at St Hugh's College, University of Oxford.

He Baogang is Lecturer in Politics in the Department of Political Science, University of Tasmania, and author of *The Democratization of*

1996) China (Routledge, 1996). He has co-authored and co-translated several books, including a Chinese translation of John Rawls's *A Theory of Justice*, and has published extensively in journals such as *The Australian Journal of Political Science, Social Philosophy and Policies, Journal of Contemporary China, Thesis Eleven, China Information, The Current World Leaders*, and *Issues and Studies*. In 1995 he was awarded the Mayer Prize by the Australian Political Science Association for the best article published in its journal.

Ariel Heryanto was until recently a Lecturer in the Postgraduate Program, Development Studies at Universitas Kristen Satya Wacana, Indonesia. Currently he writes as a freelance columnist for several major dailies and news magazines in Indonesia. He authored *Language of Development and Development of Language* (Pacific Linguistics), contributed to and edited *Perdebatan Sastra Kontekstual* (Rajawali), and has written chapters for several volumes and articles in journals on diverse topics, including the middle classes, student movements, postmodernism, nationalism, ethnicity, media, lifestyle, language, and ideology.

Kevin Hewison is Foundation Professor of Asian Languages and Societies at the University of New England, Armidale, New South Wales, and a fellow of the Asia Research Centre at Murdoch University, Western Australia. He has held other positions at universities in Thailand, Australia and Papua New Guinea and has been a consultant to a number of agencies in Thailand, Vietnam and the Lao PDR. He is the author of *Bankers and Bureaucrats* (Yale) and *Power and Politics in Thailand* (Journal of Contemporary Asia Publishers), joint author of *Village Life in Thailand: Culture and Transition in the Northeast* (Mooban Press), and joint editor of *Southeast Asia in the 1980s* (Allen & Unwin) and *Southeast Asia in the 1990s* (Allen & Unwin). He is also a contributor to journals, including *Journal of Contemporary Asia, Asian Survey, Bulletin of Concerned Asian Scholars, World Politics, Tiers Monde*, and *The Pacific Review*.

James V. Jesudason is Lecturer in Sociology at the National University of Singapore. He is the author of *Ethnicity and the Economy: the State, Chinese Business, and Multinationals in Malaysia* (Oxford University Press) and has published various articles on civil society, politics, and ethnicity in Malaysia. His current research interests include democratisation and state–market interactions in Southeast and East Asia.

Shelley Rigger is Assistant Professor in Politics at Davidson College, North Carolina. She recently completed a Ph.D. on institutional reform and electoral politics in Taiwan and has written on contemporary politics in Taiwan for academic journals, including *Issues and Studies*.

Garry Rodan is Senior Research Fellow of the Asia Research Centre at Murdoch University, Western Australia. He is on leave from Murdoch University's Politics Programme where he is a senior lecturer. He is author of *The Political Economy of Singapore's Industrialisation* (Macmillan and St Martin's Press), editor of *Singapore Changes Guard* (Longman), and joint editor of *Southeast Asia in the 1990s* (Allen & Unwin).

Preface

Industrialisation and the growth of the middle classes in East and Southeast Asia have raised expectations for the extension of civil societies in this region. According to some writers, the social transformations sweeping industrialising Asia spell the beginning of the end for authoritarian rule. In this view, social pluralism will sooner or later translate into political pluralism and the margin for political opposition, notably in the form of political parties, will widen accordingly. But *Political Oppositions in Industrialising Asia* suggests that the endeavours to establish greater space for political parties, and civil societies that feed into these organisations, are only part of the attempts to extend the avenues for contesting state power. Indeed, forces unconnected to the formal political process and often outside civil society are in many cases central to political oppositions influencing directions in these societies. Furthermore, where civil society is being extended, this is the work of a variety of social and political forces with divergent agendas. The common equation in much of the literature that links the expansion of civil society with the advance of liberal democracy is certainly questioned in this collection of essays.

The volume is introduced in Chapter 1 through a survey of theoretical debates and issues pertaining to political oppositions in general and in East and Southeast Asia in particular. This discussion is intended to expose the reader to a number of propositions and arguments for reflection and consideration throughout the subsequent reading of this book. Various points in this chapter centre on an appeal for recognition of the diverse forms and significances of political oppositions, especially those outside the realms of institutionalised party politics. A careful differentiation of the various political elements of emerging civil societies in industrialising Asia is also urged, so that elitist and authoritarian strands of civil society are also rendered visible. Furthermore, I argue that the expansion of civil society is a particular form of political accommodation by the state to emerging social forces, and that other responses, including a reformulation and consolidation of the state itself, are possible – either in conjunction with or instead of an expansion of civil society.

In Chapter 2, Hewison and Rodan challenge the prevailing association of civil society with advanced economic development, pointing out that within Southeast Asia some of the more vibrant periods of civil society occurred during times of comparatively rudimentary economic development. These periods were followed, however, by repressive state measures to close off independent political space. Their analysis is centred on a historical survey of extra-parliamentary political contestation and of the strategic role of the Left in these earlier episodes in civil society. However, the contemporary phase of political contestation has a distinct character: a wider variety of social forces, including elements of the emerging business and middle classes, and organisations giving expression to new interests and views. Importantly, these forces are essentially a source of political moderation and the Left's accustomed historical position of strategic leadership is absent.

In Chapter 3, on Thailand, Hewison argues that the advent of capitalist development has brought with it an expansion and diversification of business and middle classes with an ambiguous oppositional character. Their commitment to 'democratisation' is interest-driven and qualified. Parliamentary rule holds out the promise of keeping political activism disciplined, controlled, and within limits at the same time as curbing the arbitrariness of military rule. However, should the parliamentary regime fail to deliver a supportive economic climate, promoting business confidence and public transparency, it may abandon its support for it – even if it continues to oppose an authoritarian military regime.

In Chapter 4, I argue that in Singapore it is the extension of the state which is the prime political response to the increasingly diversified social forces accompanying rapid industrialisation. This has involved extensions and refinements to the mechanisms for political co-optation, many of which target a middle class that is a major beneficiary of the established elitist structures. But while the middle class may therefore be largely receptive to such overtures, there are also some limited and tentative attempts to establish independent political spaces. Importantly, though, avenues for organised, independent political contestation by, and on behalf of, the underprivileged in Singapore remain extremely difficult. Concerns about widening material inequalities have translated into increased electoral support for formal opponents of the ruling People's Action Party. These parties are, however, limited structures and will continue to be so in the absence of a civil society with which to connect.

In his analysis of Malaysia in Chapter 5, Jesudason also cautions against underestimating the capacity of the contemporary state to adjust to social and economic change. In particular, he contends that Malaysia has a 'syncretic state' which frames the nature of opposition; political opposition is, according to Jesudason, a refraction of the syncretic state. The syncretic state, he argues, is a particular historical configuration which combines democratic procedures and coercive practices to absorb the diverse ideological orientations and interests ensuing from social transformations. Ideologies of ethnicity and religion are central elements of the process which militates against effective oppositional coalitions inside and outside party politics. Those social organisations in which ethnicity has been least central as an organising principle, and which have exerted an impact in fostering public debate on government policy, have had significant middle-class involvement and leadership: lawyers and other professionals attempting to advance concerns about civil rights, environmental degradation, women's rights, corruption, and the social consequences of economic development. However, Jesudason sees these as limited and moderate political forces and argues that only with an unlikely loss of coherence within the ruling United Malay National Organisation (UMNO) and the syncretic state is significant political change possible.

In Chapter 6, Chan shows how emerging social forces from the middle and business classes are forming new political oppositions in China. However, rather than being a possible omen for a general political liberalisation, this development represents 'a grand coalition of elites' and an attempt to pre-empt more autonomous and organised political opposition. Essentially, intellectuals and entrepreneurs, whose technical knowledge and capital are important to the capitalist revolution under way, are afforded avenues to pursue their interests. They do this via the so-called 'Democratic Parties' (DPs) and the All China Federation of Industry and Commerce (ACFIC), both of which are represented in the National People's Congress and the Chinese People's Political Consultative Committee (CPPCC). These elements of the new rich have a common interest in political stability during the social upheavals involved in economic restructuring so adversely affecting millions of peasants and workers. Any aspirations for 'democracy' by this new rich are therefore limited to this social category.

In the subsequent chapter, He takes up the issue of a distinct category of oppositionists that has emerged since the advent of China's open door policy and proliferated after the 1989 Tiananmen Square incident:

the overseas opposition movement (OOM) of dissidents based outside China. The social base of these dissidents is narrow, since they almost exclusively comprise exiled students and scholars. However, particularly since 1989 the organisational bases of the movement have diversified considerably. In examining the OOM's links with China and a variety of international organisations, He considers the notion of a transnational civil society, concluding that the movement is not an unequivocal component of this because its preoccupations are about Chinese national issues. Nevertheless, the OOM exerts an influence over western governments' policies on China, even if it reaches a limited domestic Chinese audience. Like Chan, He emphasises that behind the rhetoric about democracy from these oppositionists lies a strong elitism.

The first of the two chapters on Indonesia, by Aspinall, maintains that political opposition now enjoys a broader base than in recent decades, with the corporatist state beginning to strain under the weight of a more socially diverse population. The expanding middle class is an important element of this and through various non-government organisations (NGOs) it has more organisational autonomy than in earlier periods of the New Order. However, labour activism has also emerged to complicate the task of state management of social forces. This unrest has converged with middle-class activism, with increasing organisational participation by students in these disputes, through a range of developmental NGOs. Attempts to build independent organisational bases within labour, in direct opposition to corporatist structures, continue to invite concerted state repression. However, this has not been entirely at the expense of corporatism, since Aspinall notes that avenues for collaboration with government have been extended for advocates of reformist, neo-populist economic development through the National Planning Board. Nor have opposition political parties been revived as a result of recent social transformations and associated attempts to develop civil society.

Heryanto's chapter on Indonesia echoes Jesudason's view on Malaysia, that significant political change in the foreseeable future is much more likely to be the result of tensions internal to the regime itself rather than enforced by opposition. Heryanto sees the New Order as a regime of declining hegemony and points to increasing public discontent as indicative of diminished political control. However, this discontent and public protestation are fragmented, and not harnessed by a counter-hegemonic leadership. Despite this overall assessment, Heryanto's analysis identifies the emergence of significant activism by both the middle and working classes in contemporary Indonesia. Significantly, the student movement is integrating itself with peasant and worker organisations, often via developmental and other NGOs. So the urban middle class is increasingly forming political coalitions with less privileged sectors, and playing a strategic role in labour activism. Nevertheless, Heryanto argues that these links are still *ad hoc*, often clandestine and insecure.

In their chapter on South Korea, Dalton and Cotton examine a case where electoral politics replaced an authoritarian military regime in 1987. Yet while the lead-up to this included radical labour and student movements, the post-1987 period has been characterised by a proliferation of diverse, and comparatively moderate, social movements. Part of the explanation for this lies in the failure of political parties to transcend the limitations associated with personality-based factionalism and regionalism – both of which curtail the capacity to respond to concerns of emerging social forces. New social movements (NSMs) championing environmental, feminist, consumer, and human rights causes have thus begun to exert a significant oppositional influence and assume a key role in debate over public policy. These movements are largely middle-class based, advocating a more balanced approach to industrial growth, social welfare, and the environment, but not calling into question the legitimacy of the political system itself. The portrayal by Dalton and Cotton of contemporary South Korea is therefore one of significantly increased political pluralism, though one that political parties have been unable to harness adequately.

Like the two chapters on Indonesia, Rigger's chapter on Taiwan explores the contemporary challenges to, and erosion of, established corporatist structures in the face of social transformations associated with industrialisation. These structures, referred to by Rigger as 'mobilisational authoritarianism', went beyond the incorporation of socio-economic interests to include municipal elites and prominent citizens through the sponsorship of local elections. The Kuomintang's broad cultivation of clientelistic networks cutting across class lines undermined broad-based oppositional movements or coalitions. This was compounded, argues Rigger, by the inextricable connection between advocacy of political reform and demands for ethnic justice for the majority of Taiwanese. However, Taiwan's economic development has translated into the growth of independent professionals, entrepreneurs, and employees of small-to-medium-sized enterprises (SME) beyond the corporatist clutches of the state. Marginalisation of some economic sectors due to restructuring, and assorted public concerns over environmental degradation, inflated housing prices, inadequate consumer safeguards and social welfare have further complicated political control. Thus, the 1980s witnessed a rapid expansion of social movements as the Republic of China (ROC) proved incapable of assimilating new social forces. Political parties in Taiwan have, however, been unable to capitalise on social and protest movements.

Political Oppositions in Industrialising Asia focuses on the impact on political oppositions of new social forces generated by industrialisation in East and Southeast Asia. Here 'political opposition' is understood to mean more than just political parties but to include social movements, non-government organisations, and social and cultural organisations that systematically attempt to influence public policy. The attempt in this volume to identify and analyse political oppositions from this perspective necessarily calls into question a number of influential theoretical assumptions in the literature. The study comes at a time, too, when arguments emphasising political contestation as alien to 'Asian culture' enjoy support in academic and popular debates. Yet this volume reveals the range and diversity of political contestations in East and Southeast Asia. Understanding the sources and natures of such contestations is essential to a comprehension of the political dynamics in these societies.

Garry Rodan

Acknowledgements

This project received funding support from the Asia Research Centre at Murdoch University and the assistance of various personnel at the administrative and production levels of the manuscript's preparation. For this I am grateful, as I am for the intellectual contribution of colleagues in the Centre and in the Politics Programme at Murdoch University to workshops and seminars tied with this project. Special thanks must go, however, to the following individuals for their contributions to the materialisation of this volume: Del Blakeway, Helen Bradbury, Kevin Hewison, Amanda Miller, Janet Payne, Richard Robison, and Robert Roche. To the contributors themselves, whose commitment and co-operation throughout the project were first rate, I am also thankful. Finally, as always, completing the task was assisted by the understanding and support of Jane Tarrant during the most demanding periods of the manuscript's preparation.

Garry Rodan

1 Theorising political opposition in East and Southeast Asia

*Garry Rodan**

INTRODUCTION

In the 1970s, political opposition in various parts of East and Southeast Asia was primarily characterised by peasant insurgencies and radical student movements questioning the very basis of the capitalist path to development. Their campaigns were often conducted outside constitutional processes. Since the mid-1980s, however, capitalism and industrialisation have firmly taken root in the region, and capitalism's ascendancy is not in question. As a consequence, the nature of political opposition, the forms through which it is conducted, and the actors involved have undergone a transformation. Extra-constitutional challenges are limited, and the predominant agendas of political oppositions in the region have decidedly narrowed to more reformist goals. The new reformers are drawn from new social forces generated by the very processes of rapid capitalist industrialisation, including elements from across a range of classes: bourgeois, middle, and working classes.[1] To differing extents and by varying means, they are shaping the contests over power in the region's dynamic societies.

Also since the mid-1980s, the demise of various dictatorships or military regimes and the establishment or resurrection of elections in Eastern Europe, Latin America, and Asia have prompted a spate of works questioning the long-term viability of authoritarian rule in general. A host of writers began enthusiastically documenting and analysing what was generally characterised as 'democratisation'. A significant component of this literature involves reconsideration of the relationship between economic development and political change. This has been fuelled to no small degree by recent political transformations in the newly industrialising countries (NICs), notably those of the comparatively mature industrial economies of South Korea, Taiwan, and Hong Kong. Would these winds of change soon be repeated in authoritarian societies elsewhere undergoing rapid industrialisation?

This question was answered with an enthusiastic affirmative by modernisation theorists whose credibility had taken a battering. Earlier they had depicted market economies and liberal democratic polities as mutually reinforcing, but the development experience of the late industrialising countries of Asia and Latin America had been at odds with this proposition. The sudden political upheavals provided an opportunity for these theorists to salvage something from the debate. To be sure, contemporary modernisation accounts of the causal link between capitalist development and political change are more sophisticated and qualified than previous attempts. They came in the wake of the influential thesis on transitions from authoritarian rule by O'Donnell and Schmitter (1986) and O'Donnell, Schmitter, and Whitehead (1986), which rejected any general theory of social or economic determination of political outcomes in favour of voluntarist approaches. These emphasised the importance of agency and processes of negotiation and strategy building. Variables such as culture, institutions, and political leadership, for example, are seen in the revised modernisation literature to complicate the forward march of 'democracy' and mediate the political effects of economic development (Pye 1985; Huntington 1991; Lipset 1993, 1990; Marks 1992; Diamond 1989, 1993; Case 1994).[2] The emphases vary somewhat within this framework, but economic development is nevertheless understood to generate fundamental changes in social structure, including the creation of an extensive and diverse middle class, that exert pressures for political pluralism. At the very least, authoritarian regimes will become increasingly difficult to reproduce, according to these analysts.

Modernisation theorists have not been alone in prophesying problems for authoritarian regimes experiencing the advent of accelerated economic development. Literature on 'developmental authoritarianism' argues that late-industrialising countries require a stage of authoritarian rule to kick start industrial growth, but after the initial phase this political regime constrains capitalism. Marxists have also argued that authoritarian regimes are ill-suited to the task of resolving friction between competing fractions of capital in more advanced phases of capital accumulation (Harris 1986). They, too, point to changing centres of economic and social power including a strategically important middle class of professionals and technicians who have economic independence from the state (Robison 1986). The attainment of bourgeois hegemony in the social and economic spheres lessens the need for coercive political structures.

Debates about the continued feasibility of authoritarian rule in late-industrialising countries have been influenced by broader events and intellectual trends. With the dramatic collapse of various East European socialist regimes, presiding over economic decay rather than economic buoyancy, the Cold War was suddenly defunct. For some, the momentous turn of events culminated in the unquestionable triumph of liberalism, a veritable end of history (Fukuyama 1992a). In this context, state-centred analyses came under fire for deflecting attention from important social phenomena which lay behind the unpredicted speed and extent of transformation in Eastern Europe. A related resurgence of analytical interest in the concept of civil society among liberal theorists has been joined by Marxists and other critical theorists looking beyond the state. The decline of state socialism brought with it disclosures about the extent of repression and abuse of office which embarrassed many socialist scholars. In political terms, this has led to a new emphasis on decentralisation and non-state forms of organisation. In analytical terms, it has steered theorists towards usages of the concept of civil society that differ significantly from Marx's own.

Against the above background, two very powerful themes are discernible in this vast body of literature on political change in late industrialising countries of East and Southeast Asia. The first of these is a propensity to equate the challenge to, or demise of, authoritarian rule with the advance of 'democracy'. This concept is generally employed unproblematically, but implicitly endorses a liberal democratic or formalistic definition of the term. For some writers, the existence of elections appears to be the benchmark of 'democracy', for others a more detailed conception of competitive party politics is articulated. But extra-parliamentary activity not servicing formal political institutions is under-theorised. At a time when popular participation and interest in political parties appear to have waned in established liberal democracies while social movements and interest associations disengaged from the formal political process gather momentum (see Schmitter and Karl 1991: 80), we should surely remain circumspect about oppositional forms elsewhere. Much of this literature is consistent with a linear conception of history, sitting comfortably with Fukuyama's notion of liberalism's imminent global triumph.

This does not mean that writers, including Fukuyama himself, have entirely dismissed the possibility that political change in late-industrialising countries of Asia or elsewhere might deviate from the liberal democratic model. But liberal democracy remains the point of reference for these analyses, deviations from it explained in terms of *obstacles* to this seemingly natural and irrepressible historical force. Of these 'obstacles', culture features thematically in the literature, and forms the basis of the prevailing attempts to conceptualise alternatives to liberal democracy. Ironically, such attempts resonate with the message of authoritarian leaders about 'Asian values'. This emphasises the 'differentness' of Asians and is employed to dismiss domestic political challenges as 'un-Asian' (Rodan 1995).

A second theme to the literature is a not unrelated romanticisation of civil society which is depicted as the natural domain of personal and group freedoms, implicitly contrasted with the state as a set of naturally coercive power relationships. There is often an unstated assumption attached to this that the rise of civil society is fundamentally a middle-class phenomenon. Civil society is championed not just for its supposed intrinsic merit as the locus of free-minded and mutually co-operative groups and individuals beyond the state's purvey, but more particularly as an essential precondition for political parties to be genuinely competitive and meaningful conduits of the popular will. This tendency in the literature downplays the significance of gross inequalities of power and resources that are to be found within civil society. It is the nature of civil society as much as the fact of it that matters to the prospect and direction of political change. Certainly not all opposition to authoritarian regimes in East and Southeast Asia is imbued with liberal democratic values or aspirations.

Moreover, the analytical and normative insistence on a state–civil society separation diverts attention from the critically important point that civil societies cannot exist as alternatives to states – only in relation to them. Civil society presupposes the state. The state provides the legal framework underwriting the independent political space of civil society. But attempts to reinforce or challenge the inequalities of civil society also involve the state in different ways – whether to enhance, consolidate, or diminish the power of particular social groups. The state–society divide is always a difficult one to make clearly, but different historical conditions have resulted in pervasive states in much of East and Southeast Asia which make these boundaries even more problematic than in Europe and North America. The prevailing assumption is that 'strong states', by definition, are associated with 'weak societies'. This is informed by the notion that civil societies, independent of the state, are the legitimate expression of society. But societal forces are to differing extents incorporated into the state and, especially in the East and Southeast Asian context, cannot be dismissed as political entities. Rather, here co-optation is a real alternative to representation and civil society which may in many cases prove the most significant political accommodation to social diversity.

Neither of these two dominant theoretical themes in the literature encourages a detailed examination of the nature of political change occurring in industrialising East and Southeast Asia. The contest between authoritarianism and liberal democracy is part of the political struggle unfolding in the region, but it is certainly not the entirety of it. Some of these struggles do involve attempts to expand the space of civil society, though not always from 'democratic' forces. They can include religious organisations, professional bodies, trade unions, or any of a host of non-government organisations (NGOs). But they can also involve attempts to establish space for political contestation in arenas other than civil society. Organised contests over particular exercises of official power can come from within state-sponsored organisations, even if this form of opposition is not oriented towards a change of government. Co-opting social forces is not unproblematic, even in one-party states, since this often targets groups precisely for fear of their potential as political opponents. Moreover, there is a conceptual limbo in the prevailing literature between civil society and state which conceals a wide variety of organised groups of differing political significance. The danger is that new forms of political organisation and reconstitutions of state–society relations which do not correspond with the liberal democratic model will escape adequate identification and analysis.

The emphasis on extra-parliamentary political activities suggests several types of 'opposition'. At one extreme, there is political opposition intended to change fundamentally the state and society, such as Communist or Islamic fundamentalist parties or movements. Another type of opposition seeks to change the government but not the state or society in any fundamental sense. Here we would include most oppositions identified by liberal pluralist theorists. Typically, such oppositions attempt to replace one political party in government with another. Finally, there are oppositions which pursue an agenda of reform or reaction within the state and the existing government. This can be conducted by factions within the bureaucracy, the military, or various social and cultural organisations brought under the umbrella of a corporatist state. It can also be conducted by various non-government organisations outside the state but not part of formal political protest. These include non-revolutionary trade unions, social and cultural organisations, for example, which pursue policy agendas without seeking to advance the cause of a particular political party or alternate government. The importance of the various types of opposition is related both to the capacity of the state to foreclose or foster particular avenues for opposition, and the degree to which contending groups accept the state or government as legitimate.

For historical reasons, the state–society relationship in East and

Southeast Asia contrasts in certain respects with the European experience, and this has important implications for political opposition. In much of East and Southeast Asia, the state serves as the midwife of industrial capitalism which involves a different relationship between it and the bourgeoisie and civil society from that in situations where an absolutist or feudal state attempts to obstruct capitalism. Since the state in East and Southeast Asia has embraced capitalism, structures emerge that incorporate the new social forces. Hence, political activities involving these social forces are often channelled into state-sanctioned institutions. The environment for potential oppositions is quite different.

With the above in mind, this collection of essays focuses on the extent and nature of political contestation in East and Southeast Asia. The principal question under scrutiny here is not whether 'democratisation' is occurring or likely to occur as economic change and social transformations take place in these societies. Instead, the question is what do these transformations mean for the nature of political opposition. The primary objective is to specify the way in which challenges – real or in prospect – to or within authoritarian rule have resulted from the massive social changes accompanying industrialisation. In particular, we are interested in the direct and indirect roles of emerging social forces – 'new rich', comprising the bourgeoisie together with the middle class, and the working class – in the process of political opposition.

There is extensive literature focusing specifically on the question of the middle class and its significance for political development. Much of this has been inspired by the unproductive hypothesis that the middle class is intrinsically hostile to authoritarian rule. However, historically the middle class has adopted a range of political positions, sometimes siding with fascist and authoritarian regimes – as in Italy and Chile. This volume attempts to focus on the ways in which the emergence of new classes have redefined the issues around which power is contested. A new economic system that gives rise to new sources of wealth and class interest also produces new fracture lines in social and political interest and new policy issues. For example, the new middle class has organised around such issues as the quality of public utilities and services, the environment, public accountability and transparency. Their interests translate into new demands and constituencies that necessarily shape oppositional politics. But the notion that these interests are necessarily tied up with a push for political liberalism is not borne out by this volume. A central theme to emerge here is that the political impact of new classes is contingent upon their relative location in the structures of social and economic power. For example, where its interests are threatened by powerful, radical working-class movements, or where it fears social chaos, the middle class is prepared to support authoritarian regimes. Similarly, working-class political movements, the product of industrial capitalism, may take several forms, depending on the prevailing configurations of social power and political structure. They may be revolutionary oppositions, loyal oppositions, or elements of a large corporatist enterprise.

The content, site, and modus operandi of political opposition can therefore vary considerably, and these differences warrant careful attention. Within this volume, the different authors draw attention to a range of oppositions. This includes advocates of greater public accountability and transparency in government who seek to eradicate official corruption and other obstacles to a modern, efficient capitalist economy. Examples of this are to be found in the chapters to follow on Thailand, South Korea, Taiwan, and Indonesia in particular. But the reform agendas of such oppositionists from the business and middle classes do not necessarily extend to more general demands for human rights or other political reforms that would open the state up to broader social forces. Rather, assorted human rights, social justice, and welfare claims are often advanced by other oppositionists. Similarly, political parties are in some cases the principal, even if limited, articulators of political opposition – as in Singapore – but to differing extents elsewhere in East and Southeast Asia we find social movements, NGOs, interest groups such as professional organisations, as well as individual dissidents, employing various extra-parliamentary organisational and strategic means to oppose government policy. In some cases, as Dalton and Cotton demonstrate in the chapter on South Korea, parliamentary and extra-parliamentary forms appear to be developing simultaneously – even if they remain essentially disconnected avenues. In other cases, as Aspinall maintains for Indonesia, the extra-parliamentary forms are the only ones to have significantly evolved in recent times. Finally, public demonstrations and labour strikes, while conspicuously absent in Singapore, are not uncommon in South Korea, for instance, and are increasingly common in Indonesia. Yet in all of the cases in this volume, less visible challenges to government policy are common – especially where corporatist structures are either firmly established or even in the process of being extended.

The position taken in this chapter is that political opposition, whatever its form, involves the existence of political space to contest the exercise of power through government or regime. This space may be established within representative political institutions, but it is no less likely to exist outside them, and even within authoritarian regimes. Equally, but not necessarily, it may involve the existence of civil society. Accordingly, while we are obviously interested in political parties, we are no less interested in other forms of political contestation – regardless of whether or not these forms facilitate competitive party systems.

In the discussion below, which selectively examines the theoretical literature relevant to the question of social transformations in industrialising Asia and their significance for political opposition, the following substantive points will be underlined: (i) dramatic transformations in social structures accompanying industrialisation are generally resulting in changes in state–society relations, but this takes a variety of forms within East and Southeast Asia; (ii) this is a process best understood as the opening up of political space rather than as a struggle between state and civil society; (iii) economic change throws up a variety of challenges, produced not just by new forms of wealth and social power attempting to shape politics, but also by those marginalised by the new forms of development who want to resist or reverse these changes and return to idealised traditional situations.

Let us begin by examining the prevailing attempts in the literature to conceptualise political opposition and the particular challenges posed by authoritarian systems in this exercise.

LIBERAL DEMOCRACY AS THE POINT OF REFERENCE

In the classic academic works on political opposition undertaken by Dahl (1966a, 1971, 1973), the main focus is on industrialised, liberal democratic societies and the place of legally protected political parties therein. However, at the outset of the first of these works, Dahl (1966b: xi) observes that the right to such an opposition is a particularly modern phenomenon, especially in the context of electoral systems based on universal franchise. To be sure, Dahl was in no doubt about the importance of the context within which parties operate. As he stated: 'A country with universal suffrage and a completely repressive government would provide fewer opportunities for oppositions, surely, than a country with a narrow suffrage but a highly tolerant government' (Dahl 1971: 5). Furthermore, he recognised that: 'To the extent that an opposition concentrate on elections and parliamentary action, it may be powerful in unimportant encounters and feeble or even absent when key decisions are made' (Dahl 1966b: 395). Nevertheless, the questions he was fundamentally concerned with related to the factors that facilitate or obstruct this form of opposition, and the variety in the character of political oppositions taking this particular form.

In Dahl's schema, the two extremes of political regimes are polyarchic and hegemonic systems. The former he describes as 'highly inclusive and open to public contestation'(Dahl 1971: 8), which manifests in the greatest number and variety of interests represented in policy making (Dahl 1973: 9). By contrast, the latter prohibits any form of organised dissent or opposition in a highly exclusive decision-making regime. No distinction is drawn between loyal and disloyal opposition. Rather, by definition opposition is regarded as disloyal and to be repressed (Dahl 1973: 13).[3] One of Dahl's central observations is that the tolerance by authorities of opposition is linked to calculations by governments about the political costs of otherwise attempting to coerce or obstruct opponents (Dahl 1966b: xii, 1971: 15).

The tolerance or lack of tolerance towards a 'loyal' opposition is obviously a basic yardstick within this framework. The concept has its roots in eighteenth-century Britain, where the party out of power was called 'His (Her) Majesty's Loyal Opposition'. Such an opposition was understood to be loyal to the Crown, even if it was office-seeking (see Safire 1972). Most importantly, loyal opposition attempts to gain office through constitutional rather than revolutionary means. In a broad sense, this commitment materially affects the content of opposition in so far as it involves a loyalty to the institutions of the state and the associated rules and regulations for their alteration; and hence a readiness 'at any moment to come into office without a shock to the political traditions of the nation' (Lowell as quoted in Punnett 1973: 13).

Yet within these limits, loyal oppositions obviously can vary in their objectives and strategies. Dahl's distinction between structural and non-structural oppositions remains an influential one in attempting to specify this. Structural oppositions attempt to alter fundamentally the distribution of economic and social power through constitutional means. This may require some modification to the constitution, but structural opposition must make such modifications according to the rules of the constitution itself if it is to remain loyal. The difficulties this can pose have been a source of frustration and division among reformers in socialist and social democratic parties in particular. As Punnett (1973: 14) points out, however, it is not just the advocates of structural change who can be tempted to reject constitutional processes. In seeking to consolidate the basic social and economic order, the constitution can be a target of extreme right-wing groups who see liberal democracy as a threat to that order.

While there are important distinctions to be made between the different characters of political parties seeking to replace the government and the margins of tolerance for their challenge, opposition to government policies in liberal democratic systems comes from various sources and takes numerous forms, including interest groups and social movements. This has long been recognised in liberal political theory and systems theory, which understands political parties either to straddle civil society and formal institutions or to act as conduits for societal demands conveyed through civil society (see Bobbio 1989: 25). Even so, much of the interest in opposition of this sort has been in its role complementing or supporting competitive party systems rather than as opposition in its own right.

However, not all the literature so acutely privileges party politics. Definitions of democracy which extend themselves beyond mere formalism or electoralism acknowledge the importance of extra-parliamentary activities somewhat differently. Schmitter and Karl (1991: 78), for example, contend that: 'Modern democracy, in other words, offers a variety of competitive processes and channels for the expression of interests and values – associational as well as partisan, functional as well as territorial, collective as well as individual. All are integral to its practice.' Much earlier, Bertrand de Jouvenel (1966: 157) argued that: 'The means of opposition are the infrastructure of political liberty: the party of opposition is simply an element of superstructure.' He emphasised the difference between seeking to be involved in government, at any level, and seeking political representation, and warned that the biggest threat to representation was its absorption into the system of government through co-option (de Jouvenal 1966: 168). At the time, he had trade unions in mind as a clear example of the prescribed duality. Both these approaches come closer to acknowledging the plurality of oppositional forms in liberal democracies alongside, rather than in the service of, electoral politics. But they are also premised on the existence of liberal democracy.

Barker (1971: 4–6) emphasises that, in addition to the concept of 'loyal opposition' with which many liberal theorists were preoccupied, 'opposition' can also be understood as: outright resistance to the state; resistance to the power of the state when that power is exerted oppressively; resistance to the group, faction, or dynasty controlling the state; a system of constitutional checks and balances guarding against power abuse; and methods employed by citizens or groups to modify the actions of government without openly challenging that government. Like Dahl, Barker (1971) emphasises how contemporary a phenomenon, and indeed an idea, institutionalised loyal opposition is. As he argues, such an opposition is by no means synonymous with liberalism, at least not in its earlier variants expressed by such people as John Stuart Mill. Certainly Mill believed government benefited from the debate of diverse opinion in parliament, guided by reasoned, disinterested argument. Yet, rather than the formalisation of dissent through a loyal opposition and party politics, Mill placed emphasis on the critical role of a free press in scrutinising government (Barker 1971: 13–15). According to Barker (1971: 17), 'It was not the existence of an organised Opposition that liberals valued, but the freedom to oppose and criticise, a freedom which could not be properly exercised in formal organised parties.'

Barker (1971: 25–6) criticised Dahl for his overly prescriptive attachment to liberal democracy which he believed leads to insufficient differentiation of the forms and contents of oppositions in favour of a celebration of the existence of opposition *per se*.[4] A similar criticism was made of Ionescu and de Madariaga (1968) and at least the initial editions of the journal *Government and Opposition* under de Madariaga's editorship. These authors contended that: 'the presence or absence of institutionalised political opposition can become the criterion for the classification of any political society in one of two categories: liberal or dictatorial, democratic or authoritarian, pluralistic-constitutional or monolithic' (as quoted in Barker 1971: 26).

Subsequent to Barker's criticisms, an edited collection by Dahl included the work of Juan Linz and others attempting to address some of these concerns. In contrast with liberal democracies in which the major distinction was between loyal and disloyal opposition, Linz (1973) emphasised that in authoritarian regimes the major distinction was between opponents inside and outside the system; and that this was not simply a distinction between legal and illegal opposition. The concept of 'semi-opposition' was advanced by Linz in drawing this out. According to Linz (1973: 191), semi-opposition 'consists of those groups that are not dominant or represented in the governing group but that are willing to participate in power without fundamentally challenging the regime'. Such opposition is not institutionalised, as in the case of political parties, and may take seemingly apolitical forms – a religious association or an educational institution, for example. These social groups do not enjoy legal protection for their political activities and thus have a precarious existence.[5] However, the chief difference between semi-oppositions in authoritarian regimes and oppositions in a liberal democracy, according to Linz (1973: 193), lies in the absence of any accountability to some form of 'constituency'. Semi-opposition thus signifies a selective opening up of the inner circle, rather than a legitimising of interest-group politics.[6]

This concept has its problems, especially in deciphering at what point groups or individuals could be said to be 'participating in power' (Aspinall 1995: 3), or in specifying the qualitative difference between the limits on semi-oppositions on the one hand, and loyal oppositions on the other, in fostering genuinely alternative programmes. Nevertheless, Linz directs attention to the fact of limited political pluralism, and he puts the question of political co-optation into a different context. Attempts by groups and individuals to exploit contradictions within the state for pragmatic ends are rendered more visible. Recently, Stepan (1993: 64) identified five key functions of democratic opposition in authoritarian regimes: resisting integration into the regime; guarding zones of autonomy against the regime; disputing its legitimacy; raising the costs of authoritarian rule; creating a credible democratic alternative. While opposition in East and Southeast Asia may quite often fall short on such criteria, it nevertheless could be the ascendant form in most societies and the one with the best prospects of extension. Co-optation is a thematic question confronting analysts of political change in East and Southeast Asia, as this volume testifies. The studies of the different countries in this collection suggest that the capacity of corporatist structures to be modified effectively to co-opt emerging social forces diverges. Rodan's chapter on Singapore, for example, emphasises the adaptability of state corporatism and Heryanto does not rule this out as a possibility in Indonesia, whatever the current difficulties. Similarly, while Jesudason acknowledges challenges to the preservation of what he refers to as the 'syncretic state' in Malaysia he sees any fundamental loss of coherence to this as unlikely in the foreseeable future. By contrast, Rigger depicts the corporatist state in Taiwan as a set of structures that will increasingly be found wanting as complex and competing social pressures are exerted.

Although Linz and others attempted some time ago to steer attention to the particularities of political oppositions other than formal, constitutional, loyal oppositions, much of the recent interest in the prospects of political change in industrialising East and Southeast Asia remains indifferent to the conceptual challenge Linz took up. In Lawson's recent work on political opposition in Asia, for example, she contends that: 'where there is no possibility of alternation in power between governing elements and oppositional elements through a peaceful process of fair and open elections, there is no constitutional opposition, and therefore no genuine democracy' (Lawson 1993a: 194; see also Lawson 1993b). Certainly there can be no liberal democracy without constitutional opposition, but this does not necessarily mean opposition itself is entirely absent. This privileging of a particular oppositional form is understandable if we are only interested in whether liberal democracy exists, but it is not helpful if we are trying to identify the extent and nature of political oppositions *per se*. More than a decade earlier, Justus van der Kroef (1978: 621) observed that 'the more effective and, from an international point of view, the more visible form of political opposition has tended to be organised and expressed outside parliament and the electoral system'. He referred to students and segments of the intellectual community, the military, religious and ethnic groups, and Communist organisations (van der Kroef 1978: 622). There have certainly been changes in the character, contexts, and relative importance of such opposition since then, but these changes escape attention in frameworks that search only for loyal oppositions operating through parliamentary processes.

However, there have been recent attempts to characterise the political systems in East and Southeast Asian societies which break from such heavy reliance upon the dominant liberal framework. The problem is that these attempts are heavily reliant upon culturalist perspectives that conceal rather than reveal the complex dynamics in these societies.

CONCEPTUALISING ALTERNATIVES IN ASIA

Among conservative and liberal writers, cultural factors have long been an important component of political analysis (Almond and Verba 1965). Of late, though, there has been a noticeable revival of interest in political culture, at various levels of abstraction, as much of the literature addresses the question of what factors are needed to sustain 'democratisation' in those countries to have recently broken from authoritarian rule (see Huntington 1991; Dahl 1994; Diamond 1994).[7] Not all theorists share the conviction that culture is so important to the establishment of liberal democracy. Schmitter and Karl (1991: 82) argue 'that contingent consent and bounded uncertainty can emerge from the interaction between antagonistic and mutually suspicious actors and that the far more benevolent and ingrained norms of a civic culture are better thought of as a *product* and not a producer of democracy'.[8]

Nevertheless, the concept of culture has been widely employed in a fundamental way to generalise the patterns of political development. In Pye's (1985) influential thesis on Asian political culture, for instance, he clearly recognised that the liberal path of North America and Europe may not be feasible in late-industrialising countries of Asia. However, he did not see this so much as the consequence of different historical and socio-political factors generating power relations hostile to, or unreliant on, liberalism. Rather, he emphasised the durability of anti-liberal Asian political culture. Subsequently, Moody (1988) sought to demonstrate how personalism and moralism, points Pye attributed to Chinese culture, posed obstacles to liberal democracy in East Asia. Moody (1988: 12) observed: 'In East Asia there is an intellectual heritage critical of unrestrained power but no heritage of institutional limitations on power. Both the social ethos and the institutional heritage contributed to politics organised around personal groups and defined in moral terms.'

More recently, a number of authors have adopted the concept of culture ostensibly as a way round the problem of measuring political development solely against the yardstick of liberal democracy. Fukuyama (1992b: 109) himself now contends: 'there are grounds for thinking that Asian political development could turn away from democracy and take its own unique path in spite of the region's record of economic growth.' According to him, this possible 'Asian alternative' is linked to pervasive group hierarchies emanting from traditional social structures in culturally Confucian societies. While the end of history may have meant ideological and institutional convergence around the globe, cultural diversity not only remains but, according to Fukuyama, underlies divergences in economic success and social cohesion (see Fukuyama 1995a, 1995b). Similarly, Huntington (1993: 17) contends that: 'The interaction of economic progress and Asian culture appears to have generated a distinctly East Asian variety of democratic institutions.' The dominant-party systems prevalent in the region, he points out, have the formal trappings of liberal democracy, but political participation is effectively reserved for one party: 'This type of political system offers democracy without turnover. It represents an adaptation of Western democratic practices to serve not Western values of competition and change, but Asian values of consensus and stability' (Huntington 1993: 18).[19]

But while Fukuyama and Huntington acknowledge the hostility of deep-seated traditional Asian cultures to liberalism, in contrast to Pye they maintain that Asian cultures also contain some 'democratic' elements. This is an important departure from Pye's (1985) generalisation which tends to obscure divisions within and between the various Asian societies. Fukuyama (1995a), for instance, maintains that there are at least three respects in which Confucianism is compatible with 'democracy': the traditional Confucian examination system was merito-cractic and thus egalitarian in its implications: the importance attached to education; and the tolerant nature of Confucianism, given that it has coexisted with Buddhism and Christianity.[10] Similarly, based on the premise that cultures are dynamic rather than immutable and static, Huntington also holds out the prospect that, over time, democratic cultural elements could prevail in Asia. According to Huntington (1993a: 21): 'Confucian democracy may be a contradiction in terms, but democracy in a Confucian society need not be.' Huntington does not actually specify the 'democratic elements' he has in mind, but it is implicit that they are compatible with liberal democracy since no other possibility is raised. This assumption is also apparent in the criteria Fukuyama cites as indicative of democratic cultural heritages. But what is most noteworthy about the propositions by both Huntington and Fukuyama is the idea that culture either lies at the core of political differences between 'Asia' and the liberal 'west', and is therefore central to the prospects of bridging this gap, or fundamentally shapes any possible democratic political trajectory in East Asia. The effect of this is to divert attention from the question of *alternatives to liberal democracy in Asia* in favour of the idea of *'Asian' alternatives*.

This analytical importance attached to culture allows observations about the 'differentness of Asians' to be appropriated for political and ideological purposes, and even legitimates such exercises. Huntington's (1993b) not unrelated thesis about a 'clash of civilizations' supplanting the previous ideological disputes characterising the Cold War has added impetus to broad, monolithic conceptions of 'Asian culture'.[11] Select authoritarian leaders in Asia have vigorously promoted the idea of 'Asian values' to deflect pressure over human rights and employment conditions, and launch an offensive against liberalism (Mohamed and Ishihara 1995; Zakaria 1994). While this may be designed to insulate authoritarian regimes from external criticism, it also attempts to depict domestic political opponents and dissenters, who do not share these values, as 'un-Asian' and dismissible on that basis. Significantly, this rhetoric about cultural homogeneity surfaces precisely at a point when social and economic transformations in various Asian societies produce diverse interests and identities requiring some sort of political accommodation. Obviously authoritarian leaders prefer an accommodation that least threatens their positions. The theme reiterated by self-appointed spokespersons on 'Asian values' about a cultural predisposition to consensus rather than contention is an especially useful rationale for this.

While the 'Asian values' perspective is principally enunciated by a handful of authoritarian elites in Asia, this has not diminished its impact on policy makers and analysts outside the region. Many appear to take these arguments at face-value in their attempts to comprehend these societies. The appeal of cultural relativism ranges across the political spectrum, providing a basis for condemnation of 'western imperialism' as well as rationalising inaction over behaviour that elsewhere would be protested as human rights abuses (Robison 1993). Some cynically adopt the rhetoric about 'Asian values' to advance neo-liberal and conservative political agendas within established liberal democracies outside the region (Rodan 1995). As would be expected, a critical public reaction within the region to the proclamations of Lee Kuan Yew *et al.* on 'Asian values' has given some expression to the fallacy of harmony and consensus among 'Asians', including from the recently established Forum of Democratic Leaders in the Asia-Pacific (*Sydney Morning Herald*, 27 June 1995: 8). Most of these voices are, however, from relatively high-profile figures who might also be categorised as the elite: political leaders, prominent lawyers, and academics. Other divergent perspectives from within the non-government and grassroots communities of course have less access to the media to challenge the 'Asian values' line. This volume identifies many of these, revealing that the agendas they pursue include welfare, human rights, and social justice issues as well as, in the case of some developmental NGOs, the establishment of greater participatory democracy and a shift in social power. Of the essays in this collection, Aspinall's chapter on Indonesia, and Hewison and Rodan's broad survey of the Left in Southeast Asia, give greatest attention to this latter point.

The preoccupation with liberal democratic political forms thus combines with cultural arguments about a supposed 'Asian' aversion to political contestation in favour of consensus and group harmony to limit inquiry into political oppositions. The additional tendency in the literature to emphasise the strategic importance of political leadership in effecting and sustaining 'democratic' transitions serves to further devalue the analytical currency of political opposition in East and Southeast Asia. Most of this attention has centred on ruling elites and their tolerance or otherwise of political contestation (see Higley and Burton 1989; Case 1994; Marks 1992; Huntington 1991; Diamond and Plattner 1993; Scalapino 1993). The pivotal role of elites is described by Case (1994: 438) thus: 'In sum, class structures, civil society, and social structures may cut in a variety of ways. To see which way, one must investigate elites, in particular the attitudes they hold and the relations they forge with societal audiences.' The choice of the term 'audience' rather than 'forces', for example, seems to imply a passivity that emphasises an unambiguous causal relationship from the elite down. It also assumes that elites are free to make a range of choices. Huntington

(1991: 108) similarly attributes exceptional strategic significance to elite leadership in contending that: 'If he had wanted to, a political leader far less skilled than Lee Kuan Yew could have produced democracy in Singapore.'

Having argued a case for broadening the framework beyond liberal pluralism, and having found culturalist arguments unsatisfactory to this task, let us examine other theoretical material that might be more helpful.

BEYOND POLITICAL PARTIES: SOCIAL MOVEMENTS

It must be acknowledged that the preoccupation with political parties and the formal political system at the expense of other broader processes of contestation is most acute among liberal theorists writing on 'democratisation' in Asia. The extensive literature from this framework on the functioning of democracy in Western Europe and the United States, by contrast, has paid greater attention to the links between political parties and their many and varied social bases, and to the institutions through which these bases are mediated. Parties are of course not distinct from society. They respond to interests and pressures emanating from constituencies within society, constituencies with differential capacities and means to exert an influence over parties. However, while some groups attempt to exert this influence consciously and explicitly, others are less directly or explicitly connected to the formal political process. It is this latter category to which far greater attention has now turned as cynicism towards, and alienation from, the formal political process in established liberal democracies appears to have gathered momentum in recent decades and resulted in a variety of new organisational structures. Accompanying this is the emergence of a body of literature focusing on 'new social movements' (NSMs). The assumption in this literature is that NSMs are new phenomena affecting the form, locus, and nature of political opposition. While this claim may be overstated, and ultimately the effectiveness of NSMs depends upon their impact on formal political processes, this literature is nevertheless helping to broaden our conception of politics and political opposition. Let us, then, briefly survey and evaluate some of its main features.

Social movements, either as an analytical category or as social phenomena, are not new. As Shaw (1994: 651) reminds us, the study of social movements was 'the stock in trade of social historians of the eighteenth, nineteenth and early twentieth centuries'. Indeed, in the broad historical sense, social movements are a fundamentally modern rather than post-modern phenomenon, dating from the peasant revolts and workers' movements studied by these scholars to the late twentieth-century variety (Shaw 1994: 651). Scott defines a social movement as:

> a collective actor constituted by individuals who understand themselves to have common interests and, at least for some significant part of their social existence, a common identity. Such movements are distinguished from other collective actors, such as political parties and pressure groups, in that they have mass mobilisation, or the threat of mobilisation, as their prime source of social sanction, and hence of power. They are further distinguished from other collectivities, such as voluntary associations or clubs, in being chiefly concerned to defend or change society.
>
> (Scott 1990: 6)

This definition concedes the possibility of considerable diversity in the sorts of political objectives, organisational structures, ideological commitments, social bases, and extent of movements. What, then, are the distinctive characteristics of 'new' social movements?

A number of generalisations and themes can be discerned from the extensive and theoretically diverse literature. NSMs are commonly depicted as: international in character; subscribing to values that fundamentally challenge the existing social and economic order; consciously operating outside the established political structures linked to the state, especially political parties; employing mass mobilisation, or the threat thereof, as the principal political weapon; having decentralised, informal, and often transient organisational structures; and lacking an easily identifiable social base, being instead issue- and value-based movements of disparate and fluid composition (see Crook *et al.* 1993; Scott 1990).

These generalisations portray ideal categories, since each of these characteristics can only more or less apply to the various heterogeneous organisations under this banner. Included here are environmentalist, feminist, peace, anti-racist, and other movements. There is a strong emphasis on NSMs as extra-parliamentary forms of opposition and protest based on values and attitudes, as distinct from the more traditional disputes over the distribution of resources.[12] State structures in general are viewed by NSM members as easily corrupted to instrumental rather than value-based decisions. This critique supposedly informs the loose, anti-bureaucratic organisational forms attributed to NSMs.[13] Some of these NSMs are understood as potentially liberating, such as feminist movements, but many more are viewed by Habermas (1987: 392–3) as defensive, attempting to stem the incursions of the 'economic-administrative complex' on the 'lifeworld'.[14] Generally, though, they are portrayed in positive terms, a tendency which downplays movements like the Aum Supreme Truth in Japan, and the Michigan Militia and Branch Davidians in the USA.

In a sense, any mobilisation of social forces is a political act that will inevitably involve some engagement with the state. The most conspicuous cases involve formal political engagement by NSMs and the establishment of 'alternative' political parties, such as the German Greens and other ecology-oriented parties (see Kaelberer 1993). But it can take more subtle forms, such as the incorporation of feminist and anti-racist perspectives into school syllabuses via state representative and consultative committees and advisory boards. The dilemma these movements face is that, however distasteful the established structures may be to them, these have to be influenced to effect any change on the specific issues of concern. The price of success in forcing policy makers to take notice of them is an increased risk of co-optation. Not all forms of co-optation result in the same sorts of compromises over autonomy and principle, but they almost certainly generate internal disputations among movement members.

But the broader and more important theoretical point is that social movements are not completely separate social phenomena requiring a distinct analytical framework. Rather, they exist *in relation to* other elements of civil society and traditional institutions. For an understanding of their impact as political oppositions, these relational dimensions are crucial (Shaw 1994). But neither the fact of co-optation nor the importance of the institutions alongside social movements negates the significance of NSMs for political opposition.[15] In particular, the extra-parliamentary nature of these movements politicises social and cultural spheres and potentially exposes the exercise of power to broader contestation. Moreover, while the concerns expressed, such as environmentalism, cannot easily be separated from the material development of global capitalism and the class structures underlying it (Wilde 1990), these movements represent a challenge to the strategies of leftist activists which must take them as a given, not a diversion. This point is taken up in relation to Southeast Asia in Chapter 2 by Hewison and Rodan in their discussion of the contemporary activities of NGOs and political alliances involving the Left.

Alvarez and Escobar (1992) maintain that during the 1970s and 1980s various forms of social movements emerged in Latin America to assert an important influence over political life. These movements have, they argue, 'placed previously suppressed or marginalised demands on to the political agenda – claiming rights to better urban services and land, as well as to increased popular participation and more meaningful democratic participation' (Alvarez and Escobar 1992: 326). Hellman (1992) envisages that this will force some reassessment by political parties in an endeavour to capitalise on the mobilisational capacities of these movements. But within East and Southeast Asia where industrialisation has in some parts matured considerably, and where working-class-based organisations like trade unions are still subject to the repressive apparatus of the state, there is increasing evidence of non-government organisational activity. This is especially noted in the chapters on South Korea, Taiwan, and, to a lesser extent, Indonesia.

Significant variations in the range and strength of social movements in the various East and Southeast Asian societies, and the relationships between social movements and political parties, represent a major force behind the differential political trajectories unfolding in the region. These different trajectories, of course, will further expose the fallacy of the 'Asian values' emphasis on cultural commonality supposedly steering polities in the same general direction.

So the theoretical opening-up of work on political oppositions in liberal democracies has the potential to feed into more imaginative approaches to the study of oppositions under authoritarian rule. For the fruits of this to be fully realised, though, it is necessary to dispense with the influential notion that extra-parliamentary political contestation is best understood in terms of the conflicting objectives of state and civil society.

PROBLEMS WITH THE 'STATE VERSUS CIVIL SOCIETY' DICHOTOMY

The concept of civil society has a long history, throughout which it has assumed a variety of meanings (see Shils 1991; Keane 1988; Bobbio 1989; Kumar 1993; Bryant 1993; Reitzes 1994; Tester 1992; Gellner 1994). This reflects in the diverse usages of the concept's current revival. As Kumar (1993: 383) observes: 'So, today, civil society has been found in the economy and the polity; in the area between the family and the state, or the individual and the state; in the non-state institutions which organise and educate citizens for political participation; even as an expression of the whole civilising mission of modern society.' Despite these problems, the concept can be usefully employed; this is certainly not a call for it to be shelved. To be sure, civil society is the form of political space that affords the most substantive oppositional capacity and potential, within which social forces can both resist and co-operate with the state in their own interests. In qualitatively differentiating the various sorts of political space this concept is indispensable. Nevertheless, civil society is one form of political space within which oppositions can operate – not the only space.

It is not the point here to survey the various traditions represented in the literature on civil society, but rather to focus primarily on the major intellectual influences shaping the concept's usage in analysing political change and opposition. In particular, the juxtaposition of civil society against state, with a clear normative preference for the former, is a powerful contemporary theme. This has a variety of analytical consequences, including inadequate specification of the content of oppositional positions within civil society and the concealment of political oppositions operating outside this realm.

Among liberal theorists, definitions of civil society approvingly emphasise themes of independence, liberty, plurality, and voluntary action. Diamond (1994: 5), for example, defines civil society as 'the realm of organised social life that is voluntary, self-regulating, (largely) self-supporting, autonomous from the state, and bound by a legal order or set of shared rules'. He also contends that: 'To the extent that an organisation . . . seeks to monopolise a functional or political space in society, claiming that it represents the only legitimate path, it contradicts the pluralistic market-oriented nature of civil society' (Diamond 1994: 7). Similarly, Mirsky (1993: 572) describes civil society as 'a social sphere in which no single locus of authority predominates and in which men and women interact with each other in a series of overlapping relationships and associations – communal, civic, religious, economic, social, and cultural'. The understanding of civil society in residual terms *vis-à-vis* the state – as the realm of social relations not encompassed by the state – often carries with it powerful normative assumptions about this separation. As Parekh (1993: 160) points out, for liberal theorists, the state is a coercive and compulsory institution quite unlike civil society: 'coercive because it enjoys the power of life and death over its members, compulsory because its citizens are its members by birth and may not leave it, and outsiders may not enter it, without its approval'. In this view, the role of government is to maximise the liberties of self-determining agents and to facilitate their goals, not to impose grand goals separate from these. The normative attachment to civil society is at times quite explicit in the literature. Kukathas and Lovell, for instance, assert that: 'The ideological and political collapse of communism suggests that we should redirect our attention to the target of its attack: to reassert the functions of the traditions and institutions of civil society, and to ask what is necessary if its development or regeneration is to be made possible' (Kukathas and Lovell 1991: 35–6). They add that 'civil society is important because of its contributions to the constitution of human identity and the fulfilment of individual aspirations'. Others emphasise the 'civility' of this particular social realm, which is sometimes depicted as protecting liberal democracy from the inherent dangers of extremism (see Shils 1991: 14).

The celebration of civil society and political pluralism associated with it is also a feature of the post-structuralist and post-modernist literature on new social movements. Here the juxtaposition of repressive state against liberal civil society is arrived at via a somewhat different route, but the effect is fundamentally the same. According to Cohen and Arato (1992: 71), 'Post-Marxists not only register, as did Gramsci, the durability of civil society under capitalist democracies and the consequent implausibility of revolution, but maintain the normative desirability of the preservation of civil society.' They further observe that: 'All of our relevant sources view liberal democracy as a necessary condition for bringing the modern state under control' (Cohen and Arato 1992: 80). Again, the premise is the notion that the state is inherently predisposed to oppression, whereas civil society is the natural domain of liberty.

The emphasis on civil society as the dichotomous opposite of the state, and the fashionable identification by scholars with the former, entail a number of problems: the idealisation of civil society; the fostering of a zero-sum conception of the relationship between state and civil society; the obscuring of attempts to gain state power to shape relationships in civil society; and the conceptual concealment of those ambiguous but significant relationships between state and society.

First, civil society is in fact the locus of a range of inequalities based on class, gender, ethnicity, race, and sexual preference, for example, that are symptomatic of specific economic, social, and political systems of power (Wood 1990; Kumar 1993; Reitzes 1994). The 'tendency to demonise the state and deify civil society', as Reitzes (1994: 105) puts it, plays down this darker side, and ignores the fact that the internal structures and practices of autonomous organisations can be both *undemocratic* and *uncivil* – a point amply demonstrated in the organisations currently surfacing in Eastern Europe as well as those that emerged in South Africa during the 1980s (see Reintges 1990; Shubane 1992; Howe 1991; Salecl 1992). Obviously the political implications of the various elements of civil society differ according to their objectives and practices.

In rapidly industrialising East and Southeast Asia, regime opponents include reactionary elements. Economic change throws up a variety of challenges, not just those by new sources of power and wealth seeking more open and accountable public decision making. Rather, marginalised groups resistant to certain forms of change, such as the recently banned Muslim fundamentalist NGO Al Arqam in Malaysia, are motivated by concern about the erosion of traditional religious values. Moreover, a range of elitist and hierarchical structures and ideologies characterise the various organisations resurfacing and emerging in the region. Among new sources of power and wealth, the aspirations for political liberalisation can also be somewhat exclusive (see in particular Chan's chapter which stresses the exclusion of workers and peasants from the ambitions of the professional and business classes for increased political participation in China).

Second, the notion that state and civil society are essentially locked in some sort of zero-sum game is especially limiting. Stepan's (1985: 318) specification of four logical possibilities in the unfolding of power relations between state and civil society is worth reiterating: state power can be extended in zero-sum fashion to the detriment of civil society; power in both realms can be simultaneously expanded in a positive-sum game; power can simultaneously decline in both realms, in a negative-sum fashion; and, finally, the power of civil society sectors can expand while those of the state decline. The arguments of various chapters in this volume underline this range in state–society possibilities as industrialisation and social transformations advance, including the expansion of the state itself rather than civil society, as in Singapore.

Third, the connection between civil society and the state amounts to more than the latter providing the legal framework for the former to exist. The process of political contestation – whether it be over the control of formal political institutions of the state or the attempt to influence these through interest groups or social movements – often centres on competing efforts to redress or consolidate relationships in civil society. This relationship has to some extent received attention from Held (1987, 1989, 1993) and Keane (1988), who have argued the case for the mutual 'democratisation' of state and civil society.

Fourth, there is a real danger that too sharp a delineation of state and society – and the related delineation of state and civil society – conceals important and interesting aspects of state–society relationships not easily handled within this dichotomous, zero-sum framework. In particular, the way in which societal forces have been incorporated or co-opted into some sort of relationship with state structures, though not always unproblematically for policy makers and officials of the state, demands careful analysis. Gorz's (1980) observation that the state in advanced liberal democratic societies has increasingly usurped the social self-regulatory capacity of civil society at the expense of reciprocity and voluntarism partly recognises the limitations of the dominant conceptual dichotomy. Certainly, it challenges the neat association of liberal democracy with an expansive civil society. Similarly, the extensive literature on corporatism in liberal democracies variously suggests that the social forces in civil society are being subverted or selectively bolstered, through functional representations. The significance of these political forms could withstand considerable elaboration, however.

Schmitter (1992: 427) has possibly come closest to grasping the implications of state–society relations with his emphasis on the varied and discrete arenas and processes of political contestation associated with the modern state:

> First, what if a modern democracy were conceptualised, not as 'a regime', but as a composite of 'partial regimes', each of which was institutionalised around distinctive sites for the representation of social groups and the resolution of their ensuing conflicts? Parties, associations, movements, localities and various clienteles would compete and coalesce through these different channels in efforts to capture office and influence policy. Authorities with different functions and at different levels of aggregation would interact with these representatives and could legitimately claim accountability to different citizen interests (and passions).

His concept of 'partial regimes' is explicitly intended to transcend the limitations of the traditional liberal notion that political parties are the most important and influential expression of political representation *vis-à-vis* the state. Thus he steers attention to the organisational representations of class, sectoral, and professional interests which 'might intrude on the putative monopoly of political parties in the representation of social groups' (Schmitter 1992: 431). Most importantly, his notion that liberal democracies comprise assorted forms of political representation encompassing a range of institutional sites encourages a more comprehensive and detailed analysis of the political intersection of state and society. This includes development of the analysis of organisational links to the formal political process, as some writers have attempted, for example, by applying the concept of partial regimes to regulatory structures.

While Schmitter's idea of 'partial regimes' is intended to assist in defining 'democracy' by subjecting more institutional sites to scrutiny,[16] the attempt to broaden the focus of political analysis has wider implications. A fifth point, then, is that the boundaries between state and civil society are greatly complicated by the existence of a host of institutional forums that attempt to incorporate social forces – regardless of whether these forms of representation are democratic. But if these boundaries are at times obscure in established liberal democracies, they are no less problematic elsewhere where different historical contexts have resulted in a pronounced ideological assertiveness for pervasive state structures.[17] The predominant acknowledgement of this feature of so many post-colonial societies takes the form of contrasting extensive states with underdeveloped social organisations: strong state, weak society (see Blaney and Pasha 1993). It is often the ability of regimes, especially, but not only, authoritarian regimes, to incorporate organised social forces that renders them so effective in political terms. But this effectiveness does not simply derive from the negation of an organisation's independence from the state or the obstruction of other organisations in society, important as both are. Rather, it lies also in the very fact of social organisation. The point is that societal groups may be highly organised, even if not residing in civil society. Rigger's chapter on Taiwan gives this special attention.

Moreover, a sharp state–society dichotomy is not sufficiently sensitive to changes *within* polities where a pervasive state has incorporated societal forces. In Aspinall's chapter on Indonesia in this volume he refers to 'grey areas' where certain oppositional activities are undertaken, and thus touches on this problem. Ding (1994: 298) appears to be addressing a similar problem to which he applies his concept of 'institutional amphibiousness'. It has the following features:

> First, the boundaries between institutional structures are ambiguous. Institutional structures are so closely interwoven with each other in their actual operation that the formal demarcation of the scope of each other's activities or powers becomes insignificant. Secondly, the nature of individual institutions is indeterminate. An institution can be used for purposes contrary to those it is supposed to fulfil, and the same institution can simultaneously serve conflicting purposes.

This, he contends, not a civil society offensive, was the most crucial dynamic in the dramatic political changes in Eastern Europe, and was important in the build-up of dissident and oppositional forces in China leading to the 1989 Democracy Movement. For Ding, societal forces incorporated into the one-party state via 'pseudo-social organisations' can, in certain circumstances, 'convert these organisations from state agencies into instruments for the expression of ideals, or mobilisation and co-ordination of interests against the party-state' (Ding 1994: 298–9). The attraction of Ding's concept lies in its recognition of the possibility of contradictions and tensions internal to the corporatist state, as well as its recognition that the absence of a civil society does not automatically equate with a lack of social organisation. It is particularly instructive for analyses of one-party states where political oppositions may be more likely to manifest themselves outside the formal political institutions.[18]

Some authors have attempted to take this point further, in effect questioning whether there is another realm that has so far escaped adequate conceptualisation: a realm which constitutes the intersection of state and society. Habermas (1989) took this up, in a fashion, when he explored the changing nature of the 'public sphere' in advanced capitalist societies. He understood the public sphere as an intermediate space between state and society, in which both participated, that could take a variety of forms: liberal, plebeian, or regimented, for example. As he saw it, the liberal bourgeois public sphere, formed in opposition to the state, was transformed with the advent of the welfare state and the parallel development of mass society and advertising. In this process: 'State intervention in the sphere of society found its counterpart in the transfer of public functions to private corporate bodies. Likewise, the opposite process of a substitution of public authority by the power of society was connected to the extension of public authority over sectors of the private realm' (Habermas as quoted in Huang 1993: 218). This, he described as the 'societalisation' of the state and the 'statification' of society, a process that undermines the intermediate space previously constituted by a particular public sphere. But Huang (1993: 219) observes that Habermas's notion of private individuals coming together to form a public sphere in opposition to the regulatory regime of public authorities means that: 'The public sphere becomes merely an extension of (civil) society in its democratic development against the absolutist state.'

To get around this reversion to a binary opposition of state and society, Huang (1993) developed the concept of a 'third realm' as conceptually distinct from state and society. It was intended as a value-neutral category with broader application than the historically specific 'bourgeois public sphere'. Huang rejects the idea of multiple public spheres as too vague, and instead looks for something that can be applied to a range of historico-social contexts. The concept of a 'third realm' was employed by Huang to analyse changes in state–society relations in post-revolutionary China:

Beyond the boundaries of the expanded formal state apparatus, moreover, the party-state sought to extend its influence further by completely institutionalising much of the remaining third realm. Instead of relying on ad hoc collaboration between state and society, the party-state created institutional frameworks within which such collaboration was to take place. The purpose was to ensure the state's influence in those spaces it acknowledged to be intermediate between state and society.

(Huang 1993: 232)

This process involved both the penetration of existing institutions, such as the justice system, as well as new institutions such as rural collectives which were part of neither the bureaucratic state nor civil society (Huang 1993: 233). It is this conceptualisation that informs Huang's (1993: 237) caution against expectations that a society long dominated by the party-state can rapidly develop societal organisations 'genuinely separate and independent from the state'. Rather, the unfolding tensions in the third realm are the most likely dynamics to shape China's political direction for the foreseeable future. Though Ding did not adopt the same sort of trinary conception, his treatment of the ambiguous dimensions of state–society relations is not inconsistent with Huang's 'third realm'.

Useful as this concept may potentially be in steering inquiry towards empirical studies of the intersection between state and society, we should be careful to scrutinise the concept more carefully before making any wholehearted endorsement of it. In particular, to attribute to it the same analytical or political significance as the concept of civil society would overstate the case. Even if one were persuaded by the notion that such an ambiguous realm exists and has general application, it does not necessarily follow that it carries equal weight in its implications for political opposition or the analysis thereof.[19]

The idea that a modern, industrialised society can exist without a civil society, and indeed flourish economically, is a further point taken up briefly by Gellner (1994). He notes a frustration by conservatives in the established, industrialised liberal democracies who lament the absence of a holistic moral community. According to Gellner, the inherently pluralistic nature of civil society simply cannot deliver what these conservatives demand. However, there are contemporary alternatives to civil society that are capable of offering the shared vision absent in civil society, in combination with industrialisation and economic development. He sees Islam in this light, addressing the spiritual and practical needs of a disoriented urban population experiencing development-related upheaval. But China, Singapore, Taiwan, and Malaysia are also singled out as a group. As Gellner understands it, the problem of capitalist anomie is ameliorated in these societies via the discipline of authoritarian order from above and family networks from below which condition the individual's experience of the market. While the depiction of these societies as ones tightly bonded by kinship may be somewhat idealised and culturalist, Gellner does at least recognise the possibility of sustainable political alternatives to civil society in conjunction with capitalist industrialisation.

To reiterate, none of the above argument implies a normative indifference to the existence of civil society or advocates its down-grading in analytical terms.[20] It simply suggests that the state versus civil society dichotomy should not be rigidly enforced if we are trying to conceptualise the full range of political contestations in any society, particularly one-party states or 'dominant party systems' which char-acterise much of East and Southeast Asia. Other political spaces are important because their existence conditions the character of opposi-tion. The nature and significance of the co-optation of societal forces through modifications to state institutions is thus an important area of investigation. To differing extents, this co-optation introduces impor-tant dynamics to the political process, including forms of contestation, that can affect the content of public policy.

However, civil society, as a concept, must be preserved for specifying a particular form of political space. It cannot include all independent, voluntary social organisations. Instead, a distinction must be drawn between civic and civil society, the latter involving regular attempts to advance the interests of members through overt political action. As Bernhard (1993: 308) emphasises, civil society requires 'the existence of an independent public space from the exercise of state power, and then the ability of organisations within it to influence the exercise of state power'. Seen in this way, civil society is an inherently political sphere, of no less significance than formal political parties. As Rodan's chapter on Singapore argues, the ruling People's Action Party (PAP) is acutely aware of the inherently political nature of civil society, hence its adoption of legislation and a legal discourse intended to constrain the political activities of social and cultural organisations.

A final observation about the concept of civil society concerns its extra-national dimensions. The theorisation of state–civil society rela-tions has been overwhelmingly premised on the assumption that civil society, like the state, is a fundamentally national phenomenon. Yet there are both international governmental organisations (IGOs) and international non-governmental organisations (INGOs) which compli-cate the matter. International relations theory literature has for some time been interested in the former, but the latter have only recently attracted serious academic interest on any scale.[21] The emphasis in new social movements on the international character of feminist, environmentalist, human rights, and other movements has contributed to greater awareness of INGOs. Moreover, the recent accelerated growth of INGOs, now estimated at 23,000, simply compels more analytical attention (Alger 1990: 159). Many of those outside the established centres of capitalist production involve developmental organisations of a grassroots nature. As is discussed in Chapter 2, important debates have surfaced over the politicisation of the development process through some of these organisations. But there is also evidence of growing regional linkages between human rights, environmental, and other activists in Asia (see Vatikiotis 1994). The extent to which political opposition is able to draw on the international support of like-minded communities – whether they be political parties or social movements – is obviously an important empirical question. But at what point do these links qualify as part of a 'globalised' or 'international' civil society?

According to Lipschutz (1992: 398–9), we are witnessing the emergence of new political spaces as transnational networks of economic, social and cultural relations are formed for specific social and political purposes by people united by common norms. This, he stresses, is qualitatively more than accelerated international social contact brought about by new technologies. Rather: 'It is new forms of social organisation and social practice, and not hardware alone, that have global political effects' (Lipschutz 1992: 413). These forms of organisation are diminishing the state's political importance, and quite deliberately as Lipschutz (1992: 398–9) sees it: 'This civil society is "global" not only because of those connections that cross national boundaries and operate within the "global, nonterritorial region", but also as a result of a growing element of global consciousness in the way the members of global civil society act.'

While the state is by no means in its death throes, avenues for political contestation over the exercise of power are being opened up by the processes focused on by Lipschutz. The question is: how significant are they and what are the preconditions for utilising them? In Chapter 7, He Baogang embarks on a dedicated study of exiled Chinese oppositionists. In this case, international organisations and movements are mounted from abroad. He finds, however, that while they are effective in shaping international opinion and influencing host governments, the impact of these groups is ultimately restrained by severance from domestically based movements and organisations.

CONCLUSION

Given the enormity of the social transformations in East and Southeast Asia resulting from rapid capitalist industrialisation, it is indeed reasonable to anticipate political changes. However, if we are to ascertain and specify those changes, it is necessary to adopt a theoretical framework that does not exclude possibilities that may differ from the historical experiences of earlier-industrialising capitalist societies, and our own normative preferences. The triumph of liberal democracy is but one possibility for these societies, and not necessarily the most likely. Political oppositions consistent with this model are thus not the only oppositions emerging in the dynamic, late-industrialising societies in East and Southeast Asia.

As we have seen above, there are some common themes to oppositions, and the circumstances shaping them, in the industrialising countries of East and Southeast Asia. In particular, economic and social transformations associated with rapid industrialisation have precipitated political accommodations involving changes in state–society relations throughout the region. However, what is striking is the diversification in the forms of these accommodations. There is a differential mix affecting the importance and complexion of political parties, social movements, NGOs, and co-opted social organisations unfolding that is giving definition to political oppositions in the various societies in the region. We should expect the contrasting mixes in the forms and substances of oppositions in each society to produce even more divergent political trajectories as capitalist industrialisation consolidates.

The relative importance and character of civil society is an important part of this differentiation. However, oppositions eking out a measure of independent political space need not be bearers of liberal democratic values or architects of political liberalism. Indeed, their attempts to effect political change are often premised on the retention of elitist and hierarchical structures. But rather than diminishing their significance as political oppositions, this may afford them greater latitude to contest the exercise of state power openly. Similarly, authorities are able to shape the direction of civil society to encourage elements that do not challenge the fundamental social and political order. Indeed, if the prospects of civil society are in some cases brighter now in parts of East and Southeast Asia than they were in the 1970s, it has much to do with the moderating influence of new social forces limiting their criticisms to the detail rather than the essence of the economic and social system. It is precisely because this time opposition is less fundamental, particularly where it involves an expanded civil society, that it is more likely to be sustainable over the longer term.

NOTES

* I am grateful to Kevin Hewison, Richard Robison, Chua Beng Huat, and two anonymous referees for their constructive criticisms on an earlier draft of this work.

1 As is the case throughout this series of volumes, a distinction is drawn between the bourgeoisie and the middle class on the basis of the former's possession of capital and the social relationship involved in it. For elaboration on this see Richard Robison and David S. Goodman (1996) 'The New Rich in Asia, Economic Development, Social Status and Political Consciousness', in Richard Robison and David S. Goodman (eds) *The New Rich in Asia, Mobile Phones, McDonalds and Middle-class Revolution*, Routledge: London and New York, pp. 1–18.

2 Increasingly, with the focus on leadership in particular, voluntarism is emphasised in the accounts of whether or not the preconditions for change are actually realised. Diamond (1989: 3), in an acknowledgement of the transitions volumes, states that 'the choices, decisions, values, and actions of political and institutional leaders have figured prominently – and in many cases, quite clearly decisively – in the decline or fall of democracy'. He contends that, in the democratic prospects of Asian countries, 'effective and democratically-committed leadership' is of crucial importance (Diamond 1989: 49).

3 There are of course variants within these two extremes, referred to by Dahl as mixed regimes and competitive oligarchies. Mixed regimes afford a measure of space for select public contestation, including 'loyal oppositions', but barriers nevertheless exist to the full expression of political preferences. Competitive oligarchies are even more selective about the tolerance of opposition, excluding the bulk of the population which is unorganised and unrepresented but allowing some contestation amongst elites (Dahl 1973: 14–5).

4 Barker (1971: 26) draws on the following quote from Dahl to illustrate the problem:'Today one is inclined to regard the existence of an opposition party as very nearly the most distinctive characteristic of democracy itself; and we take the absence of an opposition party as evidence, if not always conclusive proof, for the absence of democracy.'

5 Linz distinguishes between legal semi-opposition and alegal and illegal opponents who operate outside the system. Alegal opposition 'refers to opponents whose activities, without being strictly illegal, have no legal sanction and run counter to the spirit if not the text of the Constitution and laws of the regime. They are outside the law: alegal' (Linz 1973: 191).

6 Linz maintains that semi-opposition is largely interest-based rather than structural. Despite occasional pretensions to the contrary, this opposition does not question the basic assumptions of the regime (Linz 1973: 191). As such, it is limited in the ability to foster genuinely alternative programmes.

7 In Huntington's book *The Third Wave: Democratization in the Late*

Twentieth Century (1991), he not only identifies a new global surge in the direction of liberal democracy since the mid-1970s, he also warns that previous waves of 'democratisation' have been followed by a wave of reversions to authoritarian rule. On this point, Dahl (1994: 18) clearly sees culture as strategic in resisting any undemocratic or anti-democratic impulses:

> Whenever a country develops an advanced market oriented society its people will be provided with many structures, incentives, skills, and opportunities that are favourable to democratic ideas and processes. But such a development does not by any means insure that they will possess a democratic culture and common identity that are strong enough to avoid severe crises or conflict, or maintain democracy when they occur.

8 According to Schmitter and Karl (1991: 82), the challenge in trying to establish liberal democracy 'is not so much to find a set of goals that command widespread consensus as to find a set of rules that embody contingent consent'. For them, all liberal democracies involve a measure of political uncertainty owing to institutionalised competition. But the rules of competition limit the bounds of that uncertainty.

9 On the basis of her observations on different regimes in the region, Chan (1993: 21–4) also posits the notion of an 'Asian democracy'. This involves free elections but characteristically has the following distinguishing features: a communitarian sense which locates the individual within the group; a greater acceptance of and respect for authority and hierarchy; a dominant-party system rather than a competitive party system; and a centralised bureaucracy and strong state. According to Chan (1993: 25), 'indigenous cultures and folkways are impossible to erase, which is why we should not expect transplanted political institutions to look exactly like their antecedents and to function in a similar way. Hence Asian democracy.'

10 This latest position by Fukuyama comes in the wake of Kim Dae Jung's (1994) rebuttal of Lee Kuan Yew's widely publicised insistence on the irreconcilability of liberal democracy and Confucianism. Kim effectively turned the cultural obstacle argument on its head, arguing that 'almost two thousand years before Locke, Chinese philosopher Meng-tzu preached similar ideas' (Kim 1994: 191). According to Kim (1994: 192), while the basic ideas and traditions requisite for 'democracy' first emerged in Asia, it was the Europeans who first 'formalized comprehensive and effective electoral democracy'.

11 This is not to overlook the fact that the finer detail of his thesis has aroused considerable controversy. See, for example, *Foreign Affairs*, 72: 4 and *Asian Studies Review*, 18: 1, both of which contain various critical responses to Huntington's thesis.

12 Habermas (1984: 392), for example, argues that: 'these new conflicts arise in domains of cultural reproduction, social integration, and socialisation' and 'The new problems have to do with quality of life, equal rights, individual self-realization, participation, and human rights'. Moreover, Crook *et al.* (1993: 151) underline that the values *per se* of NSMs are not as significant as the insistence that they serve as the uncompromising measure of all institutional and political behaviour, both in civil society and formal state institutions. Young (1994: 84) argues that this emphasis on

values makes NSMs difficult to reconcile with the liberal pluralist model of rational, self-interested individuals or collectives. Rather, ideas and principles that cannot be deduced from socio-economic positions or material self-interest play a major role.

13 NSM organisations are depicted as: small, locally based groups; organised around specific issues; having wild fluctuations in their levels of activity; often with fluid hierarchies and lacking clear systems of authority. These characteristics lead Scott (1990: 30) to suggest it might be more appropriate to use the term 'social networks' rather than organisations when describing NSMs. Importantly, the disparate nature of social movements militates against their mobilisation as a coherent oppositional force with a programmatic alternative. Some NSM theorists have looked to the ecology movement as possibly having the potential to transcend this. Here it is the rejection of technocracy and its supporting institutions and values, rather than capitalism, which is seen as the motivation for radical change (see Scott 1990: 30).

14 According to Habermas (1987: 358–9), 'The lifeworld is the unspecified reservoir from which the subsystems of the economy and state extract what they need for their reproduction: performance at work and obedience.'

15 Crook *et al.* (1993: 163–4) acknowledge the dilution effect of the above processes on NSMs, but nevertheless insist that NSMs represent an irreversible change for the politics of industrialised societies in favour of increased diversity of political processes: more open organisational structures, more diverse elites, more fluid and fragmented alliances and loyalties, and more complex networks of communication.

16 Schmitter (1992: 428) notes that competing theories and models of democracy emphasise particular institutional sites in advancing their cases, but argues that all are potentially democratic so long as 'they respect the overarching principle of citizenship and the procedural minima of civil rights, fair elections, free associability etc.'.

17 This is not to insist that we can simply differentiate the actual extent of state structures in Europe and North America from East and Southeast Asia. Arguably the biggest differences in state–society relations from one case to another centres on the form or nature of the relationship rather than the extent of it. States are at all times extensively related to societies.

18 Stepan (1985: 340) makes the complementary point that the evolution of political opposition to the state within society is shaped by the way in which the state defines its project and by the contradictions and conflicts that emerge inside the state apparatus itself.

19 This point was forcefully and convincingly made by Chua Beng-Huat in reaction to an earlier draft.

20 Some theorists, such as Tester (1992) and Kumar (1993), do see cases for abandoning the concept. Tester argues against the use of the concept civil society on the grounds that it is essentially a construct of modernity and thus carries with it questionable assumptions about an objective, external reality:

> The modern imaginations of civil society are based on a series of problems and possibilities which means that they are largely inadequate for the tasks of interpreting and creating maps of post-modernity. Civil

society will only continue to be accepted as a satisfactory imagination
to the extent that it can continue to provide easy and comforting answers
to easy and irrelevant questions.

(as quoted in Reitzes 1994: 103)

Kumar believes too much wasted energy has accompanied the renewed
interest and faith in the concept of civil society. For him, 'The establishment
of a democratic polity and a public sphere of political debate and political
activity are the primary conditions for a thriving civil society of independent
associations and an active civil life' (Kumar 1993: 391). This suggests that
it is to the institutions of the state and the reconstitution of the functioning
political society that attention should be focused. This position is not
inconsistent with the 'new institutionalism'.

21 Ironically, as Ghils (1992: 417) points out, transnational phenomena such
as religious movements pre-date the institution of the state itself.

REFERENCES

Alger, Chadwick F. (1990) 'Grass-roots Perspectives on Global Policies for
Development', *Journal of Peace Research*, 27(2): 155–68.
Almond, Gabriel A. (1993) 'Foreword' in Larry Diamond (ed.) *Political
Culture and Democracy in Developing Countries*, Boulder, Colo.: Lynne
Rienner Publishers, pp. ix–xii.
Almond, Gabriel A. and Verba, Sydney (1965) *The Civic Culture: Political
Attitudes and Democracy in Five Nations*, Boston: Little Brown.
Alvarez, Sonia E. and Escobar, Arturo (1992) 'Conclusion: Theoretical and
Political Horizons of Change in Contemporary Latin American Social
Movements', in Arturo Escobar and Sonia E. Alvarez (eds) *The Making of
Social Movements in Latin America*, Boulder, San Francisco and Oxford:
Westview Press.
Aspinall, Edward (1995) 'Opposition in Indonesia: Some Thoughts', un-
published mimeograph.
Barker, Rodney (1971) 'Introduction', in Rodney Barker (ed.) *Studies in
Opposition*, London: Macmillan, pp. 1–30.
Bernhard, Michael (1993) 'Civil Society and Democratic Transition in East
Central Europe', *Political Science Quarterly*, 108(2): 307–26.
Blaney, David L. and Pasha, Mustaphe Kamal (1993) 'Civil Society and
Democracy in the Third World: Ambiguities and Historical Possibilities',
Studies in Comparative International Development, 28(1), Spring: 3–24.
Bobbio, Norberto (1989) *Democracy and Dictatorship: the Nature and Limits
of State Power*, trans. Peter Kennealy, Cambridge: Polity Press.
Bryant, Christopher G. A. (1993) 'Social Self-organisation, Civilty and
Sociology: a Comment on Kumar's "Civil Society"', *British Journal of
Sociology*, 44(3): 397–401.
—— (1994) 'A Further Comment on Kumar's "Civil Society"', *British
Journal of Sociology*, 45(3), September: 497–9.
Case, William (1994) 'Elites and Regimes in Comparative Perspective:
Indonesia, Thailand, and Malaysia', *Governance: An International Journal
of Policy and Administration*, 7(4), July: 431–60.
Chan Heng Chee (1993) 'Democracy: Evolution and Implementation', in R.

Bartley, Chan Heng Chee, S. P. Huntington and Shijuro Ogata (1993) *Democracy and Capitalism: Asian and American Perspectives*, Singapore: Institute of Southeast Asian Studies.

Cohen, Jean L. and Arato, Andrew (1992) *Civil Society and Political Theory*, Cambridge, Mass.: MIT Press.

Crook, Stephen, Pakulski, Jan, and Waters, Malcolm (1993) *Postmodernization: Change in Advanced Society*, London: Sage Publications.

Daalder, Hans (1966) 'Government and Opposition in the New States', *Government and Opposition*, 1(2): 205–26.

Dahl, Robert A. (1966a) (ed.) *Political Oppositions in Western Democracies*, New Haven: Yale University Press.

—— (1966b) 'Epilogue', in Robert A. Dahl (ed.) *Political Oppositions in Western Democracies*, New Haven: Yale University Press, pp. 387–401.

—— (1966c) 'Preface', in Robert A. Dahl (ed.) *Political Oppositions in Western Democracies*, New Haven: Yale University Press, pp. xi–xix.

—— (1971) *Polyarchy: Participation and Opposition*, New Haven and London: Yale University Press.

—— (1973) 'Introduction', in Robert A. Dahl (ed.) *Regimes and Oppositions*, New Haven: Yale University Press, pp. 1–26.

—— (1994) 'From Authorization to Democracy via Socioeconomic Development', paper presented at the conference 'Social Development in the Asia-Pacific Region', Hong Kong.

Diamond, Larry (1989) 'Introduction: Persistence, Erosion, Breakdown, and Renewal', in Larry Diamond, Juan J. Linz, and Seymour Martin Lipset (eds) *Democracy in Developing Countries: Asia*, vol. 3, Boulder, Colo.: Lynne Rienner Publishers, pp. 1–52.

—— (1993) 'Introduction', in Larry Diamond (ed.) *Political Culture and Democracy in Developing Countries*, Boulder, Colo.: Lynne Rienner Publishers pp. 1–33.

—— (1994) 'Toward Democratic Consolidation', *Journal of Democracy*, 5(3): 4–17.

Diamond, Larry and Plattner, Marc F. (1993) 'Introduction', in Larry Diamond and Marc F. Plattner (eds) *The Global Resurgence of Democracy*, Baltimore: Johns Hopkins University Press, pp. ix–xxvi.

Ding, X. L. (1994) 'Institutional Amphibiousness and the Transition from Communism: the Case of China', *British Journal of Political Science*, 24: 293–318.

Fisher, Julie (1993) *The Road from Rio: Sustainable Development and the Nongovernmental Movement in the Third World*, Westport, Conn., and London: Praeger.

Fukuyama, Francis (1992a) *The End of History and the Last Man*, New York: Avon Books.

—— (1992b) 'Capitalism and Democracy: the Missing Link', *Journal of Democracy*, 3(3), July: 100–10.

—— (1995a) 'Confucianism Is No Bar to Asian Democracy', *Asian Wall Street Journal*, 23, May: 8.

—— (1995b) 'The Primacy of Culture', *Journal of Democracy*, 6(1), January: 7–14.

—— (1995c) *Trust: the Social Virtues and the Creation of Prosperity*, London: Hamish Hamilton.

Gellner, Ernest (1991) 'Civil Society in Historical Context', *International Social Science Journal*, 129: 495–510.

—— (1994) *Conditions of Liberty: Civil Society and its Rivals*, New York: Allen Lane/Penguin.

Ghils, Paul (1992) 'International Civil Society: International Non-Governmental Organizations in the International System', *International Social Science Journal*, 133: 417–29.

Gold, Thomas B. (1990) 'Tiananmen and Beyond: the Resurgence of Civil Society in China', *Journal of Democracy*, 1(1): 18–31.

Gorz, André (1980) *Ecology as Politics*, trans. Patsy Vigderman and Jonathon Cloud, Boston, Mass.: South End Press.

Habermas, Jurgen (1974) 'The Public Sphere: an Encyclopaedia Article (1964)', *New German Critique*, 3: 49–55.

—— (1981) 'New Social Movements', *Telos*, 49, Fall: 33–7.

—— (1984) 'Reason and the Rationalization of Society', *The Theory of Communicative Action*, vol. 1, trans. Thomas McCarthy, Boston: Beacon Press.

—— (1987) 'Lifeworld and System: a Critique of Functionalist Reason', *The Theory of Communicative Action*, vol. 2, trans. Thomas McCarthy, Boston: Beacon Press.

—— (1989) *The Structural Transformation of the Public Sphere*, trans. by Thomas Burger with the assistance of Frederick Lawrence, Cambridge, Mass.: MIT Press.

Harris, Nigel (1986) *The End of the Third World*, Penguin: Harmondsworth.

Hassall, Graham and Cooney, Sean (1993) 'Democracy and Constitutional Change in Asia', *Asian Studies Review*, 17(1), July: 2–10.

Held, David (1987) *Models of Democracy*: Cambridge: Polity Press.

—— (1989) *Political Theory and the Modern State: Essays on State, Power and Democracy*, Cambridge: Polity Press.

—— (1993) 'Democracy: from City-states to a Cosmopolitan Order?', in David Held (ed.) *Prospects for Democracy North South East West*, Cambridge: Polity Press, pp. 13– 52.

Hellman, Judith Adler (1992) 'The Study of New Social Movements in Latin America and the Question of Autonomy', in Arturo Escobar and Sonia E. Alvarez (eds) *The Making of Social Movements in Latin America: Identity, Strategy, and Democracy*, Boulder, San Francisco, Oxford: Westview Press, pp. 52–61.

Higley, John and Burton, Michael G. (1989) 'The Elite Variable in Democratic Transitions and Breakdowns', *American Sociological Review*, 54: 17–32.

Howe, Stephen (1991) 'The New Xenophobes', *New Statesman and Society*, 4(149): 12.

Huang, Philip C. C. (1993) '"Public Sphere"/"Civil Society" in China?', *Modern China*, 19(2): 216–40.

Huntington, Samuel P. (1991) *The Third Wave: Democratization in the Late Twentieth Century*, Norman and London: University of Oklahoma Press.

—— (1993a) 'Democracy's Third Wave', in Larry Diamond and Marc F. Plattner (eds) *The Global Resurgence of Democracy*, Baltimore, Md.: Johns Hopkins University Press, pp. 3–25.

—— (1993b) 'The Clash of Civilizations?', *Foreign Affairs*, 72(3): 22–49.

Ionescu, Ghita and de Madariaga, Isabel (1968) *Opposition: Past and Present of a Political Institution*, London: C.A. Wath.

Jomo, K. S. and Cheek, Ahmad Shabery (1992) 'Malaysia's Islamic Movements', in Francis Loh Kok Wah and Joel S. Kahn (eds) *Fragmented Vision: Culture and Politics in Contemporary Malaysia*, Sydney: Allen & Unwin, pp. 79–105.

de Jouvenel, Bertrand (1966) 'The Means of Contestation', trans. Valence Ionescu, *Government and Opposition*, 1(2): 155–74.

Kaelberer, Matthias (1993) 'The Emergence of Green Parties in Western Europe', *Comparative Politics*, 25(2), January: 229–43.

Keane, John (1988) *Democracy and Civil Society: On the Predicaments of European Socialism, the Prospects for Democracy, and the Problem of Controlling Social and Political Power*, London and New York: Verso Press.

Kim Dae Jung (1994) 'Is Culture Destiny?: The Myth of Asia's Anti-Democratic Values', *Foreign Affairs*, 73(6), November/December: 189–94.

—— (1995a) 'On Asian Democracy', *Asiaweek*, 28 April: 32–3.

—— (1995b) 'Asia Hungers for Democracy, Activist Laments', excerpts from a speech, *Jakarta Post*, 20 May: 4

Kukathas, Chandran and Lovell, David W. (1991) 'The Significance of Civil Society', Chandran Kukathas, David W. Lovell, and William Maley (eds) *The Transition from Socialism: State and Civil Society in the USSR*, London: Longman Cheshire.

Kumar, Krishan (1993) 'Civil Society: an Inquiry Into the Usefulness of an Historical Term', *British Journal of Sociology*, 44(3), September: 375–95.

Lawson, Stephanie (1993a) 'Conceptual Issues in the Comparative Study of Regime Change and Democratization', *Comparative Politics*, 25(2): 183–205.

—— (1993b) 'Institutionalising Peaceful Conflict: Political Opposition and the Challenge of Democratisation in Asia', *Australian Journal of International Affairs*, 47(1): 14–30.

Linz, Juan J. (1973) 'Opposition to and Under an Authoritarian Regime: the Case of Spain', in Robert A. Dahl (ed.) *Regimes and Oppositions*, New Haven Conn.: Yale University Press, pp. 171–260.

Lipschutz, Ronnie D. (1992) 'Reconstructing World Politics: the Emergence of Global Civil Society', *Millennium*, 21(3): 389–420.

Lipset, Seymour Martin (1990) 'The Centrality of Political Culture', *Journal of Democracy*, 1(4): 80–3.

—— (1993) 'The Centrality of Political Culture', in Larry Diamond and Marc F. Plattner (eds) *The Global Resurgence of Democracy*, Baltimore, Md.: Johns Hopkins University Press, pp. 134–7.

Marks, Gary (1992) 'Rational Sources of Chaos in Democratic Transition', in Gary Marks and Larry Diamond (eds) *Re-examining Democracy: Essays in Honor of Seymour Martin Lipset*, Newbury Park, Calif.: Sage Publications, pp. 47–69.

Mirsky, Yehudah (1993) 'Democratic Politics, Democratic Culture' *Orbis*, 37(4), Fall: 567–80.

Mohamed, Mahathir and Ishihara, Shintaro (1995) *The Voice of Asia*, trans. Frank Baldwin, Tokyo: Kodansha International.

Moody, Peter R. Jr (1988) *Political Opposition in Post-Confucian Society*, New York: Praeger.

O'Donnell, Guillermo (1994) 'Delegative Democracy', *Journal of Democracy*, 5(1). 55–69.

O'Donnell, Guillermo and Schmitter, Philippe C. (1986) *Transitions from Authoritarian Rule: Tentative Conclusions about Uncertain Democracies*, Baltimore, Md.: Johns Hopkins University Press.

O'Donnell, Guillermo, Schmitter, Philippe C., and Whitehead, Laurence (1986) *Transitions from Authoritarian Rule: Comparative Perspectives*, Baltimore, Md.: Johns Hopkins University Press.

Parekh, Bikhu (1993) 'The Cultural Particularity of Liberal Democracy', in David Held (ed.) *Prospects for Democracy North South East West*, Cambridge: Polity Press, pp. 156–76.

Potter, David (1993) 'Democratization in Asia', in David Held (ed.) *Prospects for Democracy, North South East West*, Cambridge: Polity Press.

Punnett, R. M. (1973) 'Her Majesty's Opposition', in *Front-Bench Opposition: the Role of the Leader of the Opposition, the Shadow Cabinet and Shadow Government in British Politics*, London: Heinemann, pp. 3–32.

Pye, Lucien H. (1985) *Asian Power and Politics: the Cultural Dimensions of Authority*, Cambridge, Mass.: Belknap Press.

Reintges, Claudia M. (1990) 'Urban Movements in South African Black Townships: a Case Study', *International Journal of Urban and Regional Research*, 14(1): 109–34.

Reitzes, Maxine (1994) 'Civil Society, the Public Sphere and the State: Reflections on Classical and Contemporary Discourses', *Theoria*, 83(84): 95–121.

Robison, Richard (1986) *Indonesia: the Rise of Capital*, Sydney: Allen & Unwin.

—— (1993) 'Mahathir Paints False Picture of Asian Region', *Australian*, 14 December.

Rodan, Garry (1995) *Ideological Convergences Across East and West: the New Conservative Offensive*, Working Paper No. 41, Aalborg, Denmark: Development Research Unit, Department of Development and Planning, Aalborg University.

Rueschemeyer, D., Stephens, E. J., and Stephens, John D. (1992) *Capitalist Development and Democracy*, Cambridge: Polity Press.

Safire, William (1972) *The New Language of Politics*, New York: Collier Books.

Salecl, Renata (1992) 'Nationalism, Anti-Semitism, and Anti-Feminism in Eastern Europe', *New German Critique*, 57, Fall: 51–65.

Scalapino, Robert A. (1993) 'Democratizing Dragons: South Korea and Taiwan', *Journal of Democracy*, 4(3), July: 70–83.

Schmitter, Philippe C. (1992) 'The Consolidation of Democracy and Representation of Social Groups', *American Behavioral Scientist*, 35(4/5): 422–49.

Schmitter, Philippe C. and Karl, Terry Lynn (1991) 'What Democracy Is . . . and Is Not', *Journal of Democracy*, 2(3), Summer: 75–88.

Scott, Alan (1990) *Ideology and the New Social Movements*, London: Unwin Hyman.

Shaw, Martin (1994) 'Civil Society and Global Politics: Beyond a Social Movements Approach', *Millennium: Journal of International Studies*, 23(3): 647–67.

Shils, Edward (1971) 'Opposition in the New States of Asia and Africa', in Rodney Barker (ed.) *Studies in Opposition*, London: Macmillan, pp. 45–78.

—— (1991) 'The Virtue of Civil Society', *Government and Opposition*, 26(1), Winter: 3–20.

Shubane, Khehla (1992) 'Civil Society in Apartheid and Post-Apartheid South Africa', *Theoria*, 33: 41.

Slater, David (1994a) 'Introduction', *Latin American Perspectives*, 21(3), Summer: 3–7.

—— (1994b) 'Power and Social Movements in the Other Occident: Latin America in an International Context', *Latin American Perspectives*, 21(2), Spring: 11–37.

Stepan, Alfred (1985) 'State Power and the Strength of Civil Society in the Southern Cone of Latin America', in Peter B. Evans, Dietrich Rueschemeyer, and Theda Skocpol (eds) *Bringing the State Back In*, Cambridge: Cambridge University Press, pp. 317–43.

—— (1993) 'On the Tasks of a Democratic Opposition', in Larry Diamond and Marc F. Plattner (eds) *The Global Resurgence of Democracy*, Baltimore: Johns Hopkins University Press: 61–9.

Stepan, Alfred and Skach, Cindy (1993) 'Constitutional Frameworks and Democratic Consolidation: Parliamentarianism versus Presidentialism', *World Politics*, 46, October: 1–22.

Tester, Keith (1992) *Civil Society*, London: Routledge.

van der Kroef, Justus M. (1978) 'Patterns of Political Opposition in Southeast Asia', *Pacific Affairs*, 51: 620–38.

Vatikiotis, Michael (1994) 'Going Regional: Advocacy Groups Look Beyond Their Own Borders', *Far Eastern Economic Review*, 20 October: 16.

Wilde, Lawrence (1990) 'Class Analysis and the Politics of New Social Movements', *Capital and Class*, 42, Winter: 55–78.

Wood, Ellen Meiksins (1990) 'The Uses and Abuses of "Civil Society"', in Ralph Miliband, Leo panitch and John Saville (eds) *Socialist Register 1990*, London: Merlin Press, pp. 60–84.

Young, Iris (1994) 'Civil Society and Social Change', *Theoria*, 83(84), October: 73–94.

Zakaria, Fareed (1994) 'Culture Is Destiny. A Conversation with Lee Kuan Yew', *Foreign Affairs*, 73(2): 109–26.

2 The ebb and flow of civil society and the decline of the Left in Southeast Asia

Kevin Hewison and Garry Rodan*

INTRODUCTION

As has been mentioned in Chapter 1, the literature on contemporary political change in East and Southeast Asia pays particular attention to the relationship between economic development and civil society. This preoccupation is not peculiar to modernisation theorists, but is found among writers from a range of theoretical positions, including Marxist authors. A striking tendency across this theoretical spectrum is a view of civil society as a progressive outcome of capitalist development. The implication in this literature is that contemporary attempts to expand the political space of civil society are either more significant or more substantive than previous attempts. Indeed, previous attempts are rarely acknowledged at all.

A significant part of the explanation for this tendency lies in the adoption of definitions of political or regime change and democracy which direct attention only to the most recent round of jockeying between the state and civil society. There is a strong association of civil society with liberal democratic political forms such as parliaments, constitutions, and legal political parties. Much is made of the functional relationship between an extensive civil society and these forms. Such perspectives downplay or ignore struggles involved in the emergence of civil society, many of which have taken place outside the confines of parliaments, constitutions, and legal political parties. The contributions of these extra-parliamentary political movements to the deepening and expansion of civil society in earlier periods have generally been overlooked in the emerging literature on democratisation and regime change.

The primary theoretical point of this chapter is to challenge the idea that any contemporary expansions in the political space that is civil society lead towards some historical end point. Instead, we view these expansions as a part of the ebb and flow of political opposition, broadly conceived, which is ongoing and certainly precedented. This is not to suggest, however, that this ebb and flow simply involves a repetition of history, for in each phase of civil society's expansion there are new dimensions. Furthermore, while the emergence of civil society is significant to the development of democracy, the political space can and has expanded even under unrepresentative regimes. These points will be demonstrated by way of a historical account of the political struggles in Southeast Asia that have periodically opened up civil society, usually followed by temporary closure due to the repressive actions of colonial and post-colonial governments. This historical account will focus specifically on the role of the 'Left' in these periodic political openings.

Before proceeding any further, let us first clarify what we mean when we refer to civil society. Civil society is an autonomous sphere 'from which political forces representing constellations of interests in society have contested state power' (Bernhard 1993: 307). The range of organisations in society may be enormous, but not all engage in overtly political activity. For example, seemingly apolitical groups can include sporting clubs as well as charitable and welfare-oriented associations – these might be considered as civic organisations.[1] Politically active groups include a range of non-state groups which may or may not be legal: political parties, trade unions, employer and professional associations, women's groups, student organisations, peasant and ethnic associations, an increasingly expansive group of politically activist non-government organisations (NGOs), and a range of social movements.[2] These groups are regularly involved in political actions which attempt to advance the interests of people, ranging from those of their members to the more general interest of wider groups in society.

The autonomy of such organisations is fundamental, even if the class interests of these groups vary widely or even support the established regime or the hegemony of the dominant classes. Only through autonomous organisations can these non-state groups have an institutionalised influence over the official political sphere.

This need for autonomy often involves the state through legal recognition, but the state may also sanction this autonomy through its inaction, by not enforcing legal restrictions on political activities. As a result of struggle, the state can be compelled to recognise a political space where autonomous self-organisation can occur outside the sphere of official politics (Bernhard 1993: 308–9). Thus, it is not the emergence of organisations that is the measure of an expanded civil society. Rather, state actors must effectively legitimate the rights of such bodies to engage in political activity and even to challenge the exercise of state power before civil society can be said to be established. Civic organisations may exist in the most authoritarian polities, but they do not then have the right to be politically activist. Social pluralism does not always translate into political pluralism.

Importantly, the state must itself establish boundaries to define the autonomous space of civil society and protect it from its own interference. In essence, the state must define what is to be considered 'political' and 'legitimate'. However, in return for being granted protected political space, the organisations and associations occupying it are expected to exert a measure of self-discipline. Where this space is not legally protected, the option exists for the state swiftly to cancel *de facto* recognition of independent political space.

The focus here on the role of the Left in the historical struggles to establish political spaces in Southeast Asia is not intended to suggest that this represents the entirety of the forces involved. However, the Left has historically played a crucially important strategic role which suitably illustrates our theoretical point. Moreover, the changing fortunes of the Left over time reveal something of the distinctiveness of the contemporary push for civil society in Southeast Asia. Among other factors, successful capitalist industrialisation has fostered not just new domestic interests and sources of power, but greater social differentiation – both have undercut traditional Left strategies and appeal. The severing of the link between nationalism and socialism, and the effective harnessing of nationalist ideology to capitalist development in Southeast Asia, have also restricted the Left in the contemporary period.

The 'Left' is a term which is often used loosely to refer to a variety of reformist movements and ideas. However, we understand the common denominator of the 'Left' to be an emphasis on alternatives to the individualism of market relationships and a commitment to values which advance public and collective interests. At one extreme this involves revolutionary social movements, grounded in class analysis and carrying a vision of an alternative social system, such as socialism or Communism. It can, however, also involve reformism of a social democratic nature which may challenge the prerogatives of capital and the market within much tighter limits, and without any serious vision of an alternative social system. Both these variants of the Left can be differentiated from liberal reformism which may champion individual human rights, the rule of law and liberal democracy, for example, without embracing collectivism and challenges to the market. Liberal reformism, nevertheless, seriously challenges authoritarian rule. In the discussion to follow, unless otherwise specified, we use the term 'the

Left' principally to refer to socialists and Communists who played a leading role in earlier struggles for civil society.

In Southeast Asia, Communist and socialist movements enjoyed their greatest influence during the anti-colonialist and nationalist struggles, and especially following the Second World War. The organisational strengths of these movements, embodying coalitions of workers, peasants, and nationalists, made them indispensable to political strategies for self-government. Indeed, as will be indicated below, the Left played a pivotal role in the development of civil society in these years. Self-identified socialists and Communists also earned the respect of many for the often courageous roles played in confronting colonial forces in this process. Even so, the influence of the Southeast Asian Left should be kept in perspective, since its ideological appeal was confined to strategic sites rather than broadly embraced by the masses.

For the purposes of this discussion, we will focus on the modern countries of Singapore, Malaysia, Thailand, Indonesia, and the Philippines, and their previous incarnations as colonies, with Thailand (previously Siam) being the non-colonial exception. We will show that the Left has been significant in giving much momentum to the development of non-state political space (what we will term civil society) in these countries. We suggest that this was particularly the case in three periods – 1920s–1930s, 1940s–1950s, and the 1970s – when the Left played a pivotal role in expanding the arena of political activity. The defeat of non-state movements saw civil society greatly reduced or even expunged by authoritarian governments, which especially targeted socialists, Communists and the labour and peasant organisations through which many of them operated.

We will go on to suggest that in the contemporary period, the political space associated with civil society is, to varying extents, again being created in the societies of Southeast Asia. However, for reasons to be set out below, it is no longer socialists and Communists who are leading this movement. Rather, a range of liberals and social reformers are playing the leading roles in establishing civil society through various non-state groups. Nevertheless, while the revolutionary Left may be overshadowed by a range of other contending political forces, this does not necessarily mean social reformism is an entirely spent force in contemporary Southeast Asia. Instead, the inequities and contradictions of the market system continue to generate social problems that cannot be alleviated by liberal reformism. The capitalist system *per se* is no longer under the sort of challenge mounted by the Left in the past, but the particular form that capitalism takes in Southeast Asia remains a matter of contest. In this context, social reformers may still exert an influence by linking with other reformers in the various campaigns to extend the space of civil society.

A BRIEF HISTORY OF CIVIL SOCIETY IN SOUTHEAST ASIA[3]

Writing in 1947, Du Bois noted three 'European streams of thought' which she considered had had a marked impact on Southeast Asian societies. These were social humanism, nationalism, and Marxism. Social humanism was seen to involve education and trade unionism, and to provide legal protection as well as introducing the ideal of the dignity of the individual. Nationalism was seen as being crucial as a powerful force against colonialism (Du Bois 1962: 42–4). Marxism was clearly linked to the rise of nationalism and anti-colonialism, and appealed to internationally linked labour. It should be remembered that Lenin's contribution to the debate on imperialism was a powerful document for those opposing colonialism. Lenin had seen the potential for revolution in Asia, writing in 1913, for example, that in the Dutch East Indies there 'was no stopping the growth of the democratic movement' (cited in Gafurov and Kim 1978: 385). Du Bois (1962: 45) explains the attractiveness of Marxism: 'its apparent reconciliation of social humanism and nationalism in colonial areas . . . its appeal to . . . intellectuals and seamen; and . . . the practical efforts of Russia, which in the 1920's was still a revolutionary nations'.

As will be indicated below, there is considerable insight in these observations. While historians have noted the impact of nationalism, little has been made of the contribution of Marxism, and the manner in which the Left took a leading role in linking anti-colonialism, nationalism, and 'social humanism'. Du Bois was writing in one of the periods where civil society was expanding, and the Left was playing a central political role. This period was, however, just one of a number of such periods.

It is obviously not possible to provide a full account of the trials and tribulations of the relationships between civil society and the state in all the countries of Southeast Asia over a period of some seventy years. Rather, we will take three broad slices through the modern history of Southeast Asia when civil society did develop, indicate the crucial roles played by the Left, and show how governments were able to limit and close this political space. We begin with the 1920s and 1930s, not a period usually considered to have been a hotbed of leftist activity in Southeast Asia.

The 1920s and 1930s

In the century up to the 1920s, the colonial governments (including the modernising Thai state) of Southeast Asia had seen and defeated numerous uprisings, most of them in the countryside. These millenarian reactions to colonial rule were, in part, a response to economic and political change. By this time, the various governments had instituted centralised and bureaucratised administrations, had marked out the geographic boundaries of colonies and nation-states, and had, by and large, established government-defined systems of law and order (see Ileto 1992: 197–248; Trocki 1992: 85). In addition, in this era of high colonialism in Southeast Asia, local economies had been reoriented to the demands of mercantilism, with trade in commodities dominating the economic relationship with the west. The focus of political activity perceptibly shifted to urban areas and civil society–state relations.

It is sometimes forgotten that the 1920s marked the beginning of a renaissance in Southeast Asia, with significant change in the ideological climate and considerable political and social ferment. This ferment represented, in part, a struggle for the expansion of the political space we call civil society. The governments of the period were unrepresentative, either an absolute monarchy as in Thailand, or colonial administrations. The ferment was a struggle to gain greater political representation and national independence (Pluvier 1974: 15–21, 72–91; Bastin and Benda 1977: 95–7).

It is noteworthy that, prior to the 1920s, non-state community (or civic) organisations were significant. Throughout Southeast Asia a large number of civic associations had emerged, especially in urban areas, to further the interests of local people and the large immigrant communities, particularly the Chinese, but also other immigrants like the Indians.

These groups were not always politically active, and were certainly not sanctioned to engage in oppositional politics: their activities were usually social, cultural, and apolitical. However, they were often utilised by the state in managing their community, acting as political compradors between the state and their constituents, who were usually non-citizens (see Skinner 1957). Nevertheless, there were times when these organisations became politicised and found themselves acting in opposition to the state. This often led to labour activism, which immediately pitted these organisations against the state. Where labour was involved, the state would quickly brand their activities as subversive, and the organisation risked being labelled as a 'secret society', which meant illegality.

In Singapore, while the British maintained social order through direct repression, their general neglect of the population's welfare had the effect of encouraging voluntary and independent organisations to fill the vacuum. Privately funded vernacular-medium schools, usually operating as night schools, were among the most numerous and significant of such organisations in Singapore, prompting the colonial state to require registration of schools and teachers and to give the government the power to regulate school activities. Apart from education, the associations provided welfare, legal, and minor infrastructural services (Turnbull 1982: 134; Chua 1993: 9–10).

But some politically significant groups also emerged. These included debating clubs, literary and study groups, and the like, which were often the training ground for nationalists. Educated locals in such groups soon found themselves confronting many of the assumptions of colonial rule while organised as 'native' associations (Steinberg 1971: 251).

Much of this growth of civic organisations took place in the period between 1890 and 1920; and by this latter date, many of them were moving beyond welfare and becoming politicised. For example, in British Burma, the Young Men's Buddhist Association became the General Council of Burmese Associations in 1920, and began agitation against the colonial government, including strikes and boycotts. In the Dutch East Indies (Indonesia), a plethora of associations had become politicised, especially student groups and religious, notably Muslim, organisations. Many of these Muslim groups in the Dutch East Indies and British Malaya were influenced by the anti-colonial sentiment of Islamic reform movements in Egypt (Steinberg 1971: 275–6, 290–8, 326).

Chinese societies and guilds were in many cases transformed into separate employer and employee organisations as capitalism developed, and ethnic workers' organisations often showed a degree of solidarity with these Chinese workers (see Stenson 1970: 34; Brown 1990). The response from administrators was, as Trocki (1992: 85) notes, the creation of 'security forces, secret police organisations and spy networks to suppress political movements and labour unions'. While unions were small and represented only a fraction of the population – most of the population were farmers – they were economically significant groups operating in strategic areas such as the ports, transport, and other activities central to trade.[4] Unions were clearly non-state centres of political activism, especially when linked to socialist, Communist, and oppositional movements as they often were, seriously challenging state power.

The 1920s and 1930s saw significant labour organisation. For example, in Thailand, the earliest recorded labour activity dates from the 1880s; and by the 1920s, labour activism led to the establishment of a workers' newspaper during a particularly vicious strike in 1923. The group behind the strike and the newspaper was to become a driving force organising both the industrial and wider political struggles of industrial workers against the absolute monarchy. This activism caused the state to confront the so-called 'labour problem' (Brown 1990: 30–73).

While the colonial and Thai states seemed prepared to be tolerant, indeed in some respects were relieved that there were a range of non-government associations promoting the collective interests of different social and ethnic groups, they appear to have felt most threatened when the developing Left joined these organisations. For example, private Chinese-language schools throughout the region were caught up in movements emanating from political conflict in China, especially after the 1911 Revolution, and became important recruiting grounds for leftist youth and student movements. A strong anti-imperialist and anti-colonial rhetoric began to emerge from these schools, and Communists were seen to control many of them. The Communist Youth League in Singapore was established in 1926, with a strong base in such schools. A similar pattern was seen in Thailand and Malaya, and the authorities closed Chinese schools and attempted to control curricula (see Turnbull 1982; Skinner 1958). But it was not just the Chinese groups which became a focus of left-wing activism. Indeed, from the early 1920s, socialist and Communist organisations had formed in Southeast Asia. For example, the Communist Party of Indonesia (Partai Kommunis Indonesia (PKI)) was formed in 1920. Following this, and in concert with developments in Vietnam and China, Communist organisations were founded throughout the region, and many of the nascent trade unions came under Left influence (van der Kroef 1980: 4–7; Cribb 1985: 251).

Some of this early activity was clearly related to the establishment of the Third International (Comintern) in 1919 and developing Soviet foreign policy. The Comintern had seen significant debate, especially between M. N. Roy and Lenin, over the relationship between Communist parties and anti-colonialism, with the latter favouring alliances with nationalist movements, while the former preferred an emphasis on developing the Communist movement. While a compromise was achieved, it was clear that local conditions also played a significant part in the strategy adopted. For example, in the Dutch East Indies the 1920s saw the strengthening of anti-colonialism and a nationalist movement within which the PKI became a leading element, developing a revolutionary strategy which placed emphasis on the anti-colonial struggle. The PKI suffered a serious setback in 1926–7 following an abortive uprising, but its influence was soon to be restored. In Thailand, where anti-colonialism was not an issue, the nascent Left was able to develop, from its origins in the Chinese community, as the absolutism of the monarchy was questioned.[5]

A major boost to the Left came with the Great Depression, when economic and social conditions deteriorated, paving the way for more concerted action. In Singapore, the Comintern-inspired South Seas General Labour Union, which was established in 1926, had been unable to make any headway. By 1930, however, organised labour and the Left advanced. The Malayan Communist Party (MCP) was established in 1930, with Singapore as its base. The economic downturn in the rubber plantations and tin mines gave considerable impetus to the MCP and its associated unions. A concerted campaign to mobilise labour, which included the formation of the Malayan General Labour Union in 1934, saw the unions become a strong base for Left activism (Starner 1965: 223; van der Kroef 1980: 13).

In the Philippines, the Depression saw the expansion of the opposition and independence movement and, in 1929, the founding of the Socialist Party, which had its own labour organisation. Supporting peasants, tenant farmers, and workers and taking a nationalist stand, the party ran in elections as the Popular Front, and increased its support between 1933 and 1937. The Communist Party (Partido Komunisat ng Philipinas (PKP)) was officially established in 1930 but banned a year later, and went underground. The socialists merged with the Communist Party in 1938 to establish an anti-fascist front (Kratoska and Batson 1992: 264–5; Richardson 1993: 386; see also McCoy and de Jesus 1982; Kerkvliet 1977: Chapters 1–2).

It is usually maintained that the Communist Party of Thailand (CPT) did not establish itself until 1942, but reports from the 1930s indicate that a variety of Communist organisations existed, particularly within the Chinese and Vietnamese communities, but including some ethnic Thais. More importantly, however, following the overthrow of the absolute monarchy in 1932, one faction of the People's Party was accused of 'Bolshevist' tendencies, especially in its relations with labour and students and in its economic policies. The government banned Communism in 1933 (van der Kroef 1980: 22; Golay *et al.* 1969: 287).

By the late 1930s, Communist and socialist movements had emerged throughout Southeast Asia, both linked and divided by ethnicity and all influenced by the nationalist, anti-colonial, and anti-imperialist movements. Even where the anti-colonial struggle was emphasised, this did not diminish an element of internationalism on the Left, evidenced by the activities of revolutionaries like Tan Malaka and Ho Chi Minh who travelled the region. An element that linked these groups was a shared distrust of western liberalism and capitalism. Certainly, the colonial experience had discredited capitalism for many Southeast Asians (Golay *et al.* 1969: 18).

It is apparent that the Left in Southeast Asia had been able to capitalise on and utilise the political space which developed in the 1920s and 1930s. Indeed, the Left was a driving force for the extension of this space. However, as the Second World War approached, there was a move to curtail some of the resultant political activity, which was seen by the authorities as a measure of rebellion. In Thailand, the military had established its control over government and moved closer to fascist regimes in Europe and Japan. In Singapore and Malaya, the colonial state felt threatened by Communism. It crushed the party in 1931, but again faced strong Communist-led worker opposition in the mid-1930s (Starner 1965: 237). Coalitions of workers and Communists were seen as a major challenge throughout the region.

The 1940s and 1950s

Immediately following the Second World War there was another period of relative political openness. While this period was sometimes short, as in Malaya, or intermittent, as in Thailand, this was a time that saw considerable political change in the region. However, the dynamic force of the period was not socialism or Communism, but nationalism. Nationalists and the Left linked to challenge colonialism and expand political space outside the state.

During the Pacific War, the early defeats inflicted on western colonialists by the Japanese gave strength to the various anti-colonial movements, and clearly showed that loyalty had not been strongly established among the subject peoples. The Japanese reinforced this through their propaganda attacking western colonialism. While not all Southeast Asians were enamoured with Japanese colonialism, and many took up arms to oppose it, the Japanese interregnum set the wheels of decolonisation in motion (Bastin and Benda 1977: 109; Pluvier 1974: 195, 198).

After the defeat of Japan, the colonial powers were slow in re-establishing their administrations, which meant that the western colonialists were seen to be replacing nationalist administrations. Not only this, but the re-ensconced colonial regimes presided over severely damaged economies. The destruction wrought on Europe meant that the colonies could not be supported, and nationalists and Communists were concerned that Southeast Asian colonies would be heavily exploited, but it was clear that any colonial re-establishment would require a greater effort than anything prior to the war. In Thailand, it was felt that the British wanted to establish a neo-colony (Pluvier 1974: 334–59; Steinberg 1971: 348; Stockwell 1992: 340–6, 351). In other words, not only was much of the economic infrastructure severely damaged, but so were the political and social structures of colonial Asia, and social change was accelerating.

Nationalists saw that the historical tide was running to their advantage. For example, the establishment of the United Nations clearly implied that decolonisation would be on the international agenda. Indeed, moves to decolonisation in the Philippines and India suggested cause for optimism. Interestingly, while the British were leaving South Asia, they appeared keenest to re-establish the colonial regimes of Southeast Asia. Not only did they do this in their own colonies, but they were instrumental in the reinstitution of colonialism in Indochina and Indonesia (Bastin and Benda 1977: 116; Stockwell 1992: 353). For nationalists, and this included most on the Left, anti-colonialism became the major political issue. Thus, much of the political rhetoric exhibited a strong anti-western tone.

The Second World War also saw Communists gain considerable credibility through their leading role in anti-Japanese resistance movements. Like their western predecessors, the Japanese were anti-Communists, and vigorously suppressed Communist movements, forcing them underground. Yet in Malaya, Singapore, Indochina, and the Philippines, Communists led or were major elements of the anti-Japanese movement (Bastin and Benda 1977: 116; Pluvier 1974: 286–311). At the end of the war these movements were in a strong and popular position, and the link between nationalism and Communism was well-established.

In addition, the increased international influence of the USSR, based on its role in the European theatre of war, gave local Communists cause for optimism. As a founding power in the United Nations, the USSR was able to provide some support for local Communists. For example, Thailand wanted to join the UN and required Soviet support, and for this the USSR sought and received the repeal of Thailand's anti-Communist law in 1946 (Insor 1963: 90).

One of the many links drawn between nationalists and the Left was in the area of economic development. The example of the Marshall Plan for the reconstruction of Western Europe gave an impetus to the idea of economic planning, suggesting that benefits could be obtained from centralised planning. The Nationalists argued that modernisation could only be achieved in the Southeast Asian countries through government investments and planning, thereby strengthening the position of the Left which had long argued for this kind of economic intervention.[6] Economic nationalism became a solid stream of Left and nationalist programmes. In the words of one commentator:

> Indigenism is also influenced by the extent to which the ideology of nationalism is socialist. Independence movements in Southeast Asia, to a substantial degree, were recruited from elements uncommitted by ownership of property or job security. Furthermore, because socialism is identified with social and economic reform in the industrial West, it appeals to nationalist elements whether evolutionary or revolutionary. This appeal is reinforced . . . by the Western socialist tradition of opposition to colonialism.
>
> (Golay *et al.* 1969: 453)

This was clear in Burma and Indonesia, and in a more limited way in Thailand, Malaya, and the Philippines. In Indonesia, for example, most of the political parties were strongly nationalist and anti-colonialist, and this was reflected in an anti-foreign capital stance. The PKI was opposed to foreign investment, but it tended to be supportive of the role of national capital, while the PSI (Indonesian Socialist Party) opposed extreme nationalism (Golay *et al.* 1969: 119–24). Many Communists were also greatly heartened by the progress made by the Communist parties in Indochina and China.

By 1950, both nationalists and the Left in Southeast Asia must have felt that the tide of history was changing. The Philippines and Indonesia had gained their independence, albeit by very different routes; Thailand had remained independent; the Chinese Communists were in power; the situation in Indochina was in the balance; Communists had launched armed struggles in Malaya and Singapore, the Philippines (the Hukbalahap rebellion), Indonesia (the Madiun affair), and Burma (van der Kroef 1980: 25–32; Pluvier 1974: Part VI).

The history of the Left in Southeast Asia often ignores the contribution made by the legal socialist movement. This ignorance stems from the fact that, by the early 1950s, most socialists had taken an anti-Communist stance, even those who were at the forefront of the Asian socialist movement. Many assumed an unusual position, supporting the Chinese Revolution while opposing Communists in Southeast Asia. This group adopted what the then Burmese Prime Minister U Ba Swe called 'revolutionary democratic Socialist methods to improve the standard of living of the masses . . .' (as quoted in the Foreword in Josey 1957). For Josey, 'Asian socialism' was about easing the underdevelopment of the region and the poverty of millions through some form of collectivism. It was interested in social welfare, and socialists 'were nationalists first', opposing colonialism and imperialism by 'democratic, egalitarian and fraternal' methods. Significantly, Asian socialism was opposed to capitalism *because* of its links with colonialism, but opposed to Communism, which it saw as totalitarian (Josey 1957: 2–5).

The connection emphasised here, between nationalism, anticolonialism, and socialist and Communist movements, was crucial. Of course, the relationship between each of these political elements varied according to local conditions. For example, the PKI, which became the largest Communist party in the non-Communist world, came to see that: 'the national movement, and later the national state, might be captured by Marxism through peaceful means and, having been captured ideologically, would naturally admit Marxists to positions of power' (Cribb 1985: 259).

However, in Malaya, the Communists had abandoned peaceful and constitutional opposition to the reinstitution of colonialism, and had embarked on an armed struggle. The MCP was unable, though, to establish fully its struggle as a nationalist movement.

Given the united front tactics commonly used against colonial powers, left-wing influence can easily be exaggerated by conflating it with nationalism and anti-colonialism. However, if socialist revolutions elsewhere have occurred with little or no consent among the population to socialist values (Colburn and Rahmato 1992: 159–73), and created problems thereafter, then the successful conclusion of nationalist struggles in Southeast Asia certainly did not advance socialist ideas, the Left soon being moved off the legal political stage, perhaps defeated by its own success. This had little to do with the success of Left ideology or values, but with the ability of the Left to build links with labour and, in some cases, the peasantry, and the west's perception of the success of International Communism.

Working and living conditions had deteriorated during the war, with food and commodity shortages and inflation common. Under such conditions worker unrest increased, with the Left and the anti-colonial movement able to capitalise on this. By 1947, for example, the MCP-dominated Singapore General Labour Unon (GLU) controlled three-quarters of the organised workforce. In Thailand, labour organisation increased, and a major labour confederation, the Central Labour Union (CLU), was formed. A new generation of labour leaders, much influenced by Marxism and close to the CPT, emerged to lead the labour unions. Their approach was attractive, and by early 1949 CLU membership was 60,000. In Indonesia, the PKI also had strong links with labour which supported its programme.[7]

The radical wing of the labour movement can be seen as a part of the rise of a more generalised Left discourse. As Reynolds (1987: 25) observed for Thailand, 'there was a distinctly Left orientation in Bangkok public discourse for a decade or so after World War II'. This was common throughout the region. For example, in Malaya and Singapore, while the colonial state attempted to repress labour after 1948, this was temporary. The fundamental grievances of students and workers, when combined with the unprecedented strength of anti-colonial feeling, were manifested in a new phase in the development of independent organisations. This involved labour, students, and, for the first time, formal political parties which geared up for the achievement of self-government. The radical unions played a critical role in mobilising the masses in this broad movement. Most of the strikes in Singapore involved demands for the release of imprisoned union officials, or were part of the broader Left strategy of keeping pressure up for full self-government (Turnbull 1982: 262).

Throughout the region, a feature of this period was the linking of a range of politically active groups within civil society. Leftist discourse, especially in labour circles, employed concepts of class, class struggle, and exploitation, seriously challenging colonialist and nationalist rhetoric which emphasised capitalist development. Significantly, while the authorities readily employed internal security forces and legislation to detain labour leaders and proscribe cultural and social organisations in which the Left was influential, these moves were not initially successful. Far more repressive measures were required. As labour conflicts continued, governments soon defined these actions as unlawful and constituting 'revolt', and anti-Communist laws were made increasingly draconian. For example, in Thailand, the 1952 Act prevented attacks on the private enterprise system and outlawed acts defined as 'creating instability, disunity, or hatred among the people, and taking part in acts of terrorism or sabotage' (Reynolds 1987: 28). This did not end labour disputes, but it did restrict left-wing influence in the labour movement. In the Philippines, once the Left's influence had been reduced, collective bargaining was expanded after 1951.

The seemingly bright prospects for the Left after the Second World War were tarnished by the Cold War and the rise of US-sponsored anti-Communism and anti-neutralism. As is well known, the US and other western powers, shocked by the 'loss' of China and Eastern Europe, and an apparent threat in Korea, moved quickly into the Cold War. Of course, Southeast Asia was concerned in this, being seen to be in the path of a southward movement of Communism (Iriye 1974: 130–91). As one US policy document explained:

> South of the ominous mass that is Red China, Thailand, along with her embattled but still free neighbors, shares a peninsula. The Communists want it. They covet its riches. . . . They consider it [Thailand] a prize base, for like an oriental scimitar, the peninsula's tip is pointed at the throat of Indonesia. . . . In Malaya, Burma and Indo-China, Communist-led rebels plunder, kill and burn.
>
> (Mutual Security Agency 1952: 1)

This Cold War mentality translated into support for actively pro-western and pro-business governments. In Thailand, for example, the US supported, through the CIA, generals in the police and army who were opposed to the Left. There is no doubt that this support for repressive political structures (the military, police, and internal security) was crucial in narrowing the political space, even for democrats and nationalists. Throughout Southeast Asia the US sustained and promoted anti-Communists: in Indochina, supporting the French, and then becoming directly involved; championing the military against Soekarno and the PKI in Indonesia; supporting Magsaysay in the Philippines, against the Huk rebellion; in Burma and Cambodia opposing leaders defined as 'dangerously neutral'; and in Malaya, supporting the British in their anti-Communist war.

This anti-Communism fitted well with the domestic agendas of increasingly authoritarian regimes whose repression was justified on the basis of developmental imperatives. The Left was increasingly identified as 'alien' and as a 'fifth column' movement, and this perspective was supported by western powers. It also found itself having to defend its political organisations, developed in the nationalist campaigns, as others moved to marginalise them from the political process and weaken their bases in civil society, most notably in trade unions. This absorbed much of the creative energy of socialist and Communist movements. Externally, the Cold War climate necessarily meant various pressures would be exerted to undermine socialist economic experiments and shore up market-oriented economies. Thus, by the mid- to late-1950s, throughout Southeast Asia, the Left, including anti-Communist socialists who had supported constitutional opposition, was being repressed or forced underground. In many places, repression resulted in an intensification of armed struggles.

The 1970s

During the 1970s, while not as regionally widespread as during the earlier periods discussed above, significant attempts were made to expand civil society. This took place in a quite different environment from that in earlier epochs: all of the countries of the region were ruled by post-colonial regimes; Communist-led armed struggles in the Philippines and Thailand appeared to be gaining strength; and the US intervention in Indochina was coming to an end, on a wave of opposition in the west. Again, it should be emphasised that much of the opposition which developed was related to conceptions of anti-imperialism and economic stagnation or decline, associated with the first oil shocks.

For example, the extreme dependence of the Singapore economy on external demand meant that the mid-1970s recession hit hard, with heavy job losses in manufacturing industries, and official unemployment reaching 4.6 per cent in 1975. The ruling People's Action Party's (PAP) tame, affiliated union organisation, the National Trades Union Congress (NTUC), was unable to represent worker interests effectively, leaving an opportunity for a short-lived revival in the student movement. The students had widened their agenda to include the promotion of civil liberties and links with workers. This prompted a swift reaction from the government, resulting in the conviction of student leaders for 'unlawful assembly' and 'rioting' and the student union funds being placed under the control of the university administration and the Ministry of Education. The student union was barred from engaging in, or making pronouncements on, matters of a political nature (Chua 1992: 14)

The role of students in Singapore was seemingly part of a pattern throughout the region. Between the late 1960s and 1975, students were active in most of the countries of the region: in Indonesia, students protested against Japanese economic domination; in the Philippines, students were active until martial law was introduced in late 1972, with the breakaway Maoist Communist Party of the Philippines formed by student leaders and intellectuals in 1968; and in Malaysia, students demonstrated in 1974. The most remarkable student activism was, however, in Thailand in 1973, when students and intellectuals brought thousands of people into the streets to overthrow a military dictatorship.

Such student activism grew, in part, out of a significant expansion of tertiary education, but also out of the changes taking place in social structures through the growth of import-substitution industrialisation (ISI). Regional governments, however, having observed western students challenging their own governments in the late 1960s, were decidedly uncomfortable with the prospect of student radicalism which they saw as subversive and manipulated by the Left. The result was that many took the Singapore road, introducing repressive measures.

These student activists did not operate in a vacuum, and the example of Thailand showed that students and intellectuals could be powerful forces for the expansion of political space. Indeed, the growth of solidarity movements between students, workers, peasants, and the downtrodden was greatly feared by the governments of the region, especially as students were seen as allies of Communists. But by the late 1970s authoritarian governments had again moved to close the political opening, and repressive regimes dominated the political stage throughout the late 1970s and into the 1980s: the Marcos dynasty and its lackeys kept the pressure on through martial law, although some concessions were made; Thailand had a military government again, although limited elections were reintroduced in the early 1980s; New Order Indonesia was still under a military-dominated government, and Soeharto appeared stronger than ever; Lee and the PAP had further entrenched themselves in Singapore, having exercised internal security legislation and other means to harass critical public commentators and all legal opposition; and the Malaysian government had cracked down on opposition groups.

For the Left, the only glimmer of hope in this political gloom might have been the establishment of self-declared socialist governments in Laos, Vietnam, and Cambodia and the expansion of Communist-led rebellions in Thailand and the Philippines. But this came to nothing. In Cambodia, the Pol Pot regime embarked on a reign of terror and hyper-nationalism which, while initially supported by many on the Left, was only concluded when Vietnam invaded. The result of this was a brief but bloody war between China and Vietnam, which threw most of the Left in Southeast Asia into confusion.[8] This confusion was amplified by the strange sight of the US and the Association of South East Asian Nations (ASEAN) supporting their former enemy, the murderous Khmer Rouge, and the Chinese in opposing Vietnam.

These strange events also had much to do with the implosion of the CPT. In 1977 the CPT could claim more than 15,000 under its banner, and was waging an armed struggle, apparently with considerable success, reinforced by thousands who had fled right-wing repression after the 1976 coup. However, the CPT, dominated by a leadership allied to China, had been unable to incorporate the young and idealistic revolutionaries from urban areas. In supporting the Khmer Rouge and China, the CPT lost its bases in Vietnam and Laos, and then 'lost' its internal debate with students and intellectuals who willingly accepted a government amnesty. By the early 1980s, the CPT was dead. Only in the Philippines, where antagonism to Marcos united the opposition in a way not seen since the Second World War, did an armed struggle continue and grow. Even here, however, there were splits within the party.[9]

It should also be noted that the changing nature of international production had a major impact in the region. The tendency of international capital, beginning in the 1960s, was to transfer labour-intensive manufacturing production to the developing world to exploit lower labour costs. Not only did this boost economic growth in East Asia (Hong Kong, Taiwan, and South Korea), but it also proved timely for Southeast Asia. For example, following the mid-1960s failure of the political merger with Malaysia, Singapore's policy makers realised that with no prospect for a larger market for manufactured goods – the basis of Singapore's import-substitution industrialisation strategy – a different strategy was required. Singapore led the way, to be followed by Malaysia, Thailand, and, to a lesser extent, Indonesia and the Philippines, in moving to a more export-oriented industrialisation (EOI) strategy.

Such a move in production did not cause the decline of the Left; indeed, since the move from ISI to EOI actually expanded the industrial workforce, it might have been expected that this would enhance the Left's political potential. However, as the region's states moved to create their comparative advantage as low-wage manufacturing sites, independent unions were smashed, seriously weakening the Left (Fröbel *et al.* 1980; Deyo 1981; Rodan 1989).

At the same time, three other nails appeared poised to be driven into the coffin of the Left in Southeast Asia: first, the move to 'market socialism' in China; second, the political and economic collapse in Eastern Europe; and third, the amazing economic success of the capitalist Southeast Asian countries (with the Philippines the partial exception), in stark contrast to the stagnation of the Indochinese countries. But, as we have already suggested, this is not the end of history, and there is reason to embark on a deeper analysis of political and economic change and the political prospects for the Left.

THE LEFT AND CONTEMPORARY SOUTHEAST ASIA

As noted at the beginning of this chapter, the 1980s and 1990s appear bleak for the Left in Southeast Asia. We have also noted that the most enduring of Left strategies has involved the support of labour. This area of activism has been seen by various kinds of regimes as a powerful threat. So the rapid economic development of Southeast Asia, driven by strong, local capitalist classes, might have been expected to present an opportunity for the Left, organising among the growing working class. Yet this has not been the case. Why?

An important point to emphasise is that changes to the global political economy have facilitated a positive capitalist alternative for developing countries which has greatly undercut socialism's potential appeal in the region. One of these was, of course, the search by international capital for the low-cost manufacturing export bases which began in the 1960s. More recently, the conceptualisation by international capital of the global economy in terms of three economic regions – Europe, North America, and the Asia-Pacific – has meant a 'regional focus' (Ng and Sudo 1991). This emphasises the importance of honing operations to the peculiarities of local markets and affords more autonomy to transnational corporations' (TNC) subsidiaries. Consequently, Asia is elevated from the status of a site for low-cost production to be exported to consumer markets elsewhere to a crucial set of markets in its own right. Commensurate with this is a preparedness by TNCs to invest in higher value-added products and processes – both within and beyond the manufacturing sector – than was previously the case. In conjunction with the internationalisation of capital emanating from the region and the forging of structural linkages between the different regional economies, this investment pattern further bolsters capitalism in the region.

This process appears to be deepening capitalist accumulation, giving rise to a capitalist development alternative in Southeast Asia.[10] For the argument here, the significant issue is that remarkable capitalist economic development (with the exception of the Philippines) has been achieved with associated authoritarianism. Indeed, Southeast Asian leaders have used economic success to boost their political legitimacy and to justify authoritarian regimes in Thailand, Singapore, and Indonesia. Furthermore, capitalist development has been rendered a source of nationalist pride – in stark contrast from the earlier phases of civil society expansion.

So it is not just the negative example of state-led socialist experiments around the world that has reduced the appeal of socialism in Southeast Asia, but the demonstrable achievements of capitalism in Asia and the seemingly bright prospects it holds for the future. This has been especially noticeable in Thailand. Many of those who joined the CPT in the 1970s and 1980s have returned to urban life to become successful business people, suggesting that Communism was a dead-end. They argue that the best they can now hope for is a capitalism with some heart, meaning that some of its rough, exploitative edges are taken off. In essence, 'socialism as collectivism' is no longer a supportable goal, even for some on the Left, and has been replaced by a growing interest in more limited but laudable political goals including human rights, liberty, constitutions, and representative forms.

Paradoxically, it is the success of capitalist revolutions and the decline of socialist models which have raised the prospect of political change. The social transformations in Southeast Asian societies have not only involved the expansion of capitalist and working classes, but the emergence of sizeable middle classes, with each of these classes being segmented (see Robison and Goodman 1995). The social, political, and cultural manifestations of this process are complex, and there is a literature which sees pressures for new organisational forms to protect and advance the particular interests of these strata as an unavoidable byproduct of economic development.

As we have already argued, the historical evidence contradicts the assumption that the development of civil society in capitalist societies is a progressive and incremental outcome of economic growth. Rather, civil society has ebbed and flowed in the region throughout this century. For us, the significance of the current social transformations brought by advanced forms of capitalist accumulation lies in the nature of new social groups. As we have seen, at different periods in the histories of Southeast Asian societies, a range of social groups have succeeded in expanding the political space outside the state, even if this space has subsequently been closed as authoritarian regimes have reasserted their dominance.

Whereas independent labour organisations have been central to this periodic reconstitution of civil society in the past, what is significant in the current expansion of civil society is the greater social differentiation characterising the groups involved. It is important to acknowledge the expanding complexity of Southeast Asian social structures. The increasingly numerous and differentiated middle class encompasses a range of professionals, public and private bureaucrats, and the self-employed. The growth of this class is generated out of expanded capitalist development, which also sees an ever more complex bourgeois class engaged in diverse domestic and global accumulation strategies. Not surprisingly, these processes generate new political aspirations and demands, some of which reflect the new material conditions. Hence, environmental and consumer organisations, for instance, have joined professional and employer associations to establish their identity in civil society.

From the mid-1980s, there has been a rapid expansion of business and professional organisations in many parts of Southeast Asia. In Indonesia and Thailand at least, some of these groups have achieved considerable political power. A new literature, much of it placing a heavy emphasis on instrumental relationships between business and government, has emerged in recent years in recognition of this. MacIntyre (1992) has demonstrated that industry associations and business groups have been able to use the Indonesian state's corporatist structures to derive benefits which are for their members, not for the state. This, he argues, involves an expansion of political representation. For Thailand, MacIntyre (1990: 32–3) suggests that the representation of organised business on joint government bodies has allowed it to deal directly and independently with government and to shape policy. Anek, also writing on Thailand, argues that business associations have become autonomous of the state, acting as interest groups, that organised business has had a significant influence on the pattern of economic development, and that like 'South Korea, Taiwan and Singapore', there are '. . . close and supportive relations between the government and organised business' (Anek 1992: 15).[11]

Even in Singapore, and despite the government's brusque treatment of non-state groups in the 1980s, notably the Law Society and lay religious organisations (Rodan 1993: 91–6), some middle-class and professional organisations have emerged or become more active since the late 1980s. The most notable of these have been the Nature Society of Singapore, the Association of Women for Action and Research, and the Association of Muslim Professionals. The evolution of these three groups reflects a perception that existing political structures inadequately accommodate distinctive views and interests.

As we stressed earlier (p. 41), following Bernhard (1993), the existence of autonomous organisations requires the sanction of the state. This means that the existence of some of these organisations can be highly conditional: as soon as the state defines their activities as political, they are in trouble. This is especially so in Singapore, where legislation means they face the threat of deregistration should they be seen to pose a challenge to the PAP's authority by acting 'politically'. Equally, the threat of being co-opted by the government is real, and corporatism has meant that it is sometimes difficult to distinguish between state and non-state organisations. For example, in Thailand, the government ordered the establishment of provincial chambers of commerce, while claiming that they are private and voluntary (Anek 1992).

Nevertheless, and despite the moderate political objectives of many of these organisations, some do represent attempts to negotiate increased political space, separate from the state's extensive bureaucratic structures. Through the demarcation of this non-state space, some form of political contestation becomes possible. This is true even if, in order to avoid proscription and co-optation, contestation can be neither confrontational nor particularly public. Even so, owing to the class nature of the constituencies and leaderships of these organisations, which are disproportionately middle class, contestation will inevitably be circumspect. Many of them also proclaim, as they must, a non-ideological position, and it is fair to say that they see themselves in this light.

At the same time, the position of independent labour organisations has substantially altered. In the past, linkages between labour and political opposition movements have posed a challenge to authoritarian regimes, both colonial and post-colonial. But the legacy of decades of authoritarian rule has been seriously destabilising for labour. The institutionalised incorporation of labour into the structures of the state is now well advanced throughout the region, and the existence of independent labour organisations is everywhere threatened. This is not to say that all unions were co-opted by the state. For instance, in the Philippines a vigorous independent movement exists, and attempts continue to establish independent unions in Thailand, Malaysia and Indonesia.

Today, the underprivileged, who are not often wage labourers, find their interests being represented by groups outside labour movements. NGOs are not only leading this, but are also critical avenues for expanding the political space of civil society. Significantly, though, the agendas and constituencies of such independent organisations do not afford labour the control and influence offered by trade unions. None of this rules out the possibility of the Left shaping politics in contemporary Southeast Asia, but it does suggest that the sites of struggle will be varied, as will the political alliances involving the Left. Neither are the sites of struggle necessarily going to be the constitutional oppositions and political parties. After all, the experience in Southeast Asia has been that parliaments and elections do not necessarily mean increased popular representation. The rise of capitalism, middle classes, and electoral politics can increase representation for some classes, but not necessarily for the masses.[12]

In Southeast Asia there are various opposition groups and movements outside this narrow, party-political focus, and many of these operate in a manner which distinguishes them from the influence or lobby groups so central to liberal-pluralist democratic theory. Specifically, they are activist and do not appear to act as more or less narrow advocacy groups, for they marshal support from a range of groups and classes in society. Good examples of this kind of non-state group are the activist development NGOs which have become important political actors since the early 1980s.

There has been considerable enthusiasm concerning the political potential of NGOs. For example, Jones (1993: 70), writing of Southeast Asia, argues that: 'NGOs . . . have been chipping away at entrenched power structures. . . . They have played a critical role in forcing governments to listen to the demands of the poor, the marginalised and the abused.'

Not all analysts are so enthusiastic, pointing out that many NGOs are not non-governmental at all, having been co-opted by government, and noting that many are self-interested and self-promoting.[13] Indeed, the roles of NGOs in Southeast Asia vary, from high-profile activism in the Philippines and Thailand, to a more moderate role in Indonesia and Malaysia, a very limited one in Singapore, and virtual non-existence in Burma and Laos. Even allowing for this, the political role of NGOs has been remarkable.

In theory, NGOs are defined as voluntary and non-profit-making associations with development-oriented goals. Therefore, NGOs are not necessarily defined as political opposition by governments, at least initially. Indeed, NGOs often shy away from institutionalised relationships with political parties, arguing that these can be no more than their allies, not their leaders (Rahmena 1989: 7; see also Clark 1991: 18). However, as NGOs have matured and so-called grassroots development strategies have emerged, so their political role has been delineated. While not all NGOs are politically radical in Southeast Asia, many have experienced a degree of radicalisation.

It is often argued that this radicalisation is due to the nature of their development activities. Sasono (1989: 19) points out that most NGOs are not 'the grassroots', but in fact are most often drawn from 'urban intellectuals and middle class groups', and are certainly not social movements. Despite this, he argues that they act in a *class-biased* manner, working for the poor and taking risks, knowing the economic and political costs involved.

A new development NGO ideology has evolved out of their work. Many have learnt that development practice cannot be neutral and that *empowerment* of the poor, disorganised, and disenfranchised is the key to 'real' development. To the extent that these organisations exploit their location in civil society to agitate for an empowerment of underprivileged classes, they represent a force for substantive democracy, and one through which Left values can be promoted. While they do not constitute social or political movements, they have the potential to act as a catalyst for them through the legitimation of class-based action. In this sense, they are not so much alternatives to more traditional Left organisations, such as trade unions, as complements to them. In addition, poverty has been defined as a political issue, as it has a lot to do with powerlessness. NGOs have learnt that development projects are more successful 'if they are based on people's own analysis of the problems they face and their solutions' (Clark 1991: 102). In essence, this suggests an approach to participation, representation, and collective action, where political action on a national or even international stage is necessary.

In other words, their ideology and methodologies create an imperative for NGOs to expand the political space at all levels of their operations. As has been demonstrated in all of the countries of Southeast Asia, this can involve the building of oppositional coalitions between unions, development groups, women, religious groups, and environmentalists. Most importantly, and like the Left in earlier periods, NGOs assist dissidents by maintaining an intellectual life, providing space for ideological debate (Padron 1987: 75).

The oppositional status of NGOs is demonstrated where authoritarian regimes have been replaced by more representative forms, as in Thailand and the Philippines. In Thailand, NGOs played leading and co-ordinating roles in the events of 1991 and 1992 which eventually led to the demise of yet another military government. Earlier, in 1986, NGOs played a similar role in overthrowing the Marcos regime.[14] Significantly, following these events, many of these NGOs still find themselves having to challenge government at all levels, supporting the poor and arguing for greater representation and participation in policy making at all levels. Much of this tension between NGOs and governments arises from differing approaches to development.

Clearly, then, the current struggle to re-establish civil society in Southeast Asia involves quite different circumstances for the Left. Some of these circumstances relate to the fact that capitalism in the region is now both embedded and flourishing, but there are also more universal factors concerning the currency of socialism and Communism. Even in the established liberal democracies outside Southeast Asia, quite extensive re-evaluation of and by the Left is leading to similar conclusions. Miliband (1994: 141) observed, for example, that 'no single organization of the Left will ever again be able to claim to represent all movements of protest and pressure, as Communist parties (and, less emphatically, social democratic parties as well) once did'. Instead, Miliband acknowledged that diverse social movements have emerged, forming 'an important element of the coalition of forces which has to be constructed on the Left'. But at the same time, the challenge for socialists is to explain that 'radical demands, for democratisation, for equal rights, for the creation of communities of citizens, can only partially be met, if they can be met at all, within the existing structures of power and privilege . . .' (Miliband 1994: 157). The case for a transformation of the capitalist state remains, since no other agency has 'the power to tackle the multiple blights of capitalism', but, significantly, Miliband adopted a comparatively inclusive notion of 'the Left'.

Giddens (1994), similarly, does not believe the prospects for the Left are completely gloomy within the established liberal democracies, but goes even further in revising the notion of what 'the Left' actually means in the contemporary context. While he sees importance in retaining core socialist values, this is part of a broader emphasis on a philosophic conservatism involving a range of social movements trying to defend previous reformist gains and the environment from the onslaught of neo-liberalism. Moreover, he contends that a new radical politics needs, among other things, to accommodate aspirations and needs for autonomy and independence as well as selective forms of social collectivism. However, Giddens has in mind a very different notion of individualism here from that associated with the market. According to Giddens (1994: 13), 'In a world of high reflexivity, an individual must achieve a certain degree of autonomy of action as a condition of being able to survive and forge a life; but autonomy is not the same as egoism and moreover implies reciprocity and interdependence.'[15] Without entering into an evaluation of Giddens's approach, he is clearly attempting to reconcile a complex variety of political positions and, in so doing, opens up the notion of 'the Left' even further than Miliband.

This apparent 'watering down' of the Left is also reflected in Gorz's notion that what distinguishes the Left now is its insistence on social limits on the application of economic rationality. However, the eradication of economic rationality altogether is dismissed as impossible, or likely to lead to a totalitarian society (Gorz 1994; 1991; 1989). Similarly, Kallscheuer (1995: 136) maintains that today, to be 'Left' is to subscribe to a strong version of liberalism which delivers checks and balances 'not only between the branches of administration, legislation and the courts, but between the various spheres of social activity, judgement and distribution which are economic, cultural and religious life'. He calls for economic values to be counterbalanced by Left values of egalitarianism. As Kallscheuer (1995: 138) sees it, these values could be deployed to address the social consequences of modernity, namely the autonomisation of several subsystems of rationality, without suppressing individual preference and choice. The post-modernist embrace of pluralism of course leads to a championing of liberalism. Mouffe (1995: 296) calls for a 'complete reversal of Left identity' in which the values of homogeneity, equality, and harmony are replaced by pluralism, difference, and heterogeneity. Individual freedom and liberty, Mouffe maintains, should be elevated to at least the same status as equality.

As we have seen above, within Southeast Asia the traditional Left is also having to contend with the difficulties of social differentiation associated with industrialisation, although this is a comparatively embryonic process. A more fundamental problem has been the concerted obstruction of independent trade unions, while the expansion of wage labour continues apace. Most importantly, in Southeast Asia, as elsewhere, capitalism has not had a complete victory. Rather, with the rapid maturation of capitalism, the social shortcomings and contradictions of market relations increasingly manifest themselves in political problems for governments in the region. Many of the existing conflicts and disputes in Southeast Asia are fundamentally about the naked exploitation and oppression of capitalism, both in the human and environmental dimensions. Where economic development is most advanced, increased conspicuous consumption only highlights material inequalities. It also remains to be seen whether regimes in Southeast Asia will be able to limit the provision of public goods within such a climate. Pressures are certainly building for the provision of social infrastructures that are unlikely to be generated by the private market. So the potential still exists for influence to be exerted by social democratic ideas based around a coalition of social forces, rather than through a mass organisation.

In addition, heightened resentment of authoritarian political structures among the relatively privileged classes is also evident. Indeed, the demands people are making are not for socialism, but for representation in policy making. It is this dynamic which underlies the recent development of independent organisations and the push for an expanded civil society. However, the different elements of the Left have particular views on issues of representation and participation, so debates about these concepts could create an opportunity for the Left to regain some influence.

CONCLUSION

As the historical survey of the Left in Southeast Asia illustrates, the current attempt to expand the space of civil society is only the latest, rather than the first, such attempt. The economic triumph of capitalism in Southeast Asia is certainly critical in creating this latest historical opportunity, but it is not the sole determinant of it. Nor does it set in train an inexorable, even if protracted, force for political pluralism and liberal democracy. Rather, it represents another historical opportunity for the establishment of a more expansive civil society which, as before, includes, but does not guarantee, these possibilities.

What is different about this particular attempt which does relate to capitalist development is the possibility that on this occasion the political space will be more resilient and less vulnerable to repression than it has been in the past. This is because important elements within the capitalist and middle classes appear to be supportive of the current expansion of political space and increased representation for their interests. In the past, the dominant classes were often supportive of authoritarian reversals, since they perceived the push for increased political space as being led by working-class organisations, supported by Communists and socialists. This political space, however, can be genuinely independent without necessarily embodying liberal democracy.

This discussion has identified some emerging non-state organisations whose class composition predisposes them towards rather limited forms of contestation over state power. They are jockeying within the political system to operate as interest or lobby groups and are vulnerable to co-optation. Others, namely the activist NGOs, demonstrate broader objectives and are more removed from the constitutional political process. The Left's accustomed position as a strategic leader in the struggle for civil society is absent this time around, although the social and environmental consequences of capitalist development will continue to generate concerns which are central to the Left. To exert an influence over the political responses to those concerns, the Left has little option but to work through the various organisations attempting to articulate these concerns, rather than bring them under the umbrella of a broad social movement. What the current juncture in political contestation underlines is that, while the history of civil society in Southeast Asia has ebbed and flowed, its complexion is not neatly reproduced from one phase to the next.

NOTES

* The authors thank John Girling, Andrew Brown, Jane Hutchison, and two anonymous referees for their comments and criticisms. We also thank Merlin Press Limited and Leo Panitch for permission to use material from an earlier version of this chapter published by them. Finally, we are grateful for research assistance provided by Damen Keevers.

1 Civic groups may become politically active. For example, such associations might attempt to influence public policy in narrow ways, however removed from formal political processes they may be. It should also be noted that some civic organisations can often play important class functions. For example, sporting clubs might provide for solidarity among workers.

2 We are not entering the debate on social movements. It remains to be assessed whether any of the groups discussed in the context of Southeast Asia constitute social movements – see the definition in Scott (1990: 6).

3 We are very much aware that the interpretation we propose here is new, and requires far more research and documentation than we can provide in this chapter. Here, we can only suggest some lines that further research might take up.

4 It is worth pointing out that the so-called 'intermediate groups' were not particularly significant in this period largely due to the nature of the economy. Trade and government service were the employers of these professional groups, but these sectors did not require large workforces, and many who did occupy these positions were expatriate professionals or privileged Southeast Asians. This meant they were unlikely to fill the ranks of the anti-colonial movement, although there were some significant exceptions.

5 On the Comintern, see Knight (1985: 53–9) and Moraes (1958: 45–7). For Indonesia, see Cribb (1985: 253–6), while for Thailand, see Barmé (1993).

6 On the planning imperative, see Josey (1957: 5–6).

7 For Malaya and Singapore in this period, see Stenson (1970: chapters 2–4), while the Indonesian case is in Golay *et. al.* (1969: 198–9). For Thailand, see Hewison and Brown (1993: 12–14).

8 For examples of Left support for Pol Pot, see Caldwell (1977: 169–72) and Amin (1977: 147–52). Regarding the wars see Evans and Rowley (1984). For the politics of Cambodia under Pol Pot see Vickery (1984, 1986).

9 A useful discussion of the Communist Party of Thailand can be found in Chai-Anan *et al.* (1990). The Philippines case is explained in Lane (1993: 24).

10 It is not appropriate to embark on a long discussion of this development as we and others have done this extensively elsewhere. See Rodan (1989), Higgott and Robison (1985), Robison (1986), Hewison (1989), and McVey (1992).

11 For a critique of this genre, see Hewison (1992: 261–5).

12 On oppositions as parties see Lawson (1993a: 192–3; 1993b: 15–30). For a brief discussion of electoral politics and lack of representation in Thailand see Hewison (1993).

13 For discussions of NGOs, see Kothari (1989: 40–58) and Sasono (1989: 14–26). Rahnema (1989: 9), makes an obvious point when he warns that there is a tendency to create a false view of NGOs, seeing them as implicitly 'good' because they are non-state. In the Philippines, NGOs have been incorporated within the structures of local government, and this co-optation of NGOs by the state and international agencies like the World Bank has led to a debate concerning the independence of NGOs – see Brillantes (1992).

14 On Thailand in 1992 see Paisal *et al.* (1992: 54–72); for the Philippines see Lane (1990).

68   *Kevin Hewison and Garry Rodan*

15 By social reflexivity, Giddens (1994: 6) is referring to the process of
individuals having to filter all sorts of information and having to routinely
act upon it in a 'detraditionalizing society'. Whether, in fact, this process
described by Giddens is peculiar to advanced capitalist societies is,
however, open to question.

REFERENCES

Amin, Samir (1977) *Imperialism and Unequal Development*, New York:
Monthly Review Press.
Anek, Laothamatas (1992) *Business Associations and the New Political
Economy of Thailand: From Bureaucratic Polity to Liberal Corporatism*,
Singapore: Institute of Southeast Asian Studies.
Barmé, Scot (1993) *Luang Wichit Wathakan and the Creation of a Thai Identity*,
Singapore: Institute of Southeast Asian Studies.
Bastin, John and Benda, Harry J. (1977) *A History of Modern Southeast Asia*,
Sydney: Prentice-Hall.
Bernhard, Michael (1993) 'Civil Society and Democratic Transition in East
Central Europe', *Political Science Quarterly*, 108(2): 307–26.
Brillantes, Alex B. Jr (1992) 'Local Governments and NGOs [in] the Philip-
pines: Development Issues and Challenges', paper presented to the Fourth
International Philippine Studies Conference, Canberra, July.
Brown, Andrew (1990) 'The Industrial Working Class and the State in Thailand:
an Introductory Analysis', MA thesis, Australian National University.
Caldwell, Malcolm (1977) *The Wealth of Some Nations*, London: Zed Press.
Chai-Anan Samudavanija, Kusuma Snitwongse, and Sichit Bunbongkarn,
(1990) *From Armed Suppression to Political Offensive*, Bangkok: Institute
of Security and International Studies, Chulalongkorn University.
Chua Beng-Huat (1993) 'The Changing Shape of Civil Society in Singapore',
Commentary, 11(1): 9–14.
Chua Mui Hoong (1992) 'Campus Activism? What Activism?', *The Straits
Times*, weekly overseas edition, 25 January: 14.
Clark, John (1991) *Democratising Development. The Role of Voluntary
Organizations*, London: Earthscan Publications.
Colburn, Forrest D. and Rahmato, Dessalegn (1992) 'Rethinking Socialism in
the Third World', *Third World Quarterly*, 13(1): 159–73.
Cribb, Robert (1985) 'The Indonesian Marxist Tradition', in Colin Mackerras
and Nick Knight (eds) *Marxism in Asia*, New York: St Martin's Press.
Deyo, Frederic (1981) *Dependent Development and Industrial Order: An Asian
Case Study*, New York: Praeger.
Du Bois, Cora (1962) *Social Forces in Southeast Asia*, Cambridge, Mass.:
Harvard University Press.
Evans, Grant and Rowley, Kelvin (1984) *Red Brotherhood at War. Indochina
Since the Fall of Saigon*, London: Verso.
Fröbel, F., Jürgen, H., and Kreye, O. (1980) *The New International Division of
Labour*, Cambridge: Cambridge University Press.
Gafurov, B. G. and Kim G. F. (eds) (1978) *Lenin and National Liberation in
the East*, Moscow: Progress Publishers.
Giddens, Anthony (1994) *Beyond Left and Right: the Future of Radical Politics*,
Cambridge: Polity Press.

Girling, John (1988) 'Development and Democracy in Southeast Asia', *The Pacific Review*, 1(4): 332–40.

Golay, Frank H., Anspach, Ralph, Pfanner, M. Ruth, and Ayal, Eliezer B. (1969) *Underdevelopment and Economic Nationalism in Southeast Asia*, Ithaca, NY: Cornell University Press.

Gorz, André (1989) *Critique of Economic Reason*, London: Verso.

—— (1991) 'The New Agenda', in Robin Blackburn (ed.) *After the Fall: the Failure of Communism and the Future of Socialism*, London and New York: Verso, pp. 287–97.

—— (1994) *Capitalism, Socialism, Ecology*, trans. Chirs Turner, London and New York: Verso.

Harris, Nigel (1988) 'New Bourgeoisies', *The Journal of Development Studies*, 24(2): 237–49.

Hewison, Kevin (1989) *Power and Politics in Thailand*, Manila: JCA Press.

—— (1992) 'Liberal Corporatism and the Return of Pluralism in Thai Political Studies', *Asian Studies Review*, 16(2): 261–5.

—— (1993) 'Of Regimes, State and Pluralities: Thai Politics Enters the 1990s', in K. Hewison, R. Robison and G. Rodan (eds) *Southeast Asia in the 1990s*, Sydney: Allen & Unwin, pp. 159–89.

Hewison, Kevin and Brown, Andrew (1993) *Labour and Unions in an Industrialising Thailand: a Brief History*, Working Paper No. 22, Perth: Asia Research Centre, Murdoch University.

Hewison, Kevin, Robison, Richard, and Rodan, Garry (eds) (1993) *Southeast Asia in the 1990s*, Sydney: Allen & Unwin.

Higgott, Richard and Robison, Richard (eds) (1985) *Southeast Asia. Essays in the Political Economy of Structural Change*, London: Routledge & Kegan Paul.

Huntington, Samuel (1991) *The Third Wave: Democratization in the Late Twentieth Century*, Norman: University of Oklahoma Press.

Ileto, Reynaldo (1992) 'Religion and Anti-Colonial Movements', in Nicholas Tarling (ed.) *The Cambridge History of Southeast Asia*, vol. 2, Cambridge: Cambridge University Press.

Insor, D. (pseud.) (1963) *Thailand. A Political, Social and Economic Analysis*, London: George Allen & Unwin.

Iriye, Akira (1974) *The Cold War in Asia: A Historical Introduction*, Englewood Cliffs, NJ: Prentice-Hall.

Jones, Sidney (1993) 'The Organic Growth. Asian NGOs Have Come Into Their Own', *Thai Development Newsletter*, 22: 70.

Josey, Alex (1957) *Socialism in Asia*, Singapore: Donald Moore.

Kallscheuer, Otto (1995) 'On Labels and Reasons: the Communitarian Approach – Some European Comments', in Michael Walzer (ed.) *Toward a Global Civil Society*, Oxford: Berghahn Books, pp. 133–148.

Kerkvliet, Benedict J. (1977) *The Huk Rebellion. A Study of Peasant Revolt in the Philippines*, Berkeley: University of California Press.

Knight, Nick (1985) 'Leninism, Stalinism and the Comintern', in Colin Mackerras and Nick Knight (eds) *Marxism in Asia*, New York: St Martin's Press.

Kothari, Rajni (1989) 'The NGOs, the State and World Capitalism', *New Asian Visions*, 6(1): 40–58.

Kratoska, Paul and Batson, Ben (1992) 'Nationalism and Modernist Reform', in Nicholas Tarling (ed.) *The Cambridge History of Southeast Asia*, vol. 2, Cambridge: Cambridge University Press.

Lane, Max (1990) *The Urban Mass Movement in the Philippines, 1983–1987*, Canberra: Research School of Pacific Studies, Australian National University.

—— (1993) 'Philippine Students and Peasants Reorganise', *Green Left*, 29 September.

Lawson, Stephanie (1993a) 'Conceptual Issues in the Comparative Study of Regime Change and Democratization', *Comparative Politics*, 25(2): 183–205.

—— (1993b) 'Institutionalising Peaceful Conflict: Political Opposition and the Challenge of Democratisation in Asia', *Australian Journal of International Affairs*, 47(1): 14–30.

McCoy, Alfred W. and de Jesus, Ed. C. (eds) (1982) *Philippine Social History: Global Trade and Local Transformations*, Sydney: George Allen & Unwin.

MacIntyre, Andrew (1990) *Business–Government Relations in Industrialising East Asia: South Korea and Thailand*, Australia–Asia Paper no. 53, Nathan: Centre for the Study of Australia–Asia Relations, Griffith University.

—— (1992) *Business and Politics in Indonesia*, Sydney: Allen & Unwin.

McVey, Ruth (ed.) (1990) *Southeast Asian Capitalists*, Ithaca, NY: Southeast Asia Program, Cornell University.

Miliband, Ralph (1994) *Socialism for a Sceptical Age*, London: Polity Press.

Moraes, Frank (1958) *Yonder One World. A Study of Asia and the West*, New York: Macmillan.

Mouffe, Chantal (1995) 'Pluralism and the Left Identity', in Michael Walzer (ed.) *Toward a Global Civil Society*, Oxford: Berghahn Books, pp. 295–300.

Mutual Security Agency (1952) *East Meets West in Thailand*, Washington DC.

Ng, C. Y. and Sudo, S. (1991) *Development Trends in the Asia-Pacific*, Singapore: Institute of Southeast Asian Studies.

Padron, Mario (1987) 'Non-Governmental Development Organizations: From Development Aid to Development Co-operation', *World Development*, 15 (Special Supplement): 69–78.

Pluvier, J. M. (1974) *South-East Asia from Colonialism to Independence*, Kuala Lumpur: Oxford University Press.

Pye, Lucien (1990) 'Political Science and the Crisis of Authoritarianism', *American Political Science Review*, 84(1): 3–19.

Rahnema, Majid (1989) 'Shifting [*sic*] the Wheat From the Chaff', *New Asian Visions*, 6(1): 5–13.

Reynolds, Craig J. (1987) *Thai Radical Discourse. The Real Face of Thai Feudalism Today*, Ithaca, NY: Studies on Southeast Asia, Cornell University.

Richardson, Jim (1993) 'Review Article: The Millenarian-Populist Aspects of Filipino Marxism', *Journal of Contemporary Asia*, 23(3): 382–95.

Robison, Richard (1986) *Indonesia: the Rise of Capital*, Sydney: Allen & Unwin.

—— (1988) 'Authoritarian States, Capital-Owning Classes, and the Politics of Newly Industrializing Countries: the Case of Indonesia', *World Politics*, 41(1): 52–74.

Robison, Richard and Goodman, David (eds) (1995) *The New Rich in Asia: Mobile Phones, McDonalds and Middle-class Revolution*, London: Routledge.

Rodan, Garry (1989) *The Political Economy of Singapore's Industrialization: National State and International Capital,* London: Macmillan.

—— (1993) 'Preserving the One-Party State in Contemporary Singapore', in Kevin Hewison, Richard Robison, and Gary Rodan (eds) *Southeast Asia in the 1990s: Authoritarianism, Democracy and Capitalism,* Sydney: Allen & Unwin.

Rueschemeyer, D., Stephens, E. H., and Stephens, J. D. (1992) *Capitalist Development and Democracy,* Cambridge: Polity Press.

Sasono, Adi (1989) 'NGOs [*sic*] Roles and Social Movement in Developing Democracy: the South-East Asian Experiences', *New Asian Visions,* 6(1): 14–26.

Scott, Alan (1990) *Ideology and the New Social Movements,* London: Unwin Hyman.

Skinner, G. William (1957) *Chinese Society in Thailand: an Analytical History,* Ithaca, NY: Cornell University Press.

—— (1958) *Leadership and Power in the Chinese Community of Thailand,* Ithaca, NY: Cornell University Press.

Paisal, Sricharatchanya *et al.* (1992) *Uprising in May: Catalyst for Change,* Bangkok: The Post Publishing Co.

Starner, Francis L. (1965) 'Communism in Malaysia. A Multifront Struggle', in Robert A. Scalapino (ed.) *The Communist Revolution in Asia. Tactics, Goals, and Achievements,* Englewood Cliffs, NJ: Prentice-Hall, p. 223.

Steinberg, David Joel (1971) *In Search of Southeast Asia: a Modern History,* New York: Praeger.

Stenson, M. R. (1970) *Industrial Conflict in Malaya,* London: Oxford University Press.

Stockwell, A. J. (1992) 'Southeast Asia in War and Peace: the End of European Colonial Empires', in Nicholas Tarling (ed.) *The Cambridge History of Southeast Asia,* vol. 2, Cambridge: Cambridge University Press, pp. 329–85.

Trocki, Carl A. (1992) 'Political Structures in the Nineteenth and Early Twentieth Centuries,' in Nicholas Tarling (ed.) *The Cambridge History of Southeast Asia,* vol. 2, Cambridge: Cambridge University Press, p. 85.

Turnbull, C. M. (1982) *A History of Singapore 1819–1975,* Kuala Lumpur: Oxford University Press.

van der Kroef, Justus M. (1980) *Communism in South-East Asia,* Berkeley: University of California Press.

—— (1984) 'Introduction: Structure and Theoretical Analysis of Opposition Movements in Southeast Asia', *Journal of Asian Affairs,* 9 (Special Studies No. 154): 1–26.

Vickery, Michael (1984) *Cambodia: 1975–1982,* Boston: South End Press.

—— (1986) *Kampuchea. Politics, Economics and Society,* Sydney: Allen & Unwin.

Wood, Ellen Meiksins (1990) 'The Uses and Abuses of "Civil Society"', in Ralph Miliband, Leo Panitch, and John Saville (eds) *Socialist Register 1990,* London: Merlin Press.

3 Political oppositions and regime change in Thailand

*Kevin Hewison**

In a country where the analysis of political events has always seemed remarkably difficult and complicated, the period since Thailand's military overthrew the civilian government led by Chatichai Choonhavan, in February 1991, has been more than usually perplexing. This chapter provides an analysis which attempts to unravel the tumultuous events since that military takeover, based on theoretical lines set out in Chapters 1 and 2 of this collection.

In May 1992 the streets of Bangkok witnessed the most extreme political violence since October 1976, as hundreds of thousands of Bangkokians rose up against the military. To the world, it seemed that the middle and business classes had risen in revolt. The image projected by the world's media was of wealthy demonstrators, more at home in air-conditioned offices, taking to the streets to challenge heavily armed troops. The implication drawn was that political change was being driven by classes which had expanded and been shaped through rapid economic growth. In other words, 'free markets' were seen to have given rise to expanding and wealthy urban classes which had decided they wanted a political voice.[1] The military's attempt to maintain their control over the political agenda has been viewed as an effort to obstruct this quest for greater representation.

This perspective, albeit in more sophisticated form, has emerged in the academic literature on democratisation in Thailand (see Anek n.d.; various chapters in Sangsit and Pasuk 1993). In essence, many of these analysts appear to agree that economic development has seen the consolidation of the business and middle classes and the development of their political influence, and that this will result in expanded political pluralism; some see this as heralding the rise of civil society. The emergence of these classes, together with a technically educated population, are seen as central factors in the creation of new, non-state centres of power and a greater receptiveness to liberal and democratic ideals. In this view, the emergence of political opposition is seen essentially as a late evolutionary process, and inextricably linked to the expansion of the capitalist economy. The tenor of this view can be gauged from the following statement by a group of academic petitioners opposing the 1991 military coup:

> Thailand's economy has become larger, more complex, and more closely linked to the world economy. Such an economic system can progress further only within a liberal economic and political framework, which permits everyone the freedom to participate and to organise to claim their economic rights. . . . Thailand has become a complex, plural society. The democratic system . . . provides every individual an equal opportunity to voice opinions and to participate in determining the future course of the country without domination by any one privileged group.
>
> (cited in *Journal of Contemporary Asia*, 21(4), 1991: 563–4)

Following the approach outlined in the first two chapters of this collection, I intend to indicate that the development of political opposition is a far more complex matter than this literature, both popular and academic, indicates. Indeed, it will be shown that the history of democratisation in Thailand indicates that political opposition has been more pervasive than is usually acknowledged. In addition, it indicates that the 'new classes' (the middle and business classes) owe a political debt to previous opposition movements, even allowing for the quite ambiguous relationship between these classes and contemporary political oppositions.

POLITICAL OPPOSITIONS

In considering political opposition in this chapter it is important to specify the links between state, regime, and civil society when conceptualising the political space in which oppositions operate. There is also a need to view political space historically. This is certainly a wider context than that indicated in recent 'end-of-history' arguments, which tend to portray the expansion of political space (or civil society) as a democratic end-game (see Fukuyama 1992). In addition, it is important to go beyond what is now an increasingly common approach, by both Marxists and modernisation theorists, which looks for a more or less direct relationship between economic development and political change, especially democratisation and the emergence of civil society (see Diamond 1994). This approach, containing more nuances than can be discussed here, basically argues that economic expansion leads to the inexorable breakdown of authoritarianism as growth and modernisation expand civil society, challenging the centralised political structures of authoritarianism. The emergence of a middle class and a more technically educated population is often seen as being especially significant in this process (see Girling 1988: 332). Interestingly, the kind of democracy or representation thought likely to emerge is not dissimilar to the optimistic pluralist propositions of the 1950s and 1960s, involving parliaments, voting and consent, political parties, and constitutions (see Lawson 1993: 20).

The unfortunate outcome of this is to downplay the significance of the political activism and opposition which occurs outside these institutions. As was shown in Chapter 2, the problem is that the *extra-parliamentary struggles* have sometimes been the *only* political opposition. These perspectives also tend to present the relationship between economic development and the emergence of civil society and pluralist political systems in a unilinear, unproblematic, and deterministic manner.

In this chapter, civil society is conceived as an area of political space which is an autonomous sphere 'from which political forces representing constellations of interests in society have contested state power' (Bernhard 1993: 307). The political space required for civil society can be seen to ebb and flow, and may exist under a wide range of political regimes, even, as Bernhard (1993: 326) notes, in some authoritarian systems. In the struggles for the expansion of political space, the activities of oppositions are central, for it is these groups which challenge and deal with the regime. Political oppositions are, by their nature, multi-faceted, and will often include political parties and parliaments, but also activist groups such as trade unions, employer and professional associations, women's groups, student organisations, peasant and ethnic associations, an increasingly expansive group of non-government organisations (NGOs), and a range of social movements. These oppositions, engaged in extended political and social struggle, will often reproduce many of the class inequalities of the society in which they operate, and not all will necessarily be democratic or participatory in their organisation or practice (see Wood 1991).

The breadth of political space and the definition of whether this is 'legitimate' depend on the acceptance or sanction of the state apparatus. This regime will recognise, through struggle, official sanction, or simply inaction, a political space of autonomous organisation outside the sphere of official politics. Thus political opposition is important in the expansion and consolidation of political space, but its relationship to regime and government does not necessarily require the institutions of parliamentary representation. Political space is a site of conflict, struggle, and strife, as well as of negotiation and agreement; it is an arena of contestation. However, this contestation will not always challenge the state, especially where an expanded political space is considered a legitimate part of political activity.

CHALLENGES TO THE THAI REGIME AND STATE

Thailand's polity has often been described in terms which indicate that it is relatively unchanging or slowly evolving, emphasising the continuities in political life while downplaying conflict. Riggs (1966) described the Thai 'bureaucratic polity' in this manner, and it has only been in the last decade that mainstream theorists have begun to question this characterisation seriously. Indeed, writers such as Anek (1992a) do not suggest that Riggs's theoretical position was flawed, just that it is an obsolete picture of contemporary Thailand. The notion that rapid political change and the emergence of civil society are recent phenomena is often expressed. For example, an astute observer of the Thai political scene, Chai-Anan Samudavanija (1989: 313–14), argues that 'pressure-group politics' did not emerge until the early 1970s. Where the concept of 'civil society' is introduced into the analysis, theorists have viewed it in essentially pluralist terms, as an aggregation of non-state pressure and interest groups and a recent development in Thailand (e.g. Prudhisan 1992). Many attribute great political and social significance to business and the middle class, especially as they are seen as major sources of pressure-group politics and the fount of increased democratisation (see Anek n.d.: Chapter 3; and Chai-Anan 1990a: 72–3). Even those who are critical of middle-class and business politics see the emergence of civil society as a virtually inevitable historical end point (Thirayut 1993: 188–98).

Such perspectives rely on a normative definition of politics and neglect considerable political activism in Thailand in each decade since at least the 1920s. This is not the place for an extended history of political opposition in Thailand, but some discussion is necessary in order to avoid the presentation of the post-1991 period as an extraordinary time or as a historical end point.

A brief overview of the development of political space in Thailand, 1918–91

It is common for modern Thai politics to be presented as having been, until recently, an activity of a politicised elite, dominated by the civil and military bureaucracies.[2] The latter are seen to have been ascendant for long periods, having established and maintained an authoritarian regime for most of the period since the overthrow of the absolute monarchy in 1932.

While there can be no doubt that the military have been a major political force, this should not be permitted to obscure the significant political activism which was evident throughout much of the period usually considered as having been dominated by military authoritarianism. Recent studies indicate that there was a significant expansion of political space in the 1920s, with a vigorous press and considerable debate concerning the nature of politics and the constitution of society (Lockhart 1990; Nakharin 1992; Copeland 1994). There was considerable criticism of the monarchy and absolutism at this time. This period of expanded political space continued from about 1918 until the change of regime in 1932, despite attempts by the government of the last of the absolute monarchs to close the space.[3]

Political activism expanded remarkably immediately after the overthrow of the monarchy by the People's Party, led by Pridi Phanomyong. This group initially received considerable support from workers, students, and other urban groups. The years 1932 and 1933 saw much debate and political manoeuvring, especially as there were conflicts between radical and conservative elements within the new government, concerning such issues as economic policy and political representation. Interestingly, debates in the first-ever National Assembly were vigorous, reflecting the broadening of political space. In addition, the monarchists were not finished, and in 1933 there was an armed royalist rebellion, which the government was able to defeat only after heavy fighting. Significantly, the constitutional regime received strong public support. Basically, the combined impact of the 1932 overthrow of the absolute monarchy, the 1933 defeat of the royalist rebellion, and the founding of a parliament and constitution represented the establishment of a new government, a new regime, and the further entrenching of a new state. Not only were the absolutist political regime and its highly personalised government dominated by royal relatives, with the nobility thrown out, but the development of a new social, ideological, economic, and political logic of power, best described as capitalist, was enhanced.

Ironically, it was the restorationist rebellion and the ongoing conflict between royalists and anti-royalists over the next decade that led to a considerable narrowing of political space (resulting in an increased political profile for the military) as the People's Party struggled to entrench its constitutional regime. Despite this narrowing of political space, debate continued within the National Assembly. By 1938 the military were firmly in control, and some, including Prime Minister Phibun Songkhram, were attracted by the examples of fascist regimes in Germany and Italy, and by the expansion of Japan's militarism. Fascist thought had been attractive for some time and this increased,[4] and the government began to introduce policies which smacked of authoritarianism.

These tendencies continued until the end of the Second World War when, with the military in decline, Pridi and his supporters reasserted civilian rule. Again, the political space was expanded as civilian politicians re-established themselves. For the first time political opposition began to be expressed through competing political parties, with royalists dominating the Progressives and Democrats, opposed to a coalition around Pridi. In opposing the military, Pridi found it necessary to make concessions to the royalists. However, they had not forgotten his leadership of the 1932 coup or the insults the People's Party dealt the monarchy, and mounted a campaign against him. They used the political space created by Pridi's government against him, and were even prepared to deal with the military. When the young King Ananda Mahidol died in mysterious circumstances in mid-1946, a situation was created which allowed the military to mount a coup and again narrow the political space created by the civilian government.

The period following the 1947 coup is usually portrayed as one of military dominance (see Girling 1981: 108–11). This is true to a degree, as the period was marked by considerable manoeuvring between various military and police leaders. However, this competition also permitted the maintenance of a limited political space as no one group established its supremacy. In addition, parliament continued to operate, and while tame compared to earlier years, managed to articulate concerns about government policy. The press, business organisations, and unions were also able to provide some opposition. However, it was in 1955 that political opposition was again able to flower. In an effort to regain the political initiative from his rivals, Prime Minister Phibun embarked on a democracy campaign which was to lead to an election in 1957. Thais appreciated the expansion of democratic space, and vigorous debates developed in the local press and at Bangkok's own Speakers' Corner, Sanam Luang. As the election campaign continued, it appears that Police Chief Phao Sriyanond was not prepared to take any chances on the result, and rigged it so that the government party won (see Thak 1974: 140–1; Wilson 1962: 31–2).

Considerable public dissatisfaction and even demonstrations followed the election result. This permitted Army General Sarit Thanarat to stage a coup which significantly altered the face of modern Thai politics. Sarit abolished parliament and the constitution, outlawed political parties and unions, and founded a 'Revolutionary Party' to maintain a highly authoritarian regime. Sarit's dictatorship was vigorous in repressing all opposition, and in addition to exiling political opponents, introduced summary executions of alleged Communists, arsonists, and others identified as opponents, while making economic development, rather than politics, the key to his rule. This was the beginning of a period of authoritarianism which has coloured the perception of many regarding the military's political role in the post-1932 period. It should be remembered that this period extended from 1958 to the early 1970s.

Sarit also began a process which left an indelible mark on Thai politics – the rehabilitation of the monarchy. While the institution had remained symbolic after 1932, the various governments had done much to raise the profile of non-royal elements of state ideology. Sarit gave no indication that political activity was to be tolerated or that the trappings of parliament and constitution were to be reintroduced. As an alternative to these institutions, Sarit used the inexperienced king to raise the regime's profile, resurrecting the monarchy as a traditional political institution which embodied a paternalistic notion of representation (see Thak 1979: 309–24). Effectively, Sarit's coup abolished the constitutional regime, replacing it with an authoritarian one. But it did more. The Sarit regime moulded a state which incorporated capitalist developmentalism and authoritarianism with a technocratic logic to the organisation and operation of the state apparatus.

When Sarit succumbed to liver disease in 1963, his deputies, Generals Thanom Kittikachorn and Prapass Charusathiarana, continued his authoritarian style of rule for a decade. Politics in the 1960s saw the consolidation of anti-Communism as the rationale for the maintenance of repressive policies. Anti-Communism was used to tarnish virtually all opponents, including those who called for a constitution and parliamentary forms. This was reinforced internationally by the Cold War, and especially by US intervention in Indochina and its use of bases in Thailand. As the US's commitment to the region and Thailand declined, the military's control of the political sphere began to show cracks, and greater political space began to be created. There were demands for a more independent foreign policy, and pressure for the promulgation of a constitution increased. After a decade of 'drafting', one was finally produced in 1968. However, the elections which followed, the first since 1957, were again marred by accusations of rigging, tarnishing the government's reputation. There followed a series of allegations of corruption in high places and campaigns for increased political representation. The military attempted to close political space completely by getting rid of a fractious parliament through a coup in 1971. But this was unsuccessful, as much of the increased political activism was outside parliament, and increasingly involved students and academics, who led the campaign against the government and its regime. Increased repression failed, and in October 1973 a student-led rebellion brought hundreds of thousands onto Bangkok's streets. The regime Sarit had established was doomed, along with the government.

The 1973–6 period of civilian rule was one of great political conflict and competition, where the political space was as wide as it has ever been in Thailand (see Morell and Chai-Anan 1981; Girling 1981). Part of the reason for this was that no government could fully establish itself, especially as the constitutional and parliamentary regime was not and could not be entrenched. The conflicts which developed became increasingly violent as competition between Right and Left grew more intense. This overtook the ability of government to control the extensive political space which had been established. In part, the failure of government to establish such control was due to the instability of the parliamentary regime which meant revolving-door government and uncontrolled and unbounded political space. This led to the military coup of October 1976 which meant a reassertion of authoritarianism and anti-Communism, albeit through a civilian government which lasted a year.

The period from late 1977 to 1988 saw the evolution of a constitutional and parliamentary regime under various governments led by ex-military leaders. The period witnessed a deliberate attempt by the governments of General Kriangsak Chomanan and General Prem Tinsulanond to loosen the authoritarianism of the 1976–7 period. This included an expansion of the role of parliament and political parties. Part of the reason for this expansion of political space was that the authoritarianism of the previous government had proved divisive, driving political opposition into the arms of the underground Communist Party which was mounting an increasingly effective guerrilla war. The electoral outcome was the 1989 formation of the elected coalition government led by Chatichai Choonhavan, the first elected Prime Minister since 1976. Behind this there had been a development and consolidation of party politics.

This outline should indicate that the emergence of political space is not simply a recent phenomenon in Thailand. It indicates that the ebb and flow of this space has been the result of political struggles and the actions and reactions of governments, each period of expansion being historically significant. The point is that the contemporary expansion of political space is not to be seen as a historical oddity or as a political end point.

The expansion of political space in contemporary Thailand

The remarkable events of 1992 are symbolic of the re-emergence of political space in contemporary Thailand. The period from the mid-1980s through the 1990s has heralded great political change within Thai society, and the first significant growth of parliamentary politics since the 1930s. It will be argued that the full significance of these changes is that the transformations taking place have not only challenged the regime, but herald a transformation of the state, despite conservative resistance. But what is the challenge and where does it come from?

It cannot be denied that Thailand is continuing to undergo an extensive capitalist economic revolution, a process which is irreversibly changing society. These changes are occurring at an apparently ever accelerating rate, and class relations and politics both reflect these transformations and are part of them. Capitalists, who make up only a small percentage of the population, are firmly in control of the economy, and have been for a considerable time (see Hewison 1989a). The economy they dominate is oriented to the commercial and industrial sectors, and as its base has expanded it has demanded a greater range of skills, resulting in a more complex division of labour. The impact of the capitalist revolution is not, of course, merely an economic phenomenon, for it has marked impacts on social organisation and life and on the ideological cement of society.

To observe that Thailand's state is now unequivocally capitalist does not demand much theory, especially as capitalism is the world's dominant economic system, and its logic permeates social and political organisation virtually everywhere. However, as the world's myriad political systems indicate, this capitalist logic and the capitalist state do not demand any particular kind of regime; capitalist economic activity can be seen to operate effectively under authoritarian and liberal democratic regimes, among others. The question to be asked for Thailand is: what has happened to the Thai state to require that a parliamentary regime be established in the 1990s?

It is important to understand that the 1991 military coup, which overthrew Chatichai's civilian government, did not represent an attack on the state or simply against the government. Rather, it was an attack on the civilian-dominated parliamentary regime and its associated political space. This is clear when the coup makers' targets are considered. The state, existing behind the government and regime, and its basic elements, were not threatened by the military: bureaucratism and technocratism, law, and the country's symbols of Nation, Religion, and Monarchy were in no way challenged. Rather, the coup was an attack on the parliamentary regime and the political space it afforded.

The military targeted the significant institutions of this system: the constitution, parliament, members of parliament (MPs), and the manner in which the regime and government operated were targeted. The principal motive appears to have been to bring decision making back into the bureaucracy, away from civilian politicians. It is clear that these military and civil bureaucratic groups were concerned that previously disenfranchised groups were having an impact on government decisions, for example the environmental movement (see Project for Ecological Recovery 1991; Hirsch and Lohmann 1989) and NGOs working with farmers in a range of areas (see Quinn 1995: 20). There was also great concern that decision making in areas such as foreign policy was being removed from the military high command and the technocrats of the ministries, and given to parliament and cabinet (see Hewison 1993). In other words, the conservative elements of the bureaucracy appear to have been intent on limiting political participation at all levels, by re-establishing the centrality of technocratic decision making.

Significantly, the 1991 coup saw no assault on capitalists or capitalist values, as had occurred, for example, during the 1981 Young Turks' failed coup (see *Prachammit*, 30 May 1981). Rather, the Chatichai government and the regime it represented were overthrown because, paradoxically, they were identified as unleashing forces that threatened the amalgam constituting the state. It may seem odd that Chatichai's government and its parliamentary regime were seen as so challenging. After all, they appeared to represent the end of a capitalist development process, its values and methods, which had been formally and firmly set in train under Sarit in the late 1950s (see Thak 1979: Chapter 5). Indeed, the military and civil bureaucracies were vanguard developers (see Tarr 1991; Hewison 1989a). However, it was evident to conservative groups, especially those in the military, that the parliamentary regime, represented by the Chatichai government, was not just developing capitalism as an economic system, but was fostering societal forces which were moving the state towards a new logic whereby the capitalist state would include notions of political participation. This was at variance with the conservative definition of state, of governance, and of social and bureaucratic hierarchy.[5] In other words, the 1991 coup attempted to maintain the conservative capitalist state by ridding itself of the civilian government and the parliamentary regime. The conservatives' new, hand-picked government, drawn from military and civilian managers and business, was meant to keep the lid on these social new forces (*Far Eastern Economic Review (FEER)*, 21 March 1991; *Matichon sutsapda*, 17 March 1991).

Anderson (1990: 40) observes that the period since 1973 may be seen as that of 'the struggle of the bourgeoisie to develop and sustain its new political power . . . *against threats from the left and right*' (emphasis added). As was noted above, the threat from the Left had been largely defeated by the mid-1980s (Tarr 1991: 34). The far Right, with its tendency to fascist dictatorship, had been held off since 1977. However, the conservative military and civil bureaucracy, while supportive of capitalism, did this within the context of an authoritarian political system, favouring some well-connected capitalists over others, and making decisions on grounds which were not always clear and which tended to entrench the interests of these bureaucracies and their managers. However, this kind of narrow political base was less effective as Thailand's capitalism expanded significantly in the 1980s and 1990s. This expansion included an international orientation, increasing interest in regional investment, and a growth of competitive domestic capital, challenging Bangkok-based finance capital.[6] For these conservatives, the Chatichai government, the parliamentary form, and the logic of its operations represented the essence of the capitalist revolution and embodied the spirit of change in society, and promised political participation which was wider than the technocratic authoritarianism they preferred.

This movement opposed the manner in which officials had defined their interests as national interests, with no regard for democratic interests (that is, the interests of the 'common people'). Concepts such as order, stability, tradition, hierarchy and knowing one's place in it, and unity, symbolically entwined in the national shibboleth, 'Nation, Religion, Monarchy', have defined the exercise of legitimate power (Girling 1981: 147–8). Civilian control of political decision making, especially as bureaucratic decisions were increasingly controlled by elected MPs, was anathema to the conservative managers of the civil and military bureaucracies (on this conservatism, see Hewison 1993). The coup sought to redress this, maintain the conservative capitalist state, jettison the regime, and narrow political space. Thus, following the 1991 coup, General Suchinda Kraprayoon made it clear that any opposition to the National Peace-Keeping Council (NPKC), which ran the coup, amounted to an attack on the Thai nation and would be met with force (cited in Bandhit 1991: 235).

Taking this interpretation further, the May 1992 uprising appears as a 'counter-revolt' against a conservative, authoritarian, technocratic, and military-dominated coterie. The counter-revolt sought to re-establish legitimate political space and a parliamentary regime where elected politicians were dominant. In suggesting this interpretation, attention may be usefully directed to the increasing plurality within civil society. This is significant, for such pluralities have, in themselves, directly challenged the way the state is constituted and the manner in which senior military and civil officials have defined legitimate political activity (see Chai-Anan 1990b: 186). Among other things, these changes have seen the emergence of the middle class as a significant social stratum. What appears to have happened, in the period from the 1991 coup to the May 1992 uprising, is that people who may be identified as the 'middle class' or as 'new social forces' have begun to cast their authority over both economic and political activity. But why should they do this in 1991–2, especially when military authoritarianism has served them well in the past? A number of factors may be suggested in accounting for this.

First, as has been shown elsewhere, until the 1980s, Left and labour organisations were central to the periodic and regular opposition to authoritarian regimes (Hewison and Brown 1994; Hewison and Rodan 1994). The alliance of labour and the Left in opposing repression was challenging to the military authoritarianism, and also to the capitalist and middle classes. This challenge saw the middle class collaborate with capitalists and the state in defeating radical forces. In the past, challenges to state authority and calls for the opening of political space could easily be labelled 'Communist', 'subversive', or 'alien'. Writing of the Communist Party of Thailand (CPT), Chai-Anan (1993: 271) argues that the challenges it posed 'were *total* . . . because they were diametrically opposed to existing ideology, value and belief systems, as well as society's political, economic, and social institutions'. However, with the demise of the Left, the middle class is not now faced with political alternatives which are essentially those of the Left and which appear radical; rather, elements of the middle class are themselves proposing reforms. For the first time there is an opposition which cannot easily be portrayed as illegitimate, and this makes it a particularly potent challenge to the 'old order'.

Second, there is an element of 'market position' which must be considered for the middle class in the current epoch. The successful servicing of contemporary capitalism requires not only supervisors, but an ever-expanding range of professionals and semi-professionals – engineers, computer technicians, nurses, and the like. This has histori-cally been a relatively small demand, when trade and its finance represented the dominant economic activity, and the requirement for clerks and professionals in the private sector was limited. It was only in the centralising state that there was significant demand. However, as industrial development expanded and urban society grew, the demand for professionals and other middle-class employees mushroomed, both in the public and private sectors: in 1937 there were fewer than 50,000 professionals listed in the national census, increasing to over 350,000 (23 per cent female) in 1960 and to 2.35 million (46 per cent female) in 1990 (*Thailand Statistical Yearbook*, various editions). Other estimates place the middle-class category in employment statistics – professional and technical, administrative, executive and managerial, clerical, services, and sales – at much higher levels. For example, Pasuk (1992: 3) argues that the total number had reached five million by the late 1980s. And, for the first time, the private sector employed the majority of well-educated middle-class workers.

In the past, with a relatively weak market position, the middle class was in a kind of 'natural' economic and political alliance with the capitalist class and especially the state bureaucracy. However, by the mid-1980s, this situation had changed. By this time, there was a large unmet demand for professional and technical skills (see *The Nation*, 12 September 1988, 12 May 1989). This has meant that not only are middle-class salaries increasing, but there is also some loosening of the political and ideological nexus between the middle class and their capitalist employers, at least for the time being. The continuing expansion of capitalist enterprise suggests that the current high demand for middle-class services will continue for some time. As mentioned above (pp. 83–4) Thailand's middle class now finds itself in a strong market position which has some potentially significant political implications, especially for emerging activism. Because the professional skills of elements of the middle class are in strong demand, a degree of economic and political independence – from the dominant capitalist class and state – has emerged.

As in the economy, contemporary political activism is now characterised by a greater differentiation of participants, many of them drawn from the middle class. The 1980s and 1990s have seen environmental and consumer organisations join professional and employer associations operating in the political sphere. The May 1992 events have been characterised as a middle-class revolt, but this has been shown to be an exaggeration, at least in class terms (see Somsak 1992; Vorovidh 1993). Even so, it must be said that the popular perception of the middle-class influence on the events is significant. The ready support of many middle-class people for the demonstrations contrasts starkly with the position of organised capitalists, who were slow in throwing their support behind the demonstrators. Pasuk (1992: 5) notes that it took some time before 'modern business came to see that authoritarianism bent on fascism could have . . . disastrous effects on their business interests'. It might have been supposed that, in the interests of investor confidence, business would have continued to accept military dominance. In Pasuk's view, however, business leaders opposed authoritarianism, on account of their assessment that the military threatened their economic interests, and for the first time they gave open support to the institutions of parliamentary democracy.

For the middle class, there was not the same economic imperative at work. Anek (1992b: 18) observes that the: 'middle class did not appear to believe that democracy could take care of its own faults and flaws. . . . They rejected authoritarianism *only in principle*, while in practice holding that there could be good authoritarian rule' (emphasis added).

Indeed, he suggests that middle-class people might have thrown their lot in with the military again, as they had done in 1991, especially as they tend to hold popularly elected politicians in low esteem, even though, as noted above, they tend to respect the idea of elections and parliament. The fact that the middle class did not object to the overthrow of the elected government in 1991 was testament to the fact that this government was seen to be corrupt and incompetent. For the middle class, good government appears to be about competence and, as Anek (1992b: 20, 25) points out, this does not necessarily require elections. He argues convincingly that the middle class only rejected the military when it was clear that it too was intent on cementing its own political position, apparently for economic gain. The conservative military group demonstrated that it was prepared to make deals with corrupt figures, showing that it too lacked integrity when it came to expanding its own economic base.

All of this indicates that in the early 1990s there was a greater diversity of political orientation possible for both the business and middle classes. The result was the coalition of groups which came together in May 1992 to overthrow the military-led government. Middle-class elements were an important constituent of this, and also threw their support behind the electoral process which resulted from the tumultuous events, seeking an honest and professional government which could implement policy effectively. The outcome was a coalition of 'clean' political parties, led by the apparently honest and long-serving MP, Chuan Leekpai. Chuan epitomised the middle class: a sober and quiet professional with Sino-Thai ancestry who had worked his way up the political ladder; while not a particularly strong personality, he seemed a man of integrity. He led the country's oldest political party, formed by monarchists in the mid-1940s, but now drawing much of its support from the urban middle class. It appeared that the middle class had its government in place.

Of course, this is not the end of the story, as this government was as much a representative of the capitalist class as it was of the middle class.[7] The various parties in the coalition reflected this, and there have been the inevitable conflicts between them, and between the government and representatives of the old order. Like that of the Chatichai period, the Chuan government, which survived from late 1992 to mid-1995, is symbolic of the wider challenge to the state. This generalised challenge is clearly demonstrated by the fact that many of those who supported the overthrow of the military regime and the election of the Chuan government continued to find themselves in opposition during its period in power. Indeed, when Chuan's own Democrat Party was accused of harbouring ministers and members who had benefited from land reform deals which were said to be corrupt, many groups which had supported his rise to power did not oppose the moves which led to the fall of his government (see *Bangkok Post*, 1–20 May 1995). This illustrates that opposition to the government is not necessarily opposition to the parliamentary regime. In other words, political struggle continues, parliamentary government in place or not.

AFTER 1992

The discussion to this point should indicate that Thai social and political life has reached a watershed. In a period of rapid change a new 'logic' of social and political forces is emerging to challenge and redesign the Thai state. But what is this logic?

As noted above (p. 73), political theorists have argued that increased social complexity, rapid economic growth, and the development of capitalism give rise to pressures for parliamentary regimes. It is often held that the parliamentary form of state power is the most appropriate model of political rule for capitalist societies. Anderson (1990: 40) argues that parliamentary democracy is the 'style of regime with which all ambitious, prosperous and self-confident bourgeoisies feel most comfortable, precisely because it maximises their power and minimises that of their competitors'.

The general thrust of these perspectives appears to describe the Thai experience, but, at the same time, it needs to be stated that capitalists are not necessarily democrats, and do not actually need parliaments or representation. Capitalist development and industrialisation, likewise, do not require any particular political form. Indeed, Thailand's experience would appear to confirm these points: Thai capitalism has made great strides under political arrangements which have been neither representative nor participatory.

Capitalists are not natural enemies of political conservatives. Indeed, they may well be considered allies – in the past capitalists have entered into numerous political and economic alliances with the monarchy, aristocracy, military, and bureaucracy. As Marx and Engels (1973: 72–9) noted almost 150 years ago, the history of the bourgeoisie is one of alliance and coalition as it emerges eventually to become a truly *revolutionary* force. One might suggest that 1992 represents a significant step along this road.

Another line of argument, noted above (p. 75), has been to suggest that the middle class is a force for democracy. In my view, this is a misrepresentation. Again, democracy or parliamentary forms do not appear to be specifically necessary for this class. Indeed, Anek (1992b), quoted previously, makes this point. Further, Chai-Anan (1992: 35) notes that socio-economic change enabled 'the middle class . . . to participate more in bureaucratic politics rather than to fundamentally change . . . [its] nature'. So, in Thailand, there is no reason to assume that either the middle class or the capitalist class is *naturally* interested in a democratic, representative, or participatory regime.

There has always been, as noted above (p. 71), great concern expressed whenever elections have appeared 'rigged', and this no doubt applied in 1992. However, as I have suggested, what has happened is that a remarkable period of social and political change has resulted in a period of relative political and economic independence – from both the state apparatus and the capitalist class – for those identified as 'middle class'. Similarly, the very rapid globalisation of business enterprise has provided the capitalist class with a greater degree of flexibility in its investment strategies, reducing its dependence on national economic policy. At the same time, the dependence of small capitalists on finance capital has been reduced. A good example is seen in the operations of the Securities Exchange of Thailand (SET), which has only become attractive to local and international investors since regulatory legislation has been strengthened. The importance of the SET in mobilising capital, loosening the grip domestic banks have had on finance and industry, must be emphasised. The banks, always close to technocratic decision makers and the military, were the traditional business leaders and were not necessarily interested in competition or in the development of new businesses. The ability to raise capital through the SET has allowed a range of new companies and business groups to emerge.

Paradoxically, this relative independence and flexibility have come at a time when the political interests of the middle and capitalist classes seem to have converged. Their interests are served by their increased political representation and influence over policy making. As was reported recently (*Manager*, July 1992: 20–5), business wants order, transparency in decision making, economic growth, responsibility, predictability, openness, and access. Such desires have been translated to and from international agency policy in recent years, emphasising broad-based participation, accountability, transparency, market mechanisms, public-sector management, and an effective legal system.[8] These were qualities which conservative military and civil bureaucrats were not interested in or capable of delivering.

In other words, the middle class's interests appear to have become compatible with those of the bourgeoisie, while still reflecting the developing pluralities and complexities noted above. This congruence of interests demands political arrangements which challenge the regime and, by extension, the nature of the state and the ideology which cements the relationships between the institutions of the state apparatus. The Chatichai government exemplified the challenge to these. This challenge produced the reaction by military conservatives. Their victory over other cliques within the army, and the support they received from senior bureaucrats, represented a triumph, if momentary, of an old guard. Their 1991 coup represented an adamant objection to what they perceived as a relentless chipping away at the edifice which is the Thai state, the national interest, and, not coincidentally, their privileges, perquisites, and status. The coup represented many things, including inter-clique rivalry, but also a last-ditch bid to shore up their increasingly anachronistic position against the charge of the new business and middle class. Their defeat, and the election of the Chuan coalition government, represented another step towards a more thoroughly bourgeois polity.

Business is now in the process of further entrenching its class rule through its alliance with the middle class. This challenges not only the state, demanding that it be reshaped, but also the conservatives who assign to themselves the task of protecting the existing state. No class can merely take hold of the existing state and use it for its own purposes, and certainly not a class which is as internally competitive as the capitalist class. In Thailand, however, the capitalist and middle classes will continue the restructuring of the state, its apparatus, the logic of its operations, and its ideology. By its nature this process will continue to pose a threat to conservative values, the old order and institutions, and entrenched interests. In contemporary Thailand, it is clear that the current interests of both capital and the middle class will be best served by a functional democratic electoral system, once described by one of its opponents as:

> the best possible political shell for capitalism, and, therefore, once capital has gained control of this very best shell . . . it establishes its power so securely, so firmly, that *no* change, either of persons, of institutions, or of parties . . . can shake it.

> (Lenin 1973: 16)

There can be little doubt that parliamentary rule, if it can contain opposition within its seemingly representative institutions,[9] effectively taming opposition which challenges the logic of the capitalist economy, will gain the support of both the Thai capitalist and middle classes.

Parliamentary rule promises a political space where activism is defined within certain boundaries and governed by rules which offer the prospect of preventing opposition from becoming undisciplined and uncontrolled. The problem for the middle and business classes is that, as has been demonstrated in this chapter, there is no simple way to read off political liberalisation against economic development. This was demonstrated in the first post-1992 election, and provides a suitable 'conclusion' for this chapter.

The 1995 election resulted when Chuan's government, made up of parties which had opposed the military and its regime, and the longest-serving civilian-led government, found itself accused of corruption. The early election saw Chuan's coalition defeated by parties which had been, by and large, willing to co-operate with the military in 1992. The new coalition, led by the Chart Thai Party's Banharn Silpa-Archa, was the subject of immediate criticism regarding, among other things, massive vote buying during the election campaign, the potential for further corruption, the influence of quasi-criminal elements ('dark influences' or *chao pho*), its reluctance regarding political and constitutional reform, and the appointment of politicians with 'tainted' backgrounds.[10]

Many in the middle class, and especially academics and the press, led the criticism of the Banharn government and, especially, the cabinet, even if many in this class must have voted for parties in the coalition. Business was more circumspect, attempting to gain guarantees that economic and fiscal policy would not be manipulated, seeking a working relationship. Here is the necessary ambiguity noted above: business and middle classes may prefer a parliamentary regime, but capitalist economic development can take place under many kinds of regime, and it remains to be seen if these classes will continue their support if their class interests – represented by a supportive economic climate, business confidence, and transparency – are seen to be somehow threatened or compromised. The historical path to democratic forms was set well before 1992. Business and the middle classes may have supported this form in 1992, and there is little doubt that they will continue to oppose a return to the conservatism of military authoritarianism, but there is no *necessary* commitment to parliamentary forms.

NOTES

* The author thanks Andrew Brown, Garry Rodan, Paul Healy, and anonymous referees for their comments on an earlier draft. They are unlikely to be completely satisfied with this much revised final version, even though it has been greatly improved through their efforts. This chapter extends, refines, and revises theoretical issues first raised in Hewison (1993), and draws on ideas included in Hewison and Rodan (1994).

1 This approach is one which has again become popular in the general literature on development and democratisation (see Almond 1991; Diamond 1989).
2 For a general theoretical critique, see Hewison (1989b: Chapter 2).
3 The perspective set out in this and the following paragraphs is not one that may easily be found in the literature. My interpretation is based on the following sources: *Bangkok Times* and *Bangkok Times Weekly Review* (1918–35); *Siam Rath Weekly Review* (1955–8); *Bangkok Post* and *Bangkok World* (1957–94); Barmé (1993); Brailey (1986); various essays in Chai-Anan and Suwadi (1979); Charivat (1985); Copeland (1994); Lockhart (1990); Murashima *et al.* (1986); Suthachai (1989); Thak (1979); and Thompson (1967). Unpublished research completed by Scot Barmé and Andrew Brown has also been useful in completing this section.
4 Nationalist ideologue *Luang* Wichit Wathakan was influenced (Barmé 1993: 78, 87), and Italian fascists visited Thailand in the 1930s, sponsored by a local Italian fascist-dominated organisation (Thompson 1967: 216–7).
5 For a fuller discussion of this ideology see Chai-Anan *et al.* (n.d.: 127–68) and Thak (1979).
6 On the internationalisation of Thai capital and regional investment see Chaiyong Limthongkul Foundation (1994). For information on non-Bangkok-based business see Hewison and Maniemai (1994).
7 In purely instrumentalist terms this can be seen in the predominance of business people in government and cabinet. Official figures indicate that at least 45.5 per cent of national MPs were business people, while the unofficial figure would be closer to 65 per cent, as it is for provincial and municipal assemblies (see Khana kammakan 1992: 117). A large percentage of those in the various Chuan cabinets have been from a business background.

8 This particular list could be drawn from any number of documents from policy organisations including the World Bank, United Nations agencies, and Thai organisations like the Thailand Development Research Institute (see Christensen 1992). For a similar list, from a human rights activist, see Vitit (1993).

9 The question of whether the Thai electoral system is representative cannot be discussed here, but for some thoughts see Hewison (1993).

10 On the accusations of corruption in the Chuan government, see reports of the May 1995 censure debate in, for example, *Bangkok Post*, 15 May 1995. The criticisms of the new Banharn government were clear immediately following the elections – see, for example, *Bangkok Post*, 3 July 1995.

REFERENCES

Almond, Gabriel A. (1991) 'Capitalism and Democracy', *PS: Political Science and Politics*, 24(3): 467–74.

Anderson, Ben (1990) 'Murder and Progress in Modern Siam', *New Left Review*, 181: 33–48.

Anek Laothamatas (1992a) *Business Associations and the New Political Economy of Thailand: From Bureaucratic Polity to Liberal Corporatism*, Singapore: Institute of Southeast Asian Studies.

—— (1992b) 'Sleeping Giant Awakes?: the Middle Class in Thai Politics', paper presented to the Conference on Democratic Experiences in Southeast Asian Countries, Thammasat University-Rangsit, Bangkok, 7–8 December.

—— (n.d.) *'Mob mue thue': chonchan klang lae nak thurakit kap phatthanakan prachathipatai*, Bangkok: Matichon.

Bandhit Thammatreerat (1991) 'Chiwit khabuan kan sahaphap raengngan thai phaidai rabop ro. so. cho.', in Bandhit Thammatreerat (ed.) *Chomna raengngan thai*, Bangkok: Arom Phongphangan Foundation.

Barmé, Scot (1993) *Luang Wichit Wathakan and the Creation of a Thai Identity*, Singapore: Institute of Southeast Asian Studies.

Bernhard, Michael (1993) 'Civil Society and Democratic Transition in East Central Europe', *Political Science Quarterly*, 108(2): 307–26.

Brailey, Nigel (1986) *Thailand and the Fall of Singapore. A Frustrated Asian Revolution*, Boulder, Colo.: Westview Press.

Chai-Anan Samudavanija (1989) 'Thailand: a Stable Semi-Democracy', in Larry Diamond, Juan L. Linz, and Seymour Martin Lipset (eds) *Democracy in Developing Countries: Asia*, Boulder, Colo.: Lynne Rienner Publishers, pp. 305–46.

—— (1990a) *Rat kap sangkhom: trai laksana rat thai nai phahu sangkhom sayam*, Boulder, Colo.: Chulalongkorn University Press.

—— (1990b) 'The Military and Modern Thai Political System', in Pinit Ratanakul and U Kyaw Than (eds) *Development, Modernization, and Tradition in Southeast Asia: Lessons from Thailand*, Bangkok: Mahidol University, pp. 185–9.

—— (1992) 'Thailand', *Economic Reform Today*, Summer: 35–6.

—— (1993) 'The New Military and Democracy in Thailand', in Larry Diamond (ed.) *Political Culture and Democracy in Developing Countries*, Boulder, Colo.: Lynne Rienner Publishers, pp. 269–93.

Chai-Anan Samudavanija, and Suwadi Charoenphong (eds) (1979) *Kanmuang – kan pokkhrong thai samai mai: ruam ngan wichai thang prawatisat lae rattasat*, Bangkok: Social Science Association of Thailand.

Chai-Anan Samudavanija, Kusuma Snitwongse and Suchit Bunbongkarn (n.d.) *From Armed Suppression to Political Offensive: Attitudinal Transformation of Thai Military Officers Since 1976*, Bangkok: Institute of Security and International Studies, Chulalongkorn University.

Chaiyong Limthongkul Foundation (eds) (1994) *Asia's New Growth Circles Conference*, Bangkok: Chaiyong Limthongkul Foundation and Asia Inc.

Charivat Santaputra (1985) *Thai Foreign Policy, 1932–1946*, Bangkok: Thai Khadi Institute.

Christensen, Scott (1992) 'The Public Policy Process and Political Change in Thailand: a Summary of Observations', *TDRI Quarterly Review*, 7(1): 21–6.

Copeland, Mathew Phillip (1994) 'Contested Nationalism and the 1932 Overthrow of the Absolute Monarchy in Siam', Ph.D. thesis, Canberra: Australian National University.

Diamond, Larry (1989) 'Introduction: Persistence, Erosion, Breakdown and Renewal', in Larry Diamond, Juan J. Linz, and Seymour Martin Lipset (eds) *Democracy in Developing Countries: Asia*, Boulder, Colo.: Lynne Rienner Publishers.

—— (1994) 'Rethinking Civil Society. Toward Democratic Consolidation', *Journal of Democracy*, 5(3): 4–17.

Diamond, Larry, Juan J. Linz, and Seymour Martin Lipset (eds) (1989) *Democracy in Developing Countries: Asia*, Boulder: Lynne Rienner Publishers.

Fukuyama, Francis (1992) *The End of History and the Last Man*, London: Hamish Hamilton.

Girling, John L. S. (1981) *Thailand: Society and Politics*, Ithaca, NY: Cornell University Press.

—— (1988) 'Development and Democracy in Southeast Asia', *The Pacific Review*, 1(4): 332–40.

Hewison, Kevin (1989a) *Bankers and Bureaucrats: Capital and the Role of the State in Thailand*, Monograph No. 34, New Haven, Conn.: Yale University Southeast Asia.

—— (1989b) *Politics and Power in Thailand*, Manila: Journal of Contemporary Asia Publishers.

—— (1993) 'Of Regimes, State and Pluralities: Thai Politics Enters the 1990s', in Kevin Hewison, Richard Robison, and Garry Rodan (eds) *Southeast Asia in the 1990s: Authoritarianism, Democracy and Capitalism*, Sydney: Allen & Unwin, pp. 159–90.

Hewison, Kevin and Brown, A. (1994) 'Labour and Unions in an Industrialising Thailand', *Journal of Contemporary Asia*, 24(4): 483–514.

Hewison, Kevin and Maniemai Thongyou (1994) *The New Generation of Provincial Business People in Northeastern Thailand*, Working Paper No. 16, Perth: Asia Research Centre, Murdoch University.

Hewison, Kevin and Rodan, G. (1994) 'The Decline of the Left in South East Asia', in Ralph Miliband and Leo Panitch (eds) *Socialist Register 1994*, London: Merlin Press, pp. 235–62.

Hirsch, Philip and Lohmann, Larry (1989) 'Contemporary Politics of Environment in Thailand', *Asian Survey*, 29(4): 439–51.

Khana kammakan ditdam lae sotsong dulae kan luaktang samachik sapha phuthaen ratsadon (1992) *Kan luaktang samachik sapha phuthaen ratsadon*, Bangkok: Khana thamngan fai wichakan.

Lawson, Stephanie (1993) 'Institutionalising Peaceful Conflict: Political Opposition and the Challenge of Democratisation in Asia,' *Australian Journal of International Affairs*, 47(1): 15–30.

Lenin, V. I. (ed.) (1973) *State and Revolution*, Peking: Foreign Languages Press.

Lockhart, Bruce McFarland (1990) 'Monarchy in Siam and Vietnam, 1925–1946', Ph.D. dissertation, Cornell University.

Marx, Karl and Engels, Frederick (eds) (1973) 'Manifesto of the Communist Party', in D. Fernbach (ed.) *Karl Marx: the Revolutions of 1848*, Harmondsworth: Penguin, pp. 62–98.

Morell, David and Chai-Anan Samudavanija (1981) *Political Conflict in Thailand. Reform, Reaction, Revolution*, Cambridge, Mass.: Oelgeschlager, Gunn & Hain.

Murashima, Eiji, Nakharin Mektrairat, and Chalermkiet Phiu-nual (1986) *Political Thoughts of the Thai Military in Historical Perspective*, Joint Research Report Series No. 55, Tokyo: Institute of Developing Economies.

Nakharin Mektrairat (1992) *Kan pattiwat sayam pho. so. 2475*, Bangkok: Social Science and Humanities Promotion Foundation.

Pasuk Phongpaichit (1992) 'The Thai Middle Class and the Military: Social Perspectives in the Aftermath of May 1992', paper presented to the Annual Conference of the ANU Thai Studies Group, Australian National University, Canberra, 18 October.

Project for Ecological Recovery (1991) 'The People's Forum', unpublished paper, Bangkok, 13–17 October.

Prudhisan Jumbala (1992) *Nation-Building and Democratization in Thailand: a Political History*, Bangkok: Chulalongkorn University Social Research Institute.

Quinn, Rapin (1995) 'Community Culture and Movements: the Thai NGO Responses to Agricultural Commercialisation in a Northern Thai Village', *Thai-Yunnan Newsletter*, 28: 17–22.

Riggs, Fred W. (1966) *Thailand: the Modernization of a Bureaucratic Polity*, Honolulu: East–West Center Press.

Sangsit Piriyarangsan and Pasuk Phongpaichit (eds) (1993) *Chonchan klang bon krasae prachathipatai thai*, Bangkok: Political Economy Centre, Faculty of Economics, Chulalongkorn University.

Somsak Kosaisuk (1992) *Khabuankan raengngan phrutsapha mahahot*, Bangkok: Friedrich Ebert Stiftung, Labour Museum Project, and Arom Pongphangan Foundation.

Suthachai Yimprasoet (1989) 'Kan khluanwai thang kanmuang thi dodam rattaban samai chomphon plaek phibun songkhram (pho. so. 2491–2500)', MA thesis, Graduate School, Chulalongkorn University.

Tarr, Shane P. (1991) 'The Nature of Military Intervention in the Countryside of Surat Thani, Southern Thailand', *Bulletin of Concerned Asian Scholars*, 23(3): 34–50.

Thak Chaloemtiarana (1979) *Thailand: the Politics of Despotic Paternalism*, Bangkok: Social Science Association of Thailand and Thai Khadi Institute.

Thirayut Bunmi (1993) *Sangkhom khemkhaeng*, Bangkok: Mingmit Publishers.

Thompson, Virginia (ed.) (1967) *Thailand: the New Siam*, New York: Paragon Books.

Vitit Muntarbhorn (1993) *Human Rights in Southeast Asia. A Challenge for the 21st Century*, Bangkok: The Kernial S. Sandhu Memorial Lecture, The Chaiyong Limthongkul Foundation.

Vorovidh Charoenlert (1993) 'Chonchan klang kap hetkan phrutsaphakhom: fai prachathipatai ru ratbatikan', in Sangsit and Pasuk (eds) *Chonchan klang bon krasae prachathipatai thai*, Bangkok: Political Economy Centre, Faculty of Economics, Chulalongkorn University, pp. 117–54.

Wilson, David A. (1962) *Politics in Thailand*, Ithaca: Cornell University Press.

Wood, Ellen Meiksins (1991) 'The Uses and Abuses of "Civil Society"', in Ralph Miliband, Leo Panitch, and John Saville (eds) *Socialist Register 1990*, London: Merlin Press, pp. 60–84.

4 State–society relations and political opposition in Singapore

*Garry Rodan**

INTRODUCTION

In this chapter the relationships between economic development, civil society, and political opposition are explored through an examination of one of the most dynamic and economically advanced Asian newly industrialising countries (NICs) – Singapore. This study demonstrates that the link between economic development and the expansion of civil society is more problematic and contingent than is often conceded in the literature. In particular, it challenges the idea of civil society as something of an incremental but progressive historical process associated with economic development, an idea already brought into question in the introductory chapter and the survey of historical political developments in Southeast Asia by Hewison and Rodan in Chapter 2.

Certainly, the social transformations associated with rapid industrialisation and increasingly sophisticated economic development in Singapore are contributing to a significant reworking of state–society relations, with important implications for both parliamentary and extra-parliamentary political opposition and dissent. However, to date, the major feature of this reworking is the expanding realm of the state through the extension and refinement of the mechanisms of political co-optation, not the evolution of a more expansive civil society. Progress towards genuinely independent social organisations engaged in regular and legally enshrined political contests over the exercise of state power has been limited in Singapore, despite the emergence of a very sizeable and diverse middle class.

This extended co-optation involves modifications to the political system to incorporate sectional interests, the establishment of new relations with business and ethnic communities, and other institutional initiatives and rhetorical appeals. New corporatist forms of political organisation are being introduced to 'manage' emerging social forces.

The chief objective is to reconcile a *de facto* one-party state to a new social reality. Despite the existence of various political parties, the People's Action Party (PAP) has an effective monopoly of state power in Singapore. The relationships that define the state reflect and consolidate the interests of only one party. Furthermore, the PAP simply does not entertain the notion of a 'loyal' opposition, regardless of the unthreatening nature of the opposition parties, most of which either embrace key aspects of PAP ideology or struggle to conceptualise alternatives. The new initiatives in co-optation thus provide carefully defined alternative avenues for contestation consistent with the elitist structures and ideologies built up over past decades by the PAP. However, they are intended as alternatives not just to opposition parties, as vehicles for contending views, but to any independent organisation attempting to influence political decision making.

The rhetoric which has accompanied these initiatives has nevertheless emphasised a new era in Singapore politics: one of greater tolerance and openness (see the *Straits Times* (*ST*), 8 May 1990: 1; *Straits Times Weekly Overseas Edition* (*STWOE*), 13 January 1990: 1, 16 June 1990: 1, 7, 30 June 1990: 13). While the government's intention may be to harness social diversity to the maintenance of authoritarian rule, there have been limited and tentative, but nevertheless significant, cases where individuals and organisations have tried to exploit that rhetoric to expand the space for a measure of independent political activity. In the ensuing attempt by the PAP to clarify its position, the 'political' and the 'non-political' are sharply delineated and encapsulated in a legal discourse. This discourse reflects a suspicion of, and hostility to, extra-parliamentary forms of political contestation. By their nature, the control of these forms is more problematic than formal political institutions.

Significantly, in those limited cases where implicit official tolerance of extra-parliamentary political activities has occurred, it has involved predominantly middle-class groups with moderate political objectives, notably in the areas of conservation and women's interests. There is an aspiration among an element of the middle class in Singapore for greater opportunity to contribute to public policy without operating through government-controlled organisations. However, in Singapore the middle class is a major beneficiary of the PAP state, in both material and non-material terms. Indeed, the economic growth and associated social development achieved under the PAP has generated significant social bases of support, especially among the middle class. The gripes of the middle class are thus particularistic rather than general or fundamental. The government's handling of these limited pressures has been ambiguous, sometimes tolerating critical public comment, at other times not. By and large, though, this has tended to fall short of the rhetoric on political change. Ironically, the middle class in Singapore represents a potential force for a civil society that legitimates PAP rule. But the PAP leadership appears to be a victim of its own ideology, convinced of the paramount importance of its direct and absolute political control, and has difficulty recognising this potential.

The PAP may in some respects be a little unsure how to handle perceived middle-class dissent, but it remains perfectly clear how to manage any political attempts to advance the interests of the under-privileged via independent organisations. They continue to feel the full force of the state's repressive apparatus such as internal security legislation, especially where cross-class alliances are involved. The state in Singapore retains a considerable ability to define the limits and complexion of civil society through its empowering of some organisations and obstruction of others, a capacity Rueschemeyer *et al.* (1992) have discussed more generally of states. Therefore, widening inequalities in income and wealth and associated grievances felt by the working class expose the representational shortcomings of the state-controlled National Trades Union Congress (NTUC) without translating into alternative, independent organisational bases.

While major breakthroughs in the development of civil society are yet to happen in Singapore, by the standards of the city-state's electoral history, opposition political parties have made significant vote gains since the early 1980s. But this does not reflect a transformation in the organisational capacities of these parties, or a greatly reduced level of reticence among the population about the personal repercussions of involvement with them. Moreover, the extent to which these parties actually constitute 'opposition' to the PAP and provide meaningful alternatives remains questionable. In particular, the elitist ideological premises of the PAP make their mark on these organisations. It must be acknowledged, though, that the rapid economic growth over which the PAP has presided, in fostering significant bases of social support, has served to limit the receptiveness for alternative politics. Repression and ideological hegemony by the PAP are by no means the sole basis of its political success. Nevertheless, opposition parties are fundamentally hamstrung by the absence of an extensive and dynamic civil society with which to form organic links, a situation that would only be compounded if the PAP's strategy of greater co-optation succeeds.[1]

ECONOMIC DEVELOPMENT AND CLASS TRANSFORMATIONS

The adoption in Singapore of an export-oriented industrialisation strategy in the mid-1960s laid the basis of the city-state's impressive economic development. Propitious external circumstances were combined with domestic social and political conditions conducive to manufacturing investment geared to global markets. One of these local factors was the absence of a domestic bourgeoisie entrenched in import-substitution industrial production and capable of exerting a political influence to frustrate reform (Rodan 1989). Thus, direct manufactured exports, negligible in the first half of the 1960s, jumped to a value of S$47,520 million by 1990. Steep increases in foreign investment have fuelled the bulk of this. Whereas foreign investment amounted to a mere S$157 million in 1965, by 1990 it reached S$23,903 million (Economic Development Board 1981, 1992; Department of Statistics 1983). The ensuing industrial development generated considerable demand in wage labour, thereby alleviating unemployment and laying the basis for general material improvements for the population. The PAP's social policies, particularly in public housing, added further to these improvements and the party's electoral appeal.

Critical as the manufacturing sector has been to Singapore's development, since the early 1980s the economy has been maturing and diversifying. Activities in the services sector, notably financial and business services, are assuming increasing importance. This has been actively encouraged by the government, both because it recognises there are objective limits to the possibilities of extending the manufacturing production in Singapore and because an acute dependence on this sector has left the economy highly vulnerable to the vicissitudes of global demand. In particular, the electronics industry has been susceptible to fluctuations in demand from American consumers. Thus, there has been a concerted attempt by the government to foster greater integration with the rapidly expanding regional economies. This is expected to assist with sectoral diversification and further technological upgrading of the economy.

Discussions of class transformations in the NICs have tended to pay special attention to the burgeoning ranks of the middle class, however defined. In Singapore's case, there can be no denying that its rapid industrialisation has generated a sizeable middle class; even the most conservative measure has it approaching one-quarter of the workforce and more than doubling since 1970 (Rodan 1993a: 53–7). Professionals such as managers, computer personnel, and advertising workers have expanded alongside the 'traditional' administrative elite in the civil service (Mak 1993: 326). Yet the Singapore state itself has made a significant contribution to middle-class expansion, chiefly through its extensive economic role and profit-oriented statutory boards. The professional skills demanded here are weighted heavily in favour of those relevant to the functioning, administration, and accounting of the economy. This, in conjunction with the PAP ideology of meritocracy which accords the various technical specialisations of the middle class an exceptional social status, fosters mutual interests and values between the development-minded PAP and large sections of the middle class.

The most conspicuous development in Singapore's private sector since the mid-1980s has been the influx of foreign-based international capital associated with export-oriented industrialisation. But the government also now exerts a crucial impact on the structure of the domestic economy, and so vast is the capital of Singapore's government-linked companies that they are increasingly embarking on internationalised accumulation strategies.[2] For some of the established domestic private capital groups, the offshore ventures led by the state open up new avenues, either by bolstering investment abroad or by providing the first real such opportunity.[3] However, for the bulk of Singapore's domestic-based private sector in commerce, services, and manufacturing, offshore investment is not a serious option. The current economic trajectory thus involves widening disparities between the different fractions of capital in Singapore.

Although Singapore's rapid industrialisation has also generated a significant increase in the working class, since the 1980s manufacturing production has become more capital-intensive. Hence, the share of the total domestic workforce in manufacturing dropped from 30 per cent to 28 per cent between 1980 and 1990 (Department of Statistics 1991), and white-collar areas of working-class employment have become more important. The stocks of the domestic working class have also been augmented by guest labour from abroad, concentrated in the construction and manufacturing sectors, and also employed as domestic maids for the bourgeoisie and middle class. However, this in no way renders the working class marginal to the dynamics of Singapore's political economy. Rather, after decades of rapid upward social mobility, anxieties about income and wealth differentials are rising among blue- and white-collar sections of the working class as the structural barriers to large-scale mobility begin to assert themselves (see Medhi 1994; Rodan 1993a).

In broad terms, then, Singapore's dramatic economic transformation has been accompanied by significant developments in social structure. The city-state now has a more socially differentiated population and the objective preconditions exist for new, separate identities and organisational structures in society. Against this background, let us consider pressures on the one-party state in Singapore and the prospects for oppositional politics as a result of the emergence of new social forces.

THE ONE-PARTY STATE IN A NEW SOCIAL CONTEXT

As explained in Chapter 2, as in other societies in Southeast Asia, there have been periodic advances and retreats in the attempt in Singapore to forge a civil society. In Singapore, from the 1930s onwards, trade unions and student organisations intermittently enjoyed significant independent political space, especially during the 1950s when the student and labour movements proved a potent combined anti-colonial force. Indeed, they were the organisational backbone of the emerging political parties, especially those outside the tutelage of the authorities. Even where colonial regimes were at their most repressive in Singapore, organised leftist opposition movements survived in some form or another, however clandestine their operations. By contrast, the PAP's brand of authoritarian rule has been effective in direct repression of political opposition and in carefully defining the limits to political space outside the state.

As is well documented (Deyo 1981; Rodan 1989; Rosa 1990), organised labour was the first casualty in this. By the late 1960s, independent organised labour was virtually irrelevant in Singapore and the state-sponsored NTUC was actively mobilising its affiliated organisations behind government policies.[4] This undercut the social basis of the PAP's major political opponent, the Barisan Sosialis (BS). But a more pervasive, even if less conspicuous, measure for blunting political opposition was introduced through the Societies Act (1967). This followed a spate of student movement activism, but was subsequently bolstered and strictly enforced to bar any 'political' engagement by organisations not specifically registered for such purposes. This legislation effectively outlawed pressure group formation and severely curtailed public debate.

The Societies Act, by inference, marks out a very expansive political monopoly for the PAP state. Apart from blatantly restricting the ability of voluntary, independent organisations to pursue their collective interests, this legislation has obstructed opposition political parties in their efforts to develop an alternative programme. Unable to forge links with interest groups, they are significantly limited in their access to policy expertise and the ability to mobilise political support. Yet the PAP has been able to harness a host of state and para-statal organisations for its party-political purposes, many of them specifically created for community-level scrutiny and propagandising for the PAP (Seah 1973). Indeed, the successful candidate in the 1993 presidential election, Ong Teng Cheong, was nominated by the NTUC leadership which subsequently mobilised support for Ong through that organisation (*Straits Times Weekly Edition* (*STWE*), 14 August 1993: 14). Engagement in 'politics' by organisations not strictly established for that purpose is not so much the problem, but rather engagement in non-PAP or anti-PAP politics.

A number of incidents from the mid to late 1980s suggested that the PAP's determination to restrict civil society had not fundamentally altered. One was the amendment to the Newspaper and Printing Presses Act in 1986 which empowered the Minister of Communication and Information to limit the circulation of publications considered 'engaging in the domestic politics of Singapore' (*Asiaweek*, 15 June 1986: 20). This was used against *Time*, *Asiaweek*, the *Asian Wall Street Journal*, and the *Far Eastern Economic Review*. However, when the Law Society publicly questioned this legislation on the grounds it contained 'ambiguities' and afforded the Minister considerable powers, it was sternly rebuked by the Minister, Wong Kan Seng, and reminded that professional organisations should not 'get involved in issues of public policy which do not effect their professional interests' (Wong as quoted in *Asian Wall Street Journal*, 2 June 1986: 7). Subsequently, legislative amendments to Acts covering the legal and other professions were introduced to enforce this position further. These were intended to clarify in greater detail the boundaries between the 'political' and the 'non-political'.

The most resilient and defiant of independent organisations during the period of consolidating the *de facto* one-party state has been the Jehovah's Witnesses religious sect, banned in 1972 on the grounds that its existence was prejudicial to public welfare and order. Their members refuse to do military service, salute the national flag, or swear oaths of allegiance to the state. Despite deregistration and the detention and court-martialling of more than 100 members for failing to undertake national service, the movement has continued to grow, with an almost threefold increase in membership since 1982 to around 2,000. Thus, in early 1995, police raided four separate private residences, seizing sect magazines and literature, and arresting sixty-nine people with a view to charges under the Societies Act (*Sunday Times* (Singapore), 26 February 1995: 1).

The spectacular return to the use of the Internal Security Act (ISA) in 1987 to detain twenty-two so-called 'Marxist conspirators' was also motivated by a concern about independent organisations going beyond their brief. Detainees included members of Catholic organisations such as the Young Christian Workers' Movement, the Catholic Welfare Centre, and the Catholic Centre for Foreign Workers which were condemned as 'cover' organisations for political agitation (*Far Eastern Economic Review* (*FEER*), 4 June 1987: 8–9; Haas 1989: 59–63). In their work and publications they addressed issues such as retrenchment, wage and social security levels, the conditions of guest workers, and other matters of special pertinence to the poorer and more vulnerable sections of a working class largely denied independent organisational bases. The showdown with the Church also led to the expulsion of several missionaries and the dissolution of the Christian Conference of Asia for allegedly involving itself in Singapore's domestic politics (*FEER*, 14 January 1988: 22). The government subsequently passed the Maintenance of Religious Harmony Act in 1990 to reinforce its insistence on a separation of religious faith and social activism. The severity of the response to lay Church activities highlighted PAP sensitivity to non-government organisation (NGO) activity involving grassroots links with the underprivileged and attempts to represent such politically marginalised groups (Rodan 1993b).

CO-OPTATION AND THE EXPANDING REALM OF THE STATE

Alongside the continued official discouragement of certain 'political' activities by NGOs, government pronouncements about the need for greater political consultation and less paternalism gathered momentum throughout the 1980s. Goh Chok Tong, then Deputy Prime Minister, projected himself and his generation of colleagues taking over the party's reins as forces for change in the manner, if not the content, of Singapore politics. The attendant rhetoric about 'opening up' was born from a sustained deterioration in the PAP's electoral dominance since the early 1980s. The *post mortem* on the 1984 general election, which resulted in a 12 per cent swing against the government, focused on the rapidly expanding, younger middle-class constituency and its alienation from the government (Chua 1994: 659). As a result, mechanisms to effect political co-optation have been considerably extended in an attempt to divert the disaffected from oppositional politics. Initiatives in this vein include: the Feedback Unit (an extra-parliamentary body established within the Ministry of Community Development to take suggestions from the public and explain policies at grassroots level);

the adoption of Government Parliamentary Committees through which experts in the community could be incorporated into legislative processes; and a Nominated Member of Parliament (NMP) scheme whereby parliament can appoint up to six people with special expertise to serve two-year terms in parliament (Rodan 1992: 5–9).

The NMP scheme is the most significant of these co-optation initiatives. Appointments have included individuals associated with domestic business, labour, and women's and ethnic organisations. While these appointments are dressed up as acknowledgements of individual merit and non-partisanship, they implicitly recognise the inadequacy of existing structures of political representation, including the NTUC. After the initial batch of appointments in 1990, most of the current six NMPs have been as active in parliament as the elected opposition MPs (see *STWE*, 18 June 1994: 15), to differing extents raising issues on behalf of unofficial 'constituencies'. Kanwaljit Soin, an orthopaedic surgeon and feminist, has done most to give the scheme credibility. Not only has she dominated oral and written question time in parliament, she has at times shaped the agenda of public debate by questioning the government over issues such as domestic violence against women and the unequal conditions applying to women employed in the civil service. In 1995 she introduced a private member's Bill – The Family Violence Bill – into parliament. Soin's advocacy for women has exposed weaknesses in the opposition parties' commitment and performance in this area. During their terms, NMPs Robert Chua, president of the Singapore Manufacturers' Association, and Chia Shi Teck, managing director of the Hesche garment chain, also raised a number of concerns held by domestic manufacturers and entrepreneurs. Chia has at times been a voice for the smaller companies who cannot fit into the government's economic vision of greater offshore activity by domestic-based capital (see Ministry of Finance 1993).[5]

The incorporation of business into these new structures comes on the heels of more organised attempts since the mid-1980s by the locally based private sector to have its various interests represented in official decision making. The establishment in 1986 of the Association of Small and Medium Enterprises to represent the collective interests of small-scale enterprises was a significant initiative in this direction (Chalmers 1992). Given the government's objectives of upgrading the domestic economy and co-ordinating its offshore push, there is a certain utility in more institutionalised incorporation of the domestic bourgeoisie into processes of consultation. Moreover, the control the government exerts over the economy places the bulk of the domestic bourgeoisie in a vulnerable position, necessarily conditioning political strategies to shape policy.

The potential of the NMP scheme to reinforce rather than challenge the government's policy agenda is exemplified by an initiative by NMP Walter Woon. In 1994, Woon became the first person since independence to submit a private member's Bill – the Maintenance of Parents Bill. Under this proposed legislation, parents can legally force their children to support them adequately in old age (*STWE*, 30 July 1994: 15). It received strong PAP support since it neatly complements the government's ideological aversion to greater direct state welfare and its championing of 'traditional family values'.[6] However, since it was Woon's initiative, the political flak for the PAP was less than otherwise might have been the case.

Most importantly, the NMP scheme reinforces the PAP's technocratic and elitist view of politics ahead of a politics of representation (Rodan 1993c). According to this view, decision making should be left to the most rational and capable individuals, freed from the pressures and constraints of interest groups and partisan considerations. In Singapore, 'capability' is widely and closely associated with professional qualifications, an association the current stock of NMPs may have helped to consolidate. Journalists have seized on the comparison between elected and nominated MPs to emphasise the poor calibre of the government's opponents, echoing a recurrent PAP theme. As one enthusiastic endorsement from a journalist put it in the *Straits Times*: 'If indeed this is indicative of the contribution of future NMPs relative to their opposition counterparts, Singaporeans ought to ponder if they will be served better with more NMPs' (*STWE*, 16 July 1994: 15).

There are a number of more ambiguous and tentative moves in the direction of modifying the structures of the state to accommodate different social forces. In particular, these include the management of political pressures associated with rising inequalities, with the state creatively harnessing community organisations to its own agenda.

In what at the time marked an important challenge to the PAP, the Association of Muslim Professionals (AMP) was established in 1990 out of frustration with Mendaki, the officially sanctioned council representing the Muslim community. In essence, Mendaki was seen as too dominated by PAP MPs and therefore unable independently to defend and promote the interests of the Malay community, whose socioeconomic progress still significantly lagged behind that of ethnic Chinese. In this case, the government appears to have tolerated a new organisation rather than further alienate the Malay community, a large proportion of which abandoned the government at the 1988 general election (Chua 1991: 659; Singh 1992). However, the 1994 NMP appointments included AMP's director, Imran Mohammed, thus keeping the door open for the organisation to work within the system.

The government's preparedness to sanction a measure of independence for the AMP was also related to a clear preference for the socio-economic problems of the underprivileged to be conceptualised in ethnic rather than class terms. Through financial and other support for the AMP's welfare programmes, the government has been able to minimise direct state welfare and promote political moderation. With the government's active encouragement, the Indian and Chinese communities subsequently established organisations – the Singapore Indian Development Association (SINDA), and the Chinese Development Assistance Council (CDAC) – to assist the needy in their own ethnic communities. All three organisations receive matching funds and various subsidies for infrastructure from the government (see Brown 1993).

In the context of growing disquiet about rising living costs and increasing inequalities in wealth and income distribution, the Cost Review Committee report of 1993 also proposed that the role and resources of the state-sponsored Consumers' Association of Singapore (CASE) be bolstered. The idea is that CASE should effectively become a permanent cost review committee. At the time, CASE was already receiving S$150,000 a year in government funding. Since its inception in 1971, PAP MPs have played a pivotal role on the organisation's executive. CASE contrasts with the politically activist Consumer Association of Penang (CPA) in Malaysia, which jealously guards its separation from government and business, and enjoys an independent financial base, mainly through the sale of publications (see *STWE*, 9 October 1993: 14). In 1995, CASE came in for public criticism for voluntarily entering a debate over the cost of mobile handphones to defend retailers and service providers.[7]

What these different reforms and initiatives reflect is a thematic attempt by the PAP to politically accommodate increasingly complex and divergent social interests without conceding independent political space for opposition and dissent. If there is to be 'opposition', the aim is to steer it through manageable institutions and keep it within strict limits. The critical premise to sanctioned engagement in public debate is the notion that such contributions should assist the PAP in government, not contest the government's control over the political agenda. As Deputy Prime Minister Lee Hsien Loong recently explained, there should be no need for dissent:

If we have good people, we will try to co-opt them into the PAP and make them part of the system. . . . If good people are forced to join the opposition then I think we have already failed. . . . We've done the wrong thing. Why aren't they able to join us? What are we doing wrong? So I'm not sure we want to go in that direction.

(as quoted in *STWE*, 30 July 1994: 2)

The Deputy Prime Minister's quote suggests that one-party rule remains a given in the PAP's conception of the politically possible in Singapore.

THE RISE OF CIVIL SOCIETY?

While the state may have been able to sponsor close ties with some of the recently established social organisations, and this is the political trajectory preferred by the PAP, there are limited cases of other organisations both exerting an influence over public policy and managing to retain their independence from the state. The most noteworthy of these organisations are the Nature Society of Singapore (NSS) and the Association of Women for Action and Research (AWARE). Similarly, the arts have become an interesting arena of late for critical social and political comment by individuals. While we should not overstate the significance of these developments, since they are certainly the exception rather than the rule, they do indicate aspirations from at least some elements of the middle class for independent political spaces, encouraged possibly by the government's own rhetoric about greater political tolerance. The government thus increasingly finds itself having to clarify the limits to this.

The NSS is not a new organisation, its origins dating from 1954,[8] but its membership has been boosted since the mid to late 1980s, by increased environmental consciousness among the expanding middle class. Total membership now stands at about 2,200, nearly 70 per cent of which is comprised of people in professional, senior administrative, managerial, executive, or supervisory employment (see Table 4.1). The NSS has constructively criticised government policy through detailed submissions to government departments and selective letter writing to the editorial pages of the daily English-language newspaper, the *Straits Times*. The organisation has had an impact on government policy, starting with its role in persuading the government in 1988 to reserve 87 hectares of degraded mangrove at Sungei Buloh for a bird sanctuary. The land had actually been zoned for an agro-technology park prior to this decision. Subsequently, in 1990, the government's *Green Plan* incorporated much of the content contained in the 152-page *Master*

Plan for Conservation of Nature in Singapore (Malayan Nature Society 1990), submitted to the authorities by the NSS. In another case, following the release of its own environmental impact assessment arguing against a proposed golf course at the Lower Peirce reservoir catchment area (Nature Society of Singapore 1992), the government decided to put the project on hold (*ST*, 2 October 1993: 23). The NSS also succeeded in convincing the Mass Rapid Transit (MRT) to divert a proposed line to avoid disturbing the natural habitat of bird life in Senoko (*ST*, 20 June 1991).

Table 4.1 Occupational characteristics of NSS and AWARE memberships (percentages)

Occupation	NSS	AWARE
Business	2.83	0.92
Professional and technical	50.98	44.79
Administrative, managerial, executive and supervisory	17.21	15.74
Clerical, sales, and services	16.12	11.13
Production, agricultural and other	1.31	17.10
Homemaker	5.45	1.90
Student	6.32	7.33

Source: Membership records, NSS and AWARE

AWARE, with a membership of nearly 700, has a much shorter history than the NSS, since it was only established in 1985. Its membership is predominantly made up of professional women between the ages of 30 and 50 (*Sunday Times* (Singapore), 19 February 1995: Focus Page Six). As Table 4.1 shows, a little over 60 per cent of its membership is in professional, senior administrative, managerial, executive, or supervisory employment categories. Internally, AWARE is characterised by a high level of participatory democracy through the activities of various subcommittees. Generally, it employs a similar approach to the NSS in trying to shape government decision making, although it has at times adopted a comparatively aggressive public stance, as it did against the government's procreation policies in the late 1980s and, to a lesser extent, in a controversy in 1993 over unequal benefits to female public servants. Reflecting the interests of its overwhelmingly middle-class membership, the focus of AWARE has until the early 1990s been primarily on issues associated with the public, as opposed to private, work of women. But there now appears to be a conscious attempt to appeal to a wider constituency and to move beyond a narrow class base. AWARE has, for instance, taken up the issue of the conditions of foreign maids with the Ministry of Labour, arguing for contractual improvements that would, among other things, more adequately protect maids from arbitrary abuses by employers. Significantly, in recognition of the government's sensitivity to debate on such topics, this has been done through correspondence rather than a public campaign.

Since former AWARE president Kanwaljit Soin has been serving as an NMP, the temptation has existed for this organisation to direct some of its energies unofficially through this avenue. The difficulty here is striking a balance between capitalising on the advantages of this connection in the hope of influencing parliamentary activity, yet retaining credibility as a genuinely independent organisation.

The first general point to make about these organisations is that their capacity to undertake restricted 'political' activities is partly contingent on acceptance that such engagement with the government is not presented as oppositional. As has been pointed out (p. 100), legally these organisations have a very carefully defined existence under the Societies Act and face the possibility of deregistration should they pose a serious challenge to the PAP's authority to make public policy. This reality is ever present in the minds of organisation members and was given lucid expression by the president of the NSS, Wee Yeow Chin, following the NSS's apparent success in 'lobbying' the government over the golf course proposal. Declaring that the NSS was not a 'pressure group', Wee elaborated: 'We like to see ourselves as a group of nature enthusiasts interested in studying the environment around us, enjoying it, and passing on our knowledge to others.' He continued, emphasising: 'We are level-headed and look at things rationally' (as quoted in *ST*, 2 October 1993: 23).

This sort of comment is indicative of the nervousness and insecurity inside independent organisations undertaking informal political activities. The open public acknowledgement of the government's sole authority to make policy is presumably designed to reassure the authorities that there is no engagement in 'politics'. When the government takes notice of independent organisations in public policy, gratitude is the appropriate sentiment to express. Notice has been taken principally because these groups are seen to have demonstrated some technical knowledge functional to sound policy. Their arguments and protestations can thus be reconciled with the technocratic regime. But assertions of an organisation's right to help shape public policy, let alone to contest the PAP over it, can be sure to arouse a rebuke or worse. Not surprisingly, important divisions exist within these organisations over how to manage this process and just how far to go in testing the government's tolerance for political engagement.

The fear of proscription may well have been determinant in the strategy used by conservationists in their campaign in late 1994 against Ministry of National Development plans to develop some 70 hectares of land in Senoko. Senoko had been designated a five-star nature site in the Nature Society's *Master Plan* (Briffett 1990) in recognition of its rich bio-diversity supporting extensive bird life. Even the Urban Redevelopment Authority's (1991) master plan, *Living the Next Lap*, had designated Senoko both a 'bird sanctuary' and a 'nature park'. However, the Acting Minister for National Development, Lim Hng Kiang, declared in 1994 that the area would be developed for housing and industrial purposes. This time, opposition to the government's proposal was mobilised through a single-issue movement called Friends of Senoko rather than through the NSS. Though NSS members were involved in this campaign, including the co-ordinator Ho Hua Chew, Friends of Senoko was a cross-class, community exercise in which a number of high-profile public figures assumed strategic roles.[9] The appeal to have core areas reserved for a nature park amassed 25,000 signatures in a petition presented to Prime Minister Goh. While the appeal was unsuccessful, a number of significant points were demonstrated by Friends of Senoko. The collection of so many signatures on a petition in Singapore, which requires committing a personal identification number, evidenced an unprecedented preparedness to identify publicly with a challenge to government policy. Furthermore, support was genuinely broad-based, demonstrating that environmental concerns could not be dismissed as 'middle class'. Finally, the organisational form and spontaneous nature of Friends of Senoko may well constitute a new model for certain oppositional activities that avoids the vulnerability of formally registered NGOs in Singapore.

The second point to emphasise about both the NSS and AWARE is that, despite disclaimers by activists themselves, the activities of these organisations are clearly political: they involve concerted and regular attempts to influence government policy on behalf of members. What matters, then, is not so much whether their activities are political, but whether the PAP perceives them as politically threatening. The care taken to avoid a confrontational style and the eschewing of any sympathies or connections with the PAP's party-political opponents is part of the formula for survival. But these organisations have also been able to present their entry into the public arena as consistent with government discourse about consultation, consensus, and the welcoming of technical expertise that assist policy.

On this point, the PAP's broader ideological campaigns extolling the virtues of a distinctive 'Asian democracy' (Goh 1989) as a counter to the transplanting of 'western liberalism' raise similar problems of political management. Concepts of 'consensus' and 'communitarianism' assume a central place in this 'Asian alternative' to political confrontation and contestation. But as Chua (1993: 14) has observed, this language may yet come back to haunt the PAP if widespread expectations of new consultative structures are raised. After all, genuine consensus requires a political process that gives adequate expression to differences in the first instance. It remains to be seen whether this can be done in practice without damage to the prevailing elitist assumptions about good government as fundamentally a technical process best handled by competent individuals.

While both the NSS and AWARE are careful not to challenge explicitly the notion that politics should be the preserve of formally constituted political organisations, a couple of organisations were registered under the Societies Act in 1994 which have stated aims to foster political debate outside the strict realms of party politics. These are The Roundtable and the Socratic Circle. The former is a small group of young professionals and business people with no particular agenda but united in the view that political discussion should be open to the public. Their proposal is to operate as a discussion group and think-tank, with no claim to represent any broad societal interests (Lim 1995). The latter is another small, predominantly middle-class, discussion group with its origins in the National University of Singapore Democratic Socialist Club. But according to the organisation's chairman, Gerard Lim, participants of any ideological persuasion are welcome to join the Socratic Circle (*STWE*, 29 October 1994: 15). The organisation's constitution emphasises the 'cultivation of social and political awareness amongst its members'. Significantly, registration of the Socratic Circle was delayed as authorities insisted on a constitution barring members of political parties from eligibility.[10] Nevertheless, what is interesting about the emergence of these organisations – however small and substantively unthreatening they may be to the PAP – is that they represent a desire for greater independent political spaces, not necessarily as a means to the end of contesting the PAP so much as an end in itself.

In view of the above analysis, it is interesting to reflect on the increase in local artistic productions in Singapore that contain some measure of social and political comment. This development is sometimes pointed to as indication that tight political controls are generally being loosened in Singapore (see *Asiaweek*, 29 September 1993: 44). Others have made the point that the government's determination to exploit more fully the commercial potential of the arts can work in favour of a slightly greater margin for contentious work (see Patterson 1994: 62). This commercial objective has led to the establishment of a new statutory board, the National Arts Council (NAC).[11] According to the Minister for Information and the Arts, George Yeo (as quoted in *STWOE*, 6 July 1991: 4): 'For the arts to flourish, we need a tripartite working relationship between the arts community, the private sector and the Government', and the NAC is expected to facilitate this. Whether a corporatist model is sufficient to achieve a vibrant artistic industry remains to be seen. In any case, are there signs that individuals, through the arts, can exercise greater scope for critical expression than is possible through social organisations? Are the arts less amenable to political co-optation?

English-medium theatre has been the most significant avenue for what critical social and political comment has been made recently through art. This is especially significant since dramatists from the Third Stage, a theatre company set up in 1983, were among those detained in 1987 under the ISA in the so-called 'Marxist conspiracy'. It was charged that plays such as *Oh! Singapore* and *Esperanza* ('Hope'), the latter focusing on the plight of Filipino maids in Singapore, aroused 'disaffection with the existing social and political system' (*Asiaweek*, 13 September 1987: 20). Despite this setback, by the early 1990s a range of local playwrights and theatre companies, the most notable being TheatreWorks and The Necessary Stage, were presenting critical observations about social and, to a lesser extent, formal political life in Singapore.

Some of these works touch on the excessive social engineering and rigid bureaucratisation within Singapore, the question of gender, and existing social taboos relating to sexuality.[12] One recent play, *Undercover* by Tan Tarn How, appears to be a satirical and critical portrayal of the Internal Security Department – even if it is not mentioned by name. According to Yeo (1994: 49), we are witnessing 'a new phase in the Singapore theatre in which new and younger playwrights in their twenties and thirties show a determination to tackle controversial themes, and in the process, test the limits of both audience and authority'.[13]

This observation certainly bears relevance to controversies arising out of acts by Josef Ng Sing Chor and Shannon Tham Kuok Leong during a week-long arts festival organised by The Artists' Village and Fifth Passage in late December 1993. Ng's performance centred on the arrest of twelve men for allegedly committing homosexual solicitations and the way the press covered the matter. Part of Ng's act involved him cutting his pubic hair, with his back to the audience and clad only in swimming briefs. Tham's performance protested against the 'sensationalised' reporting of the festival, The Artists' General Assembly, by the

New Paper, Singapore's daily English-language afternoon newspaper. His act included the symbolic burning of a page of the *New Paper* and featured induced vomiting (see Kwok 1995).

The National Arts Council denounced the acts as vulgar and without artistic content, adding that organisations fostering such acts could not expect support from it. In what followed, not only did the police charge Ng with committing an obscene act in public and the organiser with holding a performance in contravention of a licence,[14] but Ng and Tham were barred from future public performances. The government's concern over the two acts was that the performances 'may be exploited to agitate the audiences on volatile social issues or to propagate the beliefs and messages of deviant social or religious groups, or as a means of subversion' (as quoted in *ST*, 22 January 1994: 3). The Minister of Information and the Arts, George Yeo, elaborated:

> It is not good for the arts in Singapore to become politicised. While art, especially theatre, cannot avoid commenting on social and political conditions in society, in Singapore art should not be used to promote particular causes, and certainly not in a covert way. Otherwise the government will be forced to regulate such performances as a form of political activity.
>
> (as quoted in *Parliamentary Debates Singapore*, 23 February 1994: column 375)

A joint statement from the Ministries of Home Affairs and of Information and the Arts also declared new restrictions on 'performance art', a category into which Ng's and Tham's acts fall, and 'forum theatre'. Both art forms, by virtue of their emphasis on improvisation and audience interaction, pose difficulties for control-minded authorities.[15]

In the wake of these events, an edition of the National University of Singapore Society (NUSS) journal, *Commentary*, which contained critical examination of the limits to cultural and artistic expression in Singapore and support for the above artists, was aborted following reservations about the content by the NUSS management committee. While this incident has been portrayed by some as an act of self-censorship (see *STWE*, 19 November 1994: 23), there was also speculation about external pressure to control the content of the journal more effectively.[16] The previous two editions of the journal had the themes of, first, civil society and, second, democracy, giving expression to the views and debates of a small but articulate intellectual community which takes these issues seriously.

Further indication of the apparent gulf between government rhetoric about increased political tolerance and the practice of the authorities was evidenced in the reaction to newspaper articles in late 1994 by Singapore novelist Catherine Lim, critical of government policy and Prime Minister Goh.[17] In the second of these, she referred to the irreconcilability of two contrasting styles within the government – the more consultative, open leadership style espoused by Goh and the more authoritarian style associated with his predecessors. She lamented the triumph of the latter and questioned Goh's authority within the government: 'Singapore is like a family in which the Senior Minister is Stern Father and he [Goh] is Oldest Brother, presumably in a mediatory capacity' (*Sunday Times* (Singapore), 20 November 1994: 12).

The Prime Minister's press secretary, Chan Heng Wing, attempted to take stock of events over the last year or so, and clarify the extent and nature of political space being opened up by Goh. Initially, he emphasised that the Prime Minister remained committed to consultation and consensus, but that he 'cannot allow journalists, novelists, short-story writers or theatre groups to set the political agenda from outside the political arena' (*ST*, 10 December 1994: 13). He advised Lim to follow the example of British novelist Jeffrey Archer and enter formal politics if she intended to continue making political comment. However, public reaction through the columns of the *Straits Times* prompted a sequel by Chan (*STWE*, 31 December 1994: 23), who insisted that there was a real opening up of political space, but that the Prime Minister 'has been placing out-of-bounds markers to define the limits of the space he is expanding'. Given its size and fragility, Singapore could not afford its government to be 'continually criticised, vilified and ridiculed in the media, and pressured by lobbyists as in America' (Chan in *STWE*, 31 December 1994: 23). The government would continue to make room for 'minority intellectual interests, provided majority sentiments are not offended' (Chan in *STWE*, 31 December 1994: 23).[18] Goh also modified his insistence that critics should join political parties, emphasising instead that once individuals attacked the government or attempted to have it change policies or shift the political agenda, they would be regarded as having entered the political fray and treated accordingly. As he told parliament: 'If you land us a blow on our jaw, you must expect a counter-blow on your solar plexus' (as quoted in the *West Australian*, 25 January 1995: 20). The reaction, he added, would take into account the tone of criticism, a point echoed in Yeo's call for suitable respect for authority in public challenges: 'You must make distinctions – what is high, what is low, what is above, what is below – and then we can have a debate, we can have a discussion' (as quoted in *ST*, 20 February 1995: 19).

What we see, then, is a curious combination of political forms and practices unfolding to accommodate greater social plurality. Concurrent with long-standing repressive structures and new forms of co-optation, some attempts have been made by certain groups and individuals to secure space for political contestation outside these parameters. Where such attempts have succeeded, this has involved basically middle-class groups in very limited and conditional space with a tenuous existence. Apart from the PAP's internal uncertainty, and possible divisions, over the exact margin for political contestation it is prepared to tolerate, the government also appears to see political mileage in periodically clamping down on English-educated liberal elements as a way of demonstrating its bona fides as the custodian of the working class. After all, it is the working class which has recently shown the greater preparedness to abandon the PAP at the polls (see Rodan 1993a; Singh 1992). But just how much of a threat does the formal political opposition in Singapore pose to the ruling party and can it continue its progressive increase in electoral support begun in the early 1980s?

OPPOSITION POLITICAL PARTIES

As is clear from the above, opposition electoral gains have been achieved in spite of the absence of a broader civil society upon which to draw. In addition to this constraint, there are numerous problems for opposition parties in competing with the PAP in elections. First, they cannot match the PAP's strategic propaganda advantage of the very sympathetic government-owned and controlled domestic media.[19] Second, there is a strong fear of persecution for involvement with opposition parties. The long list of candidates and activists taken to court by government members serves as a strong negative example to would-be participants in the political process.[20] The sacking of a National University of Singapore academic, Chee Soon Juan, for alleged misuse of research funds, not long after he contested the December 1992 by-election in Marine Parade, has only reinforced the belief that opposition politics remains a personally risky affair.[21] In a city-state where the PAP government is a substantial employer and commercial contractor, there is a perception that careers and business interests can easily be jeopardised by association, however indirect, with opposition parties. Consequently, in spite of the broader social transformations within Singapore, the opposition ranks tend to be over-represented by marginalised people with comparatively little to lose, or self-employed people who have comparative independence, such as small business people or lawyers. Third, while it thus becomes a self-fulfilling prophecy on the PAP's part that the calibre of the opposition is limited, there are also substantial problems internal to the opposition camp that hamper it and raise serious doubts about its potential for the foreseeable future. By virtue of their limited size and elitist structures, opposition parties remain highly vulnerable to personality-based disputes at the executive level.

Despite the systematic intimidation facing the PAP's political opponents, and their limitations in personnel, organisational, and programmatic terms, as Table 4.2 indicates, they nevertheless attracted nearly 40 per cent of the total vote at the 1991 elections. This preparedness to support opposition candidates has increased as a growing number of Singaporeans perceive rising material inequalities and take the only meaningful avenue open to protest against this.

Table 4.2 Major parties' shares of total valid votes, 1980–91 (percentages)

	PAP	*WP*	*SDP*
1980	77.7	13.1	1.8
1984	64.8	25.4	3.7
1988	63.2	16.7	11.8
1991	61.0	14.3	12.0

Source: *Sunday Times*, 1 September 1991: 9

Although there are twenty-two registered opposition political parties in Singapore, many of these have ceased to operate and very few of them are consistently active in contesting elections and promoting their causes.[22] Those that are include the Singapore Democractic Party (SDP), the Workers' Party (WP), National Solidarity Party (NSP), Singapore National Malay Organisation (PKMS) and the Singapore Justice Party. Only the WP and the SDP have actually won seats from the government since the BS abandoned the parliamentary process in 1966. All of these parties, however, are very limited in structures and resources, and are comparatively dormant between elections. Given that the PAP usually provides little more than the minimum required nine days' notice of election, campaigning itself is often a brief affair. Co-operation between opposition parties in determining who will contest which electorate has thus been one way of maximising limited resources. This strategy was most effective in the 1991 general election when the government was uncontested in just over half (forty-one) of the total (eighty-one) seats. On this basis, the PAP could not play on the usual idea of 'a freak result' (i.e. the 'accidental' removal of the government through 'protest' votes); thus the desirability or otherwise of opposition *per se* came into central focus (Singh 1992).

The official memberships of the SDP and the WP approximate to 280 and 2,600 respectively (Registrar of Societies 1995), but the WP figure is a cumulative one which does not separate past from current, paid-up membership. Party cadres number around forty-five for the SDP and sixty-five for the WP. At best, however, fewer than 100 members (including cadres) within either party could be described as active. But if the limited personnel involved are striking features of the two parties, even more remarkable are the organisational structures: both are elitist along PAP lines. As in the PAP model, the executives of the SDP and the WP appoint cadres, who in turn elect the executive.[23] There is thus a significant centralisation of power within each party's structure. So in organisational practice, neither party gives expression to a democratic alternative to the PAP.

Another parallel between the PAP and the major opposition parties is the premium placed on the recruitment of professionals as election candidates.[24] In the 1991 elections the SDP fielded only candidates with tertiary education qualifications, even though professionals comprised a minuscule percentage of the party's total membership (see Vennevald 1992: 8). Part of the SDP's public celebration at the time it attracted neuropsychologist and Ph.D. Chee Soon Juan into its ranks in the early 1990s was related to this emphasis on educational qualifications. Certainly the bulk of the general population has internalised the PAP's ideology of meritocracy, and measures the suitability of candidates almost exclusively in these terms. Opposition parties cannot ignore this reality. However, there has been no questioning of this elitism or strategy by the SDP to widen the electorate's expectations of political candidates. Rather, considerable energy has gone into trying to match the PAP's credentialism.

By contrast with the SDP, the WP can stake some sort of claim to a conscious ideological position. As its name would suggest, the WP projects itself as the custodian of the working class. Both the WP and the SDP have working-class and lower-middle-class support bases, but a marginally greater proportion of WP membership and leadership emanates from blue-collar backgrounds compared with the SDP (see Vennevald 1992: 11). The WP was formed in 1957 by David Marshall when there was a vibrant trade union movement, although the more radical elements of the labour movement were at that time aligned with the PAP.[25] Nevertheless, the party has over the years espoused a philosophical commitment to a social democratic conception of social justice. In this vein, a reasonably detailed party manifesto, largely the work of party secretary-general Joshua Jeyaretnam,[26] outlines a series of proposed programmes to improve the conditions for lower-income earners and generally to enhance civil liberties. The rigid streaming within the education system is also challenged. But at the same time, it emphasises the need for 'responsible trade unionism' and asserts that 'Trade unions must never be so powerful as to promote sectional interests at the expense of the rest of society' (Workers' Party 1994: 11–12). This sort of language reflects both the political moderation of the WP and the ideological hegemony of the PAP, which seems so often to have oppositionists on the defensive. WP Member of Parliament Low Thia Khiang, for instance, has declared he is not in favour of a minimum wage (*STWE*, 2 October 1993: 5). Since Low appears poised to succeed the ageing Jeyaretnam at the party's helm at some future point, this might accentuate the pragmatic direction of the WP. Low, a small business person who was educated at the former Chinese-medium Nanyang University, has cultivated support among the ethnic Chinese working class and appears less wedded to the social democratic ideas influencing London-trained lawyer Jeyaretnam.[27]

Table 4.3 Comparative electoral performances of the WP and SDP in general elections, 1980–91

WP

	1980	1984	1988*	1991
Seats contested	8	15	32	13
Seats won	0	1	0	1
% of votes in constituencies contested	29.2%	41.9%	38.5%	41.1%

SDP

	1980	1984	1988	1991
Seats contested	3	4	18	9
Seats won	0	1	1	3
% of votes in constituencies contested	30.7%	46.1%	39.5%	48.6%

Source: *STWOE*, 1 September 1991: 24
Note: *Workers' Party merged with Barisan Sosialis and Singapore United Front

The SDP was only established in 1980 under the leadership of Chiam See Tong, who has held the seat of Potong Pasir since 1984. A party manifesto did not actually materialise until 1994 when the party's acting secretary-general, Chee Soon Juan, authored *Dare to Change* (1994). This was subsequently endorsed as the SDP's official document but, as with the WP's equivalent, it could not be said to be the end product of widespread party involvement and debate. Nevertheless, as Table 4.3 demonstrates, in the 1991 election the SDP surpassed the WP in both its share of total votes and the number of parliamentary seats. It has achieved this without any clear ideological or philosophical stance articulated to the electorate. Rather, under Chiam, the SDP has campaigned heavily around the desirability of a check against government arrogance, thus actively cultivating the so-called 'protest vote'. It has also played on the theme of excessive government charges in areas like health, education, and transport.[28] However, SDP MPs have been careful to distance their calls for more government spending on health, education, and housing from 'welfarism', a concept so maligned by the PAP.[29]

Neither major opposition party, then, directly contests the ruling party's central ideological concepts. This does not necessarily indicate a conscious endorsement of PAP ideology, but it does at least reflect an inability to formulate alternatives: surely an important measure of the PAP's ideological hegemony.

Ironically, instead of electoral gains by the SDP laying the basis for a more concerted opposition push in the 1990s, at least in the short term it has given rise to a fractious atmosphere. Immediately after the 1991 elections the SDP promoted itself as the symbol of an emerging two-party, not multi-party, system. Predictably this was an annoyance to the other parties (see *ST*, 13 December 1992: 22). But more significantly, an internal SDP dispute threw the party into temporary disarray. Party founder Chiam resigned as secretary-general in May 1993 and subsequently made a public attack on a number of the party's central executive committee (CEC) members. This culminated in Chiam's expulsion from the party in August, a decision which he challenged and which was overturned through the courts later that year. He was thus reinstated as an ordinary SDP member which ensured that, under the constitution, he retained his parliamentary seat. Such was the turmoil in the SDP that pro-Chiam SDP members held their own meeting in August. The gathering voted to retract Chiam's expulsion, dissolve the CEC responsible for it, and elect a new one in its place. However, pro-Chiam forces lost a further legal battle to have the SDP leadership, now chaired by Ling How Doong, declared null and void. The net effect was that Chiam and his allies had to wait for the next biennial party conference, in January 1995, for a chance to wrest executive control from the other faction. However, they were to fail.

It was thus no surprise when, in mid-1994, Chiam's sympathiser, Sin Kek Tong, registered an application to form an entirely new party – the

Singapore People's Party (SPP). According to Sin, the SPP would be a 'moderate version of the SDP' (*ST*, 6 July 1994: 3). This 'moderation' was elaborated on when Sin (as quoted in *STWE*, 24 December 1994: 15) declared: 'We see no ideological conflict with the ruling party. We see no need to be confrontational for no good reason. . . . For opposition politicians, the greatest challenge is to admit that the PAP is a good government.' Like the SDP and the WP, the SPP also emulates the PAP cadre system. The SPP invited Chiam to join the SPP when parliament is next dissolved (*ST*, 22 November 1994: 19), since under the constitution he would lose his seat if he left the SDP in the meantime. At the time of writing, Chiam has not publicly declared his intentions, but his strong personal following in Potong Pasir means that he could also feasibly consider contesting the seat as an independent.

The Chiam fiasco reflected differences between himself and the CEC that had previously been manageable, even if that meant him being outvoted within the executive on various matters. His preference for tight control over the party was complicated by the SDP's electoral success,[30] since it translated not only into other SDP MPs but the establishment of further opposition town councils. This opened up avenues for alternative power bases within the party. It was, however, Chiam's unsuccessful attempt to censure Chee Soon Juan for conducting a hunger strike in protest against being dismissed from the National University of Singapore which brought matters to a head (*STWOE*, 19 June 1993: 24). For Chiam, Chee personified a less obedient style he feared was gaining ground in the SDP. Furthermore, Chee was committed both to widening the agenda of public debate and contesting the PAP's policies more forcefully than was usual in the SDP under Chiam. In particular, Chee challenged the PAP on the fundamental and sensitive issue of rising inequalities,[31] a theme initially, but less systematically, taken up by party colleague Ling How Doong.[32] He has also led an aggressive public challenge to the PAP over its close relations with the military regime in Myanmar and proposed the establishment of a human rights commission in Singapore to 'ensure the Government does not abuse its powers' (*STWE*, 30 July: 5).

At one level, the SDP's recent turmoil might be seen as a necessary price to be paid in its transformation to a more serious alternative to the PAP which is less personality-based and more programme-based. Chee might be seen as a potential catalyst in this scenario. Certainly Chee's persistence in the wake of financially crippling lawsuits against him and the loss of his university position does suggest a dedication to the cause of opposition politics. The highly personalised attacks directed at him from the PAP seem to indicate an equal dedication to neutralise him.[33] However, if the SDP is to mount and sustain a more meaningful challenge, it will have to undergo major reform, including not just a better-developed programme but the establishment of less elitist internal party structures. There is still no sign of this. Moreover, it would appear that even Chiam's SDP adversaries have reservations about some of Chee's directions, and his influence within the SDP in broadening the policy agenda may be waning.[34]

Broadly, the significance of the social transformation of Singapore for opposition political parties has been indirect rather than direct. Like the PAP, the opposition parties place strategic emphasis on securing professional candidates, but the middle class is disinclined towards involvement in political parties in general and opposition parties in particular.[35] But the emergence of a sizeable and relatively privileged middle class has heightened awareness of income and wealth differentials among the less privileged. At the current juncture, neither the government nor opposition parties want to be seen as pandering to the middle class. Based on the assumption that issues like environmentalism and gender equality are the preserve of the middle class, the opposition parties have made no serious attempts to base their appeal on these concerns. Rather, they concentrate on what they see as the bread-and-butter issues central to the working class. While at one level this is entirely understandable, since the middle class is a 'natural' constituency for the PAP, the broad-based support for the Friends of Senoko campaign, for instance, challenges this neat conceptual dichotomy, demonstrating that large numbers of working people place a high value on Singapore's natural environment.[36] If opposition parties are to exploit more effectively the political potential of changing identities and interests associated with Singapore's social and economic transformation, a more sophisticated strategy is required.

CONCLUSION

We see from the above that while economic development has indeed set in train new social forces, the political manifestations of this are complex. Certainly important processes of political change are taking place in Singapore, but these do not yet include the re-emergence of a substantive sphere of non-state political space. Rather, the predominant direction of political change has been towards an expansion of the state itself. New and more specific forms of political co-optation are being developed in response to the challenges of increasing social differentiation and rising material inequalities. While this response may generate contradictions, it remains to be seen whether these are unmanageable and whether or not the government's attempts to alleviate material inequalities are successful. It is certainly not inevitable that social pluralism arising out of advanced capitalist production in Singapopre will translate into a more expansive civil society – especially one that attempts to overturn hierarchical and elitist structures.

We have also seen, though, that some very conditional independent political spaces have surfaced as select groups and individuals project their activities in line with official rhetoric about greater openness. Toleration of political activities by 'non-political' organisations is occurring in spite of the Societies Act, but these spaces are tenuous, lacking the state's explicit legal protection emphasised by Bernhard (1993) in his notion of civil society. The threat of their closure constantly looms. Nor do they involve horizontal ties between different sectors of society (Stepan 1985: 336), least of all with political parties. These social forces are politically weak and unable to impose themselves on the state. Nevertheless, the process currently in train will still require periodic clarification from the government on the limits to the political space available to them.

The few independent groups attempting to influence public policy have very moderate political objectives. This is important in their current ability to undertake informal political activities. If there is to be a greater political relaxation in future, this factor will be central. In previous phases in Singapore's history when social forces have attempted to assert themselves politically through independent organisations, a radically led working class has been pivotal. The current phase is different, with a relatively privileged and conservative middle class pursuing independent political space. Neither the interests of the PAP nor capital are fundamentally threatened by such a development. Importantly, the elitism that has been institutionalised by the PAP does not appear to be under direct challenge from these groups.

In the absence of a more expansive civil society in Singapore, opposition parties will remain relatively isolated social entities and limited political forces. But as we have seen, these parties are also constrained as 'oppositional' by their inability to develop alternatives to key aspects of PAP ideology. Indeed, whether oppositional forces operate inside or outside the formal political system, alternatives to elitist values and structures would be necessary if authoritarianism in Singapore were to be effectively challenged. What the above account underlines is that authoritarian rule in Singapore may be far more adaptable to dramatic social transformations than is generally recognised. Its long-term future is by no means assured, but projections of imminent demise are certainly premature.

NOTES

* I thank Kevin Hewison and two anonymous referees for helpful critical comments on an earlier draft of this work. I am also grateful to the various individuals within social and political organisations in Singapore who co-operated during my research.

1 The concept of civil society employed here is consistent with that advocated in Chapter 2 which draws on Bernhard (1993). It involves systematic attempts to exert an influence over the exercise of state power by independent organisations. Therefore, these organisations, quite distinct from civic organisations, are routinely engaged in political attempts to advance members' interests. However, in addition to the legally recognised independent political space emphasised by Bernhard, civil society can include independent political spaces that are tolerated and given *de facto* rather than formal legal recognition.

2 Much of this has a regional focus and involves projects requiring significant intergovernmental negotiations; this has involved China, Vietnam, and the so-called Growth Triangle embracing the neighbouring states of Johore in Malaysia and the Riau Islands of Indonesia.

3 Overseas investments in the hotel and tourist development industries feature prominently among domestic-based groups.

4 Of the current eighty-two registered employee trade unions (Department of Statistics 1994: 71), only nine are not affiliated with the NTUC: Airline Pilots' Association; Film Industrial Employee Union of Singapore; Reuter Local Employees' Union; Senior Officers' Association of the PUB; Singapore Catering Services Staff and Workers' Trade Union; Singapore Motor Workshop Employees' Union; Singapore Middle School Chinese Teachers' Union; Singapore Tobacco Employees' Union; Singapore Transport Vessels Workers' Association.

5 As of 1996, Stephen Lee, president of the Singapore National Employers' Federation and managing director of Great Malaysia Textile Manufacturing, is also an NMP.

6 The government is greatly concerned about demographic trends towards an ageing population and the welfare implications of this. Lee Kuan Yew has suggested that at some later point it might be sensible to give two votes to married men with children. That way, according to Lee, the bias of the electorate would be corrected in favour of taxpayers who would have to foot the bill to support greater welfare (*Straits Times Weekly Edition* (*STWE*), 14 May 1994: 6).

7 In letters to the Forum pages of the *Straits Times*, writers complained about the costs of handphones, and subsequently diabetes test strips, in Singapore compared with Australia. Executive director of CASE Tan Bee Lan replied with the view that: 'Consumers in Singapore cannot expect to earn high salaries and have low cost for their goods and services' (*ST*, 3 June 1995: 35). One contributor took CASE to task for the methodology underlying this position (see *ST*, 6 June 1995: 28) and also maintained that 'CASE, as an independent association for all consumers here, should be more objective and look seriously into the real reasons behind the absurd price difference' (see *ST*, 14 June 1994: 28). Another contended that a consumers' association has 'both an educative and a protective function', but that 'affordability' is

a personal choice which CASE need not debate (see *ST*, 14 June 1995: 28). Even the editorial of the *Straits Times* (22 June 1995: 28) weighed in with criticism of CASE for appearing to defend big business ahead of consumers.

8   Between 1954 and 1991 it was known as the Malayan Nature Society (MNS) and acted as a Singapore branch of the parent organisation. Formal separation and a name change occurred in 1991.

9   This included playwright Kuo Pau Kun, NMP Kanwaljit Soin and prominent architect Tay Kheng Soon.

10 Thus, neither the Socratic Circle nor The Roundtable permits members of political parties to join their organisation.

11 One of the NAC's major functions is pairing artists with corporate sponsors and providing its own direct subsidies.

12 Two plays in the mould of critiques of social engineering and bureaucratisation by TheatreWorks' Kuo Pau Kun, a former political detainee, are *The Coffin Is Too Big for the Hole* and *No Parking on Odd Days*. Examples of plays addressing the gender issue include Ovidia Yu's *The Woman in the Tree in the Hill* and *Three Fat Virgins Unassembled*, and Eleanor Wong's three plays *The Joust, Exit*, and *Mergers and Accusations*. Both Yu and Wong deal with lesbianism in their works. Significant examples of work focusing on taboos regarding sexuality include Michael Chiang's *Private Parts*, which deals with transsexuality, and David Henry Hwang's *M Butterfly* on homosexuality, as well as the works of Yu and Wong on lesbianism.

13 Robert Yeo is a leading Singapore playwright/producer and also a member of the Censorship Review Committee.

14 The show went over the time specified on the permit.

15 Performance art operates from a working script rather than a tight script, allowing considerable scope for spontaneity. Forum theatre was developed by the Brazilian Augusto Boal through his Theatre of the Oppressed programme. It employs a technique of involving the audience in scenes intended to overcome oppressions meaningful to the participants. See Yeo (1994: 58–9).

16 It was reported in the *Sun* (Malaysia) that the academic and media communities in Singapore were speculating about 'a letter by a prominent academic addressed to cabinet supposedly denouncing individuals in the press and cultural establishments as "cultural subversives"'. See Kuttan (1995: 4).

17 The two articles were 'The PAP and the People – A Great Affective Divide', *STWE*, 10 September 1994: 13, and 'One Government, Two Styles', *Sunday Times* (Singapore), 20 November 1994: 12.

18 Chan reminded readers of the Prime Minister's observations after the 1991 election which contrasted the views of 'vocal English-educated liberals' and 'the more conservative views of the HDB majority'.

19 The editor of the *Straits Times*, Leslie Fong, publicly acknowledges his pro-government stance and makes no apology for it. For comments by Fong and a general discussion of the press in Singapore see *Asiaweek*, 25 September 1992: 45–55.

20 The most noteworthy case is that of J. B. Jeyaretnam whose most recent spat with Lee Kuan Yew cost him a total of S$740,000 in damages and costs after he was found guilty of defamation for comments at an election rally

in 1988. However, since 1972, eleven separate civil actions have been taken against known opposition figures.

21 When Chee came forward to contest the by-election, he was the first academic to run as an opponent to the government since the 1960s. His then SDP chief, Chiam See Tong, described him as the 'most courageous person in Singapore today' (as quoted in the *Straits Times Weekly Overseas Edition (STWOE)*, 12 December 1992: 5).

22 The retention of these parties as registered organisations does enable the government to point to an apparently healthy degree of political pluralism.

23 Under their respective constitutions, the SDP Central Executive Committee (CEC) comprises up to twelve elected members and six co-opted members; the WP can have up to fifteen appointed Council members and a further six co-opted positions.

24 This observation is partly based on interviews with the executive leaders of the WP and SDP.

25 The party remained dormant for much of the 1960s, but was revived in 1971 by Joshua Jeyaretnam.

26 This manifesto was first produced for the 1988 election and subsequently updated in 1994. See WP (1994).

27 One of the significant features of the 1991 election results was that all three new opposition MPs – Low, SDP's Cheo Chai Chen and Ling How Doong – were not only bilingual, speaking Mandarin and English, but also had a command of Chinese dialects. Since then, the PAP has decided to promote the use of dialects by its own MPs and candidates, where possible.

28 The SDP produced a one-page leaflet for the 1991 election, entitled *SDP Election Message*, which itemised some of the cost increases in these areas and also compared government charges in health with those for comparable services in the private sector.

29 See the speech by SDP MP for Nee Soon Central, Cheo Chai Chen, in *Parliamentary Debates Singapore*, 59(9), 10 March 1992, columns 683–4.

30 Chiam is on record as having likened a political party to a military outfit, contending that it is necessary for one person to give the orders. See *STWE*, 17 July 1993: 7.

31 Chee's attacks on inequalities led to the charge from the PAP that he was peddling the 'politics of envy'. See Chee's letter to the Forum column of the *Straits Times* on 17 February 1993 and a subsequent response by 2nd Organising Secretary of the PAP Matthias Yao in *STWOE*, 27 February 1993: 23 and comments in parliament by Prime Minister Goh reported in *STWOE*, 13 March 1993: 5.

32 Ling pushed this theme in the 1991 election campaign.

33 See the exchanges between Chee and Yao in *STWE*, 6 August 1994: 23; 13 August 1994: 23; 27 August 1994: 23; 8 October 1994: 23, and the coverage of this debate in *STWE*, 1 October 1994: 14.

34 Interviews with Chee's executive colleagues revealed some apprehension over his challenges to the PAP on human rights and foreign policy questions.

35 The PAP itself is worried about the implications of this for its own organisational future. In 1993, the party's youth wing was revitalised and renamed Young PAP. At the time, Young PAP's chairman, George Yeo, offered the inducement that people joining Young PAP could take positions different from the party's central leadership. See *ST*, 26 April 1993: 20.

36 Unlike wealthier Singaporeans, they have less ability to travel abroad to compensate for any downgrading of the domestic natural environment.

REFERENCES

Bernhard, Michael (1993) 'Civil Society and Democratic Transition in East Central Europe', *Political Science Quarterly*, 108(2): 307–26.

Briffett, Clive (ed.) (1990) *Master Plan for the Conservation of Nature in Singapore*, Singapore: Malayan Nature Society.

Brown, David (1993) 'The Corporatist Management of Ethnicity in Contemporary Singapore', in Garry Rodan (ed.) *Singapore Changes Guard: Social, Political and Economic Directions*, Melbourne: Longman Cheshire, pp. 16–33.

Chalmers, Ian (1992) 'Loosening State Control in Singapore: the Emergence of Local Capital as a Political Force', *Southeast Asian Journal of Social Science*, 20(2): 57–84.

Chee Soon Juan (1994) *Dare to Change*, Singapore: Singapore Democratic Party.

Chua Beng-Huat (1991) 'Singapore 1990: Celebrating the End of an Era', *Southeast Asian Affairs 1991*, Singapore: Institute of Southeast Asian Studies, pp. 253–66.

—— (1993) 'Towards a Non-Liberal Communitarian Democracy', unpublished paper presented at Murdoch University, Perth, 9 June.

—— (1994) 'Arrested Development: Democratisation in Singapore', *Third World Quarterly*, 15(4): 655–68.

Department of Statistics, Singapore (1983) *Economic and Social Statistics Singapore 1960–1982*, Singapore: Department of Statistics.

—— (1991) *Census of Population 1990: Advance Data Release*, Singapore: Department of Statistics.

—— (1994) *Yearbook of Statistics Singapore 1993*, Singapore: Department of Statistics.

Deyo, Frederic (1981) *Dependent Development and Industrial Order: an Asian Case Study*, New York: Praeger.

Economic Development Board, Singapore (1981) *Annual Report 1980/1981*, Singapore: Economic Development Board.

—— (1992) *Economic Development Board Yearbook 1991/92*, Singapore: Economic Development Board.

Goh Chok Tong (1989) 'The National Identity – A Direction and Identity for Singapore', *Speeches*, 13(1): 26–38.

Haas, Michael (1989) 'The Politics of Singapore in the 1980s', *Journal of Contemporary Asia*, 19(1): 48–76.

Hewison, Kevin and Rodan, Garry (1994) 'The Decline of the Left in Southeast Asia', *The Socialist Register 1994*, London: Merlin Press, pp. 235–62.

Kuttan, Sharaad (1995) 'The Big Chill', *Sun* (Malaysia), 28 February 1995: 4–6 (magazine section).

Kwok Kian-Woon (1995) 'Singapore: Consolidating the New Political Economy', *Southeast Asian Affairs 1995*, Singapore: Institute of Southeast Asian Studies, pp. 291–308.

Mak Lau-Fong (1993) 'The Rise of the Singapore Middle Class: an Analytical Framework', in Hsin-Huang Michael Hsiao (ed.) *Discovery of the Middle*

Classes in East Asia, Taipei: Institute of Ethnology, Academia Sinica, pp. 307–36.

Lim, Raymond (1995) 'Lowering the Barriers to a More Open Society', *Straits Times*, 7 September: 27.

Malayan Nature Society (1990) *Master Plan for the Conservation of Nature in Singapore*, Singapore: Malayan Nature Society.

Medhi, Krongkaew (1994) 'Income Distribution in East Asian Developing Countries: an Update', *Asian-Pacific Economic Literature*, 8(2): 58–73.

Ministry of Finance, Republic of Singapore (1993) *Final Report of the Committee to Promote Enterprise Overseas*, Singapore: SNP Publishers.

Nature Society of Singapore (1992) *Proposed Golf Course at Lower Peirce Reservoir: an Environmental Impact Assessment*, Singapore: Department of Botany, National University of Singapore.

Patterson, William (1994) 'Sexual Minorities on the Singaporean Stage', *Theatre in Southeast Asia*, 25: 61–72.

Registrar of Societies, Singapore, statements from various organisations for different years.

Rodan, Garry (1989) *The Political Economy of Singapore's Industrialisation*, London: Macmillan.

—— (1992) 'Singapore's Leadership Transition: Erosion or Refinement of Authoritarian Rule?', *Bulletin of Concerned Asian Scholars*, 24(1): 3–17.

—— (1993a) 'The Growth of Singapore's Middle Class and its Political Significance', in Garry Rodan (ed.) *Singapore Changes Guard: Social, Political and Economic Directions in the 1990s*, New York: St Martin's Press, pp. 52–71.

—— (1993b) 'Preserving the One-Party State in Contemporary Singapore', in Kevin Hewison, Richard Robison, and Garry Rodan (eds) *Southeast Asia in the 1990s: Authoritarianism, Democracy and Capitalism*, Sydney: Allen & Unwin, pp. 75–108.

—— (1993c) 'Elections Without Representation: the Singapore Experience Under the PAP', paper presented at the conference 'Elections in Southeast Asia: Meaning and Practice', Woodrow Wilson International Center, Washington, DC, 16–18 September.

Rosa, Linda (1990) 'The Singapore State and Trade Union Incorporation', *Journal of Contemporary Asia*, 20(4): 487–508.

Rueschemeyer, Dietrich, Stephens, Evelyn Huber, and Stephens, John D. (1992) *Capitalist Development and Democracy*, Cambridge: Polity Press.

Seah Chee Meow (1973) *Community Centres in Singapore*, Singapore: Singapore University Press.

Singh, Bilveer (1992) *Whither PAP's Dominance? An Analysis of Singapore's 1991 General Elections*, Petaling Jaya: Pelanduk Publications.

Stepan, Alfred (1985) 'State Power and the Strength of Civil Society in the Southern Cone of Latin America', in Peter B. Evans, Dietrich Rueschemeyer and Theda Skocpol (eds) *Bringing the State Back In*, Cambridge: Cambridge University Press, pp. 317–43.

Urban Redevelopment Authority (1991) *Living the Next Lap: Towards a Tropical City of Excellence*, Singapore: Urban Redevelopment Authority.

Vennevald, Werner (1992) 'Opposition in Singapore: Chances and Limits of Political Transition of an Efficient One-Party State', unpublished mimeograph.

Workers' Party (WP) (1994) *Towards a Caring Society: the Programme of the Workers' Party 1994*, Singapore: Workers' Party.

Yeo, Robert (1994) 'Theatre and Censorship in Singapore', *Theatre in Southeast Asia*, 25: 49–60.

5 The syncretic state and the structuring of oppositional politics in Malaysia

James V. Jesudason

INTRODUCTION: EXPLAINING THE CONTAINMENT OF DEMOCRACY

One of the interesting puzzles about Malaysia is that its political system has not become more democratic over the last twenty-five years. The indicators of political and civil rights used by Freedom House show a gradual restriction of 'freedom' since the early 1970s (Means 1991: 309). A recent country compilation of the state of human rights by Charles Humana puts Malaysia in the company of Colombia, Mexico, Honduras, and Singapore, all of which ranked below Brazil, Côte d'Ivoire, Senegal, and Jamaica (Humana 1992: xvii–xix). Widely regarded in the 1960s as more democratic than a host of East Asian countries such as South Korea, Taiwan, and Thailand, Malaysia has fallen behind them in recent years. It is ironic that many non-electoral, authoritarian regimes in Southeast and East Asia have experienced greater democratic consolidation in recent years than some of the long-standing electoral regimes in the region.

However, there is no reason to believe that the Barisan Nasional or National Front Coalition, underpinned by the United Malays National Organization (UMNO), is politically unstable. In fact, recent analyses of Malaysia have been at pains to demonstrate that the regime's departure from democratic norms and practices does not signal any imminent crisis of legitimacy. In Crouch's formulation, for example, the 'neither democratic nor authoritarian' regime in Malaysia is a product of a rough balance between social groups which have a stake in the *status quo* and those groups which desire greater democratisation (Crouch 1993: 147–50). William Case also says that the Malaysian regime, which he labels as a 'semi-democracy' (Case 1993: 184),[1] is secure and 'in contrast to many countries that have recently undergone regime change . . . may persist unchanged for a considerable period'. While the terms used by Crouch and Case lack analytical precision, both authors do caution against retaining optimistic notions that economic development, by generating an enlarged middle class and working class, inexorably produces pressures for democratic change (see Girling 1988).

Malaysia has seen massive changes in the social structure without accompanying increases in political competition. The broader middle class expanded from 20 per cent of the working population in 1970 to about 33.5 per cent in 1993; production workers increased from 11.6 per cent to 28.5 per cent while the agricultural population fell from 44.1 per cent to 25.4 per cent in the same period. Changes in the Malay social structure were even more dramatic: the middle class expanded from 13 per cent to 28 per cent, the working class from 7.8 per cent to 25.5 per cent, while the agricultural population declined from 65.2 per cent to 33.5 per cent between 1970 and 1993.[2]

I do not wish to suggest that Malaysian politics has been static. The many works on the country do point to active and ongoing processes of political co-optation, gerrymandering, selective coercion (see Barra-clough 1985; Crouch 1992; Means 1991: 135–6, 296, 307, 316), coalition building, and the adroit use of ethnic appeals and economic patronage to secure power for UMNO and its partners. Nevertheless, there is a shape and logic to the Malaysian political system, including its longevity, that is better explained in more analytical terms.

I argue that politics in Malaysia and, more specifically, the role of oppositional forces must be understood in terms of the particular type of state that has come into being in the country. This state, which I label syncretic, is a product of a particular historical-structural configuration that has allowed the power holders to combine a broad array of economic, ideological, and coercive elements in managing the society, including limiting the effectiveness of the opposition as a democratising force. Although there is a dialectical relation between state and society, I will adopt a state-centred perspective in understanding democratic development in Malaysia, in contrast to society-centred perspectives which view political change as derivative of social and economic change. Skocpol (1985: 27) makes a persuasive case for the state-centred approach: 'the formation, let alone the political capacities, of such apparently purely socioeconomic phenomena as interest groups and classes depends in significant measure on the structures and activities of the very states the social actors, in turn, seek to influence.'

Since the particular historical state-society configuration matters significantly, it is not very useful to counterpose the attributes of social groups and classes, such as the working, middle, or capitalist classes in Malaysia or elsewhere in Asia with equivalent social actors in Europe.

Just like comparing apples with oranges, it is not clear what is to be gained from the effort. This problem is found in Jones and Brown's (1994) otherwise engaging analysis of the 'myth' of the liberalising middle class in Singapore, a class seen as having none of the characteristics of the pioneering, liberalising middle class of Europe. While setting out to criticise modernisation theory, the analysis ends up adopting a neo-Parsonian framework that sees values and ideologies as sustaining the polity. Little is said about how state structures and power constrain the capacity of the middle class to act politically or how social identities are products of particular historical patterns of state development.

The syncretic state, whose features and development are markedly different from the western state, has centrally framed the nature of oppositional politics in Malaysia, whether the formal opposition parties or groups in civil society. Opposition political parties have great difficulty developing a coherent programmatic alternative to the ruling regime, because the state has a powerful ability to absorb diverse ideological orientations and interests in society, leaving only narrow constituencies for the opposition to cultivate. The political behaviour of the middle classes and new rich also needs to be understood in terms of the historical development and political practices of the state, which have made it superfluous for them to articulate the ideologies associated with their counterparts of a different time and place. However, I do not wish to take a narrow state-centred view in examining political opposition in Malaysia, because there is a role for modernisation approaches which see the development of the middle class as exerting some democratic pressure on the state. Some elements within the class – though not the whole of it – are able to articulate important public issues and open up limited spaces of negotiation. Unlike the formal opposition, the groups of civil society are less trapped by ethnic and religious issues because their concern is not with the immediate gaining of political power. In the final analysis, however, fundamental political change is only likely to come from the loss of coherence of the syncretic state rather than from direct and immediate pressures in civil society. Such a loss of coherence, though by no means inevitable, could come from the increasing difficulty of managing cultural identities and economic interests generated by ongoing economic and social-structural changes.

THE SYNCRETIC STATE: GENERAL FEATURES AND IMPLICATIONS

I describe the Malaysian state as syncretic because it combines a variety of ideological orientations and political practices in managing the society. The syncretic state operates at a multi-dimensional level, mixing coercive elements with electoral and democratic procedures; it propagates religion in society as it pursues secular economic goals; it engages in ethnic mobilisation while inculcating national feeling; and it pursues a combination of economic practices ranging from liberal capitalism, state economic intervention, to rentier arrangements. These features are in important ways a product of the externally implanted nature of the colonial state and the colonial capitalist economy. Early political development theorists, such as Stein Rokkan (1975), would have probably regarded the composite nature of this state as a brittle amalgam, stemming from the unsolved problems of political development in post-colonial systems.

The western state, in contrast, had met the various 'challenges' of state development prior to mass politics, producing a more streamlined state ruling over secular and culturally unified societies. However, the stability of the Barisan and its precursor, the Alliance Party, belies the fears of political development theorists. The management of syncretism can be cumbersome and crisis-ridden, but if successfully done, it allows for a high degree of regime dominance.

The key elements of the syncretic state in Malaysia, which I will examine in turn, are: democratic legitimacy and coercion; religion, ethnicity, and capitalism; and technocratic managerialism and the segmented economy.

One of the interesting aspects of the syncretic state has been its ability to mix democratic procedures and coercive practices. Both features are legacies of the colonial period. The externally implanted nature of the colonial state made it superfluous for the state elites to establish a negotiated space between state and society to seek approval from the subject population for state-building tasks. According to Tilly (1985: 186), each imposition of taxation and control in the west 'constrained the rulers themselves, making them vulnerable to courts, assemblies, to withdrawals of credit, services, and expertise'. The highly top–down process of state building under colonialism made it possible for post-colonial states to 'harbor powerful, unconstrained organisations that easily overshadow all other organisations within their territories' (Tilly 1985: 186).

The departing British colonial officials in Malaysia nonetheless expected the new state elites to assume and maintain power through electoral and constitutional means. When the Malay UMNO-dominated ruling coalition took over control of the colonial state, it was relatively easy to keep power through electoral mechanisms. The elites were able to use and build upon the vast powers and resources of the colonial state to integrate vertically significant groups in society. Democratic processes did not lead to a civil society with strong class identities, and in fact class politics declined in comparison to the colonial period. It was not just the suppression of the Communist Party in the late 1940s and 1950s that weakened strong class organisations and identities. The rapid way in which the franchise was made available to all eligible citizens, regardless of class, education, and gender, was also not conducive to strong class organisations and identities. In Europe, the fight for political inclusion was a staggered process, leading each excluded group, such as the working class and women, to form autonomous organisations, to forge alliances with other classes, and to develop a common identity. In Malaysia, however, the main source of contention over the vote was along ethnic lines, the franchise being almost automatic for the Malay population and more restricted for the non-Malays. Not surprisingly, the expansion of the polity spawned ethnic organisations and identities rather than class organisations and consciousness.

Democratic procedures, though highly manipulated by the political elite, have nonetheless given legitimacy to the dominant party. The Malaysian state elite's ability to shape electoral arrangements to its decisive advantage appears to corroborate the argument made by Piven and Cloward that electoral-representative arrangements can be highly effective mechanisms of elite control (Piven and Cloward 1977: 15–18). Case (1993: 204) makes a similar point in regard to Malaysia when he says: 'elites operating a semi-democracy may offer enough electoral activities that they forge greater political legitimacy than authoritarianism allows, but by avoiding the policy immobilism identified with full democracy, they may earn performance legitimacy also.'

The semblance of democratic legitimacy allows coercion to be used as an effective political strategy, particularly when it is meted out within the bounds of legality. Barraclough (1985: 820) expertly shows how emergency powers have been used against opposition state governments while the Internal Security Act has been used to detain individual opponents of the government. Coercion was used most persistently in the past against class-based opposition, especially Left parties, but from the 1980s the trend has been to use it against Islamic opponents of the regime. What is interesting in Malaysia is that 'coercion has, for most part, been accepted by the general population as legitimate' (Barraclough 1985: 820). Unlike the authoritarian phases in South Korea, Taiwan, and the Philippines, the mix of coercion and electoral proceduralism in Malaysia protects the dominant party from collective resentment building up to the point of effecting regime change.

One of the feats of the ruling coalition in managing the syncretic state has been its remarkable ability to combine a mix of ideological orientations, allowing the political leadership to blur the lines between state and society. In the internally generated process of western state formation, the rulers found it necessary to compete with and privatise religion in their state-building efforts. By building a wall between Church and state, the private sphere was not only sheltered from unwanted incursions, but the public sphere was also freed from insoluble conflicts among competing religious orientations (Holmes 1988: 23). In the externally implanted state, however, the public use of religion can be useful for the regime, because the process of state development did not have to overcome pre-existing supra-religious organisations and transnational religious attachments. Peletz (1993: 78) has argued that there has been a 'progressive empowering of state-controlled Islamic hierarchies' in Malaysia which began with colonial rule but has continued strongly in the post-colonial state. The leaders, by claiming to uphold and promote Islam in public, are able to blur the distinction between the public and private domains. This is highly advantageous for regime power, although it can sometimes lead to internal conflict over what is true Islam.

Ethnicity has also been effectively harnessed by the regime to secure rule, which differs again from the European experience. The long process of state development there led to relative cultural homogeneity among the population, though the process was never complete. The idea of nationhood was always more than just a territorial notion, encompassing, as well, democratic ideas of citizenship (Mann 1993: 249). The implanted colonial state in contrast did not need to homogenise the population to establish territorial control. In fact ethnic differentiation was part of the colonial project, where even labour and the bourgeoisie had to be imported from outside sources. It is not surprising that the notion of citizenship in Malaysia at independence was little more than a territorial idea, giving individuals the right to stay in the territory but with no presumption of equal rights among the ethnically diverse population. The post-colonial regime has always claimed to secure the interests of the Malay population, whose self-reference is *bumiputera* (literally, sons of the soil).

Clearly the efficacy of ethnic appeals has not been a simple process of manipulation by the political elite. The real anxieties among broad elements of the Malay population over their ability to compete economically with the sizeable Chinese minority has given legitimacy to the power holders as protectors of Malay interests. The steering of ethnic identities is not static, however, and has changed according to political and economic circumstances. In the latest phase, starting from 1991, the government of Dr Mahathir Mohamed has encouraged the Malays to become Melayu Baru (new Malay), a rejuvenated ethnic identity that is able to meet the challenges of global economic competition with greater self-confidence.

However, the dominant Malay elite has included co-operative party elites from the Chinese and Indian groups in the ruling coalition as a means of portraying a multi-racial image. While mobilising ethnic attachments, the UMNO leaders have also been able to contain outright non-Malay rebellion through high-growth policies and selective co-optation.

Whether in the management of ethnic or of religious identities, the regime has been careful not to compromise the basic rationality of the capitalist economy. Economic policies, while favouring Malays, have been modified from time to time to ensure that no long-term damage is inflicted on the economy. The government has also been concerned to project a modernist interpretation of Islam. Islam's symbols are powerfully upheld publicly, and some concessions have been made to Islamic economic practices, such as establishing Islamic banking, but versions of Islamic thinking that are anti-consumerist and socialistic in orientation have been contained.

The colonial state, for all its *laissez-faire* ideology, was a proto-developmentalist institution that played a critical role in capitalist development. The post-colonial state in Malaysia has followed the legacy of the colonial state. Major shifts in economic policy have seldom been the outcome of conflicts among groups in civil society but a product of the state's reflexive monitoring of internal and external economic and political conditions. The same ruling coalition in Malaysia has overseen primary-export production, import-substitution industrialisation, export-oriented manufacturing, economic statism, and privatisation. Even in the mildly redistributionist policies of the Malaysian state, such as the public provision of amenities, medical services, housing, and specific anti-poverty programmes, the impetus has originated not from the pressures of redistributionist coalitions or organised social groups, but from regime calculations on the electoral pay-offs of these provisions.

The state's managerial role in the economy has made many ideologies that were crucial for major economic transformations in the west redundant in Malaysian development. Capitalism, economic liberalism, and social democracy were ideologies advanced by specific groups for specific interests. These were products of civil society. Late-developing states have incorporated these ideological formulations as part of state planning through the conscious adoption of foreign models and examples. The major consequence of the state's economic managerialism is that competing economic ideologies or economic alliances do not develop in civil society, constricting one axis of democratic contestation.

What is also very interesting about the state's economic syncretism is the segmented approach of the state to various economic actors. The economy is divided into separate parcels that serve different purposes. There is a rentier segment for accumulating resources for political patronage (Gomez 1991), a protected sector for politically important small and aspiring business men, a quasi-monopolistic segment for well-connected business men and large state companies, and a sizeable competitive arena comprising multinationals, local Chinese companies, and a few Malay companies to ensure national competitiveness. The size of the segments has varied depending on political and economic conditions, and currently the state elites are expanding the competitive sector more vigorously. Although there are some conflicts within these segments, each of these groups is dependent on the state to meet its particular interests. The partitioning of the market allows the state to incorporate a large assortment of business groups with a stake in the regime.

In general, then, the syncretic state has significant capabilities to structure state–society relations. It not only operates by a mix of features in a particular dimension – such as coercion and democracy – but it works simultaneously on a variety of fronts. The ruling coalition is able to secure majority support by propagating encompassing, non-negotiable identities and ideologies, such as religion and ethnicity. These vertically structured ideologies crowd out secular identities and ideologies based on class politics and notions of autonomy from the state, promoting a clientelist consciousness that undercuts the development of effective alliances and ideologies against the regime.

SYNCRETIC STATE AND OPPOSITION POLITICS

The syncretic state is the limiting structure in which politics must be viewed in Malaysia. The kinds of ideologies opposition parties advance, the possibilities of alliance formation, the orientations and political activities of the middle classes, and the very identity of social actors are refractions of this state. Formal opposition parties are limited in their ability to articulate an alternative politics in Malaysia because their political approaches and strategies are essentially a reaction to the terms set by the syncretic state. The main opposition parties do get support from those segments of the population that do not benefit from the regime's policies, but none of them are able to forge an effective coalition to replace the Barisan Nasional. In developing on these observations, I will pursue three main propositions in the section to follow.

First, the main opposition parties mobilise different segments of the population at the more extreme poles of the syncretic state. Their party platforms are usually an exaggeration of a particular feature of the existing state such as more vigorously defending ethnic rights, promoting a theocratic state, and in some cases pressing for a stronger, economically redistributionist policy.

Second, since each opposition party tries to challenge a specific property of the syncretic state, the opposition parties end up highly polarised from one another. The major parties are not able to arrive at an ideological consensus to replace the Barisan, and co-operate only for instrumental purposes, such as making common criticisms of the corrupt practices of the government or agreeing not to split the opposition vote during elections.

Third, opposition parties help to reproduce the syncretic state. Their role in challenging or breaking down the ethnic and religious segmentation is feeble. Some of the main opposition parties, by advocating a theocratic state, or ethnic rights, have in fact anti-democratic implications for the society.

The orientations of opposition political parties

In illustrating the above propositions I will look at three of the main opposition parties: Parti Islam SeMalaysia or PAS (Pan-Malaysia Islamic Party); Parti Melayu Semangat '46; and the Democratic Action Party (DAP).

The PAS was formed in 1951, and was the major rival to the UMNO until the formation of Semangat '46 in 1987. The strategy of the PAS has been to challenge the western-educated UMNO leaders by out-bidding them on matters of Malay rights and religion. Many of the PAS's early founders had been members of the UMNO's religious bureau in the initial years of the party but had objected to the UMNO confining its religious efforts to just one bureau of the party, wanting instead to see a greater commitment to a post-independence Islamic state (Jomo and Cheek 1992: 93). In the 1960s, the PAS's religious bent was held in the background, as the party attacked the UMNO for conceding too much to Chinese economic and cultural interests (such as preserving English in schools). When the UMNO swung to promote Malay capital accumulation, Islam, and the Malay language in a vigorous way in the 1970s and 1980s, the PAS, to prevent itself from being undercut, began strongly to advocate the literal interpretation of Islam as a basis of the society. The PAS leaders started to attack the government for its failure to set up a theocratic state and implement *hudud* laws (the Islamic penal code).

The PAS has the active support of about 30 per cent of the Malay population, most of whom are rural, but there is some middle-class sympathy for the party in urban areas (Singh 1991: 724). Such an electoral base does corroborate Brown's (1994: 222) insight that the language of ethnicity and ethno-religion in Malaysia must be seen as a culturally available vehicle for the expression of class interests. It is important, however, not to stretch the point too far. It was revealed in interview that PAS leaders had confidence that their supporters, particularly in Kelantan state, where the party is in control, would rather forgo material inducements offered by the UMNO than accept the corrupt, materialistic, and pleasure-seeking life that the UMNO offers. I learned from PAS leaders that the UMNO might be able, through vote buying, to swing the result of an election in Kelantan their way only if there was a 50:50 split in the electorate.[3] Other less morally based parties, such as Semangat, report that the UMNO can make up for a 10 to 15 per cent deficit through 'money' politics.[4]

The danger for the PAS is that it will remain a party of choice for some pockets of the nation when its goal is to govern the country. Its recent moves to impose *hudud* laws in Kelantan, and impose strict controls over dietary behaviour and dress, including restrictions on the non-Muslim population, have alarmed non-Muslims and many anxious Muslims elsewhere. The PAS had been trying to convince non-Muslims since the late 1980s that their interests would be protected under Islam, and even played up the fact that its constitution did not stipulate a theocratic state, only an Islamic way of life. Many Chinese in Malay-majority areas, who saw little benefit in voting for the Barisan, did show an interest in the PAS. But the PAS, which continued to attack the Barisan for not being really Islamic, was dared by the Prime Minister to set up a theocratic state in Kelantan. This dare seems to have pushed the PAS in a direction it might not have originally planned on. The party leaders' simplicity and sincerity in attacking corruption, material deprivation, and government abuse from an Islamic moral position did meet the interests of many villagers and the lower rungs of the Malay middle class. But now the PAS will be primarily associated with Islamic theocracy, a position it had articulated but never quite pursued with vigour until pressed by the regime.

Semangat '46 came into being in the aftermath of a severe economic recession in 1985 and 1986. This recession deeply hurt the balancing act between the rentier, protected, and competitive economic sectors. Government expenditure cutbacks hurt patronage mechanisms, hitting Malay small and medium-sized business men, who began to complain that the Mahathir government only catered to well-connected Malay tycoons (Khoo 1992: 61–5). Internal dissent began to brew in the UMNO, and in 1987 Tengku Razaleigh, the Minister of Trade and Industry and long-time aspirant to premiership, challenged Dr Mahathir for the party presidency. Through a thicket of events, the UMNO split into two, with one-half, UMNO Baru, led by Dr Mahathir and the other, Semangat '46, led by Tengku Razaleigh.

For the first time there was a major split among the western-educated Malay elite, and many middle-class citizens hoped that it would lead to a two-party system in the country. Semangat began to court the trade unions, and civil rights groups, and forged co-operative relationships with non-Malay opposition parties as well as the PAS. Hopes ran high when the party won a by-election against the UMNO in 1988.

However, as the economy picked up in the late 1980s, the fortunes of Semangat began to wane rapidly. In the 1990 elections, the party won only eight out of the fifty-nine parliamentary seats it contested. Major defections back to the UMNO have since occurred among Semangat's notables, particularly those involved in business. The deeper problem for Semangat was that it was courting the same constituency as the UMNO but did not have the resources to offer a better economic deal. The party's platform was a laudable one which promised the independence of the judiciary, the repeal of unjust and repressive laws, the elimination of business investments by political parties, and the restoration of workers' rights (Khong 1991: 12). While these issues attracted some Malay middle-class support, much of the Malay population, from the middle classes to the villagers, did not regard Semangat as better placed to channel benefits to them than the UMNO.

After its poor performance, the leaders of Semangat thought it would be more fruitful to drop its multi-ethnic, social democratic rhetoric, and tried to cultivate a narrow Malay ethnic constituency. Rather than embark on a long-term strategy of building a new syncretic alternative to the UMNO and its allies, they were led by the logic of competition to try to outbid UMNO by playing the familiar game of appealing to ethnicity. In 1994 Semangat renamed itself the Parti Melayu Semangat '46, to stress its Malay nature. Semangat appeared to want to take on the role of the PAS in the 1960s, since the latter shifted its focus to the establishment of a theocratic state. Semangat's leaders were trying to rekindle Malay fears for their position in the country by arguing that the UMNO's dismantling of the powers of the sultans weakened an essential constitutional guarantee for Malay special privileges. To underscore the point, they asserted that the UMNO's new pro-growth policies had strengthened the Chinese business position while causing a decline of Malay share ownership from 19.2 per cent in 1988 to 18.2 per cent in 1992 (*Mid-Term Review of the Sixth Malaysia Plan 1991–1995* 1993: 67, table 3–57).

The behaviour of Semangat is consistent with our proposition that the syncretic state pushes opposition parties to adopt a more extreme form of its basic properties. In the process, these parties end up cultivating a narrow base, forgoing a broader vision of politics.

The DAP has traditionally addressed itself to that aspect of the syncretic state which gave a representative role to co-operative Chinese-based parties such as the Malaysian Chinese Association and later the Gerakan. As if the flip-side of the PAS, the DAP attacked the conservative, business-oriented Chinese wing of the Alliance/Barisan regime for its feeble advocacy of Chinese educational, cultural, and lower-class interests. In the 1960s, it espoused an egalitarian, democratic, and secular programme based on the concept of 'Malaysian Malaysia', which was seen as a 'political code word attacking the system of Malay "special rights" that had been incorporated into the Constitution' (Means 1991: 5).

The majority of the Chinese population and some segments of the Indian population have consistently voted for the DAP. Although the DAP never had access to patronage, this was largely irrelevant to its supporters who seldom benefited from direct state largess and were not dependent on the state for jobs. Support for the DAP has been a reflection of the relative weakness of the syncretic state in absorbing Chinese interests. This in turn has kept the party focused on Chinese issues, such as fighting to preserve Chinese education and resisting Islamisation in the country.

Although the government has labelled it a Chinese chauvinist party, the DAP's role of exposing scandals, and its attempt to help urban squatters of all ethnic groups threatened by land acquisition, have made it more acceptable as a legitimate opposition party in the eyes of urban Malays. Since 1990, the party has tried more strenuously to attract Malay support as there are decreasing numbers of constituencies which have Chinese voters as the predominant group. However, in terms of direct voting support, the party cannot rely on the Malays, who prefer to see the DAP as a watchdog rather than as a power broker.

In the final analysis, the DAP is constrained by the ethnic structures of the syncretic state. By relying mostly on the Chinese middle class and working class, it cannot become a central party in Malaysia that can hope to displace the existing regime. The new moves by the Barisan to liberalise Chinese education, and to embrace China as an economic ally, have predisposed some segments of the Chinese community to the government. It would not be surprising to see the erosion of the DAP in politics with the party ending up only as a means to legitimise the electoral procedures of the regime and to prevent the worst abuses.

The problem of oppositional alliances

Since opposition parties tend to end up with segmented political bases, it is only through a wider coalition that they could possibly pose a threat to the Barisan. Yet this wider coalition has to amalgamate a more diverse set of interests than is found in the syncretic state. I now examine the effort in the 1990 election to form just such a coalition, and the essential problems of such arrangements.

When Tengku Razaleigh and his key supporters were outmanoeuvred by Dr Mahathir in controlling the UMNO, they went about forging a broad alliance to replace the Barisan Nasional in anticipation of the 1990 elections. Semangat' 46 formed a partnership with the PAS and two minor Malay-based parties under the rubric of Angkatan Perpaduan Ummah (APU) (Singh 1991: 726). Semangat, as a new party, wanted to claim roots in the Malay tradition while PAS wanted to tone down its fundamentalist, extremist image (Khong 1991: 9). On the urban flank, Razaleigh wanted the DAP to join the opposition alliance to capture the urban Chinese vote. However, the PAS refused a formal alliance with the DAP which had criticised its Islamisation programme and feared any alliance would negate its participation in APU based on Malay unity and Islam. Semangat, instead, formed a separate alliance with the DAP along with two smaller parties under the umbrella of Gagasan Rakyat. However, there was an implicit understanding that the supporters of the parties in the two parallel alliances would vote for each other in their particular constituencies.

On the ground, however, there were numerous problems. Whatever broad platform had been developed by the leadership was jettisoned in the campaigns as politicians made appeals to particularistic issues in fighting the Barisan. Party activists and voters, long socialised to view each other with suspicion, found it hard to co-operate at the constituency level. The lack of a common vision took its toll on the alliance. For the average voter, the idea of a two-party system was attractive in the abstract but few had a clear sense of how an alternative government might work. This unease was exploited intensely and successfully by the UMNO in the media, which portrayed Semangat's alliance with the DAP and another breakaway party, the Parti Bersatu Sabah, an East Malaysian party dominated by Kadazan Catholics, as threatening Malay rights and Islam. In the elections, Semangat performed poorly, while the DAP did not do any better than previously. The prime beneficiary was the PAS, which managed to capture the state government of Kelantan; however, the critical internal problem was the lack of ideological and programmatic unity among the opposition.

The opposition was unable to articulate a vision of democracy that went beyond attacking the specific malpractices of the regime. Semangat's subsequent appeal to Malay rights and the use of ethnic scare tactics suggest that its earlier advocacy of democracy was for instrumental purposes. In private, Party leaders justified their stance, claiming that the party needs to engage in short-term political tactics, but this position could not inspire confidence that they had an alternative vision of a democratic and multi-racial society. Indeed, in May 1996, Tengku Razaleigh announced he would be leaving Semangat and rejoining UMNO, and that he expected others in the party to do likewise (*The Economist* 18 May 1996: 38).

For the leaders of the PAS, democracy was not even an ultimate value. They viewed democracy as a desirable political system only in a secular context.[5] If an Islamic state ever came into being, it could not be reversed; however, not even non-Muslims would want another system once they had experienced the virtues of Islamic theocracy. The PAS also expressed dissatisfaction with the concept of majority rule because it potentially allowed morally wrong tenets to be enacted, such as according homosexuals the right to their lifestyle. Democracy's protection of individual choice was also anathema because it seemed to presume that the individual was somehow all-knowing. In essence, PAS conceived democracy and Islam as two competing forms of moral community.

After the 1990 elections, each opposition party decided it would be better to revert to its own narrow base of support. A rift developed between the PAS and Semangat over the powers of royalty. The PAS voted with the government in 1994 to restrict the powers of the sultans and the monarch further, while Semangat abstained. In late 1994, the DAP called off any alliance with the PAS, having earlier supported the PAS government of Kelantan against accusations by the Barisan that it was restricting alcohol consumption among non-Muslims.

The opposition has been unable to come up with their own syncretism to match that of the Barisan Nasional. The imminent danger for regime opponents is that they will end up participating in politics without any real influence at the national level, and with only the possibility of gaining power at the state level in a few places such as Kelantan and Sabah. The most recent elections in April 1995 support the argument advanced here that the syncretic state has the effect of marginalising the opposition. The continuation of high growth rates since the last elections and the active courting of the urban Chinese vote saw the National Front government significantly improve its electoral position. In contrast to the general decline of dominant parties in Japan, Scandinavia, and India, the component parties of the National Front boosted their share of the popular vote quite remarkably from 53 per cent to 63 per cent, while their proportion of parliamentary seats increased from 71 per cent to 84 per cent (*Asiaweek*, 5 May 1995: 20). The DAP, which focused its campaign on Chinese-majority constituencies, particularly in Penang, was severely weakened, winning only nine seats compared to twenty in 1990. The PAS and Semangat '46 managed to retain their position in the Malay Muslim-dominated state of Kelantan but by reduced margins. The initial reaction of the opposition parties was to blame their poor showing on gerrymandering by the National Front, and the flagrant one-sidedness of the national media in discrediting them. But the despondency and disbelief with which the opposition leaders reacted to the results demonstrated clearly that their problems went deeper than having to operate in an electoral system in which the rules were stacked against them; so much so that the future of Semangat in 1996 was in question. It was obvious that they could not collectively present a broader vision of politics which appealed to a larger electoral base, managing only to win in certain niches where religious and ethnic considerations were foremost.

The weakness of the opposition, and here I am referring to the non-religious parties of the DAP and Semangat '46, cannot be attributed simply to its leaders making tactical mistakes and suffering from a deficit of personal vision. Opposition parties are not able to transcend the religious and ethnic ideologies that arise from the interaction between the syncretic state and society, making it difficult for class-based interests to take root in the society, which Lipset (1960) saw as providing political parties with the support base needed to sustain democratic competition in capitalist societies. The weakness of any discourse on class politics gives a powerful advantage to the ruling coalition, particularly under conditions of high economic growth. Despite the inherent difficulties facing the opposition, the 1995 elections nonetheless contain an important lesson for the DAP and Semangat. Both had abandoned the 1990 electoral alliance because the result did not meet their excessively high expectations of quick political success. In retrospect, the attempted alliance in 1990 was not such a failure after all, considering the rout suffered this time around when their strategies focused on making appeals targeted at particular states and constituencies. In 1990 the *ad hoc* campaign platform at least captured the imagination of a larger segment of the population by attempting to advance, if not entirely convincingly, a viable multiracial, democratic, non-corrupt, and more redistributionist alternative to the existing regime. The mistake in 1995 was to think that criticisms of governmental corruption and the lavish lifestyles and peccadilloes of government leaders, or quibbling about marginal changes in Malay wealth ownership figures, constituted serious oppositional politics.

The enfeeblement of class politics

The labour movement in Malaysia has been progressively weakened over time, cramped by the destruction of the Communist Left in the 1950s, the pattern of franchise extension which favoured ethnic loyalties, strict regulation of trade union activities, and restrictions on the political activities of union leaders. By building on ethnic loyalties through selective benefits to the Malay population, the regime has been able to ignore unionised workers as class actors. Only 17 per cent of wage earners belonged to unions in 1990 (Crouch 1993: 147), and the percentage has been falling. Despite expectations that the increasing size of the Malay urban proletariat would cause a shift from ethnic to class politics, the degree of ethnic attachment continues to be very strong among the working class. Quite clearly, class identities are not the mechanical product of the capitalist work experience. Workers, like everyone else, have multiple identities, making the macro-political context critical in accentuating or activating a particular identity.

The racial and religious structures of the syncretic state have deeply penetrated the union movement. Despite Boulanger's (1992: 331) heroic portrayal of local unionists as successfully resisting the national 'ethnic paradigm' by co-operating over common concerns at the firm level, her own study shows a high degree of ethnic suspicion and stereotyping among the workers. In Ackerman's (1986: 162) study of a shoe workers' union, she finds that the fight for benefits takes interesting racial forms: the Indians fought for a holiday for Deepavali, while Malays wanted a paid holiday for Awal Muharram, a Muslim holiday.

At the national level, the main labour confederation, the Malaysian

Trade Union Congress (MTUC), has also been made ineffective by the wider nature of ethnic politics in the country. The MTUC has considered, but avoided, a direct political role as a workers' party because of the diverse political and ethnic orientations among its members. Since many of them are supporters of the UMNO, the leaders fear that turning the movement into an oppositional force could tear it apart.[6] Instead, individual leaders have joined various opposition parties such as the DAP and Semangat. For example, V. David, a prominent leader of the MTUC, had been a DAP Member of Parliament. In early 1990, the president of the MTUC, Zainal Rampak, joined Semangat, which had promised to support the union's basic labour programme that included a minimum wage, the recognition of a national federation of electronics workers, a five-day working week, and additional fringe benefits (*New Straits Times (NST)*, 8 May 1990: 29) In 1990, Ahmad Nor, the president of CUEPACS, the federation of public-sector unions, resigned his post to form the Social Democratic Party, and after it collapsed, joined the DAP as an office holder. This was a significant departure for both the DAP and Ahmad Nor, in that a prominent Malay had joined the party.

The government's response to the politicisation of the trade unions in the late 1980s and early 1990s was to split the union movement, encourage the formation of compliant unions linked to the government, isolate the MTUC, and make leaders with opposition ties sever their political links. A great source of annoyance to the government was the attempt by some union leaders to link up with American Federation of Labor-Congress of Industrial Organizations (AFL-CIO) to press for recognition of a national union of electronics workers. The AFL-CIO was threatened by low-cost producers in Asia, and was on the look-out to link Generalised System of Preferences (GSP) status as well as trade benefits to labour conditions in competitor countries. Labour's greatest leverage over the government was the pressure applied by foreign unions and not its own domestic capacities. This has made the government employ more subtle means of control, such as excluding the MTUC from a number of tripartite bodies, including the National Labour Advisory Council (NLAC) and the board of the Employees' Provident Fund. To improve relations with the government, Zainal Rampak resigned from Semangat in May 1994, saying that he was putting aside his conviction that trade unionism was inseparable from politics (*NST*, 2 May 1994: 5).

The other strategy of the regime has been to encourage the formation of a rival federation of unions to the MTUC. In 1989, the Prime Minister warned that a new union might be necessary if the MTUC became political. But plans were already afoot. The Malaysian Chinese Association (MCA) Minister of Labour took the initiative of encouraging the National Union of Newspaper Workers, whose general secretary had close ties to the MCA, to form a separate federation. The UMNO leadership then followed up by inviting the Manual Group of the Public Sector to join the new federation, along with the National Union of Bank Employees (NUBE). NUBE had been a pillar of the MTUC but began to fall out with it when its leader lost the contest for MTUC vice president. The new union, the Malaysian Labour Organization (MLO), quickly acquired a membership of 100,000 through defections from the MTUC, but the numbers have flattened out since. The MLO, whose constitution forbids political involvement, has done the government's bidding in embarking on the formation of in-house unions.

The broader structural problem of the labour movement has been the state's syncretist developmental role. The state has either initiated changes in economic policy in response to economic conditions, or developed an amalgam of strategies for the different fractions of capital. There is no process of pluralist competition between business groups to shape national economic policies. It thus becomes superfluous for business groups to open up democratic space to mobilise allies in the labour movement. This further isolates the working class.

THE LIMITS AND POSSIBILITIES OF THE NEW RICH

A number of scholars have argued that the middle class and the bourgeoisie have not played a democratising role in Malaysia because of internal ethnic divisions (Crouch 1993: 151; Girling 1988: 333). This explanation is not incorrect but limited. The post-colonial state, as well as the syncretic state, constrains the new rich to an instrumental orientation to life. In general, the middle class does not like authoritarian structures, which accounts for their active role in civil society in Thailand, the Philippines, South Korea, and Taiwan. But when members of this class are given a semblance of participation or are entrapped in electoral mechanisms, their capacity and desire for further democratisation are limited. Nonetheless, there are middle-class individuals and organisations in Malaysia that have been interested in democratic and social reform. These groups do help in some reform efforts and do expand the sphere of negotiation in society. But they are limited in their ability to move the syncretic state towards a more competitive political system.

The state and the encapsulation of the new rich

It is futile to compare the behaviour of the middle classes of the post-colonial state with those in eighteenth- and nineteenth-century Europe, because they are different historical actors. Small strategic groups, such as intellectuals, lawyers, and journalists in nineteenth-century Europe, were able to enjoy great influence in shaping both the state and civil society. State elites and lawyers interacted to shape the constitutional development of the European state, forming a nexus of interests that made it possible for a structure of horizontal accountability to develop between state and society. The role of professional groups in shaping European society was not just a product of capitalist development. In the late medieval period, professional groups had developed a strong sense of corporate identity and culture (Clough 1982). The critical actors of civil society in Europe, such as lawyers, the intelligentsia, artisans, schoolteachers, priests, were active agents in creating the sites they occupied, from the university to law-making.

The Malaysian middle class, whose emergence was an after-effect of colonial state formation, has not been able to shape political development in the same ways as their 'counterparts' in the West.[7] The key sites of civil society were often set up from above by the state. For instance, the university, the constitution, the broadcasting media, the organs of discursive literacy, and even Muslim religious institutions have been established through either state design or funding. The emergence and political capacities of the middle class must be understood in the light of their location in these highly structured and controlled sites.

It is not surprising that the broader middle class has been primarily consumerist and career-oriented. Professor Mahadzir Mat Khir of the University of Malaya, in an interview with the *Straits Times* of Singapore (Life Section, 13 July 1994: 4), says this about the middle class in Malaysia:

> The advent of the middle class in Europe saw society becoming highly intellectualized. They placed high priority on fine arts such as music, literature and plays, and had a thirst for knowledge. In Malaysia, growing prosperity has seen an interest in such matters, but instead of the search for knowledge, it is more snob appeal that motivates the middle class here.

Although the behaviour of the contemporary western middle class may not be very different, they are nonetheless heirs to the participative traditions and institutions set up by their forebears. The historical sequencing of state development in the post-colonial world has produced a different kind of middle class, whose capacity for and interest in creating liberal institutions are relatively weak. Even among intellectuals in the universities, the predominant concern is to teach and to make extra money through consultancies. For others, leaving the university and going into business is a prime attraction, and is often combined with a career in one of the ethnic parties in the ruling coalition. Only a meagre number have gone into opposition politics or joined public-interest organisations with the aim of invigorating the institutions of civil society.[8]

One can readily understand why an ideology like liberalism, which has been so closely associated with the emerging bourgeoisie and certain segments of the middle class in Europe, is irrelevant to the post-colonial middle class. The fight for individual and political autonomy in Europe was aimed at opening a widened sphere of free choice and lifestyles, unencumbered by considerations of status and birth. Even the concept of property, as Habermas (1989: 85) reminds us, was infused with a politico-philosophical understanding of liberty and was never just understood as material wealth. For the contemporary middle class in the Third World, a relatively wide choice in consumer lifestyles and consumption has become available without the philosophical and political underpinnings of liberalism and individual autonomy. Anyone who has lived in both the west and East Asia will know that commodity fetishism – which now includes acquiring such cultural commodities as golf club memberships and attending Pavarotti concerts – is more powerful in Asia than in the west. Liberal impulses have been channelled into Adam Smith's free market, where people find individual realisation as sovereign consumers rather than as Mill's politically sovereign citizens. A relevant anecdote is the following: when I asked a middle-class professional whether he was angered by the banning of *Schindler's List* in Malaysia on the grounds of its alleged pro-Semitic leanings, his reply was, 'It does not matter. The video version will be out on the streets soon.'

The Malaysian middle class's political stance has also been the product of the syncretic state. For one thing, the functioning of statist democracy, by allowing for electoral participation, is largely considered legitimate. In Saravanamuttu's (1992: 56–8) survey of office holders in various ethnic organisations (an indicator of general middle-class sentiments), he finds that 91 per cent of Malays agree or agree very strongly with the statement that the system of elections is just. A relatively high 59 per cent of the Chinese and 62 per cent of the Indians are also in agreement. It is not as though the middle classes do not care about democracy because in answer to another question, the respondents of all ethnic groups chose 'democracy' as the most important issue articulated by political parties. However, their view of democracy does not appear to be a liberal one; it appears, rather, to be one which gives considerable latitude to the winners of elections to rule as they please.

Although increasingly becoming participants in the consumerist culture, the middle-class groups are also hampered politically by their internal differentiation and unequal relations to the syncretic state. The state has symbolically affirmed the special position of the Malays in society, and in material terms has made vigorous efforts to sponsor Malay mobility into the middle and capitalist classes. The state's role in patrolling religious boundaries, particularly by way of rules preventing exit options for Muslims, precludes the free negotiation and blending of ethnic and religious identities. The result is that the numerous political and social organisations of the middle class tend to be ethnically based, with only a few being multi-racial. Many of these organisations, such as the Peninsula Malay Students Union, the Malaysian Association of Youth Clubs, the National Muslim Youth Movement, and Dong Jiao Zong (Chinese Educationalist Movement), are linked up to the main ethnic parties. These ethnic and religious divisions make it difficult for the different ethnic groups to unite on common middle-class concerns, such as governmental corruption, poor educational facilities, or urban congestion. The Malay middle class, for example, has shown private concern over charges of corruption and the allocation of contracts to well-connected individuals (*Malaysian Business*, 16 November 1993: 17; *Asiaweek*, 26 October 1994: 27). But they are in a dilemma because they are also the prime beneficiaries of government policies. A former Member of Parliament, Tawfik Tun Ismail, notes that increasing affluence among the Malay middle classes has made them uninterested in politics:

> Politics played a great role in creating the middle class, but at the same time, it created in them a disinterest in politics. They did not want to rock the boat by being vocal. They wanted to ensure that their rice bowl is not jeopardized.
>
> (as quoted in *Straits Times (ST)*, 13 July 1994: 4)

Turning to the capitalist class, Crouch has argued that they have played a limited role in democratisation because their evolution has been dependent on the state (1993: 141). Only the Chinese bourgeoisie has had some independence, and has thwarted extreme statist economic policies. The other groups, such as state enterprises and the Malay bourgeoisie, are extremely dependent on the state, and have contributed to its authoritarian features. Crouch's implicit premise, that the middle and capitalist classes are important in democratisation, cannot be accepted so casually. Recent work on comparative and historical analyses on democracy have confirmed the proposition that the bourgeoisie has played a weak role in democratisation (Therborn 1977; Rueschemeyer *et al.* 1992: 269–75).

Chinese business groups did protest against encroachments on their business practices in the 1970s and 1980s, as the syncretic state embarked on cultivating the development of a Malay and state bourgeoisie in the era of the New Economic Policy. The Chinese bourgeoisie in general, particularly its small to medium-scale members, wanted a reduction in statist economic expansion and an end to restrictive economic regulations. The Chinese capitalists bargained with the state for a more favourable reapportionment of economic incentives and share of the economy but never challenged the basic politico-economic system. The basic feature of the state in Malaysia, despite its rentier and patronage practices, has been its consistent pursuit of the developmentalist logic. The state has played a fundamental role in disciplining labour and fostering capitalist development. In the current phase of economic deregulation which began in 1986, closer links have been established between the state and Chinese capital. This change has been the result of increased international competition, the state's attempt to trim down budgetary deficits, and the rise of an increasingly confident Malay corporate class with a stake in high growth. In 1991, the Malaysian Business Council was formed to forge tighter co-operation and the exchange of ideas between the state and capital. The resistance of Chinese business to the state has considerably decreased. There are now new and close ties between the top business men of all ethnic groups. However, there has been no clear change to the political system as a result of this new identity of interests among the bourgeoisie, whether in a more authoritarian or democratic direction. It is safe to say that the bourgeoisie is unlikely to press for political democratisation if economic liberalisation can be obtained without it.

Middle-class reformism and civil society

There are small fractions of the middle class in Malaysia that have been active agents in the development of a civil society. The process of economic modernisation has resulted in the expansion of the intellectual and professional strata, out of which has come the leadership of civil society organisations in the country. But this is as far as modernisation theory can take us, for it is not the general middle class that is the relevant political actor, but the specific visions and heroic acts of individuals within it that have mattered most in Malaysian civil society. The general fortunes of civil society have been tied less to the inexorable process of economic growth, as suggested by Girling (1988: 332), than to the space allowed by the state for its development.

The notion of civil society adopted here goes beyond the usual one of an intermediate sector between the state and the family. I want to consider only those organisations that seek to advance a generalised public interest, not by aiming to take over political power directly, but by trying to influence and criticise state policies (Chazan 1992: 287). There are many organisations that fit this criterion in Malaysia. The prominent ones include Aliran (the Penang-based reform movement), the Environmental Protection Society of Malaysia (EPSM), the Selangor Graduates Society, the Consumer Association of Penang (CAP), Sahabat Alam Malaysia (Friends of the Earth Malaysia), the National Council of Women's Organisations, the Association of Women Lawyers, the Malaysian Council of Churches, the Catholic Resources Centre, Sisters in Islam and the civil rights group, Suaram. There are a few others, such as the Federation of Malaysian Consumer Associations (FOMCA), that are linked to the state but sometimes articulate an independent position.

The rise of many of these associations can be traced to the immediate aftermath of post-1969 politics, when the UMNO became more hegemonic in the polity, and the influence of non-Malay political parties waned. Saravanamuttu (1989: 245) has argued that the impetus to civil society came from the failure of political parties in Malaysia to fulfil 'their historical mission as traditional interest articulators' since they have only excelled as ethnic mobilisers. There was, however, a significant ethnic component to the rise of associational activity since most of the founders and members of civil society groups were often non-Malay. The exclusivity of the UMNO, the weakness of non-Malay ethnic parties, and the preoccupation with ethnicity led a small group of Indian and Chinese intellectuals and professionals to seek an alternative forum to raise public issues. Moreover, as the practices of the state became less transparent with the centralisation of power, and as the media became more tightly controlled, the politically interested middle class also sought new sources of information and analysis. Specific actions of the state also triggered the activism of civil society. Most of these revolved around malpractice and corruption in government, and its environmental policies. The 1980s saw a series of major financial abuses taking place, such as the Bank Bumiputra Finance scandal, the irregular buying and selling of companies by top ministers, and the government's contract-awarding process (*Aliran Monthly*, March 1995: 24–6). The major episodes of environmental protest concerned the siting of a radioactive waste dump in a Chinese community in Perak, and government-sponsored construction of huge dams that caused massive deforestation and threatened the native land rights of the people in Sarawak.

Intellectuals have supplied a high percentage of the leadership in many of these organisations. They have tended to focus on publishing magazines to inform the western-educated middle class about a variety of issues from civil rights violations, environmental degradation, corruption, the universal values of religion, and the human meaning of development. Lawyers have been the most active among professional groups involved in associational activity, and their concerns have been in protecting civil rights, pushing for legislation favourable to women, and conducting forums on human rights and civil liberties. There have been very few business people, engineers, and accountants actively involved in the activities of civil society. It is only by coincidence that some unusually passionate men such as Gurmit Singh of EPSM, and S. M. Idris of the CAP and Sahabat Alam, happen to be an engineer and a business person respectively.

There are some telling features of these public-interest organisations which reflect the limitations imposed by the syncretic state on civil society. Malay membership in these organisations has tended to be smaller than that of non-Malays, since most prefer not to take an overtly critical stance against the government. The reform groups with significant Malay participation have usually worked closely with the government, for example the government-funded Federation of Malaysian Consumer Associations and the National Council of Women. The other characteristic of these groups has been their heavy dependence on a few key figures, and it is not uncommon to see one dominant figure who not only founds an organisation but also plays a vital role in running it, often over a span of one or two decades. Examples include Gurmit Singh, Martin Khor, and S. M. Idris (of both CAP and Sahabat Alam), and Chandra Muzzafar, once a key figure in Aliran. Many of these men have been willing to face verbal attacks, intimidation, and sometimes imprisonment by the regime. Passion, hard work, and bravery have been in short supply in the middle class, and though some segments are interested in public issues, few are prepared to play an activist role.

Because of the thin middle class base for the development of civil society, many organisations face the problem of being very dependent on external funds and international backing. External pressure from organisations such as Amnesty International, the Worldwide Fund for Nature, the AFL-CIO, the International Labour Organization (ILO), and foreign professional associations have sometimes given added leverage to civil society. But the negative aspect of relying on global linkages is that domestic organisations can be labelled by the government as being manipulated by foreign interests. In addition, an unfortunate side-effect of foreign dependence is that it causes rivalry between interest groups for global funds; this has sometimes led to suspicion and lack of co-operation within civil society groups. Some of the leaders of these interest groups, because of their skill in mobilising funds, enjoy a high degree of dominance in their organisations, which may be less than democratically run.

Yet the distinctive aspect of civil society compared to electoral parties has been the relative insignificance of ethnicity as the organising principle. The goals are not directly to advance ethnic interests but broader issues, from the environment to human rights. Malays have some involvement in most of the public-interest organisations and they form an increasing readership of the publications put out by these groups. For example, 30 per cent of the readers of Aliran's publication are Malays. Of the eighty members of the Environmental Protection Society of Malaysia, about 20 to 25 per cent are Malay, 35 to 40 per cent Chinese, and 30 per cent Indian.[9]

The activism of groups has waxed and waned depending on the regime's threat perception of critical activity in society. The relatively thin base of support has meant that they do not enjoy much leverage *vis-à-vis* the government, and are hence at the mercy of the coercive practices of the state. The period of greatest activism was the mid-1980s when many civil society organisations linked up with each other, as well as outside bodies such as the Bar Council of Malaysia, and the DAP, to defend themselves against restrictive legislation on their activities, severe curtailments on press freedom, and unprecedented assaults on the judiciary (Means 1991: 136–45, 234–43). On the environment, associations such as Aliran, Sahabat Alam, and the Environmental Protection Society participated in the formation of various *ad hoc* groups, such as the Papan Support Group and the Perak Anti-Radioactive Committee, to defend and work closely with communities affected by government policies. This period of activism coincided with the pronounced recession in Malaysia in the mid-1980s and the growing splits within the UMNO. The state's vulnerable position provided some space for organisation and mobilisation. But this same vulnerability resulted in the state unleashing its coercive powers in late 1987 by arresting 106 people under the Internal Security Act: the rationale was that a dangerous climate for racial riots was building up. Among those arrested were leaders of opposition parties as well as activists from a vast spectrum of public interest groups, religious bodies, trade unions, and professional associations. While ethnic tensions were indeed building up, often instigated by regime leaders themselves, the detentions were a useful way to tame public interest groups, some of which the Prime Minister had specifically named a year earlier as enemies of the state, such as Aliran, the CAP, the EPSM, the Selangor Graduates Society, and the Malaysian Bar Council (Means 1991: 194).

In the post-1987 climate, civil society has become more cautious and less activist. For the most part, public interest groups have avoided direct links with opposition political parties and have stressed that their activities are non-political. The frequency of public forums has also decreased. The memory of arrests of prominent activists has loomed over these organisations. The regime's ability to restrict discursive activity in society by blacking out the activities and discussions of public interest groups in the highly controlled media has cut their umbilical link with the potentially participatory segment of the middle class. Equally debilitating has been the economic boom conditions since 1988. Many activists complain that the middle class has developed a more accepting and complacent attitude towards society, turning themselves inward into private cultural and religious pursuits. The middle-class cultivation of the self, extending to the preoccupation with children, has become the new praxis.

There are a few groups like Aliran that attempt to keep a critical discourse going through their own publications and forums. The aim is less to change or mobilise against current practices than to preserve an analytical consciousness that might assert itself in more conducive circumstances. Most of the consumer and environmental groups, through school education programmes and courses for civil servants, also wish to raise public consciousness. For the most part public interest organisations have worked within the parameters set by the state. In fact the more accommodating groups have often obtained more concessions from the state than groups more openly critical and independent of it. One example of civil society's role in pushing for moderate reform was the passage of the Domestic Violence Act in May 1994 after eight years of lobbying by women's groups. Although more change-oriented women's groups dismissed the Bill as highly inadequate in establishing domestic violence as a specific crime needing its own set of penalties and enforcement procedures, the Act in principle recognised domestic violence as a crime. What was interesting was the role of politically well-connected groups in convincing the relevant ministers to come up with the legislation.[10] When the leaders of the Association of Women Lawyers tried to persuade the government of the need for a Domestic

Violence Bill, there was much confusion within the ministries over which had jurisdiction over domestic violence. Interestingly, it was civil society groups that made the government understand its own *modus operandi*, locating the relevant ministry as the Ministry of National Unity and Social Development, and prompting its minister to take an active hand in the legislation.

In consumer affairs, the Federation of Malaysian Consumer Associations (FOMCA), an association of mainly Malay university lecturers funded by the Ministry of Domestic and Consumer Affairs, has given added leverage to government in dealing with manufacturers that have overcharged the public or acted unfairly towards consumers. The efforts of consumer associations offset somewhat the powerful influence of manufacturing and trade associations, whose financial strength gives them much sway over top government leaders and officials. FOMCA's activities sometimes conflict with the government's position, for example over the need for strict product liability legislation, but on the whole the organisation helps the government by monitoring prices and allows it to earn goodwill by showing that it responds positively to 'reformable' issues.

Even more vociferous groups like the Environmental Protection Society of Malaysia have had to reconcile themselves to 'critical co-operation' with the government. The government under Dr Mahathir is seen as fixated on capitalist development, and showing little consideration for the social and environmental consequences; hence it is deemed wiser to avoid confrontation. The EPSM has decided to work with the Department of the Environment to help monitor the Environmental Quality Act, and push for an independent body to ensure the impartiality of Environmental Impact Assessment (EIA) studies. According to its leader, the EPSM still reserves the right to criticise activities detrimental to the environment but will focus on educating government officials and company executives on sustainable development and the environment.

One of the dangers for civil society is the new nationalist agenda of the Prime Minister who has embarked on a strong tirade against the 'west' for their policies on human rights, the environment, and security matters, as well as the behaviour of their media. The new nationalism has swept along individuals who were once critical of the government's developmental policies and approach to human rights. The long-standing leader of Aliran, Chandra Muzzafar, who has since founded the Just World Trust, has closely allied himself with the top leadership and has directed his moral energy at criticising perceived western arrogance and hegemony. The CAP, once critical of the government's approach to the environment, has also jumped on the anti-west band-wagon, attacking western countries for their hypocrisy in criticising Third World countries for environmental damage when they consume the bulk of the world's resources. Anti-westernism has all the dangers of engendering a new hypocrisy among the leaders of NGOs, which allows them to proclaim that they are pursuing a moral cause while directing their attack at safe targets.

Civil society in Malaysia has raised social consciousness over key public issues in a way that the formal opposition has never done. But the legitimate arena for its activities has expanded and contracted depending on the state's threat perception of public interest groups. Unfortunately, civil society does not have the leverage to carve out its own democratic space in the public sphere because of the historical process of political development in Malaysia. The new accommodating stand of some public interest groups is perhaps a necessary stage for the further development of civil society in Malaysia. Establishing regularised relations between state and civil society, even at the cost of playing down important public issues, might create a setting whereby neither perceives the other to be a threat, allowing for the gradual consolidation of civil society.

CONCLUSION: THE TRANSFORMATION OF THE SYNCRETIC STATE?

The syncretic state has played a fundamental role in structuring politics in Malaysia. Its roots are in the externally implanted nature of state development in Malaysia, which has produced a pattern of state–society relations that departs fundamentally from the ideal-typical western model, leading to distinct class capacities, ideologies, and identities in society. A major consequence of the state's syncretic approach has been the immobilisation of effective ideologies and alliances which might have challenged the ruling regime and moved it in a more democratic direction.

Future political changes in the country are more likely to come from the loss of coherence of the ruling coalition, particularly the UMNO, than from a more effective political opposition. New political tensions, uncertainties, and opportunities could conceivably arise from the failure of the state elites to manage the various syncretic elements that have facilitated its dominance. The UMNO has been very effective in mediating social-structural transformation in ways which strengthen its position, but there could be limits to its ability to manage ongoing social changes indefinitely. A number of cracks could occur in its political management.

First, the emergence of the Malay middle class and the corporate class could lead to problems in the UMNO's use of Malay ethnicity as an ideology of rule. There are indications that ethnicity has become less salient for the Malay corporate class as its ability to accumulate becomes increasingly based on general economic growth rather than direct state sponsorship. Even the Malay middle class has developed an instrumental attitude to the UMNO, and is showing evidence of shedding its deep ethnic attachment to the party. As many as 400,000 of more than two million UMNO members have failed to register to vote, many of them from the rich and middle-class strata. The leaders of the UMNO have expressed bewilderment at this development, having expected the party to become even stronger as Malays became better off (*NST*, 16 May 1994: 2). Perhaps prosperity and the misgivings about 'money politics' and corruption have exacerbated their political apathy. But a more interesting dialectic might be operating. The UMNO's role in giving Malays greater confidence in their abilities seems to have made the well-off among them see the party as less of an ethnic protector over time. This class is not turning against the UMNO or embracing other political parties, but this does appear to be a chink in its ethnic armour.

Second, the UMNO has always given public prominence to Islam as a way of claiming guardianship over the religion, providing the party with a powerful source of legitimacy. But state-sponsored religions are also inherently problematic to manage because sect formation and deviations from governmental definitions of 'correct religion' become politicised and threatening to the regime. The heavy-handed banning of the Al-Arqam sect as a deviationist group in August 1994 is a case in point. The movement, which claimed a membership of 60,000, had set out to create an Islamic society, rejecting the religious stances of both the PAS and UMNO (*NST*, 6 August 1994: 22). The internal regulation of Islam has led to the use of coercion against ways of being a Muslim other than government-decreed ones. The regime's protection of Islam from the proselytising activities of other religions has received universal assent from Malaysian Muslims, but the terrain has shifted to the more difficult task of managing internal differences within Islam. Excessive reliance on coercion for religious management could potentially delegitimise the regime by undermining its claims to democratic practice as well as raising questions about the validity of the government's own interpretation of Islam. In Malaysia the use of force has usually had the tacit support of the majority because it has been used selectively and sequentially. Large sections of the population have not perceived the regime as a harsh, authoritarian state, as the Thais, South Koreans, and Filipinos perceived their pre-democratic regimes. The danger for the regime is that it might be moving towards the coercive pole of the spectrum, in which a broader array of groups might come under pressure from the state. These include opposition parties, labour unions, middle-class public interest organisations, and religious groups. The result might be that perceptions of the regime's essential democratic form might shrink over time.

Third, with the possibly shrinking pay-off of ethnicity and religion as bases for the UMNO's legitimacy, the party's claim to the right to rule will have to be based on the nation's economic performance. The long-standing economic record and the present boom conditions have served it well, but any future decline in growth could have serious consequences for the UMNO and the Barisan. Even with high growth the UMNO is not free from internal factional conflicts and disaffection from certain segments of the population. A retardation in growth for any length of time will have system-wide ramifications not only because it would be inherently delegitimating, but also because the party might not then be able to claim the cover of being the protector of the Malays.

I have laid out some possible fault-lines in the state, with no implication either that the regime cannot solve them in the future or that an imminent change in the political system is on the cards. The UMNO has since 1994 undertaken to cultivate a cleaner image by coming up with new amendments to its constitution to limit vote buying and corruption. It is also coming up with new syncretic possibilities, such as opening the party to non-Malay Muslims and the non-Muslim *bumiputera* of East Malaysia, and is willing to consider giving associate UMNO membership to individuals from the tiny Portuguese and Baba communities. New syncretic possibilities could replace the loss of old formulas of political rule.

The key point, however, is that it is going to be the unravelling of the regime that will make for political changes, not the behaviour of the political opposition. Even if the regime fails on all counts, one cannot expect a smooth transition to a more liberal or democratic system. My analysis of the formal political opposition parties shows that they are incapable of providing a coherent alternative to the current regime. In other words, they are unlikely to capitalise on a crisis, economic or otherwise, to bring effective political stability and a new democratic society. Civil society groups have a greater repository of alternative ideas and visions that could favour democratic politics. However, the base from which they operate is very thin and they are not sufficiently interlinked under a political party – due to regime controls rather than by choice – to offer an immediate programmatic alternative to the regime.

NOTES

1 For a different approach, see Jesudason (1995).
2 Data compiled from *Mid-Term Review of the Sixth Malaysia Plan 1991–1995* (1993: 65, Table 3.3) and *Third Malaysia Plan* (1976: 182, Tables 9–7). The middle class is defined as persons in professional, technical, administrative, managerial, clerical and sales sectors.
3 Information obtained from interview with a PAS party official, Kuala Lumpar, May 1994.
4 Information obtained from interview with Semangat '46 official, Kuala Lumpur, May 1994. Dr Mahathir Mohamd has himself expressed worry about the role of money politics, particularly over UMNO politicians offering material inducements to get positions in the party. See *Aliran Monthly*, March 1995: 13.
5 Interview with a PAS official.
6 Information obtained from interview with an MTUC official, May 1994.
7 According to Mann (1993: 65), lawyers had a corporate identity reducible to neither state nor society, while the law had an emergent power in Europe which even absolute rulers did not like to be seen infringing.
8 Personal communication with a lecturer in a leading Malaysian university, September 1994.
9 Information obtained from officials in the EPSM and Aliran, May 1994.
10 Information obtained from officials in the National Council of Women and Association of Women Lawyers, May 1994.

REFERENCES

Ackerman, Susan (1986) ' Ethnicity and Trade Unionism in Malaysia: a Case Study of a Shoe Workers' Union', in Raymond Lee (ed.) *Ethnicity and Ethnic Relations in Malaysia*, De Kalb, Northern Illinois University, Center for Southeast Asian Studies, pp. 145–67.
Barraclough, Simon (1985) 'The Dynamics of Coercion in the Malaysian Political Process', *Modern Asian Studies*, 19(4), October: 797–822.
Boulanger, Clare L. (1992) 'Ethnic Order and Working Class Strategies in West Malaysia', *Journal of Contemporary Asia*, 22(3): 322–34.
Brown, David (1994) *The State and Ethnic Politics in Southeast Asia*, London: Routledge.
Case, William (1993) 'Semi-Democracy in Malaysia: Withstanding the Pressures for Regime Change', *Pacific Affairs*, 66: 183–205.
Chazan, Naomi (1992) 'Africa's Democratic Challenge: Strengthening Civil Society and the State', *World Policy Journal*, 9(2): 279–308.
Clough, Cecil H. (ed.) (1992) *Profession, Vocation, and Culture in Later Medieval England*, Liverpool: Liverpool University Press.
Crouch, Harold (1992) 'Authoritarian Trends, the UMNO Split and the Limits

to State Power', in J. S. Kahn and Francis Loh (eds) *Fragmented Vision: Culture and Politics in Contemporary Malaysia*, Sydney, Allen & Unwin: pp. 21–43.

—— (1993) 'Malaysia: Neither Authoritarian nor Democratic', in K. Hewison, R. Robison, and G. Rodan (eds) *Southeast Asia in the 1990s: Authoritarianism, Democracy and Capitalism*, St Leonards: Allen & Unwin, pp. 133–58.

Girling, John (1988) 'Development and Democracy in Southeast Asia', *Pacific Review*, 1(4): 332–40.

Gomez, Edmund Terrence (1991) *Money Politics in the Barisan Nasional*, Kuala Lumpur: Forum.

Habermas, Jurgen (1989) *The Structural Transformation of the Public Sphere: an Inquiry into a Category of Bourgeois Society*, Cambridge, Mass.: MIT Press.

Holmes, Stephen (1988) 'Gag Rules or the Politics of Omission', in Jon Elster and Rune Slagstad (eds) *Constitutionalism and Democracy*, Cambridge: Cambridge University Press, pp. 19–58.

Humana, Charles (ed.) (1992) *World Human Rights Guide*, Oxford: Oxford University Press.

Jesudason, James (1995) 'Statist Democracy and the Limits Civil Society in Malaysia' *Journal of Commonwealth and Comparative Politics*,, 33(3): 335–56.

Jomo, K. S. and Cheek, Ahmad Shabery (1992) 'Malaysia's Islamic Movements', in J. S. Kahn, and Francis Loh (eds) *Fragmented Vision: Culture and Politics in Contemporary Malaysia*, Sydney: Allen & Unwin, pp. 79–106.

Jones, David M. and Brown, David (1994) 'Singapore and the Myth of the Liberalizing Middle Class', *Pacific Review*, 7(1): 79–87.

Khong Kim Hoong (1991) *Malaysia's General Election 1990: Continuity, Change, and Ethnic Politics*, Research Notes and Discussion Paper no. 74, Singapore: Institute of Southeast Asian Studies.

Khoo Kay Jin (1992) 'The Grand Vision: Mahathir and Modernization', in J. S. Kahn and Francis Loh (eds) *Fragmented Vision: Culture and Politics in Contemporary Malaysia*, Sydney: Allen & Unwin, pp. 44–76.

Lipset, Seymour M. (1960) *Political Man*, Garden City: Anchor Books.

Mann, Michael (1993) *The Sources of Social Power (vol. 2): The Rise of Classes and Nation-States, 1760–1914*, Cambridge: Cambridge University Press.

Means, Gordon P. (1991) *Malaysian Politics: the Second Generation*, Singapore: Oxford University Press.

Mid-Term Review of the Sixth Malaysia Plan 1991–1995, (1993) Kuala Lumpur: Percetakan Nasional Malaysia Berhad.

Peletz, Michael G. (1993) 'Sacred Texts and Dangerous Words: the Politics of Law and Cultural Rationalization in Malaysia', *Comparative Studies in Society and History*, 35(1): 66–109.

Piven, Frances F. and Cloward, Richard A. (1977) *Poor People's Movements: Why They Succeed, How They Fail*, New York: Vintage.

Rokkan, Stein (1975) 'Dimensions of State Formation and Nation-Building: a Possible Paradigm for Research on Variations within Europe', in Charles Tilly (ed.) *The Formation of National States in Western Europe*, Princeton, NJ: Princeton University Press, pp. 562–600.

Rueschemeyer, D., Stephens, E. H., and Stephens, J. D. (1992) *Capitalist Development and Democracy*, Chicago: University of Chicago Press.

Saravanamuttu, Johan (1989) 'Authoritarian Statism and Strategies for Democratization: Malaysia in the 1980s', in Peter Limqueco (ed.) *Partisan Scholarship: Essays in Honour of Renato Constuntino*, Manila and Wollongong: JCA Publishers, pp. 233–51.

—— (1992) 'The State, Ethnicity and the Class Factor: Addressing Nonviolent, Democratic Change in Malaysia', in Kumar Rupesinghe (ed.) *Internal Conflict and Governance*, New York: St Martin's Press, pp. 44–64.

Singh, Hari (1991) 'Political Change in Malaysia: the Role of Semangat' 46', *Asian Survey*, 31(8): 712–28.

Skocpol, Theda R. (1985) 'Bringing the State Back In: Strategies of Analysis in Current Research', in P. Evans, D. Rueschemeyer, and T. Skocpol (eds) *Bringing the State Back In*, New York: Cambridge University Press, pp. 3–37.

Therborn, Goran (1977) 'The Rule of Capital and the Rise of Democracy', *New Left Review*, 103, May–June: 3–41.

Third Malaysia Plan, (1976) Kuala Lumpur: Government Press.

Tilly, Charles (1985) 'War Making and State Making as Organized Crime', in P. Evans, D. Rueschemeyer, and T. Skocpol (eds) *Bringing the State Back In*, New York: Cambridge University Press, pp. 169–91.

6 The changing ruling elite and political opposition in China

Anita Chan *

China is an anomaly among the countries included in this volume. Whereas these other ruling Asian elites do not claim to be the representative of any particular social group, the People's Republic of China (PRC), established as a one-party state in 1949, explicitly claimed to be a 'dictatorship' of the proletariat. Admittedly the situation has changed in China since Mao's death. Under Mao the state was totalitarian; under Deng, it has softened to become authoritarian and only in rhetoric clings to a class-based self-definition. There is now even talk in China about learning from the 'Four Little Dragons'. Guangdong, said Deng Xiaoping, should be the 'Fifth Dragon' in the not too distant future (*Reuters*, 27 February 1992). Thus, Deng is appropriating the idea of 'new authoritarianism' that was expounded by a group of intellectuals in China in 1988–9 (Rosen and Zou 1991). 'New authoritarianism' in substance is very similar to the 'soft authoritarianism' that has formed the tenet of the Singaporean ideology: soft on the economy, but authoritarian in the political sphere (Roy 1994: 231–42). Soft authoritarianism is the commonality towards which China and some of its Southeast Asian neighbours are converging.

In its rhetoric, the Chinese Communist Party (CCP) today would prefer to characterise itself as a socialist democracy, impressing on its own people and the world *ad nauseam* that China possesses 'socialism with Chinese characteristics'. The emphasis is on the 'uniqueness' of its Chineseness, a construct that is manufactured to fend off any critical efforts to measure China against anything that is called democratic. To locate this 'uniqueness', we have to begin with an examination of the nature of the Chinese state and its oppositional social forces.

Apart from identifying where opposition in China derives from, it is important to identify what is being opposed, whether it is (i) the official ideology; (ii) specific policies but not the official ideology; or (iii) the people in power because they are not living up to the ideology they profess.

The first involves the most fundamental form of opposition, in as much as its protagonists seek to undermine the legitimising tenets of the ruling elite. It involves throwing out both the baby and the bath water. The second involves loyal opposition, where the challenge to extant power is not in the fundamentals, but limited to certain policies or the speed with which policies are being implemented. Such an opposition may seek to replace or share power with those at present monopolising it (Punnett 1973: 9–29). The third case refers to the traditional Chinese phenomenon of 'remonstration'. The remonstrators challenge neither the ideology nor the superiority of those in power. They see their own role as advising errant powers-that-be to uphold their moral integrity, while placing their own loyalty to their masters at a premium even at the risk of endangering themselves by incurring the wrath of the master (Nathan 1985: 24–5).

We shall examine briefly how these three categories manifested themselves in the decades under Mao; and then in greater detail since Deng Xiaoping's assumption of power. We shall attempt to identify which social groups, under what circumstances, and by what means have asserted their opposition to the authorities. An obvious development since the mid-1980s is that the political elite is rapidly becoming China's economic elite; and it shall also be observed that this changing nature of the ruling elite creates new class relationships and a shift in the patterns of political opposition.

THE NATURE OF THE STATE AND 'OPPOSITION' UNDER MAO AND DENG

China under Mao, like other Leninist polities, was a party-state in that there was no distinction between the ruling party and the government. Yet when Mao's personality cult was at its height, his power overrode that of the CCP. Even top national and party leaders were cowed in his presence (Teiwes 1988; Li 1994).

Between 1949 and 1976, the year Mao died, two major political upheavals shook China: the Hundred Flowers Movement (1956–7) and the Cultural Revolution (1966–9), both of which were instigated by Mao when he called on the people to speak up against the party. When huge numbers of people responded to his call, plunging the country into a frenzy of protest actions, Mao suppressed the upheavals with an iron fist and portrayed these disturbances as a vicious plot to overthrow the Chairman and the party.

Actually the protagonists of the Hundred Flowers Movement, the intellectuals, mostly acted as remonstrators.[1] Less than a decade after the revolution, many of them were genuine adherents of Marxist-Leninist-Maoist ideology (Yue and Wakeman 1985; Fang 1990). Neither was the socialist ideology under attack during the Cultural Revolution. The protagonists battled over who should be anointed the true defenders of Chairman Mao (Chan 1985). For a small minority, political disillusionment and opposition came when Mao began suppressing the movement at the end of the 1960s; for most, scepticism came considerably later.[2]

These two upheavals were products of a suppressive polity which normally provided no formal channels through which to address personal and class grievances. In theory, there was the so-called 'mass line', where dissatisfaction from the bottom could reach the top through 'mass organisations' such as the Women's Federation, the official trade union, the peasant association, the Communist Youth League, etc. There was also the system of People's Congresses, which were supposed to be the supreme legislative bodies elected by the people. In addition, under the Party's United Front Department, a Chinese People's Political Consultative Committee (CPPCC) met irregularly, this being a body of prestigious people appointed by the party to serve as 'representatives' of society's sectoral interests. The CCP was supposed to feel the pulse of society through consultation with these representatives. Above all, the party, claiming to be the vanguard of the proletariat (which in China was defined as including both workers and peasants), was supposed to be in the service of the masses, while leading them in a march towards utopian Communism.

All of this was entirely window-dressing: such bodies were absolutely devoid of power and influence. All power lay within the party, and the omnipresent 'ears and eyes' of the party, as they were called, kept unrelenting watch over all behaviour and all thinking deemed deviant. Under such a closed and suppressive state-dominated society, people dared not think unthinkable thoughts. Thus when Deng allowed pent-up anger to be released once he ascended to power at the end of the 1970s, the Democracy Wall Movement blossomed from 1979 to 1981. But the protest was not directed against the fundamental tenets of socialism. On the contrary, the general mood was supportive of Deng's promised liberalisation programme. It was neither anti-Deng nor anti-socialist. But the aspirations for personal freedom, the style, and the anti-bureaucratic content of the protests were more than Deng could tolerate. He ordered suppressive measures and threw some of the protesters into jail for ten or more years (Seymour 1980; Amnesty

International 1984). What should be underlined about this movement is that the intellectuals did not emerge within it as a leading force.

In the early 1980s, Deng and his supporters introduced a series of macro- and micro-economic reforms to lift the country out of economic stagnation. In the countryside agriculture was decollectivised and the free market allowed to flourish; this was followed by reforms in the industrial sector to give greater incentives to enterprises. Welfare socialism was to be gradually abolished so as to effect successful marketisation. China was to enter the global economy. Both foreign-funded and indigenous capitalist sectors were allowed to develop.

Economic liberalisation went hand in hand with limited political liberalisation. Individuals gained some personal and organisational political space from the reform process. Existing organisations tried to wrest more autonomy from the state, and new organisations proliferated as new social groups began to articulate their interests (Unger and Chan 1995).

In addition, political power was decentralised sectorally along bureaucratic lines and regionally to the localities. This led to the rise of bureaucratic sectoral interests, which some scholars have dubbed 'fragmented authoritarianism' (Lieberthal and Lampton 1992: 6–13). As the state transformed itself from totalitarian to authoritarian, various bureaucracies, the most organised and powerful institutions after the Communist Party, have manoeuvred for political turf, and more recently for economic turf. They have become active proponents of their own sectoral interests. Simultaneously, local governments are becoming more and more independent. Party edicts from Beijing are often thwarted by local authorities, especially in areas well-endowed with resources and local tax revenues.

On the surface, an emergent civil society is in the making in China – if civil society is defined as social groups struggling for political space *vis-à-vis* the state in a zero-sum game. However, if defined differently, as the freedom and dignity of the individual, as citizenry endowed with certain rights *vis-à-vis* the state *and* society, then whether civil society is emerging in China is debatable (Chamberlain 1994). Also debatable is whether civil society necessarily leads to a democratic political system. As argued in Rodan's analysis of Singapore in this volume (Chapter 4), the expansion of civil society can take place without dismantling authoritarian rule. As economic and political liberalisation continues to deepen, the possibility of social groupings articulating their interests and forming themselves into a political opposition of sorts becomes a threatening reality to the ruling elite. The following pages will identify the various kinds of political opposition and the strategy taken by the elite to pre-empt the development of any autonomous and organised political opposition.

POLITICAL OPPOSITION UNDER DENG

As part and parcel of the policy for limited liberalisation, the government's strategy is to pursue a policy of co-optation and inclusion of the elite groups within society; but *vis-à-vis* ordinary people, the leadership pursues a policy of exclusion.

The 'loyal opposition' in China's legislature and other forums

This kind of opposition involves two kinds of elites: portions of the intelligentsia and the new capitalists. Unlike under Mao, when intellectuals were denigrated as 'the stinking ninth category', and when anyone suspected of wanting to enjoy an income or lifestyle slightly above average was denounced as 'bourgeois', today the intellectual elites and successful entrepreneurs are portrayed in positive images and endowed with privileges in the formal political structure. The intellectuals are valued for their technical skills and the new capitalists for their adroitness in the primary accumulation of wealth. They are permitted by the party to articulate their respective interests by way of the so-called Democratic Parties (DPs) and the All China Federation of Industry and Commerce (ACFIC), which are prominently represented in the National People's Congress (NPC) and the Chinese People's Political Consultative Committee (CPPCC).

The intellectual elite

Before 1949, while the CCP on the Left and the Kuomintang (KMT) on the Right competed for power, there were groups of well-known intellectuals who would not join either. They were no less idealistic, nationalistic, or politically committed than the Communists in their opposition to right-wing KMT politics. Ideologically they tended to be liberal social democrats who wanted to realise their socialist ideals through a democratic parliamentary system. Those who were inclined more to the Left were fellow-travellers of the Communists. Yet they were elitist and never cared to cultivate a mass base: 'They were groups of figures enmeshed in a complex web based on personal relationships rather than modern political parties' (Jeans 1992: 14; see also Spar 1992; Wong 1993; Van Slyke 1967). Historians characterise them as a third force, though they did not truly contend for power. Instead, they ultimately threw in their lot with the Communists. As one historian writes of one of the best-known of these figures:

> Despite his multifarious activities on the fringes of the power structure, it was difficult for him to conceive of himself in a truly oppositional role. Indeed in their search for a new role, many of his contemporaries preferred, as did he himself, to pursue social and cultural reforms, rather than politics. Whatever their private convictions, they did not, in the final analysis, cross the boundaries of a political culture that devised for them a legitimate role as loyal opponents.
>
> (Curran 1992: 105)

After 1949, the CCP was adept at co-opting them into playing satellite roles in the polity (Seymour 1987). The United Front Department of the CCP took charge of reorganising them into the eight Democratic Parties, each of which was assigned to recruit its members from one particular grouping: (i) two of the DPs were reserved for high-level academics in the social and natural sciences;[3] (ii) two professional associations were reserved for doctors, educators, and journalists;[4] (iii) one 'party' was to incorporate business people;[5] and lastly, (iv) three were specifically for people with KMT, Taiwanese, and overseas Chinese connections.[6] The CCP imposed strict limitations on the breadth and numbers of their membership. For example, they were not allowed to recruit from small towns or villages, from among peasants, workers, or ethnic minorities. This served to reinforce and perpetuate their elitist nature. At the same time, the Party placed the heads of the DPs into high-level deputy ministerial positions, providing them with high social status and material benefits. Within a few years the DPs acquired the reputation of being 'flower vases' of the CCP.

But these once politically active idealists turned out to be unwilling to serve merely as puppets. When the Hundred Flowers Movement in 1956–7 presented an opportunity they spoke out with surprising alacrity, criticising the party for being dictatorial, debunking the collectivisation and nationalisation programmes, and castigating emerging corruption. They held discussion forums, launched recruitment drives, and actively mobilised their regional branches. Some demanded political independence and political equality with the CCP. The CCP's crackdown on the DPs was quick in coming – and thorough. Thousands of ordinary DP members were branded as anti-socialist and anti-party Rightists and sent off to the countryside or into labour camps. The DP leaders lost their government posts, but their high status at least spared them imprisonment, unlike many of their followers. The DPs were effectively silenced for the next twenty years (Hinton 1958: 39–46).

When Deng Xiaoping came to power, among the liberalisation policies he launched were moves to revive the DPs under the slogan of 'instituting multiparty co-operation under the leadership of the Chinese Communist Party' (Chi and Huang 1987: 259). With the permission of the CCP, in the 1980s, until the 1989 protest movement, all of the DPs rapidly recruited new members, doubling or even trebling in size (Table 6.1).

The largest and most prestigious of them, the Democratic League composed of high-level intellectuals and academics, expanded from 16,000 to 99,000 between 1983 and 1989. The DPs first urgently rejuvenated their ageing membership, not having recruited for more than twenty years. They engaged in proto-party activities, reaching a climax in 1988 and early 1989 when ferment in society reached new heights. DP journals advocated numerous reforms, which if put into practice would have meant the emergence of independent political parties. Some suggested rewriting the constitution to legalise the status of the DPs as political parties (see *Solidarity News (Tuanjie Bao)*, 31 January 1989; *CPPCC News (Zhengxie Bao)*, 3 March 1989). Others wanted equal status with the CCP, much as Japan's opposition parties enjoyed equal status with the Liberal Democratic Party even though the latter had monopolised the government for many terms (see *Solidarity News*, 31 January 1989). In Shanghai the municipal government began using the phrase 'non-Communist Party personage' rather than 'non-party personage' in polite recognition that there were more political parties than one, the CCP. There were calls for a more independent recruitment policy and for expansion of membership beyond the DP-restricted recruitment pool (see *CPPCC News*, 25 November 1988). Some advocated development of political party consciousness (see *CPPCC News*, 25 November 1988). Some even went further than their forefathers in the 1950s – calling for the establishment of horizontal linkages between the eight DPs. In other words, some DP members were willing to put aside their sectarian history to band into a kind of coalition *vis-à-vis* the CCP. One article specifically proposed that the DPs should collectively represent the interests of the intellectuals since the CCP claimed to represent peasants and workers (see *CPPCC News*, 5 July 1988).[7]

Top CCP leaders, such as Hu Yaobang and Zhao Ziyang of the reformist faction, were known to be supportive of the DPs. Just before the outbreak of the 1989 protest movement, Zhao was in the process of drafting a document to expand the role of the DPs in the government,

Table 6.1 Increases in membership of the DPs and ACFIC, 1983–93

	1983	1984	1988	1989	1990	1991	1992	1993
China Democratic League	16,000	50,000	81,000	99,000	89,000	99,000	106,000	110,000
The Nationalist Revolutionary Committee	18,000	20,000	37,000	39,133	40,000	40,000	40,000	42,000
China National Construction Association	24,767	25,000	46,425	50,000	46,000	50,000	53,500	56,000
China Association for Promoting Democracy	15,000	15,000	N/A	48,000	31,000	48,000	50,000	53,000
Chinese Peasants' and Workers' Democratic Party	13,770	N/A	43,000	46,000	35,000	46,000	48,000	48,000
Zhi Gong Party	2,200	1,300	N/A	10,000	8,000	10,000	10,000	10,000
September Third Study Society	11,014	25,000	40,000	45,000	40,000	47,000	48,766	50,000
Tai Meng	N/A	N/A	N/A	1,100	1,200	N/A	1,300	1,700
Total Democratic Party memberships	*100,751*	*136,300*	*247,425*	*337,133*	*289,000*	*340,000*	*356,266*	*369,000*
All China Federation of Industry and Commerce	N/A	N/A	N/A	N/A	500,000	N/A	N/A	620,000

Source: The figures for DP membership is taken from Gerry Groot, 'The Chinese Democratic Parties since T'ianamen', an unpublished paper, 1994

judiciary, and legislature (Seymour 1992: 289–91). The head of the CCP's United Front Department, which is the watchdog over the DPs, was himself a comparative liberal and encouraged democratisation within the DPs, though within limits. Encouraged by this liberal political atmosphere, in 1988 and early 1989 the Democratic League convened two forums to discuss sensitive issues. These decided to reject the leader the CCP had hand-picked for them, the famous Chinese sociologist Fei Xiaotong, and to change the League's benign motto of 'Do good work, do concrete work', to 'Democracy and science'. More personally challenging to CCP leaders was the suggestion that high-level officials' children should make public their personal bank accounts.[8] The Zhigong Party, with its wealthy overseas Chinese connections, made noises about becoming financially independent of CCP funding.

At the height of the 1989 popular protest movement some DP members came out into the streets both as individuals and as party members. From February to June various members in the top hierarchy of the DPs signed petitions calling for the release of political prisoners, urging the CCP and the government to open a dialogue with the protesting students and calling for the ideals of democracy and patriotism to be upheld. Of the fifty-seven National People's Congress (NPC) Standing Committee members who signed an open letter urging the convening of an emergency meeting to dismiss Li Peng, at least nine can be identified as coming from the top echelons of the DPs.[9] In an unprecedented development, the Beijing Autonomous Workers' Federation that emerged on Tiananmen Square went to the DPs to seek help to have their organisation legalised (Seymour 1992: 303). In short, other social groups were beginning to see the DPs as both influential and independent of the CCP.

But the DPs could not hold onto their claims to independence after the 4 June crackdown. They entirely capitulated and reverted to mouthing support for the CCP. Yet their about-turn can also be interpreted as a sign of political maturity. As the Chinese saying goes, adept politicians retreat at the right time and advance when the time is ripe. Pragmatic DP leaders preferred to lie low at a time of suppression.

The 1989 upheaval coincided with the collapse of Communism in the Soviet Union and Eastern Europe. In recognition of this, the CCP decided that to ward off further major disturbances in China, it was best to co-opt the intellectuals and professionals and to open up wider the channels for the frustrated intellectual elite to participate in the polity. Thus, at the end of 1989, the CCP issued a major document promising to promote the influence of the DPs (see *Beijing Review*, 5–11 March

1990: 14–18). Henceforth they were to be referred to as 'parties participating in government affairs' (*canzhengdang*). The phrase 'multi-party cooperation under the leadership of the CCP' was changed to 'multi-party cooperation led by the CCP'. The removal of 'under' (*xia*) is significant in that it means the DPs are no longer considered as subordinate to the CCP (Liu 1990: 7–8). The document specified, however, that the DPs were not to assume that they might have a turn at ruling the country, as 'opposition parties do not exist in China'. But there was to be more consultation between the CCP and DPs, more important government posts would be opened up to DP members, and more DP members would sit in the NPC and CPPCC (see *Beijing Review*, 19–25 February 1990: 4–5). The importance of the DPs will therefore be contingent on the ability of the NPC and CPPCC to function as they are supposed to on paper. In the next section, it will be seen that these two political institutions are indeed gradually assuming their constitutional functions. In 1993 the roles of the DPs were enshrined in the constitution (*Legal Daily (Fazhi Ribao)*, 5 April 1993).[10] In short, the DPs' agitation for power in the 1980s had paid off after the 1989 upheaval.

The DPs have come a long way since their rebirth in the early 1980s. Their willingness to play second fiddle to the CCP indicates a strong urge to build up separate identities as a 'loyal opposition'. But will they ever become really 'democratic', that is, live up to what their name implies? My reading is that they will not. The CCP's willingness to share some power with the DPs should be seen as a willingness to share a small portion of power among a larger circle of elites. Neither do the DPs have any intention of turning into mass parties. Maintaining the 'quality' of the members is an oft-cited reason for not expanding their pool of recruitment. In fact, it has become more difficult to be admitted into a DP than into the CCP, since only those who have attained a certain professional ranking are qualified to apply, whereas anyone, by the soft criterion of political commitment, can apply to join the CCP.

The three DPs that are reserved for educational, medical/ scientific, and journalistic personnel function more like professional associations. Much of their energy is directed to advancing their members own professional interests and providing them with better social services. On occasion, they tender their expert professional advice to the government on policy matters within their professional spheres. But they lack a distinct political mission.

The two most important DPs are the China Democratic League (for high-level intellectuals) and the China National Construction Association (for people involved in economic matters). The former has always been the more assertive politically. It is also by far the largest, with a membership of about 150,000 in 1994. The pool from which it can recruit members is wider. According to a high-level member in the know, the CCP is particularly sensitive to the League's activities.[11]

The China National Construction Association is made up of economists, business people, and government specialists involved in overseeing the economy. As reforming the economy has become the priority of the government, the prestige and influence of some of its leading members have increased. It is likely that over the next several years, they will move even closer to the centre of power, but whether they would want to transform the Association into a political party is doubtful. If they did, their elitist posture would deprive them of a mass base, and without the driving force of any sense of mission, given that their key members do not possess an articulated ideology, all they can do is to append themselves to the CCP's ideology. To complicate matters, this is currently in a state of flux.

The capitalists

The other elite which the CCP is willing to incorporate into its fold comprises the newborn capitalists. Generally they are referred to in China as 'entrepreneurs', in that the term 'capitalist' cannot be applied in a state which espouses 'socialism'. By social origin they are of three types: the new capitalists who rose from ground zero; the 'bureaucratic capitalists' or 'nomenklatura capitalists' who originated from the political elite and who sometimes still have one foot in the political realm; and the 'red capitalists' from the old moneyed families.

The new capitalists tend to have started off small as 'self-employed labourers' (*geti laodongzhe*), and with wealth have attained the official social status of 'entrepreneurs'. In the first half of the 1980s they were defensive about their success and felt that they were being discriminated against by government policies and corrupt local bureaucrats (Young 1991). With the 1989 Tiananmen crackdown, the precarious nature of their status became evident when the government carried out a campaign against them, ostensibly to wipe out corruption (Chan and Unger 1991: 106–26). But more recently, as their numbers and assets have increased geometrically, reaching 184,000 'entrepreneurs' by mid-1993, they have been granted a more positive official image (see *People's Run Economy (Minying jingji)*, 24 April 1994).

The nomenklatura capitalists are officials and their close kin who have amassed wealth illicitly, through corruption, nepotism, and inside deals, transforming power and state resources into private wealth. Understandably, their assets are difficult to estimate.

The 'red capitalists', too, had a better headstart than the self-employed labourers. The original 'red capitalists' came from prominent pre-revolution families of great wealth. They were used by the government under Mao in its contacts with overseas Chinese and sometimes were given official positions, hence 'red capitalists'. Under Deng they have been able to resume their business networks and in the 1990s they are hailed for helping in the effort to lift China out of economic stagnation.

The two most prominent of the 'red capitalists', Rong Yiren and Wang Guangying, are prime examples. Rong was from an extremely wealthy Shanghai family and had been appointed deputy minister of the textile industry in the 1950s. Wang's Tianjin pedigree combines wealth and power. His brother-in-law was none other than Liu Shaoqi, one of the handful of top CCP leaders (who later became Mao's arch-victim). Both Rong and Wang are eulogised today. Reportedly, Deng Xiaoping personally invited them to re-enter business and to make big money for the country (*Beijing Daily (Beijing Ribao)*, 16 May 1993; *Beijing Youth News (Beijing Qingnian Bao)*, 3 January 1993). In the 1980s, Rong headed the China International Trust and Investment Corp (CITIC), the biggest of China's 'state' investment companies, with an outpost in Hong Kong.[12] More recently, he was appointed Vice President of China. Wang, for his part, was sent to Hong Kong in 1983 to found the Guangda Company, which has emerged as a powerful state development corporation. As one indication of the ambiguity in the distinction between state and private capital, the Guangda Company, ostensibly a state enterprise, includes in its title one of the Chinese characters of Wang's name.

To incorporate the interests of these three kinds of capitalists into the political structure, the All China Federation of Industry and Commerce (ACFIC, *Gongshanglian*) was revived at the beginning of the economic reforms, with Rong as chairman. Reportedly, Rong and other former capitalists were reimbursed the interest that had been owed to them by the government for the nationalisation of their properties in the 1950s, and with part of that large sum they contributed to the financial base of the revived ACFIC. It was granted a status equivalent to a sort of ninth Democratic Party. Like the DPs, the ACFIC has been placed under the supervision of the CCP's United Front Department, and state bureaucrats were sent to establish the ACFIC headquarters and branches in the provinces. The ACFIC was to be another 'bridge' between the state and society, in this instance the country's new capitalists. The ostensible function of the ACFIC was to implement 'political education' among its members (Liu and Shen 1992: 1), but within a few years it was instead largely pursuing its own members' interests.

In May 1993, the ACFIC established a national research organisation whose ostensible mission is to conduct research about private entrepreneurs. The organisation's real purpose is to create favourable publicity on behalf of the new capitalists. The array of celebrities invited for the opening ceremony in the distant city of Taiyuan, the provincial capital of Shanxi province in central China, was a reflection of the kind of influence and support the ACFIC was seeking. Participants included important people from the judiciary, the NPC, CPPCC, and CCP, and various sectors of the government. Also included were provincial-level officials, officials from the trade and industrial sectors, well-known academics and prominent private entrepreneurs who had recently risen into the NPC and CPPCC. The 140 participants (I was the only foreigner among them) rubbed shoulders and exchanged information. They had assembled for one common purpose – to raise the status of the ACFIC and 'private entrepreneurs'. Private entrepreneurs publicly poured out their grievances about the period of post-1989 suppression. Local officials from poor provinces pleaded for help in getting more private enterprises on their feet in order to enliven their failing economies. The atmosphere reverberated with a strong sense of historical mission and solidarity. The entire national conference, costing a great deal of money, was funded by three local 'private entrepreneurs'.

As can be seen, the ACFIC, though enjoying the political status of a Democratic Party, is quite different from the DPs. It has a broad class-based constituency and a burgeoning ideology, both of which the DPs lack. Moreover, the ACFIC had 620,000 members as of the end of 1992, half of whom were private entrepreneurs before 1949. The number of ACFIC members is twice that of all the eight DPs combined.[13] The ACFIC can also afford to be financially independent, drawing on its investments and the wealth of its membership. The DPs' and the ACFIC's increased participation in politics as a 'loyal opposition' will only be meaningful if the NPC and CPPCC assume an increasingly independent stance as China's legislature and main consultative body. Their power has expanded in the past one and a half decades, though this is generally not recognised in the western press or among western China scholars. The bodies are routinely described as 'rubber stamps', as tools of the CCP, an image reinforced by photographs and television coverage of some 2,000 bored and docile-looking conference attendants raising their hands in unison when required to show support for CCP agendas.

Congresses indeed do *not* provide floors for open, heated debates or dissenting views. But the NPC and CPPCC are not as ineffectual as they seem. The CCP has granted much of China's law-making to the NPC (Tanner 1994), which is nursing its organisational strength and capacity. As O'Brien (1994: 101) would have it, the NPC is the site of 'interorganisational wrangling, bureaucratic articulation, and opportunistic organisational development'. Contrary to being a mere rubber stamp, the NPC has been exerting a moderating influence on the CCP's reform policies (O'Brien 1990). True, its members are constrained by a political culture which puts a premium on a formal show of consensus, combined with a pragmatic recognition that the CCP is in command. Thus a façade of unity at public meetings is maintained for general consumption. But once the CCP had begun instituting economic and political reforms from above, divided interests and heated debates surfaced behind closed doors, despite the continued display of unity. This is well demonstrated by my own research on the passage of Chinese labour legislation. The Labour Law, passed in July 1994, had gone through marathon debates and lobbying, entailing some three dozen drafts over the previous fifteen years. This reflected contrary interests that required political negotiations and compromises within the elite circle (Chan 1995). With the voting on Bills in the NPC no longer by public show of hands but by pushing individual buttons, nonapproval has become much easier. Though Bills are still often passed with few dissenting votes or abstentions, this can be interpreted as a willingness by those with differing views to accept amended drafts and to compromise after genuine negotiations.

The public has also taken the NPC more seriously since the late 1980s. When the NPC convenes in Beijing, it is no longer unusual to see petitioners and lobbyists trying to contact delegates. According to an NPC delegate from Hong Kong whom I interviewed, several Guangdong peasants travelled all the way to Beijing to seek his support while the NPC was in session, protesting that their land had been taken away for urban redevelopment with little compensation.[14] The NPC and CPPCC sessions, which always take place simultaneously in Beijing, have also attracted a lot of PRC and foreign press publicity. As a consequence, political dissidents, including well-known figures like Han Dongfang, Wei Jingsheng, and Wang Dan, have all used these occasions to gain worldwide publicity for their demands for democracy and human rights.[15] (Although widely known in the west by way of the

Hong Kong and western media, they do not reach the Chinese public, even within Beijing.)

Representation in the NPC and the CPPCC is determined by quotas: so many seats are assigned to each DP and each 'sector' of society. In this schema the peasants and workers are underrepresented by a large margin. This compares to the disproportionate representation for the high-level intellectuals in the DPs. I have calculated that, of the 2,081 delegates to the seventh CPPCC in 1988, at least 928 members can definitely be identified as representing the intellectuals, while a mere eighty-five sat as representatives for the 'agricultural and forestry sector', and sixty-four for the 'trade unions'. At the seventh NPC that same year, out of 2,970 delegates, the sectoral representation for workers and peasants comprised 23 per cent of the assemblage, intellectuals 23 per cent, officials 25 per cent, and the army 9 per cent. Worker and trade union representation in the NPC has been in gradual decline, from 27 per cent in 1978 to 11 per cent in 1993 (Feng 1994: 249–50). At the 1988 NPC, each rural delegate represented eight times as many 'electors' as delegates from urban areas. Worse still, these rural delegates are likely to derive from the rural moneyed elite, whose interests do not normally coincide with those of ordinary peasants (Chan 1989: 81–2). Workers and peasants are being marginalised and excluded from the formal polity at a time when the legislative and consultative bodies are becoming increasingly important.

Opposition from outside the power structure

To the CCP, to the intellectual elite, and to the capitalists who share in the power structure, a perceived threat to social and political stability comes from three sources: the peasantry, the workers, and the so-called 'dissidents'. The former two pose a worry because a good many of them have been losers under the economic reforms.

Peasants and workers

For the first few years of the reforms the peasants were among the gainers. With a return to family farming in the early 1980s, agricultural productivity rapidly increased and so did peasants' income. But these levelled off by 1985, in the wake of soaring prices for agricultural inputs and depressed government procurement prices for agricultural produce. In particular, the 120 million peasants who eke out a subsistence living in the poorest parts of China's hinterland, in regions where industrial development is negligible, are the prime victims of urban-biased and seaboard-biased government plans and local corruption. With the state budget running at a deficit and unable to support these regions, local governments have turned to extracting more and more from the peasants by imposing a myriad *ad hoc* taxes and levies on them (Chan 1989: 73–4). Worse still, year after year local governments have been issuing IOUs (known as white slips) for procured products, leaving the farmers desperate for cash. Annual orders from the central government to cease this practice have been to no avail. In 1992 and 1993, the problem came to a head. Throughout the inland provinces, peasant protests erupted. The most serious occurred in Renshou County in Sichuan Province, where 10,000 peasants occupied government offices and held out for days (Lam 1994: 2.23–2.24).

The workers' conditions are better than the peasants' because of decades of urban-biased policies. But under the enterprise reforms, marketisation, the creation of a labour market, etc., the superior status, job security, and fringe benefits of the 110 million employees of state-run enterprises are progressively crumbling. In 1989, individually and in groups such workers had come out on demonstrations. Independent trade unions sprang up in many of the cities in protest against lack of representation by the official trade union, worsening conditions of employment, and runaway inflation (Walder and Gong 1993). These protests were soon crushed with brutality in the summer of 1989, while the official press sang the praises of the 'proletariat' in an effort to salvage the party's injured legitimacy.

For a couple of years in the early 1990s, the government gingerly pushed state-owned plants to raise productivity by permitting them to lay off workers, but only to an extent that would not disrupt social stability. As of 1992, after Deng Xiaoping's famous speeches in south China eulogising the role of the private economy, China's political and economic climate underwent a dramatic change. Since then, as the non-state sector has expanded, the state sector has contracted. As the central government treasury continues to haemorrhage, state enterprises increasingly are allowed to go bankrupt. It is beyond the scope of this chapter to go into the reasons behind the economic troubles of the state enterprises, or to evaluate the merits and demerits of the bankruptcy policies. What concerns us are the social repercussions. Whereas for a number of years one-third of state factories were in the red, starting in 1994 the figure jumped to 50 per cent (*Agence France Presse*, 8 July 1994). In 1993, two million blue-collar workers lost their jobs in Heilongjiang, a province in northeast China beset by antiquated heavy-industrial state enterprises (*China Daily*, 31 May 1993). In Wuhan, a steel city where productivity is twenty times less efficient per capita than in Japan, by 1993 50,000 of the 170,000 steel workers had been laid off, with another 30,000 targeted over the next two years. In Shanghai 120,000 workers in the state industrial sector have been laid off at half pay. Of the 500,000 textile workers in Shanghai, 450,000 remain, but the target is to shrink this number to 250,000. Most affected are women above 35 years of age (*China Labour Bulletin* (Hong Kong), 3, May 1994: 8–9). Many other employees in state factories throughout China have not been paid for months because neither the state nor the local government has money available to meet the payroll.

A rash of wildcat protests erupted during 1994. Earlier worker resistance in the 1980s and the first years of the 1990s had not usually been manifested in head-on confrontations such as strikes but rather in a resort to such 'weapons of the weak' as absenteeism, go-slows, passivity, lax work ethics, and occasional sabotage.[16] Over time, however, the intensity of industrial action has been racheted up. In the first months of 1994, as the government renewed its efforts to lay off workers, or in some cases state enterprises simply had no money to pay wages, 200,000 workers in the industrial northeast and in China's interior went on strike or staged other militant actions. In the heavy-industrial city of Fushun, the local official union branches broke loose from central control and led the strikes (*China Labour Bulletin*, 3, May 1994: 8–9).

While blue-collar state workers are threatened with plant closures and unemployment, some ten million workers in the foreign-funded export-oriented industrial sector suffer another sort of problem – labouring in Dickensian conditions reminiscent of the nineteenth-century Industrial Revolution. Some workers are forced to labour from ten to twelve hours or even longer each day, with no days off for weeks on end, at low pay, in poor and unsafe working conditions, with high accident rates, performing deskilled tasks set at break-neck speed for four hours at a time with only brief scheduled toilet breaks of one to two minutes. At two firms I was told of workers being made to rotate the bed space of their back-to-back bunks with workers on other shifts.

According to a survey carried out by Guangdong Province's General Trade Union in 1994, 46 per cent of the workers surveyed normally work more than eight hours a day; 35 per cent reported that overtime is mandatory; 34 per cent said that there is no extra pay for overtime work; 32 per cent are paid a below-minimum wage. The logic of this management method is to squeeze as much surplus labour as possible out of these human machines, and to discard them once they are spent, for there is no job security or unemployment benefits.

Labour unrest here too has been coming to a head. In the special export zones, wildcat strikes on the shopfloor are increasingly common in the foreign-funded enterprises. But these are less organised than the actions taken by the state workers. They usually flare up as single, spontaneous incidents, without support from workers in nearby factories. The workers, being rural migrants, are in a much more vulnerable position. Their hope often is that the incidents will press the local union offices or government labour bureaux to respond as mediators.

Political dissidents

Throughout the Maoist period, much as in Stalinist Russia, it required extraordinary courage – to the point of foolhardiness – to exhibit any truly dissident sentiments. Horrific prison conditions or execution awaited any such effort – and there were very few takers. The political accession of Deng Xiaoping began to provide far greater room for dissent, even though considerable risks were still entailed. If well enough known, however, a dissenter could expect a measure of protection from arrest. As described by a famous former East European dissident, Vaclav Havel, such dissidents are

> a protected species who are permitted to do things others are not and whom the government may even be cultivating as a proof of its generosity; or it lends support to the illusion that since there is no more than a handful of malcontents to whom not very much is really being done; all the rest are therefore content, for were they not so, they would be dissidents too.
>
> (Vaclav Havel 1985: 59)

This category of dissident embodies the following characteristics: they have already gained a high professional status or reputation within their own countries; they openly express views either in writing or in actions that are not approved by their governments; these views are interpreted by the foreign press as 'democratic', in contradistinction to their governments' despotic and autocratic rule; though few in number, they are viewed from abroad as voices for the ordinary people who are either less brave or unable to put their thoughts down on paper; and as personalities they are deemed to be principled, idealistic, humanistic, courageous, and selfless. They are apt to be used by western democratic governments and their own governments as chess pieces in intricate diplomatic games; and this in turn is contingent on the fact that their own governments are eager to court the 'democratic' international community, and so find themselves vulnerable on charges of human-rights violations.

In China, such political dissidents emerged only when Deng Xiaoping began to open China to the outside world and to enter into dialogue with western powers. Under Mao, when China refused or was deprived of a chance to have any dealings with the western world, the same dissident activities, sometimes even staged by the same individuals who in recent years have been elevated to the status of 'dissidents', had no protection. Thus martyrs like Yu Luoke and Zhang Zhixin could be tortured and executed by the authorities in the early 1970s for speaking up against the oppressiveness of the regime, yet did not gain dissident status on the world scene. Nor were peasants' and workers' protest actions protected as dissident activities, any more than they are now. Maoist atrocities, which committed several million to death, imprisonment, or exile to China's desert regions, did not stir up as much publicity or persistent outcry from western democratic governments as when Deng today confines well-known dissidents to house arrest.

To ward off international criticism, the Deng government is employing new tactics: lavishing VIP treatment on some dissidents; or shortening their terms of incarceration; or exiling them abroad rather than to Chinese gulags, as had been the practice under Mao. Dissidents are dealt with like strategic cards, doled out one at a time when pressure from the west intensifies. Thus, in the few weeks preceding the announcement of the winner of the bid to host the Year 2000 Olympic Games, for which the PRC was a frontrunner, the Chinese government released one famous dissident every week. A similar game was played out in 1994 just before the United States Congress was to vote on whether China should continue to be granted most-favoured-nation status. In contrast, ordinary Chinese who have been caught for similar political violations, as was the case during the June 1989 crackdown, were subjected to brutal mistreatment and long jail sentences (ICFTU Briefing 1994; Han 1994).

But is the western media-created image of the Chinese dissidents as champions of democracy close to reality? Do the Chinese dissidents represent voices of the people? Are they the equivalent of the Polish intellectual dissidents at the height of the Solidarity movement who worked closely with workers and peasants as a civil society in opposition (Geremek 1992: 4)?[17] The answer is that the demonstrators on Tiananmen Square in 1989 cordoned themselves off from ordinary people, so that their elite student/intellectual movement would not be contaminated (Walder and Gong 1993; Chan 1993; Perry 1992). This elitist attitude and their aspiration to 'remonstrate' as upright intellectuals with the powers that be (Esherick and Wasserstrom 1992: 28 66) were not so different in nature from those who have chosen to enter the official channels by joining the DPs or seeking selection as delegates to the NPC and CPPCC.[18]

Among those who lost out at Tiananmen were officials who had to flee the country because CCP General Secretary Zhao Ziyang's faction had lost a power struggle within the party elite.[19] Others were imprisoned because their past protest actions were deemed too militant, despite the fact that they had recently tried to mend their ways.[20] Some had earlier tried to serve as advisers to the elite reformist political faction, which they believed could best further their interests or ideals. Yet others who had once been part of the power elite but had entered the private economic sphere and had been demanding too much liberty from the party also found themselves targets of suppression.[21]

Subsequently, many of these intellectuals, as well as the younger, as-yet-student dissidents, came to reside abroad, having fled, accepted self-exile, or been exiled by the PRC government. Their behaviour since they left China has been disappointing to their supporters: internal factional squabbling, self-serving power struggles, problematic lifestyles, and undemocratic organisational behaviour have all aroused widespread disillusionment among the overseas Chinese community. Within China, their dissident activities today have minimal influence.

Very little in their writings expresses a concern for those peasants and workers who are clearly the main losers in the reform process, except to the extent that these exiles, like the political and economic elite back home, are worried about social instability. Just as there is today little substantive difference between the ideological beliefs of the CCP and the DPs, so the ideological beliefs of these dissidents have begun to converge with the changing ideology of the CCP. One has yet to find a faction among them that openly advocates universal suffrage, though much homage has been paid to the abstract idea of democracy. So long as the Chinese economy continues to boom and political liberalisation continues, with time these dissident exiles become increasingly irrelevant to political developments in China.

Five years after the 1989 upheaval, as noted above, disturbances again broke out among peasants and workers, accompanied by another spate of dissident activities. Somewhat different from the previous dissidents, these include some intellectuals who publicly call for protection of workers' rights (*Wall Street Journal*, 4 April 1994). A group calling itself the League for the Protection of Working People of the People's Republic of China, headed by a lawyer, a law student, and a veteran Democracy Wall Movement activist, sent its charter and a five-point proposal to the president of the NPC while it was in session in March 1994 (*China Labour Bulletin*, 2, April 1994: 12–13; Human

Rights Watch/Asia 1994). The organisers were harassed and arrested. It seems finally that an equivalent of Poland's KOR (Committee to Aid the Workers), which was comprised of Polish intellectuals and played a critical role in the birth of Solidarity, is in the making in China – except for this hitch in the League's charter, which places demands on membership:

> All citizens of the People's Republic of China who accept the charter of this League, who are dedicated to the development of the cause of protecting the rights of the working people of the People's Republic of China, *who have a certain level of theoretical grounding and a reasonable ability to engage in socialist practice, may become members of the League if they apply personally and are approved by the managing directors of the League's board.*
>
> (Human Rights Watch/Asia 1994: 8; emphasis added)

In short, Chinese intellectuals still condescendingly resist making common cause with the masses even when they are willing to go to jail in defence of their rights.

THE ELITES' IDEOLOGICAL CONVERGENCE AND FUTURE SCENARIOS

Janina Frentzel-Zagorska (1992), in her comparison of Hungary's and Poland's transitions from authoritarian socialism to democracy, has posed two distinct models. The first is the Polish model in which disparate social groups blurred their distinctive interests and organised themselves under the banner of Solidarity to confront a dominant power structure – civil society versus the authoritarian state. The culture of opposition had taken such broad roots in society that finally the state capitulated and agreed to share power. The Hungarian model, in contradistinction, was characterised by three features: it was economy-centred, non-confrontational, and elite-centred (Frentzel-Zagorska 1992: 44). Here the Communist Party reformed the system and trans-formed itself to pre-empt the emergence of a coalesced opposition. To accomplish this, it formed a 'grand coalition' of the upper and middle-level party oligarchy and bureaucracy, managers of large and medium-sized companies, and the new stratum of entrepreneurs. The Hungarian reformist Communist camp, while still in power, liberalised the polity. Consequently, Hungary underwent a more controlled and evolutionary transformation (Frentzel-Zagorska 1992: 60–1).

Will China's transformation approximate to either of these models? Current developments clearly suggest the Hungarian variant. A

Solidarity-type society-wide coalition in China is unlikely, since an intellectual camp with the wherewithal to help trigger broad organised opposition is simply absent. As noted, the DPs confine themselves to representing the interests of the high-level intellectuals. They only call for democracy within the broader elite. Mass democracy is not what they are seeking. The ACFIC, for its part, enjoys support from its rank and file, but these are no ordinary citizens; they are members of the new rich who are gaining social prestige and seeking a legitimate political role. Will the DPs and the ACFIC develop into real opposition parties, as in western democratic systems? The DPs with their narrow bases probably will not, though the ACFIC on the surface appears to have that potential.

But the latter scenario is based on a misplaced perception that the ACFIC's capitalist ideology is opposed to the CCP's so-called 'social-ism'. The question remains whether the CCP's professed ideology still has any socialist content. For the time being, there is still economic socialism. But this is being eroded fast with the rapid expansion of the non-state sector. That state ownership has not been dismantled in one fell swoop is less a result of the ruling elite's 'socialist' ideals than its fears of even more rapid worker dismissals and social instability. The system today is best characterised as 'socialism with capitalist charac-teristics'. The offspring of high-level CCP officials are more eager to join the ACFIC than the CCP.[22] 'Socialism' is quietly moving towards convergence with capitalism, especially nomenklatura capitalism, as manifested in the semi-state/semi-private corporations of Rong Yiren and Wang Guangying. Among the DPs, the ACFIC and the CCP, there seems to be little fundamental disagreement over ideology. The con-tention is over how to divide up power and wealth in a way that is perceived to be fair by those eligible to participate. The DPs will be junior partners, serving as handmaidens to the new joint elite. Along with the ACFIC they have become a sort of 'loyal opposition'.[23] Their common interests lie in defending their privileged positions and maintaining 'stability' during this major overhaul in the nation's economic restructuring by ensuring that the peasantry and the workers remain acquiescent.

Thus, akin to the Hungarian model,[24] a 'grand coalition' of elites has emerged, particularly a nascent alliance between the party and the new rich. The 'civil society' that is being erected is only for the elite, to the exclusion of a large sector of the population.

The state-sector workers and once-powerful state-sector industrial bureaucracies are falling by the wayside. Joining them are workers in the non-state sector who are subjected to poor working conditions. Today, these sectors are becoming restive. So are a sizeable portion of the peasants, the rural unemployed and underemployed, who, worse off than the workers, have no representation in the polity at all. Real opposition to the elite, here understood as violent disturbances, might emerge from among these millions of losers. This threat is well understood by the 'grand coalition' of elites and by the elite 'dissidents', and it unites them in a common fear of mass disorder. They have no solutions at hand except to keep the restive sectors at arm's length, in the hope that continued economic growth will stave off mass disturbances from below.

NOTES

* Some of the findings included in this chapter are based on two field trips in 1993 and 1994, funded by the Australian Academy of Social Sciences, the Chinese Academy of Social Sciences Exchange Programme, and an Australian Research Council Small Grant. Thanks are due to Zhu Xiaoyang, Zhang Dongdong and Jiang Shu for their library research assistance in Canberra and to staff members of the Chinese Academy of Social Sciences for their assistance in helping to organise the field research in Beijing. I am grateful to Garry Rodan for his comments on an earlier draft and to Jonathan Unger for his sharp critique and copyediting.

1 A discussion on a small minority of those who went further than remonstrating will follow later in this chapter.
2 Constrained by space, this is a very truncated interpretation of the Cultural Revolution and the Red Guard Movement. For detailed analyses of the nature of the movement see Anita Chan (1982, 1985, 1992).
3 These are the China Democratic League (Minmeng) and the September Third Study Society (Jiusan xueshe).
4 They are the Chinese Peasants' and Workers' Democratic Parties (Zhongguo nonggong minzhu dang) and the China Association for Promoting Democracy (Zhongguo minzhu cujin hui). As can be seen, the names given to some of these DPs had very little to do with the specific characteristics of their memberships.
5 This is the China National Construction Association (Zhongguo minzu jianguo hui).
6 They are respectively the Revolutionary Guomindang (Guomindang Geming Weiyuanhui), the Taiwan Democratic Self-Government League (Taiwan Minzhu Zizhi Tongmeng) and the Party for Public Interest (Zhi gong Dang). They all have strong overseas Chinese ties.
7 *CPPCC News*, 5 July 1988. For more details on the DPs' activities and suggestions in the 1980s, see Seymour (1992).
8 The information on these two forums was obtained in June 1993 through interviews in Beijing with a Democratic League member who was an invited participant.
9 *FBIS-CHI-89–100* (25 May 1989). Thanks are due to Mr Zhu Xiaoyang for laboriously checking off the names of the signatories of five petitions and this open letter (from February to May) to identify those who were members

of the DPs. Because the party affiliation of some of the signatories cannot be identified, the numbers of DP members are all underestimates.

10 My interview in May 1993 with the member of the China National Construction Association who introduced this Bill to the legislature impressed on me the importance given to this victory by some of the DP leaders. Their optimism is built on the fact that henceforth they could legally participate in assemblies with the CCP on an equal footing.

11 This information was derived from interviews with the offspring of one of the most well-known founding fathers of the League.

12 CITIC Pacific, described as one of the major players on the Hong Kong investment scene, is a branch of CITIC and is now headed by Rong's son, Larry Rong. The market capitalisation of CITIC Pacific has soared from HK$1 billion in 1991 to HK$30 billion in 1993 (*International Herald Tribune*, 23 April 1993).

13 Based on a monograph compiled by the CPPCC Eighth Congress's first plenum, issued in March 1993.

14 Interview carried out in 1993. Hong Kong delegates to the NPC are appointed by the Chinese government and are considered as part of the delegation from Guangdong Province.

15 Five years after the 1989 crackdown, the spring of 1994 witnessed a resurgence of dissident activities. Signed petitions were presented to the NPC, and dissidents sought out foreign correspondents to help publicise their protest activities. See *Washington Post*, 20 March 1994; *Wall Street Journal*, 4 April 1994.

16 For earlier discussions of worker dissatisfaction and resistance, see, e.g., *Shijie Jingji Daobao* ('World Economic Herald'), 25 January 1989; *Zhongguo Xinwen* ('China News'), 4 January 1989; and Cao Xiaofeng and Zhao Zixiang, 'Duoxing Xintai: Qiye zhigong laodong jijixing diluo de yuanyin qianxi' ('The Psychology of Laziness: a Brief Analysis of the Reason for the Low Incentive of Enterprise Staff and Workers', *Shehui* ('Society'), 4, 1991: 40–2.

17 It should be noted that the solidarity born out of opposition to the Polish ruling Communist elite in the 1980s, is today fragmented and quarrelsome. Polish society is in the process of restructuring itself politically.

18 Of course, there are exceptions to this generalisation. Fang Lizhi, the famous dissident scientist who sought protection from the American Embassy in Beijing in 1989, seems to be one of the very few who advocates genuine democracy (Fang 1990). Another one would be Wei Jingsheng, China's most famous dissident who was imprisoned for almost fifteen years for his Democracy Wall Movement activities in 1980. He was released just before the announcement of the host of the Year 2000 Olympic Games, but then was resentenced to a further fifteen years.

19 For example, Su Shaozhi and Yan Jiaqi, Bao Tong and Chen Yizi.

20 The two prime examples are Chen Ziming and Wang Juntao whose activities prior to and during the 1989 movement were recorded in detail in Black and Munro (1993). They had tried time and again to be included into the reformist camp of the political elite, but had been rejected because of their activities back in the 1976 Tiananmen uprising and the 1979–80 Democracy Wall Movement.

21 Prime examples are Wan Runnan and Cao Siyuan who could be considered as champions for more independence for the new rich.

22 Information from ACFIC administrator in 1994.
23 For definitions of 'loyal opposition', see William Saffire (1978: 388–90) and R. M. Punnett (1973: 20–1). See also Chapter 1 of this volume.
24 From a different angle, Kelly and He (1992: 38) have also come to the conclusion that the Chinese transformation is closer to the Hungarian variant.

REFERENCES

Amnesty International (1984) *China: Violations of Human Rights*, London: Amnesty International.

Black, George and Munro, Robin (1993) *Black Hands of Beijing: Lives of Defiance in China's Democracy Movement*, New York: John Wiley.

Chamberlain, Heath B. (1994) 'Coming to Terms with Civil Society', *Australian Journal of Chinese Affairs*, 31, January: 113–17.

Chan, Anita (1982) 'Images of China's Social Structure: the Changing Perspectives of Canton Students', *World Politics*, 34(3): 295–323.

—— (1985) *Children of Mao: Personality Development and Political Activism in the Red Guard Generation*, London: Macmillan Press.

—— (1989) 'The Challenge to the Social Fabric', in David Goodman and Gerald Segal (eds) *China at Forty: Mid-Life Crisis?*, Oxford: Clarendon Press, pp. 66–85.

—— (1992) 'Dispelling Misconceptions About the Red Guard Movement – The Necessity to Re-examine Cultural Revolution Factionalism and Periodization', *Journal of Contemporary China*, 1(1): 61–85.

—— (1993) 'Revolution or Corporatism? Workers and Trade Unions in Post-Mao China', *Australian Journal of Chinese Affairs*, 29, January: 31–61.

—— (1995) 'The Emerging Patterns of Industrial Relations in China and the Rise of Two New Labour Movements', *China Information*, IX(4), Spring: 36–59.

Chan, Anita and Unger, Jonathan (1991) 'Voices from the Protest Movement in Chongqing, Sichuan: Class Accents and Class Tensions', in Jonathan Unger (ed.) *The Pro-Democracy Protests in China: Reports from the Provinces*, New York: M. E. Sharpe, pp. 106–26.

Chi Fallen and Huang Ha (1987) *Research on Deng Xiaoping's Thought on Political Structural Reforms* (*Deng Xiaoping zhengzhi tizhi gaige zixiang yanjiu*), Beijing: Chunqiu Publishing Company.

Curran, Thomas D. (1992) 'From Educator to Politician: Huang Yanpei and the Third Force', in Roger Jeans (ed.) *Roads Not Taken: the Struggle of Opposition Parties in Twentieth-Century China*, Boulder, Colo.: Westview Press, pp. 85–110.

Esherick, Joseph W. and Wasserstrom, Jeffrey N. (1992) 'Acting Out Democracy: Political Theater in Modern China', in Jeffrey N. Wasserstrom and Elizabeth J. Perry (eds) *Popular Protest and Political Culture in Modern China: Learning from 1989*, Boulder, Colo.: Westview Press, pp. 28–66.

Fang Lizhi (1990) *Bringing Down the Great Wall*, New York: Alfred A. Knopf.

Feng Tongqing (1994) 'An Analysis of a Survey of the Situation of Chinese Staff and Workers' (in Chinese), in Jiang Liu, Lu Xueyi, and Shan Tianlun (eds) *An Analysis and Prognosis of the Social Situation*, Beijing: Social Science Academy, pp. 237–55.

Frentzel-Zagorska, Janina (1992) 'Patterns of Transition from a One-Party State to Democracy in Poland and Hungary', in Robert F. Miller (ed.) *The Development of Civil Society in Communist Systems*, Sydney: Allen & Unwin, pp. 40–64.

Geremek, Bronislaw (1992) 'Civil Society Then and Now', *Journal of Democracy*, 3(2): 3–12.

Han Dongfang (1994) Speech delivered on behalf of *China Labor Bulletin* for the third meeting of the ICFTU Human and Trade Union Rights Committee, Brussels, 26–27 June.

Havel, Vaclav (1985) 'The Power of the Powerless', in John Keane (ed.) *The Power of the Powerless*, New York: M. E. Sharpe, pp. 23–96.

Heilmann, Sebastian (1994) 'The Social Context of Mobilization in China: Factions, Work Units and Activists during the 1976 April Fifth Movement', *China Information*, VIII(3): 1–19.

Hewison, Kevin and Rodan, Garry (1994) 'The Decline of the Left in Southeast Asia', in R. Miliband and L. Panitch (eds) *Socialist Register 1994*, London: Merlin Press, pp. 235–62.

Hinton, Harold C. (1958) 'The "Democratic Parties": End of an Experiment?', *Problems of Communism*, VII(3): 39–46.

Hu Shikai (1993) 'Representation without Democratization: the "Signature Incident" and China's National People's Congress', *Journal of Contemporary China*, 2(1), Winter–Spring: 3–34.

Human Rights Watch/Asia (1994) 'China: New Arrests Linked to Worker Rights', 6(2).

International Confederation of Free Trade Unions (ICFTU) Briefing (1994) 'Behind China's Economic Miracle: Workers' Repression', June.

Jeans, Roger B. (1992) *Roads Not Taken: the Struggle of Opposition Parties in Twentieth-Century China*, Boulder, Colo.: Westview Press.

Kelly, David and He, Baogang (1992) 'Emergent Civil Society and the Intellectuals in China', in Robert F. Miller (ed.) *The Development of Civil Society in Communist Systems*, Sydney: Allen & Unwin, pp. 24–39.

Lam, Wo-lap Willy (1994) 'Locking up the Floodgates', in Maurice Brosseau and Lo Chi Kin (eds) *China Review 1994*, Hong Kong: Chinese University Press, pp. 2.1–2.52 (Chapter 2).

Li Zhisui (1994) *The Private Life of Chairman Mao: the Memoirs of Mao's Personal Physician*, New York: Random House.

Lieberthal, Kenneth C. and Lampton, David M. (1992) *Bureaucracy, Politics, and Decision Making in Post-Mao China*, Berkeley: University of California Press.

Liu Chia-Cheng, Beda (1990) 'Political Reform: Now What?', *China News Analysis*, 1407, 1 April: 1–8.

Liu Jianyi and Shen Jianlin (1992) *Basic Knowledge of Individual and Private Economy (Geti, Ziying Jingjijichu Zhishi)*, Beijing: Huawen Press.

Mazur, Mary G. (1993) 'Intellectual Activism in China during the 1940s: Wu Han in the United Front and the Democratic League', *China Quarterly*, March: 27–53.

Mu Fu-sheng (1963) *The Wilting of the Hundred Flowers: the Chinese Intelligentsia under Mao*, New York: Praeger.

Nathan, Andrew J. (1985) *Chinese Democracy*, Berkeley: University of California Press.

O'Brien, Kevin (1990) 'Is China's National People's Congress a "Conservative" Legislature?', *Asian Survey*, XXX(8), August: 782–94.

—— (1994) 'Chinese People's Congresses and Legislative Embeddedness', *Comparative Political Studies*, 27(1), April: 80–107.

Pearson, Margaret M. (1994) 'The Janus Face of Business Associations in China: Socialist Corporatism in Foreign Enterprises', *Australian Journal of Chinese Affairs*, 31, January: 25–46.

Perry, Elizabeth (1992) 'Casting a Chinese "Democracy" Movement: the Roles of Students, Workers and Entrepreneurs', in Jeffrey N. Wasserstrom and Elizabeth J. Perry (eds) *Popular Protest and Political Culture in Modern China*, Boulder, Colo.: Westview Press, pp. 146–64.

Punnett, R. M. (1973) *Front-Bench Opposition: the Role of the Opposition, and the Shadow Cabinet and Shadow Government in British Politics*, London: Heinemann.

Rosen, Stanley and Zou, Gary (eds) (1991) 'The Chinese Debate on the New Authoritarianism (I), *Chinese Sociology and Anthropology*, 23(2), Summer.

Roy, Denny (1994) 'Singapore, China, and the "Soft Authoritarian" Challenge', *Asian Survey*, XXXIV(3): 231–42.

Saffire, William (1978) *Saffire's Political Dictionary*, New York: Random House.

Seymour, James (1980) *The Fifth Modernization in China: Human Rights Movement 1978–1979*, New York: Human Rights Publishing Group.

—— (1987) *China's Satellite Parties*, New York: M. E. Sharpe.

—— (1991) 'China's Minor Parties and the Crisis of 1989', *China Information*, V(4), Spring: 1–23.

—— (1992) 'A Half Century Later', in Roger B. Jeans (ed.) *Roads Not Taken: the Struggle of Opposition Parties in Twentieth-Century China*, Boulder, Colo.: Westview Press, pp. 289–312.

Spar, Fredric J. (1992) 'Human Rights and Political Engagement: Luo Longji in the 1930s', in Roger B. Jeans (ed.) *Roads Not Taken: the Struggle of Opposition Parties in Twentieth-Century China*, Boulder, Colo.: Westview Press, pp. 61–84.

Tanner, Murray Scot (1994) 'The Erosion of Communist Party Control over Lawmaking in China', *China Quarterly*, 138, June: 381–403.

Teiwes, Frederick C. (1988) 'Mao and His Lieutenants', *Australian Journal of Chinese Affairs*, 19/20: 1–80.

Unger, Jonathan and Chan, Anita (1995) 'China, Corporatism, and the East Asian Model', *Australian Journal of Chinese Affairs*, 33: 29–53.

Van Slyke, Lyman P. (1967) *Enemies and Friends: The United Front in Chinese Communist History*, Stanford, Calif.: Stanford University Press.

Walder, Andrew and Gong Xiaoxia (1993) 'Workers in the Tiananmen Protests: the Politics of the Beijing Workers' Autonomous Federation', *Australian Journal of Chinese Affairs*, 29, January: 1–29.

Wong Young-tsu (1993) 'The Fate of Liberalism in Revolutionary China: Chu Anping and his Circle, 1946–1950', *Modern China*, 19(4): 457–90.

Young, Susan (1991) 'Wealth but not Security: Attitudes towards Private Business in China in the 1980s', *Australian Journal of Chinese Affairs*, 25, January: 115–37.

Yue Daiyun and Wakeman, Carolyn (1985) *To the Storm: the Odyssey of a Revolutionary Chinese Woman*, Berkeley: University of California Press.

7 Chinese political opposition in exile

He Baogang *

INTRODUCTION

With the advent of economic reform the Chinese government adopted an open door policy and sent students abroad; the option of external exile was then available but seldom used by students. Not until 1983 did a group of students from mainland China studying in the United States establish the Chinese Alliance for Democracy. This marked the beginning of an era of exile politics. Exile politics has been developed with rapid domestic economic growth. Rampant corruption and high inflation accompanying economic development underlay the social support for the 1989 students' demonstration. As a result, Chinese exile politics reached a climax in the wake of 1989, when a number of renowned intellectuals and students fleeing China after the military suppression of the demonstration sought refuge in the west.[1] The Front for a Democratic China was subsequently established.

Thus Chinese politics was extended abroad, necessitating a broadening conception of the subject and a study of overseas opposition. There is already a growing literature on Chinese exiles,[2] for example journalists' reports (Awanohara 1989; Pan 1989; Pan *et al.* 1989; Lau *et al.* 1990; Mosher and Kaye 1991; Goldstein 1994) and scholarly studies (Barme 1991; Nathan 1992; Ma 1993). These provide some useful materials and insights, but they focus narrowly on Chinese exiles rather than on the organisations, and make one-sided criticisms rather than provide a fair evaluation (except for Nathan's work). A systematic and objective study is required.

This chapter aims at a more comprehensive assessment of the overseas opposition movement (OOM): its strengths, achievements, problems and failures, significance, and prospects. The intention is to discuss the main organisations of political exiles, and, particularly, to examine two kinds of link. A study of the links between the OOM and

China is crucial to understanding the nature of the influence of the OOM on China. Further discussion of the links between the OOM and a variety of international organisations enables us to consider the proposition that some elements of the OOM are being incorporated into a transnational civil society.

This chapter is structured as follows: it begins with a discussion of the main organisations of political exiles, their political objectives, overseas bases and activities in influencing domestic politics. This is followed by a discussion of the linkages between the OOM and international organisations, particularly the linkage establishing a transnational civil society; and the linkages between the OOM and China, with particular focus on the links between economic development in China and the emergence of the OOM. The chapter concludes with an overall assessment of the OOM and a discussion of its prospects.

THE VARIETY OF CONTENDING OPPOSITION GROUPS

The overseas Chinese opposition movement displays little organisational cohesion. It is dispersed in a number of organisations operating independently of one another. There are two major opposition organisations which have intentionally refrained from organising as political parties, deeming the time not ripe. The Chinese Alliance for Democracy (CAD) was established in 1983 as a follow-up to the publication of the Chinese-language magazine *China Spring* in 1982. It was founded by Wang Bingzhang – a charismatic doctor whose efforts in the democracy movement inspired comparisons with Sun Yatsen – and by people who left China in the aftermath of the crackdown on the Democracy Wall Movement. The CAD was headed by Hu Ping in 1988, Yu Dahai in 1991, and Wu Fangcheng in 1993. It was located in Queens, New York, and in the District of Columbia. It publishes *China Spring*, which produces 11,500 copies of each issue, 6,500 and 5,000 copies being printed in the US and Hong Kong respectively, and sold in major cities around the world (*CAD Newsletter*, 17, 1990: 36). June 1989 was a turning point for the organisation. Before this date, the CAD's membership was secret except for its leaders; but after June 1989, the CAD openly extended its membership.

The Front for a Democratic China (FDC), founded on 7 October 1989, is a political organisation which aims to carry forward the process of Chinese democracy with Chinese compatriots throughout the country and overseas. The FDC consists chiefly of people who fled China after 4 June 1989, and previously served as entrepreneurial officials, 'academic' advisers, or party bureaucrats. The five key founders were student leader Wu'er Kaixi, theorist Yan Jiaqi, computer entrepreneur and deposed party leader Zhao Ziyang's confidant Wan Runnan, dissident writer Liu Binyan, and former head of Zhao's Institute of Economic Structural Reform, Su Shaozhi. This line-up gave the FDC unrivalled authority and glamour (Awanohara 1989). It was headed by Yan Jiaqi, then by Wan Runnan, the former head of the Stone electronics group in Beijing. Its headquarters are in Paris, though by far the majority of its officers and members are in the US and Australia. The FDC published a Chinese magazine, *Democratic China*, whose editors were Su Xiaokang and Yuan Zhiming. The Magazine ceased in 1996.

Shortly after 4 June 1989, when the overseas democratic movement was at high tide, the leaders of the FDC saw the organisation as 'a government in exile' which might have to assume power any day. They drafted 'T Plan', a plan for taking over power in an immediate crisis in China, including measures such as how to deal with the army (*FDC Newsletter*, 5, 1990). Also, Hu Ping, the former chairperson of the CAD, suggested at the organisation's fourth convention in June 1989 that it should prepare guidelines for how to rule China.

There is another political party, the Chinese Liberal Democratic Party (CLDP), founded in Columbus, Ohio, in 1990, mostly by Chinese students and a handful of long-time activists. Its membership was about 400 in 1990, mostly Chinese students at Midwestern universities.

The number of organisations is large for a small community.[3] There has been talk of merging the CAD and the FDC, following the wishes of Taiwan's funding organisations. Most leaders of the FDC and the CAD, such as Yan Jiaqi, Hu Ping, and Xu Bangtai, think that overseas organisations should be concentrated into a single movement to increase the competitiveness of the opposition. In January 1993 in Washington, the two merged as the United Front for a Democratic China (UFDC), headed by Xu Bangtai. Unfortunately, this turned out to be a great failure. In July 1993, the telephone meeting of the board of directors of the FDC decided to maintain the autonomy of their organisation, and not merge with the CAD (*Beijing Spring*, 8, 1993: 95). The CAD did the same thing. In California in 1994, the UFDC sued FDC and CAD as illegitimate. The court, however, ruled that the three organisations are allowed to coexist.

Besides the above political organisations, there is Human Rights in China (HRIC), which focuses only on human rights issues, and is an independent, non-profit organisation. It was founded by scholars and activists such as Fu Xinyuan, Li Xiaorong, Liu Qing, and Xiao Qiang from the PRC, and located in the offices of Human Rights Watch in

New York. It does not seek political power, but aims at documenting and publicising Chinese human rights abuses, informing Chinese people about the international human rights standards and the mechanisms by which these are enforced, and assisting those persecuted and imprisoned in the PRC for non-violent exercise of their fundamental rights and freedoms. It is also a lobby group.

There is further the Foundation for Human Rights and Democracy in China, headed by Dimon Liu, in Washington DC, which assists the other organisations in fund-raising, especially *vis-à-vis* the National Endowment for Democracy (NEC), as well as helping to organise conferences and submissions to the UN Human Rights Commission, etc.

The overseas organisations consist of a series of think-tanks and specialised organisations of a more academic or intellectual cast. There may be two or three score organisations, but the more important are discussed below.

The Centre for Modern China (CMC) was founded in the US in 1990 and headed by Chen Yizi, the former director of the Institute of Economic Structural Reform (Tigaisuo), the major Zhao Ziyang think-tank. The main aims of the CMC are to draft new policies for China's future under a revived reform leadership, to bring together scholars and experts on China, to form a worldwide network for research on basic issues facing contemporary China, to promote not only theoretical research that may enrich the literature of China studies, but also practical, strategic, and policy research that may contribute to China's course towards democracy and a free economy. It has an office in New York. So far the CMC has successfully elicited the support of leading sinologists and has established wide contact with interested groups internationally. It published the *Journal of Contemporary China* (in English) and *Papers of the Centre for Modern China* (in Chinese), and has organised a few conferences. The Journal is no longer published by the CMC.

The Future of China Society is a research and discussion forum initially headed by Guan Weiyan and Su Shaozhi, well-known pro-reform academics. This society holds conferences, and focuses on broad theoretical issues like the nature of capitalism and socialism, neo-authoritarianism, and analysis of the control systems of Chinese society.[4]

The International Federation of Chinese Students and Scholars (IFCSS) is a third organisation. This is the interest group of the Chinese students in America, a strong lobby on immigration and other policy issues affecting Chinese students and scholars. As the constitution of the IFCSS states clearly, the main aim is to protect the interests of

Chinese scholars and students. The IFCSS also aims to promote democratisation in China and to protect human rights, but it does not openly oppose the Chinese Communist Party (CCP). The current president is Luo Ning, the vice president Liu Chenyan.

The exile publications are huge. Apart from *China Spring* and *Democratic China*[5] as mentioned above, there are a number of new journals and newspapers. The *News Freedom Herald* was published in Chinese in California; it aimed at breaking the news blockade on the mainland, and envisaged an overseas student and scholar audience. But publication seems to have ceased.

The bimonthly *Twenty-First Century* (*Ershiyi shiji*) appeared in late October 1990. This was mainly initiated by theorist Jin Guantao. *Twenty-First Century* aims to promote the development of Chinese pluralist culture. Its audience is Chinese intellectuals, and it serves as a forum for discussion of Chinese cultural reconstruction among intellectuals from China, Taiwan, and Hong Kong.

The *Chinese Intellectual* (*Zhishifenzi*) was founded by Liang Heng in New York on 5 October 1984. Liang moved his office to Beijing and published one issue in early 1989, but the journal was suspended in China and reappeared in the US after 4 June 1989. Currently, 7,000 copies go to mainland China, 3,000 abroad. The *Chinese Intellectual* has generally served as a forum for serious, although at times obfuscating, intellectual discussion.

In conclusion, before 1989, the CAD was a mere overseas opposition, which was kept at a certain distance by most Chinese students as their government labelled it a 'counter-revolutionary' organisation. Since June 1989, a plural structure of political organisations has emerged and developed abroad. Many organisations compete with one another to attract Chinese students and scholars who have more choices than before.

THE POLITICAL OBJECTIVES OF OPPOSITION MOVEMENTS

The objectives of the HRIC, the CMC, and the IFCSS have already been mentioned above. Here I focus on the political objectives of the FDC, the CAD, and the CLDP, and dilemmas associated with these objectives.

The political objectives of the FDC, the CAD, and the CLDP are similar: to be a 'mature opposition party' rather than a 'loyal opposition' in China. June 1989 was a watershed. Before 1989, Chinese intellectuals such as Liu Binyan advocated 'the second loyalty', a loyalty to the party and the state but with added criticism and social consciousness. This kind of 'loyal' opposition was tolerated and promoted by reformers, but was obstructed by the hardliners within the party. After 1989, all three organisations lost interest in the idea of 'loyal opposition'. Now, all claim to aim at 'transforming China's system of dictatorship, and fighting for democracy, rule-by-law, freedom, and human rights in mainland China' (*FDC Newsletter*; *China Spring*, 3, 1988: 15; *Cheng Ming*, 5, 1989: 74). It should, nevertheless, be pointed out that their ideal of democracy is elitist; that is, democracy is seen as a check-balance mechanism between professional politicians and elites, and fair competition at the top layer of the hierarchy. As far as Chinese political reforms are concerned, Yan Jiaqi, the former president of the FDC, has proposed to establish the authority of the constitution and the National People's Congress, and stressed the democratisation of the elite's power basis. For exile dissidents, mass participation is merely a side-issue.

The political aim of 'the end of one-party dictatorship' has been debated across organisational lines. Some have argued that this does not imply that the CCP should be banned. Others have argued the opposite. When the USA branch of the FDC was established on 16 February 1990, its manifesto had the specific aim: 'Down with (*dadao*) the CCP'. This implies destruction of the CCP.[6] This aim was also supported by Wu'er Kaixi, student leader and former vice president of the FDC (*Central Daily News*, 2, 19 February 1990). Nevertheless, this radical aim was rejected by the majority of the members of overseas opposition organisations. It was argued that the CCP's dictatorship should be ended, but the CCP should be allowed to exist.[7]

The means to achieve democracy have also been debated. The dominant groups in both the FDC and the CAD have been committed to a non-violent strategy. The exception here has been the CLDP which seeks to use whatever means necessary to replace the CCP in power. This implies the possible use of force, but nobody outside the organisation has any idea how such force might be brought to bear on the situation inside China from an American base (Nathan 1992).

There was division on political strategy between the FDC and CAD in 1989 and 1990. As Woei Lien Chong observed, CAD leaders such as Hu Ping aimed to 'reform outside the system' (to oppose the power monopoly of the party and even to wrest power from it), whereas some of the FDC leaders such as Wan Runnan aimed to 'reform within the system' (to maintain a dialogue with the party to persuade it to accept a multi-party system and a market economy) (Ma 1993; *CAD Newsletter*, 16: 14–18). This difference was due to the organisations' relationships with the CCP itself: the CAD was branded early on as being anti-party, while leaders of the FDC served within the party as reformers. They looked forward to the day they could go back and continue their work under enlightened leader Zhao Ziyang. This might be called *zhaoan*.[8] It was argued that the FDC would be more likely to co-operate with the CCP than the CAD in the near future, just as reformers such as Kang Youwei and Liang Qichao had co-operated more with Emperor Guangxu of the Qing than revolutionaries such as Sun Yatsen (*Nanbeiji yuekan*, 6, 1990: 55). This argument suggests that the issue of co-optation is a matter of division between the CAD and the FDC. The argument might have been true in 1989 and 1990, but it is no longer valid today. To gain support from Taiwan, Chinese students, and the Chinese communities, leaders of the FDC had to leave their position of 'reform within the system', and commit themselves to 'reform outside the system'.[9] Further, there have been cross-memberships between the CAD and the FDC, and the two organisations have been making efforts to unify. Thus, the issue of co-optation is no longer a criterion for determining the difference between the CAD and the FDC.

To build 'a great China' is an underlying goal of the Chinese overseas opposition. Nationalism has taken root among Chinese overseas opposition groups. They charge the CCP with taking a weak position in dealing with Japanese aggression over Diaoyu (Senkaku) Island (*FDC Newsletter*, 19, November 1990: 15–21; *Democratic China*, 6, February 1991: 82). They are committed to the unification of China with Taiwan and Chinese sovereignty over Tibet. This nationalist goal of building a great China presents a dilemma. They want to gain support from Taiwan and exiled Tibetans, which puts them in an ambiguous position on the boundary problem (for Yan Jiaqi's position, see *FDC Newsletter*, 16, 1990: 22). As a result, they are silent on the issue of whether they support Taiwan's effort to enter the UN; and they are in dispute with the Dalai Lama over the independence of Tibet (*Nanhan: For a Democratic China*, 2, 1989: 33; *FDC Newsletter*, 19, November 1990: 21–3; *Democratic China* (Japanese edition), 59, June 1994: 43–7; *Central Daily News*, 16 June 1990: 4). However, if overseas oppositionists openly support the independence of Taiwan and Tibet, they probably will lose some support from Chinese students and scholars. On this issue, they certainly do not have the advantage of Sun Yatsen who called for the overthrow of the Manchus and the restoration of China to the Chinese, which, at the time, unified most overseas Chinese (Schiffrin 1968: 41–4). No wonder Sun Yatsen said that overseas Chinese were 'the mother of the Chinese revolution'; but any similar remark is now seldom heard.

THE OVERSEAS BASES OF THE OOM

The main membership of the political organisations comes from the estimated 100,000 Chinese students and scholars around the world, and the overseas Chinese, *huaqiao* (on *huaqiao* support, see Pan 1989; Pan *et al.* 1989), which now totals about twenty-seven million (Ma 1993: 368). The French branch of the FDC, for example, had 100 out of 3,000 Chinese students in 1990 (Lau *et al.* 1990: 21).

However, the extent to which Chinese students and scholars support these organisations should not be overestimated. Only twenty-one and forty attended meetings of the FDC out of thirty-eight and 130 members of the Toronto and Tokyo branches respectively (*FDC Newsletter*, 19, 1990: 30, 32, 1991: 26). The actual number involved in the Canberra branch of the FDC has been even smaller. Only three or four out of about twenty members attended regular meetings or participated in activities.[10] The genuine interest of Chinese students in participating in these organisations can be questioned if we look at attitudes towards the membership fee. The CAD has been urging its members to pay their subscriptions; those who do not pay are to be regarded as automatically leaving the organisation. The FDC has also had a problem with subscriptions (US$10 for students and US$40 for salary earners, see *FDC Newsletter*, 3, 1990: 5). From March to May 1990, total membership subscriptions amounted to only US$180, compared with total donations of US$298,236 from February to June 1990 (*FDC Newsletter*, 13, 1990: 36).

The various strategies for expanding membership of the organisations are as follows. First, the CAD and the FDC carried out 'a withdrawing party campaign', a movement calling on Chinese students and scholars to withdraw from the CCP. There were 304 and 216 people who left the party on 1 July and 1 October 1989 respectively (*China Spring*, 8, 1989: 38–42; *Beijing Spring*, 9, 1993: 92). Second, in 1990, the New Jersey branch of the CAD attempted to extend its membership by waiving or reducing the subscription (then US$58), charging, for example, only once for a couple. It has, however, been very difficult to extend the membership of the CAD. Qi Guang, a leader of the Michigan branch, in a year's hard work, persuaded only dozens of Chinese students to join the CAD. He felt the task was more difficult than 'falling in love' (*CAD Newsletter*, 17: 9). It should be made clear, however, that the OOM does have certain support from Chinese students and scholars, as is suggested by the figure that, roughly speaking, 4 per cent of Chinese students and scholars are members of exile organisations.

ACTIVITIES FOR PROMOTING DOMESTIC OPPOSITION

The overseas opposition plays neither major nor minor roles in Chinese politics – not minor because overseas opposition groups are currently the only open political opposition. Thus, leaders of political groups see their role as 'guiding' Chinese democracy. Nevertheless, because they exist outside China, isolation makes it difficult to guide home activists directly, and to establish close links with people in China. Thus they play only 'supporting' roles (Yang Jianli 1992: 12–13).

The role of the CAD in the 1989 students' demonstration illustrates this view. Chen Jun, a member of the CAD, returned to China in 1987 and, in early 1989, initiated the petition movement demanding that the Chinese government release political prisoners such as Wei Jingsheng (*Baixing*, 191, March 1989: 28–9). The CAD has further supported the students' demonstration by providing financial donations and information. For example, the CAD has urged all its members around the world to send a million letters to China and make a million calls to tell the truth. It has also established the Information Centre for the Chinese Democracy Movement (*Beijing Spring*, 9: 92). However, the CAD did not organise or guide the student demonstration. The role of the CAD was limited in the 1989 events for two reasons. First, the factional fight in the CAD was then serious. Wang Bingzhang, a founder of the CAD, was expelled in January 1989. Subsequently, Wang founded a new organisation, the Chinese Liberal Democratic Party, in April 1989. Wang also sued Hu Ping and others through the American judiciary system (*Asiaweek*, 1 September 1989: 31; *Cheng Ming*, 2, 1989: 29–30; *CAD Newsletter*, 13, 19). Second, the secret nature of the CAD then limited its organisational capacity: no one knew who its members were (*FDC Newsletter*, 13, 1990: 9–11; *Beijing Spring*, 9, 1993: 97).

Mainland China is a central concern for overseas opposition organisations. The FDC was committed to spending 30 per cent of its budget on funding mainland activities, although it is not known whether or how the money is spent (*FDC Newsletter*, 16, October 1990: 6).[11] Wan Runnan sent secret members to China, and initiated various actions such as establishing a human rights organisation and the Protecting-Workers-Organisation. But the information on these moves is very limited. After 1989, the exiles' organisations took a number of measures to exert influence in China.

The overseas opposition organisations, like all opposition, focused mainly on what was wrong with the Chinese government. This was essential to the identity of Chinese political exiles. With this kind of focus, it is not surprising that some of the claims by the overseas opposition organisations have been found to be exaggerated. In extreme cases, there may even be fictitious claims (Ma 1993). Most importantly, the probability of this tends to increase with the current low tide of the overseas Chinese pro-democracy movement (Ma 1993).

In October 1989, the FDC launched a 'Fax of Freedom Campaign'. On one day alone, 12,000 copies of a pro-democracy mock-up of the *People's Daily* bombarded fax machines inside China (Lau *et al.* 1990: 21). In early 1990, the FDC, with help from French pro-Chinese democracy activists and funded by Taiwan with US$720,000, bought a boat and renamed it a *Democratic Goodness Boat* with a pirate radio station. It attempted to broadcast around the South China Sea, but the effort failed in the end due to the Chinese government's pressure on Taiwan, which withdrew its support for the action (*FDC Newsletter*, 6, 9; *China's Scholars Abroad*, 21, September 1990: 42–5). Later, in November 1990, the British and Toronto branches of the FDC sent thousands of letters and copies of *Democratic China* to China. Between January and February 1991, the German branch sent 1,000 copies of the journal *Democratic Voice* to China and sent 100 faxes to more than twenty cities in China (*FDC Newsletter*, 34, December 1991).

Human Rights in China (HRIC) produced a twenty-minute bi-weekly radio programme, broadcast to China from a station in Taiwan. Over three months in early 1994, Liu Qing and Xiao Qiang did over twenty interviews with the Chinese-language services of Voice of America, Radio France Internationale, the BBC, and the Canadian Broadcasting Corporation about the human rights situation in China (*Human Rights Forum*, Summer 1994: 3). HRIC sent a leaflet in Chinese introducing its work to a list of 1,000 law-related individuals and institutions (*Human Rights Forum*, Fall 1993: 3).

HRIC's humanitarian fund was established and designed to send money to victims of human rights abuses and their families in China. By summer 1994, about US$64,000 had been sent to around 700 people in China, with a large proportion going to former 4 June 1989 prisoners, the families of those still in prison or killed on 4 June 1989, and people wounded in the crackdown (*Human Rights Forum*, 1993–4 issues).

The CAD, the FDC, and the HRIC all collect information about prisoners and human rights abuses in China and send it to western governments and non-government organisations (NGOs), asking them to exercise more pressure on Beijing to release political prisoners. For example, when Yao Kaiwen and Gao Xiaoliang, leaders of the mainland branch of the FDC, were sentenced to ten and nine years respectively in early January 1994, the FDC organised global action to rescue them. The branches in France, the US, Germany, Australia, Japan, Sweden,

Belgium, and Norway wrote letters to political leaders of their host countries, and visited relevant officers to urge the west to exercise pressure on Beijing to release the two political prisoners.

These appeals have had some effect. As Woodman observes, an individual identified by international pressure will be protected (*Human Rights Tribute*, 2(6): 16–17). Surely, as Ma points out, in order to save face, Chinese leaders will not concede that external pressure, whether from foreign governments or overseas dissidents, has played any role in their handling of domestic opposition. At the same time, Chinese political exiles tend to attribute any better-than-expected actions by the Chinese government to the effectiveness of their voices, so as to confirm the value of their role as political exiles (Ma 1993: 379).

Intellectual work by Chinese dissidents has benefited from the scope of freedom in the west and the freedom of information which people in China do not have. Also, being overseas, political exiles are able to engage in more detached reflection. In this regard, the CMC has done a great deal. By March 1994, it had published forty-one issues discussing various policy-oriented topics. For example, a few articles are concerned with how to strengthen the capacities of the state (*Modern China Studies*, 2, 1994). Hu Ping has often published articles on theoretical and strategic issues of Chinese democracy in *China Spring* and *Beijing Spring*. There has been debate on neo-authoritarianism in the journal of *Democratic China* and in the forum of *Future of Chinese Society*. In 1992, the HRIC organised a conference on the applicability of international human rights standards to China.[12] The *Twenty-First Century Foundation* organised scholars to draft the constitution of the Federal Republic of China (*Central Daily News*, 28 February 1994).[13] Also, to work on major issues of constitutional design in China, a number of influential and distinguished Chinese scholars participated in a research programme, *Constitutionalism and China*, organised by Professors Andrew Nathan, Randle Edwards, and Louis Henkin, and funded by the Luce Foundation. Given that this kind of work cannot be done within China, at least not as efficiently, such overseas work is of great value to the Chinese intellectual enterprise.

Political exiles are oriented to going home. They are so deeply politicised by their experiences in China that life outside China is not sufficiently meaningful. They would be famous and influential in China, which they cannot be overseas (Nathan 1992).[14] They worry about being marginalised as history in China inches along without them. They also worry that even if there is a dramatic change on the mainland, they will no longer be the main players on the stage of history (Mosher and Kaye 1991: 34; Ma 1993). Further, political exiles see 'returning home' as a political right. This could exert new pressure on Beijing. It is expected that with a number of famous dissidents back in China, pressure groups could gradually form again with the participation of those who had remained behind. Thus the struggle for political and other freedoms would continue. This is a risky strategy, but one likely to generate international fame.

The Chinese government's soft policy makes 'returning home' possible. In 1991 Jiang Zeming, the present party general secretary, announced that while all overseas pro-democracy movement activists were welcome to return home, on arrival they would have to surrender themselves to the police, and a confession of guilt would be required. These are certainly unacceptable conditions for most principled dissidents (Ma 1993: 383). Certain leading exiles, for example Yuan Zhiming, the former editor of *Democratic China*, are now negotiating their return to China. They demand that the government withdraw their arrest warrants and ensure the personal safety of the returnees. Many members of the CAD and the FDC have returned to China. For example, Li Shanyuan, a member of the CAD and the director of the Voice of June 4 radio station, Shen Tong, an organiser of the Democracy for China Fund, have safely returned to China and left again.

However, returning home is only possible for individuals. Opposition organisations are not allowed in China. For Wan Runnan, the conditions for returning home are immediately contingent on the issue of rehabilitation: only when the June massacre and even the protest movement itself are officially re-evaluated and their victims rehabilitated, will it be time for the FDC to return home (*Jiushi niandai*, 2, 1990: 32–3). In other words, the verdict (*fan'an*) on the historical incident must be offically overturned before the FDC can return home.

INTERNATIONAL SUPPORT FOR OVERSEAS POLITICAL OPPOSITION

All organisations make great efforts to win support from international communities. The CAD, which runs the China Solidarity Committee, a more broadly based lobby group, set up a Washington office led by Feng Shengping. The IFCSS has lobbied Capitol Hill in an attempt to achieve some of their most immediate goals, including relaxed immigration regulations and tougher US attitudes towards the continued crackdown in China (*China Spring*, 8, 1989: 73–5; Nathan 1992).[15]

Without varied international support,[16] Chinese overseas political organisations cannot exist and develop in their host countries. The US has permitted and supported Chinese political exiles and has provided them with a reasonably hospitable environment. The French government has provided financial support. Immediately after June 1989, eighty post-Tiananmen exiles, including dependants, stayed in France as refugees (Awanohara 1989: 18). Although France made it easier for people to stay, most chose not to. People such as Chen Yizi, Yuan Zhiming, and Su Xiaokang moved to the US. The Australian government also permitted political exiles to stay, and granted most Chinese students permanent residence. Australia has the largest number of self-supporting students, 20,000–30,000. Thus, the Australian branches of the CAD and the FDC have the largest memberships, roughly, 1,000 each (FDC Newsletter, 32, September 1991: 26; Singtao Jihpao (Xingdao renbao, Australian edition), 19 December 1989: 1). The Ministry of Foreign Affairs in Germany provided DM740,000 as urgent aid for Chinese students after June 1989, and had received 280 applicants by the end of November 1989 (FDC Newsletter, 4, 1990: 25). Japan, however, made it harder for Chinese exiles to stay, although historically, the country had been a centre for Chinese dissidents such as Kang Youwei, Liang Qichao, and Sun Yatsen. Sun Yatsen was offered a free house when he was in Tokyo, and the Japanese government provided him with 450,000 yen for arms (Jansen 1967: 145–7; Schiffrin 1968: 256–74). But on this occasion, it chose not to support Chinese dissidents, and refused to extend Chinese students' visas after 1989 (Herzog 1993: 46–8). On 3 October 1990, thirty members of the FDC submitted a petition to the Japanese government asking for a 'special permit' to stay in Japan and this was granted (FDC Newsletter,17, 1990: 21–5).

Further explanation is needed to understand why the US has become a centre for Chinese exiles. In 1989, fifty-three motions concerning China were proposed in the Congress, including those supporting Chinese democrats, permitting students to stay and granting them permanent residence, and revising the immigration law to help Chinese exiles to apply for permanent residence (Beijing Spring, 9, 1993: 95). Also, a free office and free telephone in the Washington Congress were offered by one of Bush's supporters to Chinese students. This facilitated the lobbying activities of Chinese students and exiles. Lynn Chu, a lawyer and the co-ordinator of the One Hundred Group, offered advice and legislative recommendations. The National Endowment for Democracy provided financial support for those who escaped from China after June 1989 and gave money to the Future of China Society and others. In 1993, President Clinton's wife wrote a letter to the wife of Yu Zhuo to express concern and sympathy for her husband, a graduate in Wuhan who was arrested and was to be secretly sentenced for demanding rehabilitation following the 4 June events (*Beijing Spring*, 9, 1993: 86). In early 1994, President Clinton wrote a letter to United Front for a Democratic China, explaining his China policy, and promising to keep pressure on Beijing to improve its human rights record (*Central Daily News*, 24 January 1994). American universities have also played a role through individual fellowships to Chinese scholars and students, e.g. the Princeton China Initiative, the Luce Foundation, and grants at Columbia, Harvard, and elsewhere.[17]

Links between Chinese and East European political opposition organisations have also been established and developed. In early 1988, the CAD's China Solidary Committee established links with Solidarity (*Beijing Spring*, 9, 1993: 94). The CAD even donated US$1,000 to Polish and Romanian opposition groups in 1990 despite its own financial problems. In April 1990, Yan Jiaqi, the former chairperson of the FDC, and Jens Reich, the leader of the New Forum in East Germany, co-organised the Berlin International Conference, which was attended by 150 delegates from more than ten countries (*Central Daily News*, 21 April 1990; *Beijing Spring*, 10: 102).[18] The support from East European opposition groups is a moral one. The developments in Eastern Europe in late 1989 and early 1990 to some extent strengthened the exiles' traditional Chinese confidence in moral leaders. In particular, Vaclav Havel provides a role model to the sage-king (*shengwang*) (Barme 1991). He has also encouraged Chinese exiles, and given them hope. Thus, Chinese exiles are keen to learn lessons from Eastern Europe. As a result, there has been an effort to translate many East European dissident writings and major documents into Chinese.[19]

It is both practically and theoretically significant that the OOM has been incorporated into a transnational civil society, and this has supported and strengthened Chinese overseas opposition groups. A transnational civil society includes a number of international non-government organisations (INGOs) (Ghils 1992). It is thus distinct from a national civil society. The former may be considered not only as the subject of international law, but also as an active participant in the shaping of such law; while the latter may be the subject of international law, it is a less active participant in the shaping of such law. The former shapes opinion and is an autonomous actor in competition with states, while the latter may compete with its own government, but less with states in the international arena. The former is more concerned with global issues such as human rights and the global environment, and is less concerned with national sovereignty; the latter is more concerned with national issues and committed to national sovereignty. In terms of membership, the former is international, while the latter is national.

From the previous discussion of the political objectives and activities of the OOM, overseas Chinese exile organisations can be seen as a political civil society if civil society is defined as *de facto* autonomous organisations that are independent of direct political control by the state and the party. Furthermore, the OOM has been inspired by the idea of civil society: establishing a civil society in China has been adopted as a political objective by exile organisations (He 1994). There have been many discussions on the political dimension of civil society in exile journals such as *The Chinese Intellectuals* and *Twenty-First Century* (He 1994). Chinese exiles have also drawn on the idea of civil society, and the power of popular pressure groups in the transformation of European socialist states (*FDC Newsletter*, 17, 1990: 25–8). But, generally speaking, the OOM cannot be seen as an unequivocal member of an international civil society, because it has not played a role in shaping international law; it is less concerned with global issues and more concerned with Chinese national issues. The Chinese nationalism of political exiles is so strong that they place Chinese national sovereignty above global issues (see the previous discussion of the objectives of the OOM); and the memberships of the FDC and the CAD are almost exclusively Chinese.

The exception here is the HRIC. The aim of the HRIC has been influenced by NGOs. Its political opposition has taken the form not of competing for political power, but of concern for the human rights issue. Because of this non-party approach,[20] the HRIC has gained support from the Soros Open Society, the International Centre for Human Rights and Democratic Development, the European Human Rights Foundation, Human Rights Watch, Asia Watch, etc. The HRIC's budget has increased every year. Although it faces difficulties in fund-raising, it does not worry about financial problems as do other political organisations such as the FDC and the CAD.[21] Further, the HRIC is concerned not only with Chinese human rights issues but also with Asian human rights issues. For example, Xiao Qiang attended a meeting of NGO's from the Asia-Pacific region in Bangkok in February 1994; this was a continuation of the efforts, begun in 1993 at the World Conference on Human Rights, to share information and co-ordinate action among groups in the region. Importantly, the HRIC was elected to the facilitating team which will continue such activities (*Journal of Human Rights in China*, Spring 1994: 3). The HRIC also took an active role in the World Conference on Human Rights in 1993 in an attempt to reshape international documents on human rights. Significantly, the HRIC goes beyond the boundary of Chinese national sovereignty in that it supports Tibet's struggle for the right to self-determination. The membership of the HRIC's office is also international, roughly two-thirds being Chinese, a third from other nationalities. Thus, the HRIC is constitutive of, or incorporated into, a transnational civil society, although in both respects we are talking about an embryonic development.

THE LINKAGE BETWEEN THE OOM AND CHINA

Various linkages between the OOM and China, such as the OOM's political objectives and activities, oriented towards promoting a mature opposition in China, have already been discussed. Here, I will explore the linkages further. I will first relate the emergence of the OOM to economic development and social transformation in China; then discuss the crucial influence of the OOM on the Chinese government's exile policy by examining the logic of the interplay of the OOM, the Chinese government, domestic dissidents, and domestic economic and political developments.

The OOM is linked to domestic economic development and social transformation. Economic reform has changed the balance of class relations in China: the emergence of the new rich and their increasing roles in the economy and politics is accompanied by the decline of the importance of the position of the working class. Groups of both the new rich and the working class are interested in, and attracted to, the stances of oppositionists.

A group of new rich, or what people often call 'the middle class', now commands enormous resources and attempts to have a voice in the political sphere. For example, Hannan is now becoming the centre for dissidents; many of those released from jail since 1990 have gone there. They have attempted to promote political activities through their wealth and influence on economic activities – in Chinese, *yishang yangzheng*. Wan Runnan typifies this new social force. He openly encouraged the development of the middle class and financially supported the 1989 students' demonstration when he was the director of the Stone Company in China. From exile in France, he insisted that the FDC should be representative of the new middle class which, he believes, constitutes the social base for Chinese democracy (*Cheng Ming*, September 1994: 60–2). He has also kept close contact with the members of the Stone Company by telephone and through his personal aide.[22] Thus the political goals of the FDC are to establish a civil society and encourage development of a private economy as well as the middle class. All these are believed to be preconditions for opposition. Nevertheless, the political appeal of the FDC is not restricted to the new middle class, but is focused rather on the human rights issue. This is because the new middle class is ambiguous about democracy and its political role (see He 1994: 161–3); and because the human rights issue is seen as the best strategy for winning general support and attacking the Chinese government.

The political position and influence of the working class have been declining. It was once regarded as the leading class in Communist ideology. It now faces the loss of its political privileges, the possibility of unemployment, and worsening working conditions. In this context, labour activists have been defending their rights, in particular the right to form and join trade unions for the protection of their interests. When the League for the Protection of the Rights of Working People of the PRC (Working People's League) was suppressed by the police, activists like Wang Jiaqi escaped from China and joined in overseas opposition movement (see *China Rights Forum*, Fall 1994).

Economic development also influences overseas opposition. If the domestic economy is going well, political opposition organisations are usually silent. If the economy deteriorates, or if the Chinese government commits serious errors, the climate becomes favourable for overseas opposition organisations to expand, make criticisms of the Chinese government and appeal to western governments. When the Chinese government managed to improve the economy and maintain political order, the overseas political movement reached 'a low tide'. Wan Runnan was then forced to give up the dream of returning to China to take over power in the short term and to aim, instead, at establishing the FDC as 'a mature opposition' (*Central Daily News*, 22 October 1990).

As regards the Chinese government's methods of handling opposition, suppression has been dominant. The use of external exile is, however, now an alternative to direct suppression. This was new as an official policy in China in the early 1990s (Barme 1991; Ma 1993),[23] and may be explained by western pressure, internal compromise among Chinese leaders, and persuasion and pressure by the OOM as well as overseas Chinese students and scholars. For the Chinese government, the external exile policy and control over communication between the Chinese people and the rest of the world seems an effective way of neutralising the dissidents' influence. Overseas Chinese dissident voices can reach only a small number of intellectuals in the home country. Allowing dissidents to leave the country also gives the Chinese government some relief against western pressure to improve human rights in China (Ma 1993). Does the exile policy, then, help the Chinese government to reduce domestic protest?

The Chinese government's exile policy may limit the influence of certain political exiles, but generally it has failed since political protest has in no way decreased. Since 1991, domestic dissidents' movements have been growing. In 1991, sixteen people were arrested for their involvement in organising a Democratic Liberal Party. In 1993, activists changed their strategy from organising a party to demanding constitutional reform by non-violent means and supporting the CCP. This was called the *heping xianzhang* (Peace Charter) movement. There have been many petition movements. One with eleven signatures urged the government to release Qin Youmin, an organiser of the the Peace Charter movement. The other, with 350 signatures, supported a painter who had protested against police violence (*Central Daily News*, 29 January 1994). Also, thirty-eight groups collected signatures demanding the right to strike and to organise trade unions (*Central Daily News*, 25 March 1994).

The Chinese government's exile policy will inevitably fail for the following three reasons. First, the combination of party domination and capitalism promises to be economically dynamic, but will bring certain kinds of socio-economic exploitation and greater inequalities (White 1994: 91). Economic development in China has already intensified social gaps, highlighting the serious problem of unequal distribution of wealth and welfare. These gaps are now becoming wider. The iconisation of Mao Zedong at the level of popular culture in China in the early 1990s may be explained as a kind of social complaint against this unequal distribution. The party appears unable to control and reduce corruption. These are favourable conditions for producing and encouraging domestic dissidents in China and for the FDC and the CAD to attract socially discontented people.

Further, as already shown, there are various links between domestic dissidents and the OOM. Overseas organisations have been sending funding to domestic dissidents, and some of their members have gone back to China secretly to initiate political activities. Both the FDC and the CAD have secret branches in major cities in China. Some students and dissidents regard the FDC and the CAD as 'democratic symbols', and have been keen to have new information on them and even to establish links with them.[24] Chinese dissidents are also developing links with international organisations through their connections with overseas Chinese. Yu Haocheng, a legal theorist in China, has agreed to serve as a member of the board of directors of the HRIC. Family relationships also strengthen the links between the OOM and domestic dissidents. For example, Liu Nianchung, an organiser of the Peace Charter movement and the Working People's League in 1994 in China, is the brother of Liu Qing, an HRIC activist in New York.

Furthermore, an opposition-promoting mechanism is at work. It was created by the international community and overseas political organisations, and unintentionally reinforced by the exile policy. It means that those who are opposed to the Chinese government may end up better off, in either a moral or a material sense, in spite of temporary setbacks. Liu Xiaopo, a hunger striker in the 1989 Tiananmen demonstration, a *heishou* ('black hand' or behind-the-scenes organiser) of the political riots identified by the Chinese government, was among the first people to discover this mechanism. When, as a visiting scholar at Columbia University, he decided to return to China to join the students' demonstration in 1989, he felt that his return, as a moral action, would help him to gain a reputation and help him to leave China again. He was right. When he was released from jail, he was invited by both the Australian National University and Harvard University in 1993. Liu's case demonstrates that dissidents may gain a reputation or funding, or go to the west. These incentives, among other things, encourage many activists to join the opposition ranks.

AN OVERALL ASSESSMENT OF THE OOM

As shown above, the OOM has done a great deal of intellectual work, resulted in multiple organisations, and initiated many activities to support domestic dissidents. Here I would like to stress the following important achievements.

The number of Chinese intellectuals, students, and activists engaging in organised political activities has been roughly estimated at 4,000,[25] which constituted 4 per cent of the 100,000 Chinese exile population scattered worldwide by 1989. Even if there has been some minor decline in this level, Chinese political exiles have now become a powerful force. The CAD and the FDC each has about fifty branches throughout the world. Most impressive is their organisational capacity in mobilising branches and members around the world and launching actions within just a few hours through fax, e-mail, and telephone communications.

The FDC and the CAD have been vulnerable to criticism that their own organisations are not democratic (*Central Daily News*, 30 July 1990). Wan Runnan and Wang Bingzhang have been accused of being authoritarian, and there have been abuses of funding and power in the FDC and CAD.[26] This has taught activists the lesson that the OOM is liable to corruption through abuses of power and funding. It has also led to pressure for the democratisation of the OOM. Considerable emphasis has been placed on using overseas organisations to democratise the political habits of the Chinese on a small, practical scale. The CAD took nearly eight years, the FDC one year (*Jiushi niandai*, 11, 1991: 46), from being founded to begin conducting their business in democratic ways: leadership successions in the CAD and the FDC are now decided through contested elections. Boards of directors have also been established in both the FDC and the CAD to check the use of funding. Most important, an internal control system has been established and improved. The CAD introduced a three-level power system in 1989: the board of directors functions as the legislative power; the headquarters as the executive power; the supervisory committee as the juridical power that interprets the movement's constitution. The FDC has also established the rule that the chairperson and board of directors hold a power of veto over each other.

Many attempts to establish a single centralised organisation of the OOM have failed, and factionalism has fragmented the movement. Attention is being given to how to institutionalise Article 6 of the FDC constitution[27] and create a set of rules regulating factions (Wang Luo 1990; also see *FDC Newsletter*, 9, 1990). But, so far, overseas organisations of the FDC and CAD have failed to deal successfully with factionalism. There have been power struggles within some organisations, for example between Wan Runnan and Chen Yizi (*Jiushi niandai*, 10, 1990: 38–9), between Yan Jiaqi and Wan Runnan, and between the Paris and Princeton groups in the FDC, between Wang Bingzhang and Hu Ping within the CAD, and between the CAD and the FDC. This factionalism seems less to do with ideology than with personal relations (see the previous discussion of the objectives of the OOM). Furthermore, factional fighting has become the rule rather than the exception. Factionalism was and still is a key factor which has constrained the development of an effective OOM.

There is also a trade-off between the democratic procedure and the efficiency of these organisations. For Wan Runnan, democratic procedure and internal controls on power have delayed quick decision making; and efficiency has been sacrificed to democracy (*FDC Newsletter*, 17: 26).[28] Thus, rigid measures to control the membership were taken, and the responsibility of local branches to the headquarters of the FDC was emphasised (*FDC Newsletter*, 4, 1990: 3–4). But Wan Runnan was then accused of being undemocratic. Yan Jiaqi and Yuan Min disagreed with Wan Runnan's elitist line for overseas political organisations. They saw the FDC as an ordinary organisation for ordinary people (*FDC Newsletter*, 17, 1990: 12–15). Thus, for both the CAD and the FDC, how to balance democracy and efficiency is an unresolved issue. Without discipline and efficiency, they are hardly likely to offer effective opposition; without democracy, they are hardly likely to be justifiable and credible.

Finance is another serious problem. It burdens the organisations. For example, the annual salary for seven staff in the FDC headquarters in Paris was US$150,000, or roughly, US$21,429 each. Office expenses were US$10,000 per month (*FDC Newsletter*, 16, 1990: 14). By comparison, the CAD spent US $198,000 for the second half of 1989 (*CAD Newsletter*, 17, 1990: 1).

Funds come chiefly from Taiwan – specifically, from the Chinese Nationalist Party's Hai-kung-hui (Overseas Work Committee) as well as from the publishers of the two big newspapers, *China Times* and *United Daily News* (Nathan 1992: 317–19). At the 1990 convention, Wan Runnan offered a glimpse into the FDC's finances: total donations amounted to US$1.3 million, half of which came from Taiwan, with Hong Kong[29] and the US accounting for another 20 per cent (Mosher and Kaye 1991: 34).

In the first rush of sympathy after the 4 June episode, funds flowed for the dissidents. But the money – whether from the US, Taiwan, or Hong Kong – soon dried up when the exiles failed to deliver much in the way of visible results. Taiwan's money has been reduced, either due to disagreements within the country over the principle of funding, or perhaps because of a perception that the exile groups waste money, or perhaps because of the Taiwan Democratic Progressive Party's requirement that funding should be open, or for some other reason. The cut has caused some retrenchment and struggles over who receives a salary. Lack of funding silenced the Chicago-based Voice of June 4 radio project, and Chai Ling's North American fund-raising tour barely managed to cover expenses. The FDC and the CAD have now engaged in business activities such as opening restaurants and shops to raise money.

With the current tightening of political and ideological controls in China, overseas political opposition organisations have become the major articulators of Chinese dissidence. Things would be very different if this overseas democracy movement did not exist. A large influence can be exercised by even a small OOM, since the Helsinki process was, and still is, a linkage of forces at home and abroad. The significance of overseas opposition organisations lies first of all in existing – the existence of the OOM is in itself a great pressure on the Chinese government; in lobbying – this has influenced US policies on China and thereby Chinese politics; and in the intellectual work which has influenced and continues to influence the ideas of Chinese people

(Nathan, 1992). For these reasons, I reject Goldstein's (1994: 23) view that the dissident movement looks doomed to irrelevance.

There are other aspects to the significance of the OOM. Its overseas location necessitates a broadening conception of China's politics. The activities of the HRIC also demonstrate a process whereby the OOM is being incorporated into a transnational civil society. China's politics have gone beyond the national boundary. Overseas political opposition can exercise pressure on the Chinese government through linkages and co-operation with a transnational civil society, and through influence on western governments' policies on China. Chinese issues of opposition and human rights have also been internationalised. In this matter, the traditional nation-state boundary has lost its significance. All these reflect the process of political globalisation.

CONCLUDING REMARKS: THE PROSPECTS FOR THE OOM

The OOM seems to have become smaller, and faces enormous difficulty in surviving, let alone developing into a powerful force. There have been moral as well as financial crises in overseas opposition organisations, caused by factionalism and fighting for posts. This has led to the withdrawal of some support from Taiwan, western governments, non-government organisations, and Chinese students and scholars. All contribute to the increasing marginalisation of overseas opposition organisations.

Location overseas itself implies a process of marginalisation;[30] that is, Chinese political exiles have moved from the centre of Beijing and other major cities in China to peripheral overseas sites.[31] Further, location overseas highlights the question of survival for political exiles. It is because of the need to survive that some leaders of the FDC and the CAD are concerned with their own future in their host countries, and have applied for permanent residence. This weakens the moral dimension of the OOM. The FDC and the CAD claim that they are more deserving of loyalty than the existing regime; thus they are expected to conform to a higher moral standard (Ma 1993).[32] The overseas Chinese community also expects political exiles, who are struggling to return home, to live up to higher-than-average moral standards (Tang Ben 1991). Thus, when leaders of the FDC and CAD hold foreign passports and struggle for a 'democratic post', their moral claim is damaged (Ma 1993). The credit of the OOM is also undermined, because for some western and Chinese activists, the OOM has degenerated into an immigration movement.[33]

Factionalism is inescapable in the context of exile. The Chinese government is far away, and the absence of an 'immediate enemy' can hardly motivate overseas political organisations to concentrate in one organisation. Further, a concentrated movement implies a reduction in the number of organisations and jobs. But many exiles need the income the jobs provide.[34] To have one's own organisation is a quick way to gain funding, and to be a leader of an organisation gives not only status but the credentials for applying for a refugee visa, for example.

Prospects for the OOM look dim if exiles remain in the west, as is shown above by examining the logic of location overseas. But the OOM could become the prime mover behind a strong opposition if activists return to China and establish an alliance with domestic opposition activists and reformers. Today, radical economic development and social change make it extremely difficult for the party to maintain the current neo-authoritarian system. There are enormous institutional tensions between limited economic pluralism and a monolithic political structure. The contradictory coexistence of capitalism and economic pluralism with party domination will, in the end, create social disruptions. To prevent this from occurring, reformers, as Sun Liping (1992) suggests, should openly acknowledge the legitimacy of opposition to deal with popular pressure effectively. This is a lesson from the 1989 students' demonstration. If the autonomous student organisations had been officially recognised earlier, the government might have controlled the student demonstrations effectively by selecting representatives for the students. The students might not have lost control of themselves.

A political crisis in post-Deng politics, which is likely to occur, might provide an opportunity for reformers to legitimise the opposition organisations. Thus, reformers might allow and welcome back political exiles, just as Gorbachev did in 1986. If this happens, overseas opposition organisations are likely to return and become a powerful opposition within China.

NOTES

* I would like to thank the participants of the Political Oppositions in East and Southeast Asia Workshop in Murdoch University on 2 September 1994, and particularly Garry Rodan, for useful comments, and Gail Graswell, Della Owens, Su-ke Ye, Hai-chuan Chou, and Suxing Mao for their help.

1 Out of the twenty-one most wanted pro-democracy movement leaders, the Chinese have apprehended only four, and two or three others have turned themselves in. The rest are now in the west (Awanohara 1989: 20).

2 The defining characteristics of political exiles are: exit (leaving the country), voice (criticising the home regime), and the struggle to return (engaging in political activities that are meant to create circumstances favourable to exiles' return). See Ma (1993: 371).

3 Before the Tiananmen massacre, there were roughly 100 organisations of Chinese students and intellectuals in the US, based on and around university campuses throughout the country. Not all were against Beijing. Shortly after the Tiananmen incident, the number of organisations jumped to 8,000 by one count and practically all condemned the incident (Awanohara 1989: 18).

4 See Shaozhi (1992).

5 *Democratic China* was supported by Taiwan's funding. The editors only solicited and edited articles; other activities such as typesetting, printing, and posting were done in Taiwan (*FDC Newsletter*, 13, 1990: 3). Chinese exiles have not had to cope with the trauma faced by Czech, Hungarian, or even Soviet émigrés who had to create their own publishing world and linguistic environment overseas. There is the ready-made publishing industry of Hong Kong and Taiwan, and countries like the US have an extensive Chinese-language press (Barme 1991).

6 Also see San Ying, 'Democracy Must Be Opposed to the CCP' (*CAD Newsletter*, 16, November 1989: 36).

7 Wan Runnan rejected the slogan 'Down with the CCP', as advocating an impractical and unwise strategy (*China Spring* (Australian Edition), 1, 1990: 65–6).

8 *Zhaoan* is a classical Chinese expression for the subversion or co-opting of rebel leaders through promises of personal safety, an amnesty, and so on.

9 For example, Wan Runnan changed his position from supporting to rejecting the idea of neo-authoritarianism. He argued that the FDC did not seek to be a neo-authority, nor did it accept *zhaoan* (*Democratic China*, 6, February 1991: 4–6). Wan's change in position can be seen as a strategy to win support from Chinese students and from Taiwan, as an example of how the place of exile can influence the opposition's strategy.

10 Information from Gao Jie who was a local leader of the Canberra branch of the FDC.

11 The CAD spent only US$5,000 as special money for mainland activities out of the total buget of US$170,000 from February to March 1990 (*CAD Newsletter*, 19, 1990: 12).

12 See HRIC (1992) 'Conference Proceedings', *International Human Rights Standards and Chinese Human Rights Situation*, New York: HRIC.

13 See Zhang Weiguo (1994).

14 This is not to deny that a large group of Chinese students plan to stay in the west permanently, but precisely for that reason the group is less active in the overseas democractic movement (Nathan 1992).

15 Wan Runnan, the leader of the FDC, has frequently written to world leaders including the general secretary of the UN, members of congresses or parliaments of western countries, and met or visited officials to urge them to exercise pressure on Beijing (*FDC Newsletter*, 34, 1991). Liu Jinghua, a woman participating in the workers' demonstration in 1989, visited the American Federation of Labor-Congress of Industrial Organizations which has promised financial support for at least one million workers for one year

if they strike in China. This comes from my talk with Zhang Zhihong, an activist in the workers' movement.

16 Of course, there was some disillusionment with the foreign host countries after western governments returned to business-as-usual relations with China mainly for economic reasons.

17 A typical example is Professor Andrew Nathan, the director of the East Asia Institute at the University of Columbia, who has long supported Chinese exiles. He sent invitations to Chinese activists such as Guo Luoji and Yu Haocheng, and helped them to leave China. He met and supported Wang Bingzhang before he founded the CAD, knew Ni Yuxian long before he and Wang Bingzhang formed the CLDP, as well as Yan Jiaqi and Hu Ping. He has served as an advisory board member or equivalent for several organisations such as the HRIC, the CMC, the Foundation for Human Rights and Democracy in China (organisations which are more academic than political).

18 Further, the FDC sent its delegates to the World Citizen Congress held in the US in October 1990 and the Fourth Helsinki International Citizen Conference in Czechoslovakia in October 1990 (*FDC Newsletter*, no. 34, 1991). Yue Wu, an activist in the workers' movement and a member of the FDC, attended the World Workers Conference in January 1991 (*FDC Newsletter*, 34, 1991).

19 For example, for a translation of Havel, see *Democratic China*, 6, February 1992; for a translation of Jacek Kuron, a key adviser to Solidarity, see *Chinese Intellectuals*, Fall 1989: 22–3; for a translation of Janos Kis on Hungary, see *Chinese Intellectuals*, Autumn 1992: 3–10.

20 As Fang Lizhi, astrophysicist and human rights activist, comments: the HRIC is committed to an independent, non-political, and intelligent approach (*Human Rights Tribune*, Spring 1992).

21 This comes from Liu Qing, an executive of the HRIC.

22 I gained this information from my interview with some people in the Stone Company on 24 October 1994.

23 For example, the philosopher Li Zehou, and dissidents Fang Lizhi, Wang Juntao, etc., have been allowed to leave China.

24 I met five students who had just been released from jail and they expressed their interest in the overseas organisations in early 1991. The above impression was reinforced by my research trip between October and November 1994. It should be pointed out that people's opinions on the overseas organisations vary. When I talked about the overseas organisations in China in 1994, some like Zhang Xianyang, a famous theorist, doubted their role in Chinese democracy. Others like Mo Qizhong, a millionaire business man, looked down upon them. People occasionally commented that exiles should have stayed in China, and that even if they were allowed to return to China they would not play major roles. Many asked about the FDC and the CAD sympathetically. Also see Barme (1991); Ma (1993); Nathan (1992); Goldstein (1994: 23).

25 The CAD had around 1,200 members in 1990 (*CAD Newsletter*, 17, 1990: 30). But Hu Ping told Nathan that the CAD had 2,000 in 1991. The FDC increased its membership from 153 in 1989 to 2,160 in 1990, and to 2,245 in 1991 (*FDC Newsletter*, 16, 1990: 18; 32, 1991: 25). The CLDP had about

400 members in 1990. There have been withdrawals of membership, thus the total may roughly be estimated as 4,000.

26 For example, Wang Bingzhang opened a consultation company in the name of the CAD for refugee applicants. Wu'er Kaixi used public donations for personal calls. (See *Cheng Ming*, 2, 1989: 29–31; Baixing, 187, March 1989: 19.)

27 Article 6 of the constitution of the FDC acknowledges inescapable factionalism among opposition organisations. It states that internal factions should be allowed to exist and should be transparent.

28 Cao Wuqi has also argued that political organisation must entail discipline and professionalism (*FDC Newsletter*, 4, 1990: 3–4). Ding Chu and Chen Jun have further argued that the CAD as a political organisation should not adopt the three-power system; it needs discipline (*CAD Newsletter*, 17, February 1990: 37). All wanted to establish a small organisation efficiently; they attempted to introduce secret membership, and wanted to establish a professional political organisation (*Cheng Ming*, 9, 1990: 64).

29 For Hong Kong's support, see Lau (1990: 20) and *Far Eastern Economic Review* (24 August 1989: 21).

30 On the important site of opposition, see Dahl (1969).

31 The sense of periphery sees that overseas is not where the crucial and decisive battlefield will be. Only in China can they employ resources to bring about change, and confront the Chinese government directly.

32 As Yu Dahai, the former chairman of CAD, has realised, the Pro-Democracy Movement is in fact a 'moral movement' (Ma 1993: 380).

33 For the majority of overseas Chinese students and scholars, their real interests and immediate concerns are to be able to stay in their host countries and get permanent residence. To win support from the students and scholars, the FDC and the CAD lobby western governments and officials to help Chinese students and scholars to obtain permanent residence.

34 This may be unflatteringly described as 'eating steamed bread soaked in blood'.

REFERENCES

Awanohara, Susumu (1989) 'In the Land of the Tree: Exiled Dissidents Split between Revolution and Reform', *Far Eastern Economic Review*, 24 August: 18–21.

Barmé, Geremie (1991) 'Travelling Heavy: the Intellectual Baggage of the Chinese Diaspora', *Problems of Communism*, 40(1–2): 94–112.

Chong, W. L. (1989) 'Recent Activities of the Front for a Democratic China', *China Information*, 4(2): 1–27.

Dahl, Robert (1969) 'Patterns of Opposition', in Charles Cnudde and Deane Neubauer (eds) *Empirical Democratic Theory*, Chicago: Maikham Publishing Company, pp. 114–30.

Ghils, Paul (1992) 'International Civil Society: International Non-governmental Organisations in the International System', *International Social Sciences Journal*, 133: 417–31.

Goldstein, Carl (1994) 'Innocents Abroad', *Far Eastern Economic Review*, 15 September: 22–7.

He Baogang (1994) 'Dual Roles of Semi-Civil Society in Chinese Democracy', *Australian Journal of Political Science*, 29(1), March 1994: 154–71.

—— (1995) 'The Ideas of Civil Society in Mainland China and Taiwan', *Issues and Studies*, 31(6): 24–64.

Herzog, Peter (1993) *Japan's Pseudo-Democracy*, New York: New York University Press.

Jansen, Marius (1967) *The Japanese and Sun Yat-sen*, Cambridge, Mass.: Harvard University Press.

Lau, Emily, Awanohara, Susumu, and Field, Michael (1990) 'Truth from the Fax: Exiled Dissidents Secure a Platform in the West', *Far Eastern Economic Review*, 31 May: 20–1.

Ma Shuyun (1993) 'The Exile, Voice and Struggle to Return of Chinese Political Exiles', *Pacific Affairs*, 66(3), Fall: 368–89.

Mosher, Stacy and Kaye, Lincoln (1991) 'Home Thoughts Abroad: Chinese Dissidents in US Grope for Post-Tiananmen Role', *Far Eastern Economic Review*, 6 June: 34–5.

Nathan, Andrew (1992) 'Historical Perspective on Chinese Democracy: the Overseas Democracy Movement Today', in Roger Jeans (ed.) *Roads Not Taken: the Struggle of Opposition Parties in Twentieth Century China*, Boulder, Colo.: Westview Press, pp. 313–27.

Pann, Lynn (1989) 'Springtime in Paris', *Far Eastern Economic Review*, 24 August: 20.

Pan, Lynn, Balakrishnan, N., and Handley, Paul (1989) 'Stirring the Blood: Dissidents Seek Overseas Chinese Help in Ousting Leadership', *Far Eastern Economic Review*, 24 August: 16–17.

Schiffrin, Harold (1968) *Sun Yat-sen and the Origins of the Chinese Revolution*, Berkeley: University of California Press.

Shaozhi, Su (ed.) (1992) 'Conference Proceedings', *On Institutional Choice*, Princeton, NJ: Future of China Society.

Sun Liping (1992) 'Guojia yu shehui de jiegoufenhua' ('The Structural Differentiation of the State from Society'), *Zhongguo shehui kexue jikan*, Hong Kong, 1, November: 69–76.

Tang Ben (1991) 'The Moral Dignity of Democratic China's Future Leaders', *Democratic China*, 6, February: 24–9.

Wang Luo (1990) 'Lun minzhen de "paibie gongkaihua"' ('Remarks on the Publicisation of Factionalism'), *FDC Newsletter*, 15: 8–12.

White, Gordon (1994) 'Democratization and Economic Reform in China', *Australian Journal of Chinese Affairs*, 31: 73–92.

Yang Jianli (1992) 'Haihuan minyun de jiaoshe yu zhudang wenti' ('The Roles of Overseas Democracy and the Issue of the Establishment of Party'), *FDC Newsletter*, 38: 11–13.

Zhang Weiguo (ed.) (1994) *China Constitutionalism Newsletter*, San Francisco.

8 The broadening base of political opposition in Indonesia

*Edward Aspinall**

President Soeharto's New Order government is almost thirty years old. During this time, a tremendous transformation of economic, social, and political life has occurred. Economic growth, industrialisation, and the emergence of new urban classes have transfigured the social terrain in which political opposition operates. This chapter attempts to provide a brief survey of how this changing social terrain has affected the character of opposition. It argues that such changes have contributed to the broadening of the social and political base of opposition, and have put considerable strains on the corporatist model which has hitherto been employed by the New Order to contain discontent. Compared to the narrow urban middle-class opposition circles of the early New Order period, opposition activities in the 1990s have a far broader social base, as indicated most clearly by the spread of labour activism. Populist and radical political currents which were largely silent in the 1970s have re-emerged in new form. And middle-class dissent now possesses a stronger and more autonomous organisational basis, indicated primarily by the growth of non-government organisations (NGOs). All of this points to the emergence of a nascent state–civil society division. Nevertheless, opposition still faces formidable challenges, not only because of continued repression, but also because of middle-class fears of political and social disorder. Hence the government retains substantial capacity for new forms of co-optation, and much opposition is played out in the grey zone between 'state' and 'society'. In order to clarify these arguments, it is necessary first to glance back to the origins of both the present regime and its oppositions.

THE NEW ORDER COALITION

The New Order regime did not come about through a simple military coup. Rather, it was brought into being by a coalition which, although it had the army at its core, also drew on significant social support. The later years of President Soekarno's Guided Democracy was a time of profound economic, social, and political conflict. It was a time of mass-based politics and a seemingly irresistible surge to the Left, with the rapid growth of a mass-based Communist movement, class struggle in the Javanese countryside, and Soekarno himself increasingly dependent on the Left for support. Civilian opponents of the Left had an increasing siege mentality; their chief organisations were either banned (Indonesian Socialist Party (PSI) and the modernist Islamic party, Masjumi), under threat of banning (Islamic Students Association (HMI)), or being wrested away from them (Indonesian National Party (PNI)). At the same time, hyperinflation and general economic disintegration caused great hardship in middle-class circles (as in other sectors of society). The middle class and elite social layers which had emerged in the colonial and parliamentary eras were in any case small and weak, especially the indigenous capitalist class (Robison 1986). All of these circumstances gave rise to a great sense of beleaguerment and fragility in privileged social layers, whereby the military was increasingly seen as the only possible alternative to the Left.

The 30 September Movement affair of 1965, when leftist army officers kidnapped and killed a number of senior army officers, provided the trigger for the coalescence of the 'New Order coalition'. The army had two principal allies in its campaign against the PKI (Indonesian Communist Party), the rest of the Left, and Soekarno. The first was the Islamic community. The followers of the main Islamic organisations provided the bulk of the masses in the demonstrations in Jakarta and other cities, and Islamic youth participated directly in the eradication of the Left in rural areas. The second source of support was what can be described, for want of a better term, as the secular-oriented urban middle classes. Middle-class university students, journalists, legal professionals, intellectuals, economists, and others, many of whom were associated with the banned PSI or the Catholic party (although many were independent or associated with Masjumi), rallied to the army. In co-operation with military officers, they formed the Action Fronts, the most important of which were the students' and scholars' groups KAMI, KAPPI, and KASI. These groups campaigned vigorously – on the streets, through their new media publications, in the universities, and elsewhere – against the 'Old Order'. They provided crucial civilian legitimation for the military rise to power, and many of them from the outset attempted to provide the military with a policy framework. Some individuals later became prominent as members of the government party Golkar or as key technocratic ministers.

In the space of a few months after 30 September 1965, the PKI was destroyed in one of the greatest political massacres of modern times. Within two years, Soekarno had lost all effective power, and a comprehensive purge of the state apparatus of leftists and Soekarno sympathisers was nearing completion. By the late 1960s, the uncertainties of the transition period were passing, and the main contours of the new regime were clearly visible. The New Order was firmly committed to a programme of capitalist economic development, in contrast with the 'economic chaos' of the previous years. It was military-based and committed to political order, in contrast to the 'political chaos' which had reigned under its predecessor.

What did this portend for opposition? The very concept of political opposition had no place in the all-pervasive Pancasila ideology which was constructed and elaborated by the government during the 1970s and into the 1980s. According to the official view, there was no place in Indonesia for conflicting interests either within society or between society and state. Instead, state and society were portrayed as an integrated and organic whole, where deliberation and consensus replaced the divisive and conflictual politics of the past. (On *Pancasila* ideology, see, for example: Morfit 1981; Bourchier 1992, 1993; Ramage 1995.) Mass politics was to end, and a network of corporatist institutions was created to establish control over key social sectors. In the first decade of the New Order there was a sustained effort to depoliticise society, especially the lower classes. In short, these years saw the consolidation of the tremendous domination of 'state' over 'society', which in various manifestations has since dominated much analysis of Indonesian politics (for example, McVey 1982; Anderson 1983; Robison 1986).

OPPOSITION IN THE EARLY NEW ORDER: 1968–78

However, with the consolidation of the New Order regime in the late 1960s and early 1970s, the military–civilian coalition which had brought it into being began to fray. Two main clusters of issues gave rise to opposition (and have continued to do so to this day).

The first set of issues centred on themes of 'democracy', 'rule of law', 'human rights', and so on. During the transition period, when the onslaught against the Left was at its height, and not without some irony,[1] the more liberal elements in the coalition hoped that the 'New Order' they were helping to bring about would result in the formation of a *rechtsstaat*, a state based on the rule of law, where there would be respect for due process, equality before the law, the submission of authorities to legal constraints, civil liberties, and democratic norms (Lev 1978). From the late 1960s some of the new government's supporters became disillusioned with its military leaders' apparent lack of commitment to these same ideals (especially as many of these supporters-turned-critics found themselves increasingly at the receiving end of mistreatment by the security apparatus). Two early expressions of disillusionment were the boycott (*golput*) campaign organised by Arief Budiman and other students as a protest against abuses in the 1971 elections, and the formation of the Legal Aid Institute (LBH), as an agent not only to provide free legal aid for the poor, but also to act as a kind of ombudsman in cases of abuse by the state apparatus (Lembaga Bantuan Hukum 1973: 15).

The repressive-authoritarian character of the regime became increasingly clear to many of its erstwhile supporters during the 1970s, which saw the 'bulldozer tactics' of the 1971 and 1977 elections, the forced amalgamations of the political parties, and the hardening government attitudes to liberal and Islamic critics. As it became increasingly clear that the military was entrenching itself in politics for the long haul, the rule of law, human rights, and democratic themes became increasingly prominent in criticisms made of the government. Critics increasingly called for the military role to be substantially revised or reduced. For example, the student movement of 1977–8 (even more than that of 1973–4) contained strongly anti-military elements, demands for the respect of human rights, and the regularisation of state administration more generally (including in the matter of patrimonial and corrupt relations between leading state officials and private business interests). But most students were still hesitant as to how far they were willing to condemn the military, with calls for the military to 'return to the people'. Even more clearly, in the late 1970s, a group of disgruntled retired military and civilian leaders – eventually to coalesce in the Petition of Fifty group – began to make open calls for a range of democratic reforms (Jenkins 1984). But even here there were ambiguities, and this group too is most properly seen as a movement for regularisation within the framework of the existing state: its aim, as expressed in a recurring refrain in the literature it has produced, is the 'return to the original resolve of the New Order, the pure and consistent implementation of *Pancasila* and the 1945 Constitution'.

The second main cluster of issues which gave rise to opposition was economic and social in character, and centred on calls for greater social justice and distribution of the nation's wealth. From its foundation, the New Order regime pursued an economic development programme which generated high levels of growth but at the same time exacerbated many of the inequalities manifest in Indonesia's social structure. In the early years of the new regime, much of the legitimacy accorded it by middle-class layers was due to its insistently proclaimed commitment to overcoming the economic crisis of Guided Democracy, and to its promises to work away at the country's economic modernisation and to raise living standards. This source of legitimacy became even more important as many early supporters became increasingly disillusioned with the government's performance in the political sphere. Early criticisms by the military's former partners called on the government to honour its promises of rational, fair, and efficient economic development. For example, the student demonstrations of the late 1960s and the first years of the 1970s did not attack the government's economic development programme as such, but were explicitly aimed at saving it from the dangers of rising prices, mismanagement, corruption, and wasteful extravagance.

By 1973–4, it was becoming apparent to a number of critics that rather than better and cleaner implementation, a more fundamental change in economic policy was needed. These were the days of the open door policy towards foreign investment. Overseas capital, especially from Japan, was flooding into the manufacturing sector, displacing many medium and small-scale (especially Islamic) indigenous businesses. In the period leading up to the Malari affair, when on 15 January 1974 riots greeted the arrival of Japanese Prime Minister Tanaka, economists like Sarbini Sumawinata and Dorodjatun Kuntjoro Jakti played a key role in developing a populist critique of government economic policy. They promoted greater distribution of the 'fruits of development' and found a receptive audience in student and other dissident circles. Government critics began to talk in terms of the need for a development strategy which focused on basic needs, put more emphasis on rural development and employment, and criticised the government's obsession with 'simply increasing the GNP'. A focus on the neglect of the poor in development policy, plus the earlier critique of corruption at high levels, produced the harsh attacks on the corrupt alliance between foreign capital, Chinese business tycoons, and government bureaucrats which characterised the student movements of 1973–4 and, especially, 1977–8. The emerging neo-populist critique of government development policy then gave birth to a new generation of developmentalist NGOs in the late 1970s.

Five particular aspects of opposition in the first decade of the New Order deserve note. First, there was a distinction between tolerated and non-tolerated opposition. Although all manner of critics were eventually liable to be repressed, the most systematic persecution was directed at those political forces defined by the government as being beyond the pale of Pancasila orthodoxy, as representing the principal threats to national and societal unity.

The first and primary target was the Left. The New Order's principal claim to legitimacy was that it saved the nation from Communist treachery, and during the 1970s there was a sustained anti-Communist ideological campaign. Against the backdrop of the killings some years before, phrases like *bahaya laten PKI* ('latent danger of the PKI') and *ekstrim kiri* ('extreme Left') were constructed into a potent ideological edifice. In reality, the PKI had been destroyed as a potentially powerful force by the massacre, and the few surviving guerrilla remnants in Kalimantan were eliminated in the early 1970s. There were two important corollaries to the anti-Communist political atmosphere, however. First, lower-class political activity, especially the organisation of workers and peasants in defence of their class interests, was proscribed and liable to be persecuted. Depoliticisation policies were initially and most concertedly directed at the lower classes. Important measures included the 'floating mass' policy which excluded the political parties from villages, and the development of corporatist bodies to 'channel the aspirations' of labour and farmers. For most of the 1970s, fear was widespread in the lower classes and they remained largely quiescent. The second corollary was the taming of the Soekarnoist current. The PNI and other populist supporters of the former President suffered badly in the aftermath of the 1965–6 events. The left wing of the party was eliminated, many party leaders, members, and supporters were killed, imprisoned, or harassed, the party was cut off from its former base in the civil bureaucracy, there was heavy military intervention in the selection of party leaders, and finally, the party was pressed to merge into the Indonesian Democratic Party (PDI) in 1973. Suffering from the effects of fear in the rank and file, and from the paralysis brought about by incessant government-encouraged internal conflicts, the PDI itself had minimal effectiveness as an opposition force.

The second, increasingly non-tolerated opposition was the *ekstrim kanan* ('extreme Right'), which in regime terminology refers to those who seek the establishment of an Islamic state. Although Islamic groups had participated vigorously in the campaign against Soekarno and the Left, there had been considerable tension between them and the military from the outset. Significant sections of the officer corps viewed political Islam as a potentially centrifugal and disintegrative force, in part because of the Darul Islam rebellion and the constitutional debates of the 1950s. From early in the transition to the New Order, obstacles were placed in the way of Islamic groups, for example when the government vetoed the revival of Masjumi and the rehabilitation of its leaders. However, during the 1970s, local communities of believers, mosque-based networks, and even the great Islamic social organisations, Muhammadiyah and Nahdlatul Ulama (NU; respectively the principal organisations of the 'modernist' and 'traditionalist' sections of the orthodox community), tended to be more resilient to intervention from the state than were, say, the Soekarnoist organisations. Precisely because Islam was not merely a political movement, it was able to maintain its coherence and potential as a political force. And so, by the late 1970s, it appeared that Islam was developing as the most vocal and resilient voice of opposition, as evidenced by the dispute over the 1973 Marriage Bill, the energetic United Development Party (PPP) election campaign of 1977, the 1978 NU walk-out from the People's Consultative Assembly (MPR), and even the social protest *dakwah* music of singers like Rhoma Irama. This intransigence accounted for the new emphasis on the threat from the extreme Right in regime discourse by the late 1970s, with, for example, the manufacture by military intelligence of the Komando Jihad affair in the lead-up to the 1977 elections. Again, as with the proscription of Communism, there was considerable spillover, and Muslim activists with a broad range of political viewpoints were harassed or repressed.

It should be clear, then, that those most able to articulate dissent were those elements who had participated most centrally in the New Order coalition of the 1960s and who had been closest to the army at that time. Students, secular intellectuals, former Action Front activists, and even retired military and civilian officials formed the core of the dissident circles of the 1970s. Because of their former role, they had at least a modicum of political legitimacy in New Order discourse. For example, university students played a central role in opposition politics in the 1970s in large part because they had won a relatively privileged position through the role played by the main anti-Communist student organisations, and especially students from Universitas Indonesia and Institut Teknologi Bandung, in the anti-Soekarno movement. Mainstream accounts of the formation of the New Order emphasised the role played by these students and their moral and idealistic motivations. In these circumstances, it was initially difficult for the government simply to move against the new generation of student activists. Similarly, it was the newspapers which had most vigorously attacked Soekarno, such as *Mahasiswa Indonesia*, *Indonesia Raya*, *Nusantara*, and *Harian Kami*, which were the most vocal critics of corruption and other abuses of power in the early 1970s.

Thus, in the early 1970s, there developed a kind of 'dissident niche' for those middle-class and elite groups which had earlier supported the rise of the New Order. Critics in such circles were able to make more or less forthright and general criticisms of the government. In Linz's terms, they constituted an alegal or tolerated opposition, operating relatively openly but on the fringes of legality (Linz 1973: 191, fn. 35). This is not to say that they had unlimited freedom of political movement. Instead, they were increasingly subject to intermittent, low-level and unpredictable harassment. As will be discussed below, their relations with the government deteriorated sharply over the decade.

The second point concerning opposition in the 1970s is that, precisely because of their political and social origins, these middle-class dissidents and alegal opponents continued to share much in common with the regime or elements within it. Indeed, the earliest expressions of dissent made clear that they in fact wanted to save the New Order, as the following extract from a statement produced by student anti-corruption group Mahasiswa Menggugat (Students Accuse) makes clear:

> The aim of these demonstrations is not to overthrow the government, but instead they represent critical support for the government. We see dangers in the government's action [a price rise], which is destroying the good name of the government in the eyes of the little people. . . . Once again, the government should be truly convinced that the protest actions which we are taking are intended precisely to improve the image of the Soeharto government in the eyes of the little people. Because we, the students, also helped to put in place the new order, we feel that we also have responsibility for their good name.
>
> (*Sinar Harapan*, 19 January 1970)

Admittedly, this is an early and extreme example. Later in the decade there would be far greater frustration and alienation in student and other dissident circles. But it serves to underscore the point that most middle-class critics and the government continued to share an underlying commitment to economic development and political stability. These were, after all, the principal concerns which had underpinned the 1966 coalition. Critics in the 1970s wanted a more efficient, regularised, and cleaner administration which was subject to legal restraint and which put the pursuit of rational economic modernisation ahead of the private and corrupt gain of officials. One particular feature of the 1966 coalition had been the hostility to mass politics. The mobilisation of the lower classes was an integral element of daily political life under the 'Old Order', which 'New Order radicals' had seen as a primary obstacle to modernisation (especially because it was carried out by the political parties which they saw as venal, corrupt, and based on dangerous primordialism). The aversion to mass politics (often expressed as repudiation of 'chaos' or 'anarchy') continued to mark the student and intellectual opposition circles of the 1970s. This was evident in, for example, the court defence speeches of many student activists in 1978, or, somewhat earlier in the decade, Arief Budiman and others' arguments that students constituted a moral force seeking to correct government, rather than a political force seeking to overthrow or replace it.

A third point, which follows directly from this, is that opponents of the regime in the 1970s had very little in the way of an autonomous institutional base. The most vocal critics were intellectuals, journalists, and other professionals operating out of the media or in the universities. There was a handful of prominent NGOs, but most of these were established in conjunction with more liberal or supportive elements in the regime: for example, LBH was established under the sponsorship of Jakarta Governor Ali Sadikin and relied on him for funding, while LP3ES (Institute for Economic and Social Research, Education and Information) was sponsored by technocrat ministers like Soemitro Djojohadikusomo, Ali Wardhana, and Emil Salim (Eldridge 1995). In addition to the Islamic organisations touched on above, the only relatively autonomous institutional base which still survived and had the capacity to organise dissent on anything approaching a national scale was the university student councils. And in the long run, as relations with government worsened, all of these bodies became vulnerable to repression. Overall, then, the formal organisational base was weak: urban middle-class opposition in the 1970s in many respects resembled a milieu more than an organised movement. Informal networks, clique groups, personalised ties and relations, which would often cut across institutional boundaries, played a role which could not be performed by more institutionalised political forms.

The fourth important point is that, as a consequence of all these factors, there was a great overlap or blurring between opposition and government, state and civil society. It is difficult to conceive of opposition in the 1970s as simply the mobilisation of political forces from the domain of civil society outside and against the state. This was reflected in two phenomena.

In the first place, what Linz has described as 'semi-opposition' was very common: 'Semi-opposition in our sense consists of those groups that are not dominant or represented in the governing group but that are willing to participate in power without fundamentally challenging the regime' (Linz 1973: 191).

Linz's definition may itself be problematic (especially the ambiguous phrase 'participate in power'), but it is useful. From the outset, the Indonesian New Order regime was never merely narrowly military-based. The core power centres sought to co-opt and incorporate other social and political forces in a subordinated position (except the Communist and populist Left, which were eliminated). It is this characteristic which gave the phenomenon of semi-opposition such prominence. From the early 1970s, there were many niches of various kinds in official institutions for individuals and groups with views somewhat at variance with the core groups, provided the fundamentals were not challenged. And so, some groups which were early allies of the military deliberately adopted a 'work from within' strategy and entered various institutions either in the state apparatus proper or in Golkar and its subordinate institutions. From the inside, they sought to win leadership positions and influence policy making. For example, the Grup Tamblong of young 'modernising intellectuals' from Bandung joined Golkar where one of the group's leaders, Rachman Tolleng, became a member of the central leadership board. Similarly, Gabungan Usaha Perbaikan Pendidikan Islam (GUPPI; Association for the Improvement of Islamic Education) played an important role in attracting Islamic support to Golkar while at the same time its members, especially those in the Department of Religion, actively strove to modify or even oppose various government policies, such as the 1973 Marriage Bill (Cahyono 1992). For other groups, however, semi-opposition was less a choice on strategy but more of an unavoidable response to forced incorporation. The surviving political parties, for example, had little choice but to submit to the forced mergers of 1973 and to make the best of the new political conditions. Those party leaders who were even somewhat critical of the government devoted much of their energy to attempting to maintain their positions in the face of incessant internal conflicts deliberately encouraged by government intervention.

There was a second sense in which there was a blurring of the demarcation between regime and opposition: even in the dissident milieu which was beginning to emerge on the 'outside', critics of the government very much looked to the state for political opportunities and allies. The classic example was the circumstances surrounding the Malari incident in January 1974, when tensions in the regime (especially the conflict between General Soemitro representing 'military professionals' and Ali Moertopo as the chief representative of the 'business generals') coincided with mounting pressures for political and economic reform from students, intellectuals, and the liberal press.

Although the exact configuration of events remains murky, it is clear that many dissident elements attempted to take advantage of these splits to press for thoroughgoing reform. Some hoped that Soemitro would be able to take advantage of the situation and, if not take power, at least act decisively against Ali Moertopo and the other business generals (Crouch 1974, 1988: 306–17; Gunawan 1975; Cahyono 1992: 143–70). It was not surprising that dissidents should endeavour to seek out the most reform–oriented elements within the regime, given the obvious imbalance between their own political resources and those of the state, and also because of their experiences only a few years before in the civil–military alliance which ushered in the New Order.

A fifth and final point needs to be made about opposition in the 1970s. There was a progressive diminution through the decade of the space available for even the limited opposition described above. As the regime continued to consolidate and the government gained in confidence (in part because of the increase in state revenues brought about by the mid-1970s oil boom), politics became more monolithic and repressive. Limited pluralism of power centres in government gave way to a more centralised line of command tracing up to the Presidential Palace. As a result, there was less room for manoeuvre in state and corporatist institutions. This was reflected in, for example, the expulsion from Golkar and imprisonment of Tamblong leader Rachman Tolleng after Malari, or the defeat of the moderately oppositional Sanusi-Usep leadership of the PDI some years later. Harsher conditions applied also to dissent more clearly on the 'outside' of the system. There were two major crackdowns on students, other dissidents, and the press: first in 1974, in the wake of the Malari affair, and second in 1978, when student councils were finally permanently frozen.

SOCIAL TRANSFORMATION

Since the first decade of the New Order, Indonesia has undergone a profound social and economic transformation. Economic growth has been sustained at high levels, and real per capita GDP trebled between 1965 and 1990 (Hill 1994: 56). The economic crisis caused by the decline in oil prices in the early 1980s prompted a major rethink of economic nationalist and statist policies. There was a major policy shift in favour of export-oriented industrialisation, liberalisation, a greater role for the private sector, and an emphasis on manufacturing. What have been the social consequences of these changes?

In the first place, they have contributed to new tensions within the regime. As argued persuasively by Robison (1986), a new and powerful capitalist class has begun to consolidate itself from within the upper echelons of state officialdom. Leading state officials have used the opportunities availed them by their access to the levers of economic decision making over the last thirty years to engage in large-scale capital accumulation. The new 'notable' families (most importantly the Soeharto family but also those of other senior officials) have emerged as the loci of enormous political and economic power (Robison 1994). At the same time, partly as a result of this process, the political power of the military as an institution has been on the decline, although in the final analysis it retains considerable strength. There has been significant resentment in sections of the officer corps with the President, his family and his most loyal camp followers (especially Golkar chairperson and later Vice President Sudharmono in the 1980s, and powerful Research and Technology Minister B. J. Habibie in the 1990s).[2]

Second, it is indisputable that there has been important growth in the size of the urban middle class (Tanter and Young 1990). In the early years of the New Order, there was something of a hothouse atmosphere in the elite suburbs of Jakarta and the other big cities. Limited educational opportunities and the stunted post-independence economy produced a correspondingly small educated and wealthy elite. Professionals, intellectuals, and entrepreneurs moved in narrow, inward-looking, and cross-cutting social circles. Privileged groups had been made acutely conscious of their minority status by the political conflicts and officially egalitarian culture of the late Guided Democracy period. Now, the middle-class is not only a much larger and more amorphous social entity, but it is far more self-confident. A brash and exuberant middle class consumer culture is plainly visible in the shopping malls, night clubs, golf courses, business schools, and housing estates which have mushroomed in and around the big cities. And this new enthusiasm is not limited only to a few top beneficiaries of New Order economic growth: alongside luxurious shopping centres like Pondok Indah Mall and Plaza Indonesia there are many less ostentatious supermarkets which cater for the more modest tastes of the growing lower middle-class market.

It would thus seem that the potential social base of the kind of middle-class opposition which emerged in the 'dissident niche' of the 1970s is much larger in the 1990s. However, there is need for a note of caution here. First, although the social middle has grown rapidly, it still represents a small fraction of the overall population, and is surrounded on all sides by impoverished rural and urban masses.[3] Second, according to some analyses, Indonesia's middle class primarily consists of elements which represent more a social bulwark of authoritarianism, rather than the archetypal liberalising and enlightened middle class of much political theory (see, for example, Robison 1990). This is partly because of the dependence of much of the middle stratum on state resources, either directly through state employment or indirectly via patronage. Middle-class conservatism may also be attributed to an important third reason for caution, fear of social unrest and instability. Officials of the government and its ideological apparatus certainly endeavour to keep alive the memory of the conflicts of the pre-Soeharto years and constantly warn of the dangers of social explosion if political controls are loosened. It would seem likely that many in the middle classes have little interest in jeopardising the steadily increasing prosperity they have enjoyed under New Order economic growth for the sake of an uncertain project of regime change. In particular, fear of the explosive combination of lower-class resentment at the growing gap between rich and poor ('social jealousy', as it is often called) and popular anti-Sinicism is often viewed as a fear of the large ethnically Chinese section of the entrepreneurial middle and business class.[4] For many non-Islamic and secular-oriented members of the middle class, fear of unrest from below is also inextricably bound up with fear of an Islamic resurgence and a supposed desire for retribution from the frustrated and impoverished Islamic majority.

This middle-class unease is important. Economic growth has affected more than the middle and upper echelons of society. It has also been accompanied by tremendous social dislocation affecting much broader sections of the population. In particular, and of crucial importance, the years of economic liberalisation have seen a rapid burst in industrialisation, especially in labour-intensive light consumer good sectors like textiles, garments, and footwear. The industrial share of GDP is now 23 per cent compared with 5–6 per cent in the 1960s (*Far Eastern Economic Review(FEER)*, 18 May 1995: 48). Massive new industrial estates have sprung up on the outskirts of Jakarta, Bandung, Semarang, Surabaya, Medan, and other towns in and outside Java, and a correspondingly large industrial working class has come into existence, a social force which hardly existed in the early years of the New Order. This process of class formation has been brutal, involving tight labour regimentation in order to maintain Indonesia's 'comparative advantage' in wages. Similarly, capitalist development has had negative social impacts on rural society, with massive rural underemployment and unemployment, conflicts over land and other resources, and other social problems. Thus, the emergence of a new rich and upwardly mobile middle class has taken place against the backdrop of continuing social inequality and mass poverty. This gives the issue of the 'social gap' tremendous currency in contemporary Indonesian politics.

OPPOSITION IN THE LATE NEW ORDER: 1987–95

So, against this backdrop of social transformation, what have been the changes and continuities in opposition? In the first place, the same two basic sets of issues still give rise to opposition, but in even sharper form.

Since the late 1980s, and following the worldwide wave of democratisation which began in the mid-1970s (most critically for Indonesia, in the Philippines and South Korea), *demokrasi* ('democracy'), *keterbukaan* ('openness'), and *hak asasi manusia* ('human rights') have been far more unambiguously at the centre of the agenda of many regime critics than they were in the 1970s. This is clearly reflected in the student movement, for example, with defence speeches at student trials since the beginning of the 1990s making great play of the worldwide wave of democratisation. Student activist groups are now far more uniformly hostile to the very idea of military participation in government than they were in the 1970s. LBH now promotes itself increasingly not merely as a legal aid or even human rights organisation, but as the *locomotif demokratisasi* ('engine of democratisation'). Similarly, 1991 saw the formation of Forum Demokrasi, a group of prominent intellectuals openly making the case for democratic reform. Perhaps the fundamental change, however, is that since 1989 *keterbukaan* and *demokratisasi* have emerged not simply as the slogans of a narrow and marginalised alegal opposition, but (admittedly with fluctuations) as key themes of public debate, discussed and promoted by the media, academics, a wide range of 'semi-oppositional' political groups, and elements from within the government itself (notably the military group, F-ABRI, in parliament). The desire for democratic reform has become almost tangible. It was reflected in, for example, the spiralling circulation of the bold news weekly *DëTik* before it was banned in mid-1994, or the frequency of seminars discussing aspects of democratisation on the Jakarta seminar circuit. Even the spirited campaign which followed the banning of *DëTik* and two other magazines stands in stark contrast to the acquiescence which followed the media shutdowns of the 1970s.

There have been three major changes in opposition centred on economic and social justice themes. In the first place, avenues for collaboration with the government have remained open and even expanded for advocates of reformist, neo-populist economic development. The number of non-government organisations which view problems of poverty as primarily policy or technical issues has increased greatly, and so has their co-operation with various government agencies. Similarly, many academic advocates of neo-populist development have found positions within Bappenas (the National Planning Board) or other government bodies. In the second place, largely as a consequence of social changes discussed above, there has been a marked increase in the incidence and visibility of conflict involving the lower classes. Disputes over land, usually involving poor farmers resisting demands made by developers and local authorities, have become commonplace. The most marked change, however, has been in the labour sphere. There has been a great explosion in strikes, mobilisation, and illegal organising by workers. In the third place, there has been something of a convergence between this lower-class unrest and the political activity of middle-class activists. Increasing numbers of students have attempted to organise and mobilise farmers and, increasingly, workers. Many small NGOs have been formed which adopt a more combative advocacy stance, or even what is essentially a class struggle position. Indeed, the increased visibility of activity by the working class and farmers cannot be separated from the role of students and former students in NGOs who have developed mechanisms to reach out to, and organise, the poor.

THE BROADENING OPPOSITION

From this brief description, it should be clear that opposition is now more diverse than it was in the early New Order. In the 1970s, the massacre of 1965–6 was a recent memory, coercion was at a high point, and fear was widespread throughout society but especially in the lower classes. A relatively narrow dissident niche existed for former allies of the military. Now, opposition activities are broader in three respects.

Broader social base

In the 1970s, active dissidence was mostly limited to narrow intellectual and other elite circles in the big cities, especially Jakarta and Bandung. This clearly remains a crucial domain of opposition, but the social base of such activities is now far broader. This can be illustrated by two examples. The first and most graphic is the explosive spread of labour organising in the industrial estates and working-class housing suburbs which surround the big cities. It is true that labour activism is still subject to harsh repression and that most strikes put forward essentially economic demands. However, the potential political implications of the new labour activism are indicated by the increasing prominence of demands for freedom to organise unions (and even for the dissolution of factory SPSI – corporatist labour union – units) in many strikes since the early 1990s and by the alliances between workers and students or other middle-class activists which underpin many of these actions. The second example is in a more purely middle-class sphere, the student movement. In the 1970s, the student movement was very much centred in Jakarta and Bandung, especially in a handful of elite state universities. Since the re-emergence of student activism in 1988–9, although these two cities remain important, the movement is much more evenly dispersed through regional towns in Java (and is, if anything, centred in Central Java). This is in part related to the boom in tertiary education, and especially the growth of private universities and colleges in regional centres since the 1970s, which in turn has been generated by the middle-class boom and the increasing demand for entrepreneurial, managerial, and professional skills.

More heterogeneous political character

A wider range of political forces has moved into overtly oppositional political activity. In particular, there has been a re-emergence (albeit in new form) of nationalist, populist, and even leftist political moods and ideologies, precisely those political currents which were the chief victims of the 1965–6 events. In large part, these currents draw their political sustenance from the social inequalities which have accompanied and been exacerbated by New Order economic growth.

In particular, since the early 1980s a new element of defiance has been detectable in the Soekarnoist current, which had been reduced to compliance in the 1970s. This has been symbolised by the new political activism and visibility of Soekarno's children, the resurgence of enthusiastic public interest in Soekarno, and the emergence of Soekarnoist organisations and networks outside the PDI. But perhaps the most visible sign has been a certain invigoration of the PDI, which in its 1987 and 1992 election campaigns attempted more vigorously to reassert a role for itself as populist spokesperson of the *wong cilik* ('the little people') who have been sidelined by the process of national development. PDI campaigners in the 1992 election criticised the socially disastrous clove and citrus monopolies held by members of the Soeharto family, for example, and some even called for a change of President. This doubtlessly had a lot to do with conflicts within the government, with the PDI leadership reportedly receiving much encouragement and support from the group in the military who supported

Benny Moerdani (Chief of the Armed Forces from 1983 to 1988 and Defence and Security Minister from 1988 to 1993). But the enthusiastic campaign from the *arus bawah* ('undercurrent') within the PDI which saw Megawati Soekarnoputri, daughter of former President Soekarno, appointed as leader in 1993 also indicates a new level of energy and boldness in the Soekarnoist rank and file.

Indeed, the importance of the Soekarnoist current does not mainly lie in its organisational strength, but in its largely latent and unorganised mass support. Soekarnoism, or perhaps more accurately Soekarno as a symbol (and things closely associated with him, such as his family), has its greatest appeal in the lower classes, especially in urban areas.[5] The lower-class character of the PDI support base is very apparent in its election campaign rallies, or even in the largely plebeian crowds which surrounded the 1993 Surabaya congress, cheering Megawati on and shouting down her opponents. Organisationally, however, this current remains weak. Soekarnoist groups outside the PDI are atomised and factionalised. The Megawati leadership of the PDI continues to be badly circumscribed by the government's encouragement of inner-party factionalism (including the use of Communist scare campaigns) and has in any case not yet signalled any clear intention seriously to challenge the regime.

At the same time, a small new Left, or Left-populist, current is increasingly visible. This has its roots in the critique of developmentalism and militarism which evolved in student and NGO circles from the mid-1970s. This new Left is most visible in one wing of the student movement which combines the traditional student critique (abuse of power, corruption, violations of democratic norms, and so on) with class analysis, intense anti-elitism, contempt for 'mainstream' opposition and NGOs, and the organisation and mobilisation of workers and peasants. Although this current is visible in its purest form in student circles, its influence is also apparent in the many new 'transformative' NGOs which have been formed since the mid-1980s (especially those active in the workers', women's and peasant sectors) and is also felt in some of the bigger and more established NGOs such as the LBH (Thompson 1993). The new radical current has few links to members of the pre-1966 Left, however. Rather, it is a product of a long process of radicalisation in the student movement and NGOs established by student activists since the late 1970s. In this sense, it is not only a reflection of continuing social inequality, but also a consequence of the repression and marginalisation of middle-class dissent since the 1970s.

Stronger institutional base

The third development is that the organisational base of opposition, especially alegal, middle-class opposition, is now stronger and more diversified than it was two decades ago. The liberal dissident milieu of the 1970s has over the last two decades partially institutionalised itself, and it is now more realistic to talk of an embryonic state–civil society distinction. This new institutionalisation is most apparent in the huge growth of NGOs, which were mostly built by former student activists and other dissidents after the closure of student councils, the critical press, and other channels of political expression during the 1970s. NGOs are active around a huge array of issues, including alternative forms of community development and income generation for the poor, consumers' and women's rights, environmental protection, and labour and farmers' issues. Most of them promote alternative development models to poor communities, and seek to avoid confrontation with the state. But many NGOs, especially those which are active in the field of human rights, also make more or less general attacks on the government. A large number of these more critical NGOs have emerged since the late 1970s. They are a very important (perhaps the most important) vehicle for the more self-conscious middle-class critics and opponents of the regime.

This rise of an organised middle-class opposition stratum, and the pressures for democratisation emanating from it, have been reflected in the changing character of government discourse. Since the mid to late 1980s, new political forces – in addition to the 'extreme Right' and 'extreme Left' – have been increasingly identified as major threats to stability by the most bellicose security officials. In particular, the terms *ekstrim tengah* ('extreme centre') and *ekstrim lain-lain* ('other kinds of extremes') have been added to the repertoire. NGOs have also been specifically identified as a threat and new legal measures for their control have been proposed.

However, it is appropriate to introduce a note of caution concerning the oppositional potential of NGOs. As implied above, many of their leaders and members have ambivalent attitudes concerning the state and the prospects for political transformation. Most such organisations – especially those involved in 'community development' – should be seen as, at most, semi-opponents of the regime. They co-operate with state institutions in order to achieve their policy goals, although they may simultaneously criticise particular government policies or aspects of the regime and attempt to achieve policy reform in limited areas (Eldridge 1995). Indeed, the growth of NGOs has occurred not simply due to ambiguities in Indonesian law (particularly the greater autonomy from state 'guidance' for foundations, *yayasan*, compared to societal organisations, *ormas*), but also because the developmentalist aims pursued by most of them have been compatible with and able to be accommodated by the government. The very fact that developmental and other NGOs have been so generously supported by overseas funding agencies has also contributed to their domestication. The large NGOs are run by a professional stratum with a middle-class income and lifestyle – and, thus, an interest in ensuring that their organisations do not engage in illegal or otherwise too risky activity.

It is worth noting in this context that efforts to build autonomous organisational bases beyond the NGO sphere and in direct challenge to state-controlled corporatist bodies have met with more determined repression. This is especially the case where such efforts are in lower-class sectors, as evidenced by the campaign of harassment against the SBSI (Prosperous Workers' Union) since its formation in 1992, despite the fact that its chief organisers are by no means political radicals. Even the attempt to challenge the stranglehold of the PWI (Indonesian Journalists' Association) in the media by young journalists who in 1994 established the AJI (Alliance of Independent Journalists) led to sackings and arrests.

Thus, the 'niche' for tolerated opposition may have expanded greatly since the late 1980s, but it is still limited, and it is still a primarily middle-class phenomenon. Most activists have a more or less instinctive feel for the boundaries of tolerated political action beyond which their activities will attract repression. Numerous factors have a bearing, including the degree to which the oppositional activities involved are mass-based (especially if those mobilising are from the lower classes), the extent of explicit ideological challenge to *Pancasila* orthodoxy involved, the level of direct confrontation, and the particular issues raised.

Of course, the niche contracts and expands according to conditions; there is a long-term war of attrition along its boundaries. What is one day tolerated will at another time or place be repressed: the very unpredictability and randomness of repression increases its efficacy. On the other hand, activists (especially younger and more radical ones) constantly seek to stretch the boundaries, especially when political conditions seem favourable due to conflicts within the government, international pressures, or some other factor. In recent years, numerous activist groups have taken great risks to push open the boundaries into previously unimaginable areas. The first protests in Jakarta by peasants from distant areas of rural Java in the late 1980s, or the beginnings of open labour union organising from the early 1990s, for example, were assisted by student and other NGO activists. Such actions required considerable courage, were carried out in the face of steady repression, and have profoundly affected the character of contemporary political debate and action. But such activists remain a minority in middle-class alegal oppositional circles. For the larger group, the effect of the ever present threat of coercion is that they learn to identify the boundaries of state toleration and how to avoid overstepping them. One product of this has been the dominance of the NGO format in opposition circles for the last fifteen years. Because of their ostensibly 'non-political' character, NGOs offer a form of legality and a limited freedom of movement. In contrast, it is striking that since the consolidation of the three-party system in the early 1970s, there has been no open attempt either to establish a new party or revive any of the old ones; such a move would clearly contravene the law and invite repression.

THE CONTINUED BLURRING OF THE STATE–SOCIETY DISTINCTION

Alongside the signs of a nascent civil society referred to above, one feature of political life from the 1970s remains prominent, namely the blurring of government and opposition, state and civil society. The combination of rewards (primarily material) for participation, and the fear of sanctions applied to those who step outside the system, combine to produce a great deal of qualified, ambivalent, and hesitant participation-opposition, especially in those middle-class and elite social layers which have benefited materially from the government's economic development project. And so, for middle-class critics of the government, semi-opposition remains the central pattern. Most of the politically active middle classes negotiate the compromises and limitations of working within the political parties, state-sanctioned *ormas*, universities and government-sponsored research institutions, government departments, or other state institutions. The capacity of the more critical members of such bodies to play a more overtly oppositional role is severely limited by the constraints inherent to working within the system and the many rewards, material and otherwise, which accrue to those who do so. The compromises inevitably involved in such participation tend to discredit them in the eyes of both younger activists and the broader public: for example, political parties, at least until recently, were viewed in almost universally cynical regard. This is reflected in the well-known saying that the role of Dewan Perwakilan Rakyat (DPR, People's Representative Assembly), members is confined to *datang, duduk, dengar, diam, duit* ('turn up, sit down, listen, keep quiet, get paid').

But the overlapping of regime and opposition has been made particularly prominent since the late 1980s by the emergence of new tensions within the regime, especially the friction between the 'palace camp' and senior military officers referred to briefly above. There has been a remarkable rapprochement between a section of the Islamic community and the regime, or at least the Soeharto camp. This has been evidenced by, among other events, the Islamisation of the public face of the regime (including the well-publicised *haj* (pilgrimage) by Soeharto and the appointment of increasing numbers of supposedly orthodox Muslim officials and military officers), various legal and administrative reforms (such as greater recognition for Islamic courts) and, especially, the formation of the Muslim Intellectuals' Association (ICMI) in 1990. This organisation was sponsored by Soeharto, and Habibie is its General Chairperson. All of this has been a remarkable shift, given that in the late 1970s, the Islamic 'extreme Right' was increasingly defined as a threat to national stability second only to the latent danger of Communism. The new rapprochement has been made possible by the formal acceptance in the mid-1980s by the major Islamic organisations of *Pancasila* as their sole ideological base (*asas tunggal*) and hence the supposed disappearance of their basic ideological difference with the regime (Ramage 1995). Of even greater significance, however, has been the emergence of a sizeable educated Islamic middle class, in private business, academia and the professions, NGOs, and, especially, in the bureaucracy (Hefner 1993; Anwar 1993). The formation of the ICMI and other Islamisation measures can thus be seen as an attempt to respond to and co-opt a new and important social force, and in so doing to broaden the support base of the regime (especially that of the Soeharto–Habibie group) precisely at a time when the unconditional backing of all elements of the armed forces was becoming less reliable. From the perspective of the more critical of the new ICMI activists (some of whom in the 1970s were considered to be implacable opponents of the regime, others of whom play important leadership roles in moderately critical NGOs), co-operation with and support for Soeharto and Habibie has been a mechanism to gain protection for their political activities and to seek positions of greater influence within the government and bureaucracy. In this way they seek to improve the social, economic, and political position of the Muslim community, and at the same time to reduce the political role of the military, which they consider to be both the principal obstacle to democratisation and the major historic foe of Islam.

On the other hand, many secular and liberal dissidents share military concerns about the rise of (Islamic) 'primordialism'. They view President Soeharto as the primary obstacle to democratisation, and see his removal as the key prerequisite for regime restructuring. At the same time they consider that the military will inevitably play a role in such restructuring. In this context, it has been a barely concealed subtext that many such dissidents (such as Abdurahman Wahid and others in Forum Demokrasi) have envisaged 'moving forward' with the military, with the object of winning concessions in the shape of political reforms.[6] It may be preferable to support the grwoth of civil society, one argument goes, but in the end civilians may be obliged to make a painful choice between Soeharto-ICMI and the army. Many dissidents believe that they cannot promote meaningful political reform under current conditions, and instead hope to establish contacts and position themselves in such a way as to have greater influence in the event of presidential succession or death.[7]

Certainly, many political activists have attempted to make use of these divisions within the regime in order to win an expanded political space for their own activities, whether in semi-oppositional bodies like the political parties, or more clearly outside the system (Aspinall 1995). For example, there are indications that tacit or even covert support from military elements has been one of the factors which has assisted the reinvigoration of the PDI since Soerjadi became its leader in 1986.

CONCLUSION

A marked trend to monolithism in Indonesian politics in the first decade of the New Order saw the progressive repression and marginalisation of even moderate oppositional forces. Since the late 1980s, this process has begun to go into reverse. New political and social forces have emerged or been reactivated (including some which have been basically passive since early in the New Order). Although tensions within the regime have played an important part in this process, it has not been a carefully engineered or stage-managed liberalisation. There have been no fundamental political reforms, no major shift in the pattern of state corporatism or the tenor of integralist regime ideology, and groups which challenge the basic premises of '*Pancasila* democracy' continue to be repressed. It should be stressed that this chapter has not aimed to provide a complete account of all the factors which have influenced the greater levels of mobilisation in recent years and the changing face of opposition. As Ariel Heryanto points out in Chapter 9 of this volume, the regime has experienced a complex and multi-faceted crisis of hegemony. A more thorough account would have to look into, for example, the role of international influences (very important, for example, in the development of NGOs) and the factor of 'regime fatigue'.[8] Instead, this chapter has endeavoured to argue that this process partially stems from and must be understood within the context of the social dymanics generated by the very processes of New Order capitalist development. The emergence of a larger and more self-confident middle class and a new industrial working class, and the apparent exacerbation of social inequality, have had an important bearing on the shape of opposition politics. New social forces have been propelled into action, the organised base of middle-class dissent is stronger, there has been an important process of radicalisation in one section of the middle-class youth-NGO movement, and there has even been a partial re-emergence of more independent and oppositional currents within previously passive, incorporated organisations like the PDI.

Nevertheless, opposition still faces formidable odds and there is little reason to expect a fundamental reordering of regime–opposition relations, at least until the presidential succession gets fully under way. Repression remains most severe for political activities deemed to challenge '*Pancasila* ideology' and which occur in the lower classes. At the same time, intermittent repression and harassment continue to be used in order to control and limit semi-opposition and middle-class dissidence, as evidenced by recent attempts to obstruct the Megawati Soekarnoputri and Abdurahman Wahid leaderships of PDI and NU, and the continuing harassment of the most outspoken intellectuals, parliamentarians, and journalists. The ubiquity of the actuality and fear of state coercion and deep concerns about social disorder encourage passivity in the middle classes and hesitancy in many oppositional and semi-oppositional organisations, such as NGOs. The continued great disparity between the political and economic resources of state and society is reflected in the continuing prevalence of semi-opposition and in the persistent orientation by many elite dissidents and activists to one or other faction within the regime. Indeed, moves by the government to conciliate Islamic interests since the late 1980s, indicated by the formation of the ICMI, apparently signal an intent to broaden the social base of the regime. The chief target has clearly been the 'new Islamic middle class', but other attempts have been made to respond to broader middle-class concerns and to shore up middle-class support – to cite one example, the 1993 formation of the National Human Rights Commission.

NOTES

* My thanks to Dr Harold Crouch for his comments on an earlier version of this chapter.

1 Law professor Ismail Sunny and retired General A. H. Nasution regarded the first two years of the New Order as the 'best years for human rights' (Lubis 1993: 134).

2 For more discussion of these frictions see, for example, Lane (1991), Robison (1993).

3 For some estimates of the size of the middle class, see Mackie (1990).

4 See, for example, Budiman (1992). There are, however, indications that anti-Sinicism is being superseded by class antagonism at the popular level (Heryanto 1994).

5 According to Labrousse (1993: 191), a part of the Soekarno 'mythology' is that he died poor, which stands in sharp implicit contrast with the current President and his family.

6 It is striking that many of the members of Forum Demokrasi were themselves prominent members of the military–civilian coalition of 1966, especially the student action front KAMI.

7 Since the sudden removal of Benny Moerdani himself as Commander-in-Chief of the Armed Forces in 1988, the President has increasingly re-asserted his personal control over the armed forces and has moved many former Moerdani supporters and other officers whose loyalty cannot be relied upon out of their senior positions. A result has been growing pessimism in dissident circles about the potential for a reform option involving the military as a counterweight to the Soeharto camp.

8 'Regime fatigue' involves in part the simple passing of time and generational turnover. This has made an important contribution to the deterioration of relations between government and opposition, and the appearance of the nascent state–society division, and deserves particular mention. In the 1970s the bulk of the population had experienced the political turbulence of Guided Democracy and many dissidents had been personally involved in the coalition which brought the New Order to power. With the passing of a generation some of the old certainties (such as the Cold War climate and the possibility of a Communist resurgence) which seemed to give the New Order its *raison d'être* have lost their potency, and there is a greater sense of distance, alienation, and frustration with government in opposition circles and society more broadly. Thus, for example, the radicalisation of student dissent is partly because the immediate past for contemporary students was not the heady days of military-student co-operation in the 1960s, but the trend to monolithism and the increasing antipathy between student activists and authorities in the 1970s.

REFERENCES

Anderson, Benedict R. O'G. (1983) 'Old State, New Society: Indonesia's New Order in Comparative Historical Perspective', *Journal of Asian Studies*, 42(3): 477–96.

Anwar, M. Syafi'i (1993) *'Islam, Negara dan Formasi Sosial Dalam Orde Baru: Menguak Dimensi Sosio-Historis Kelahiran dan Perkembangan ICMI'*, Supplement to *Ulumul Qu'ran*, 3(3).

Aspinall, Edward (1995) 'Students and the Military: Regime Friction and Civilian Dissent in the Late Soeharto Period', *Indonesia*, 59, April: 21–44.

Bourchier, David (1992) 'Reflections on the "Integralist" Tradition of Political Thought in Indonesia', paper presented to the Ninth Biennial Conference of the Asian Studies Association of Australia, University of New England, 6–9 July.

—— (1993) 'Contradictions in the Dominant Paradigm of State Organisation in Indonesia', paper presented to the conference on Indonesia, Paradigms for the Future, Asia Research Centre, Murdoch University, July.

Budiman, Arief (1992) 'Indonesian Politics in the 1990s', in Harold Crouch and Hal Hill (eds) *Indonesia Assessment 1992, Political Perspectives on the 1990s*, Canberra: Australian National University, pp. 130–9.

Cahyono, Heru (1992) *Peranan Ulama Dalam Golkar 1971–1980: Dari Pemilu Sampai Malari*, Jakarta: Sinar Harapan.

Crouch, Harold (1974) 'The "15th January Affair" in Indonesia', *Dyason House Papers*, 1(1), August: 1–4.

—— (1988) *The Army and Politics in Indonesia*, Ithaca, NY: Cornell University Press (revised edition).

Eldridge, Philip J. (1995) *Non-Government Organisations and Democratic Participation in Indonesia*, Kuala Lumpur: Oxford University Press.

Gunawan, Andrew (1975) 'The Role of Students in the 15 January 1974 Incidents', *Southeast Asian Affairs*: 65–70.

Hefner, Robert (1993) 'Islam, State, and Civil Society: ICMI and the Struggle for the Indonesian Middle Class', *Indonesia*, 56: 1–35.

Heryanto, Ariel (1994) 'Chinese Indonesians in Public Culture: Ethnic Identities and Erasure', paper presented to the conference on Identities, Ethnicities, Nationalities in Asia and Pacific Contexts, La Trobe University, Bundoora, Australia, 7–9 July.

Hill, Hal (1994) 'The Economy', in Hal Hill (ed.) *Indonesia's New Order: the Dynamics of Socio-Economic Transformation*, Sydney: Allen & Unwin, pp. 54–122.

Jenkins, David (1984) *Suharto and His Generals: Indonesian Military Politics 1975–1983*, Ithaca, NY: Cornell Modern Indonesia Project.

Labrousse, Pierre (1993) 'The Second Life of Bung Karno: Analysis of the Myth (1978–1981)', *Indonesia*, 57: 175–96.

Lane, Max (1991) *'Openness', Political Discontent and Succession in Indonesia: Political Developments in Indonesia, 1989–91*, Brisbane: Griffith University Centre for the Study of Australia–Asia Relations, Australia-Asia Paper No. 56.

Lembaga Bantuan Hukum (1973) *Tiga Tahun Lembaga Bantuan Hukum*, Jakarta.

Lev, Daniel (1978) 'Judicial Authority and the Struggle for an Indonesian Rechtsstaat', *Law and Society Review*, 13(1): 37–71.

Linz, Juan J. (1973) 'Opposition In and Under an Authoritarian Regime: the Case of Spain', in Robert A. Dahl (ed.) *Regimes and Oppositions*, New Haven, Conn.: Yale University Press, pp. 171–259.

Lubis, Todung Mulya (1993) *In Search of Human Rights: Legal–Political Dilemmas of Indonesia's New Order, 1966–1990*, Jakarta: Gramedia.

Mackie, J. A. C. (1990) 'Money and the Middle Class', in Richard Tanter and Kenneth Young (eds) *The Politics of Middle Class Indonesia*, Clayton: Monash University Centre of Southeast Asian Studies, pp. 96–122.

McVey, Ruth (1982) 'The Beamtenstaat in Indonesia', in B. R. O'G. Anderson and A. Kahin (eds) *Interpreting Indonesian Politics: Thirteen Contributions to the Debate*, Ithaca, NY: Cornell Modern Indonesia Project, pp. 84–91.

Morfit, Michael (1981) 'Pancasila: the Indonesian State Ideology According to the New Order Government', *Asian Survey*, 21(8): 838–51.

Ramage, Douglas (1995) *Politics in Indonesia: Democracy, Islam and the Ideology of Tolerance*, London: Routledge.

Robison, Richard (1986) *Indonesia: the Rise of Capital*, Sydney: Allen & Unwin.

—— (1990) 'Problems of Analysing the Middle Class as a Political Force in Indonesia', in Richard Tanter and Kenneth Young (eds) *The Politics of Middle Class Indonesia*, Clayton: Monash University Centre for Southeast Asian Studies, pp. 127–37.

—— (1993) 'Indonesia: Tensions in State and Regime', in Kevin Hewison, Richard Robison, and Garry Rodan (eds) *Southeast Asia in the 1990s: Authoritarianism, Democracy and Capitalism*, Sydney: Allen & Unwin, pp. 39–74.

—— (1994) 'Organising the Transition: Indonesian Politics in 1993/94', in Ross H. McLeod (ed.) *Indonesia Assessment 1994: Finance as a Key Sector in Indonesia's Development*, Singapore and Canberra: Institute of Southeast Asian Studies and Research School of Pacific and Asian Studies, pp. 49–74.

Tanter, Richard and Young, Kenneth (1990) *The Politics of Middle Class Indonesia*, Clayton: Monash University Centre of Southeast Asian Studies.

Thompson, Edmund (1993) 'Practising What You Preach', *Inside Indonesia*, 36: 7–9.

9   Indonesian middle-class opposition in the 1990s

Ariel Heryanto

Indonesia's sustained economic growth since the mid-1970s has unwittingly helped to revitalise two urban-based oppositional forces. They are the industrial workers and the middle-class professionals and activists (students, lawyers, non-government organisation (NGO) activists, journalists, artists, and religious leaders). Notwithstanding their dynamism, such oppositions encounter obstacles that constrain them as movements for far-reaching social change. Having been born out of, and having to operate within, the social structure they try to challenge, these oppositional groups find themselves in a position full of dilemmas and contradictions. What follows is a brief account of these new oppositional forces in the 1990s, and the difficulties they have to overcome before any radical transformation of the existing social order can be imagined.

The main thrust of this chapter can be outlined as follows. The New Order regime achieved a hegemonic status on the basis of the extraordinary political violence in 1965–6, and the continued reproduction of widespread fear in its protracted aftermath. The 1965–6 massacre took the lives of around one million people and jeopardised the lives of millions of survivors.[1] That massive violence and subsequent terrorism provided the fundamental basis for sustained 'political stability' and successful economic development. However, the same events have generated new phenomena that increasingly undermine that basis. A new generation of middle classes and industrial workers has emerged. World capitalism incorporated Indonesia further into its structural relationships politically and economically, as well as culturally.

Despite its continued success in keeping the economy of the nation growing, the New Order regime has been in steady political decline since the mid-1980s and more obviously in the 1990s. There is no certainty what this will lead to. It may well be a transitory period for the regime to strengthen itself again and to renew its old hegemonic power with new names and personnel. For the moment, existing oppositional forces are too fragmented to exert a counter-hegemonic leadership. Attempts to make alliances among them have been made, but the result is still far from being solid. A key question to fundamental changes is whether the old hegemonic power can still be reproduced or is already exhausted.

HEGEMONIC BASIS

The massacre in the aftermath of the 1965 events, and its historical significance, remain the most determining factor in shaping contemporary Indonesia. Writings on the topic have been voluminous, but there are still more questions concerning various aspects of the events of that time. In the years immediately after, a preoccupation with sheer survival steered attention away from a full analysis. Today, discussion on the topic is still strongly proscribed by the government and voluntarily avoided by many, especially those who have been directly affected by those events.[2] Yet even though the memory of the violence remains traumatic, for various reasons (e.g. to make the pain endurable, or avoid risks) many people choose to deny or distort the violence. A nationwide campaign threatening a possible recurrence of earlier events has contributed to public acquiescence without the actual use of direct violence by state agents.

According to the official propaganda, the society runs and reproduces itself on the basis of familial harmony – deliberation and consensus (*musyawarah* and *mufakat*). Under such conditions, many non-governmental agents are compelled to collaborate in reproducing the propaganda. This does not mean that they allow themselves to be mystified, or that they can completely ignore what they believe to be 'real historical facts'. On the contrary, their conformity is a direct effect of their awareness of the past violence and its potential recurrence. New Order hegemonic state power is achieved through a combination of both the apparent and celebrated consent on the one hand, and the perceived but undiscussed coercion on the other.

In that hegemonic position, the New Order regime is able to hold authoritarian control over major political, economic, and cultural institutions. It has also managed to reproduce the conditions for its hegemonic power by the use of occasional political violence, witch-hunts, and propaganda. Without taking this into account, and unless we delude ourselves with the myth of distinct 'eastern values', it would be difficult to understand how the world's fourth most-populated nation could have tolerated an authoritarian rule for more than a quarter of a century. Likewise, it is difficult to understand why a regime feels so inclined to ratify a seemingly liberal law one day, then ignore or abuse it the next.

A presidential election is held by the Majelis Permusyawaratan Rakyat (MPR, People's Consultative Assembly), once every five years. It has always elected the same man; in fact he has been the only nomination for all six successive terms. If we look at how the Assembly is constituted, this state of affairs is understandable. The President has the power to appoint 600 out of the total 1,000 members of the Assembly. The remaining 400 are the elected members of the national parliament, the Dewan Perwakilan Rakyat (DPR). Even within the DPR, the government party Golongan Karya (Golkar, 'Functional Group'), has always won the majority of votes (around 70 per cent). All members must pass government screening tests before being eligible nominees, a requirement that poses particular difficulties for the opposition. Once appointed, Members of Parliament are subject to recall if they speak critically of the regime. In 1973 the government fused the existing ten political parties into three convenient groupings, and prohibited the establishment of new parties. Apart from Golkar, there are the Islamic-based Partai Persatuan Pembangunan (PPP, United Development Party) and the Christian Partai Demokrasi Indonesia (PDI, Indonesian Democratic Party) of predominantly secular nationalists. Given the nature of such externally motivated fusion, each of these two parties suffers from perennial frictions.

Until very recently the parliament has not proposed a single Bill to the executive. It has only once rejected proposed legislation coming from the executive. The judiciary shares the same fate. Under the Basic Law 14/1970, the Ministry of Justice (which is responsible solely to the President) has the power to control the budget of courts below the Supreme Court, to promote judges and transfer them. The same law stipulates that the President appoints and dismisses judges. Presidential Decree 82/1971 demands that all state employees be members of Korps Pegawai Negeri Indonesia (KORPRI, All Indonesia Civil Servant Corps) headed by the Minister of the Interior. Prosecution of individual citizens for peaceful political activities has been a regular activity of the courts.

Heavy surveillance and severe censorship operate in the administration of formal education at all levels, in the mass media, religious rituals, and artistic productions. Most curricula must be approved by local authorities. No electronic media are allowed, at least in theory and, until recently, in practice, to produce and broadcast their own news. Reporters and editors from print media receive regular threats.

To make the threats effective, actual closure of selected media without due legal process occurs from time to time. In certain areas or periods religious leaders have been banned from giving sermons. Theatrical productions, academic seminars, and poetry readings are all vulnerable to attempts by the police and local military authorities to control the content of texts before they can be delivered in public.

Political opposition is officially declared illegal, despite the regime's continued claim to enforce a self-styled democratic polity called '*Pancasila* Democracy'.[3] Separation of powers is officially denounced. The image of familial harmony is deployed to justify the systemic suppression of any expression of grievances and potential conflicts. Under this condition any public expression of opposition is by definition extra-legal, not simply extra-parliamentary.

Despite all the restrictions, oppositional forces regularly emerge from time to time. They have come and gone throughout the New Order rule, some with more consequences than others, but none has come near to overthrowing the regime or radically transforming the existing social order. The President-centred New Order regime remains one of the most durable in the modern world, while its steady economic success impresses many. At the time of writing in 1995, no single identifiable social force seems to have the capacity or potential seriously to challenge the regime.

In the 1990s, however, the political scene shows some changes which may develop greater significance in the years ahead. In 1994 we witnessed for the first time in New Order history several historic events. Mass rallies of hundreds of thousands of workers took place in protest against abuse of their rights. Six NGOs filed a lawsuit against the President in a case of reallocation of state funding. Another lawsuit was filed by a private corporation against the government for having banned its news magazine. The recall of vocal Members of Parliament provoked nationwide controversy in 1995.[4] Meanwhile, there were public challenges to the most sensitive ideological area, namely the official history of the 1965 coup d'état which caused the birth and swift rise to power of the New Order. These are just a few examples.

What follows is an account of these recent changes, focusing specifically on two processes: the decline of the regime's hegemonic power, and the rise of the oppositional forces. It must be noted from the outset that the two processes are not simply two sides of the same coin, one necessarily resulting from the other. The two processes are fairly independent of each other in their origins, although the effects of one in practice enhance the effects of the other. Each process has its own internal dynamics and contradictions, as well as external pressures from different sources.

The regime's waning power is more related to internal friction within the ruling elite, and to international pressures, than to the strengthening of its domestic opposition. But the consequences of the regime's decline provides more room for the consolidation of existing opposition. Conversely, the rise of the oppositional forces cannot be directly or primarily attributed simply to the regime's political recession. In one respect, the two processes have something in common: they are both taking place in a period during which global capitalism more comprehensively conditions the Indonesian domestic political economy and renders the nation-state boundary less meaningful.

I will proceed with an examination of highly publicised tension between the regime and the urban middle classes. The incident illustrates empirically the general argument outlined earlier and will thus be followed by an attempt to link it with broader processes of social change. The concluding section will consider the question of hegemonic relations during the New Order high points and their possible break-up.

THE 1994 MEDIA BANS

On 21 June 1994 the Indonesian government banned three major Jakarta-based weeklies, namely the tabloid *DëTIK* and two news magazines, *TEMPO* and *Editor*. At the time of the bans, *TEMPO* and *DëTIK* were the most prominent media in the country. Of the three, *DëTIK* had the biggest circulation, approximately 600,000, while *Editor* was the smallest, with roughly 60,000. According to *FORUM Keadilan* (3(7), 21 July 1994: 33), *TEMPO*'s circulation reached 200,000 before the government closed it down. These bans may prove to be of greater historic importance than first appearances suggested in mid-1994.

Daniel Dhakidae provides an additional note on the significance of the figures above. In his view, *DëTIK*'s achievements were miraculous. The tabloid had survived with professional dignity and no dependence on revenue from advertising – an imperative for most media in the country. In a matter of months, during its first year, *DëTIK* managed to gain the largest circulation of all print media in the country, demonstrating what had previously been thought to be impossible: that professional journalism can sell itself (Dhakidae 1994: 53). With regard to *TEMPO*, Dhakidae (1994: 55) describes it as 'the largest magazine published in national language in Asia outside India, Japan, China, Korea, and Taiwan . . . in Asia-Pacific . . . outside the USA and Russia'.

Curiously, when the June 1994 bans took place, most of the initial protest attacked the government on moral grounds and in political terms, apparently overlooking the economic dimension. This is not so surprising if we consider contemporary discourse on the press in Indonesia. In recent years Indonesians had spoken disparagingly of the national press as having become heavily and dangerously 'industrialised', as opposed to having been, presumably, 'socially engaged' during the national struggle for independence and soon afterwards.[5] Dhakidae's remark on the economic dimension of the affair is rare and of great importance. Although press bans have been regular incidents throughout the history of Indonesia, no ban has hit a press industry on the scale of the June 1994 measures.

In superficial public discourse there was a common view that the June 1994 ban punished the three publications for their extensive coverage of the bitter conflict between Research and Technology Minister Habibie and Minister of Finance Marie Muhamad over the former's controversial purchase on behalf of the government of thirty-nine former East German warships. But this is only one element of the probable reasons for the ban. Soon after it, it became clear that certain conglomerates were impatient to take over the market left by the closed publications, and intended to purchase and renew their press licence.

Legally, the government cannot ban the mass media. Several regulations still in effect stipulate that the freedom of the press should be protected. In June 1994, as in similar cases in the past, the government described its decision not as a ban, but as a revocation or cancellation of the press licence of the publications concerned. However, instead of satisfying the public, this explanation provoked protests over issues of legality. Moreover, the decision raised larger questions. First, if the government was powerful enough to close down the press on a whim and get away with it, as it had done before, why did it feel a cloak of legality was necessary? And if so, why did it not come up with something more credible? Why did the government not revoke the legal stipulation of the freedom of the press, and thus remove any trace of legal ambiguity?

The second set of questions concerns the government's motivation for announcing the provocative bans. Had the three publications really been a threat or was this 'threat' imaginary? What was the nature of the threat? Was it more economic or more political? Were there any premeditated attempts on the part of the journalists to challenge the government that had provoked a severe retaliation? What characterised the relationship between the New Order government and its detractors around the time of the ban?

These questions are extremely broad and all that can be attempted here is a partial response. First, the heavily moral overtones in the immediate outrage at the government measure strongly typifies much of the urban middle-class opposition in New Order Indonesia. This moral approach has strengths and weaknesses. While it projects the cause to the public as noble, it lacks critical analysis of the way in which industrial capitalism pervades the whole situation.

Second, the mass media serve as a crucial ground for ideological battles in this country. Although the Indonesian press has always been highly politicised, its political prominence has increased sharply in the current climate. This is partly due to the fact that the more formal political venues (party politics, parliament, judiciary, etc.) have been reduced largely to mere instruments of the ruling executive power. The new prominence of the press is also linked to its transformation into a fast-expanding industry. Major agents in the ideological battle in the press include state officials, the business community, and urban professionals. Although all are aware of the press's increased political weight, the new situation cannot be attributed to a clever design of any of these participants. None is yet in a position to dominate.

Third, the ban is one of a series of signs of the regime's paranoia, itself an indication of a decline in its power and confidence. The ban has injured the government itself as much as the press. The regime may remain in power for some time, in the absence of an effective opposition. However, it appears unprepared to face the fact that it can no longer rule with the same ease as it has for the two previous decades.

In sum, what we witness is a situation where old hegemonic power starts to decay, but no vigorous counter-hegemonic force seems yet available to take its place. It is a period of transition where an ageing regime and its emergent opposition are highly antagonistic but both are too weak to dominate fully. All of this is happening in a period where the economy is surviving fairly well, slanting progressively towards pro-market policies and privatisation *vis-à-vis* the old state protection-.sm. The June 1994 media bans should come as no surprise when considered in a broader context of political and ideological struggles in the 1990s. The bans and the response to them from the urban middle classes offer clues for a broader study of the form and direction of political opposition.

RESPONSE TO THE BANS

The ban on the three publications in June 1994 was neither new nor particularly interesting in itself. More than thirty media organisations have been 'banned' under the New Order. What is so remarkable about the event is the series of public reactions to it. For the first time in the New Order's history we encounter the following four phenomena, whose significance goes beyond the internal intricacies of the ban itself.

Nationwide demonstrations

For the first time in New Order Indonesia, the June 1994 bans provoked a long and continuous series of protests across different islands of the archipelago. These included mass demonstrations in the cities of Medan, Padang, Palembang, Bandarlampung (Sumatra), Manado, Ujung Pandang (Sulawesi), Samarinda (Kalimantan), Kuta (Bali), Mataram (Lombok), and Sampang (Madura), apart from those in Jakarta, Bandung, Yogyakarta, Semarang, Salatiga, Solo, Jombang, Surabaya, Malang, and Jember (Java). In many of these cities, several demonstrations took place in the months after the June bans. When they began in late June 1994, many of the demonstrations attracted several hundred participants. The list of protests above does not include those staged overseas.

On paper and according to officials' speeches, demonstrations are still illegal. Despite, or rather because of, this illegality, demonstrations always carry special weight in political discourse. Launching a demonstration is in itself a strong political statement, regardless of the cause and the issues presented on banners or in slogans. Heavy sentences have been given to many defendants for participating in peaceful demonstrations against the government. Demonstrations occasionally play a significant role in political change, although until June 1994 they have not usually been called in response to press bans. Before June 1994 most demonstrations against the New Order regime took place over quite different issues, with considerable gaps between them, for instance the demonstrations against the new traffic regulations in 1992–3, and those against the national lottery in 1993–4.

Demonstrations usually attract world attention according to the level of easily documented violence, rather than their historical significance. The series of demonstrations described above did involve some violence, arrests, and trials though not on a very serious scale. However, they may have greater historical significance than previous demonstrations in the country that involved more violence and material destruction. For instance, demonstrations in Jakarta (1974) against the government's foreign and economic policy were the biggest and most violent in New Order Indonesia. Next in their notorious violence is the series of demonstrations in Ujung Pandang (Sulawesi) in 1987 against the new regulation on wearing helmets for motorcyclists. In both, however, the protests were largely localised. Their impacts were fairly minimal for the costs involved.

A middle-class alliance

With the exception of the violent upheavals in 1965–6 that gave rise to the New Order regime, this is the first instance of widespread urban protests against the government by the middle classes, who are often dismissed as politically insignificant. Participation in these protests cut across divisions that have often been regarded as of major significance, apart from the geographical differences indicated above: religion, ethnicity, gender, profession, ideological orientation. In most of the demonstrations, student and NGO activists, academics, lawyers, religious leaders, artists, union leaders, and women's groups were prominent.

What I observed in the small university town of Salatiga, Central Java, may be similar to what happened in most other cities as reported in the press. In Salatiga hundreds of students set up an open forum where they and their lecturers, as well as a priest, a newspaper seller, a poet, and a member of the local legislative body, spoke to a big cheering crowd, condemning the bans. Then they marched to the local government office to present their grievances.

Public criticism of the bans also came from Members of Parliament, the President-appointed National Committee on Human Rights, mass organisations, legal aid institutions, and the Indonesian Democratic Party, as well as individual government officials and top military officers. However, all of this criticism appeared in the regular 'official' channels, such as media interviews or press releases. Regardless of their substance, such protests do not carry the political weight pertaining to the mass demonstrations.

Since the late 1980s, demonstrations have become a regular phenomenon in Indonesian politics but they develop rather sporadically or fragmentarily. In the foregoing I have suggested such discontinuity in terms of geographical difference. But a similar lack of convergence has for years been apparent among middle-class urbanites and politically conscious activists in various fields. Not only have religious, gender, or ethnic differences been obstacles to the formation of a political alliance, but tensions between passionate student activists and NGOs, and rivalries among fellow activists, have impeded attempts towards a more collaborative oppositional effort. The government's repressive bans provoked a movement of unification among opposition elements for the first time.

The significance of protests against the bans lies primarily neither in what they achieved among the demands listed in their slogans, banners, or petitions, nor merely in what they did to the government. Of more importance is what these protesters did to themselves. These urban activists experienced an unprecedented sensation of collective identity and a middle-class political consciousness that previously existed only on paper and in academic debates. It was like a child amazed by the first sight of itself in a mirror.[6]

Journalists' confrontation

Journalists took part in many of the protests mentioned above, and their participation constitutes a phenomenon with a special merit of its own. For the first time in the New Order's history, hundreds of journalists went to the streets to launch a mass protest. More significantly, this protest was launched against the government and the sole, government-sanctioned union of journalists, Persatuan Wartawan Indonesia (PWI). The defiant journalists went further by establishing an overtly opposi-tional professional association called Aliansi Jurnalis Independen (AJI, Alliance of Independent Journalists) in August 1994. In the ensuing months the government took various measures with the collaboration of intimidated press companies to suppress the AJI, and harass indi-vidual members. Several AJI reporters lost their jobs, others were removed to other positions or remote places. Despite all the pressures, the AJI continued to consolidate itself and gain support from other segments of the urban middle class in Indonesia and abroad. Under the leadership of their chief editor Goenawan Mohamad, many former employees of *TEMPO* filed a lawsuit against the government's bans. A group of lawyers filed a separate lawsuit on behalf of hundreds of individual readers of the three publications against the same govern-ment decision.

To appreciate these acts of resistance fully, a few words of back-ground information are called for. Indonesian journalists have always been close to the world of student politics and demonstrations. Many of the journalists have close personal friendships with student activists. Some journalists had been key figures in student politics in their earlier years. The special link between these two groups is visible in the media's recruitment of new reporters as well as in their style of reporting. In the eyes of many, *DëTIK* was the clearest example of this connection, being the ultimate embodiment of the spirit of youthful activism.

Despite all the above, in their professional activities and public posture, until June 1994 Indonesian journalists appeared largely as impartial reporters of incidents involving protesters (demonstrations, arrests, and trials of activists). Even in cases where their collective professional interest or individual fellow reporters suffer repressive measures from the authorities, these New Order journalists usually do not launch confrontational protests, let alone street demonstrations. Instead, they usually publicise interviews with important figures to express their grievances by proxy. In fact, the familiar self-imposed censorship reasserted itself again when certain reporters were sacked from their employment presumably for involvement in the AJI, and when the government faced legal charges as a result of its decision to ban the three publications.

In many previous press bans, journalists had not only been embarrassingly silent; worse, some had reportedly even been pleased, for reasons which cannot be proved conclusively but could involve business rivalry, differences of work ethos, or ideological orientation. The dramatic closure in 1990 of *Monitor*, the largest-circulation publication in the country ever, was a case in point. The New Order government did not intend to ban this TV guide tabloid, until a large and aggressive public demanded that it do so. Among segments of 'civil society' that endorsed the banning of *Monitor* and the prosecution of its chief editor, Arswendo Atmowiloto, were his fellow journalists.[7]

Before the reluctant government did anything to close down the publication, Jakob Oetama (a leading member of the national, government-sanctioned association of press publishers, and a key figure in the leadership of the Kompas-Gramedia Group, the biggest press empire and owner of *Monitor*) 'voluntarily' made a recommendation. He asked the Minister of Information to close down the tabloid without any due legal procedure by revoking the publication's licence (as happened in the June 1994 bans).[8] The government complied, and also prosecuted Arswendo Atmowiloto, who was sentenced to five years' imprisonment. Atmowiloto received further punishment. His employer dismissed him from the company and revoked his reporting licence.

In other and immediately related cases, a similar lack of professional solidarity has prevailed. In 1992, three top editors of the news magazine *Jakarta-Jakarta*, also owned by the Kompas-Gramedia Group, were removed from their prestigious positions by their superior. Apparently this was an attempt on the part of the company to show loyalty to the military leadership which was angry following a report of what happened in Dili, East Timor, after the killings on 12 November 1991 – a report that contrasted strikingly with the official version.[9] The case provoked no public protests from those directly affected or from anyone working in journalism or elsewhere in the country.

A few months earlier in 1992 Surya Paloh, whose daily *Prioritas* was banned by the government in 1987, made a historic first attempt to file a case to the Supreme Court asking for a judicial review of the regulation by which the Minister of Information can close any publication with a stroke of a pen. While, as expected, the Supreme Court dropped the case in 1993, it was significant that the general public and journalists' professional bodies gave Paloh no meaningful support. But the June bans made the public think again.

Government on the defensive

The press bans were one of the rare occasions when the New Order government appears to be very susceptible to pressures from the domestic opposition, and swiftly becomes apologetic about its own repressive action. This is the first and maybe the only time that a press ban has immediately been followed by a government offer to renew the publishers' licences which had just been revoked. In all previous cases, press bans were followed by months of further recrimination against the victims and intimidation of other media. The victims were blamed without a trial or opportunity for self-defence. The surviving media were expected to learn the lesson, or even to take part in publicly denouncing their fellow journalists.

What are we to make of it all? Do the four developments outlined indicate a decline of what has thus far looked like a very strong authoritarian regime? Or are they simply part of a clever strategy of governance on the part of the New Order regime? Do the same phenomena suggest the rise of middle-class political alliances? Does the weakening of the regime necessarily mean the strengthening of 'civil society'? If not, how do we understand the relationships in play in contemporary Indonesia?

There is no simple yes/no answer to these questions. The next section will deal with the questions of the government's shrinking power and the blossoming of urban middle-class politics. I will try to relate the June 1994 bans and the public response to them with several other political events in a broader context. But first I will sum up the above and introduce the arguments I will make in the following section.

The four phenomena do indicate a significant retreat of the New Order regime *vis-à-vis* 'civil society'. But this is not to suggest that the government is crumbling. In fact, no single force has yet appeared to rival the regime. I am only arguing that for reasons to be explored below, the regime has lost much of its previous prowess and the ease with which it used to handle and mishandle things. Now in order to survive, the regime is having to make more substantial concessions to the dissenting urban middle classes, giving them more room to assert their own agendas. The moment may be conducive to 'democratisation', but is an inadequate condition for it. Neither is it evident that political opposition from 'civil society' is on the rise.

If the middle classes do appear to be better consolidated and politically more assertive than before, as I believe they are, the reasons need to be sought elsewhere than simply in the decline of the government's hegemonic power. After all, the various acts of opposition to the regime described above do not portend significant changes in the main structures of New Order Indonesia. The next section will therefore submit a broader view of the recent decline of the regime and the coincidental rise of opposition movements. The question to be confronted is how social inequalities and political repression in New Order Indonesia have managed to persist and reproduce themselves, and under what conditions they can be expected to dysfunction or break down.

A DECAYING REGIME?

The four phenomena described in the preceding section can be seen as part of a train of events. In varying degrees they all display the New Order regime's continued failure to keep control of domestic discontents. This became highly visible in the first half of the 1990s, progressively accelerating in pace and intensity to the time of writing. I will illustrate this point with six successive incidents which took place over a period of several months prior to the media bans.[10]

Government Regulation No. 20/1994

Three weeks prior to the June 1994 bans, the government issued a new and no less controversial regulation. This was the most pro-market economic policy it had ever introduced, allowing 100 per cent foreign ownership of locally based new investments or the purchase of existing companies with only a 1 per cent divestment required after fifteen years. The regulation also opened major areas of infrastructure and the public sector to management by domestic and foreign private joint ventures: ports, electricity generating and distribution, telecommunications, airlines, water, railways, and the mass media. According to the constitution, all these areas are prohibited to private companies, whether foreign or domestic. With the new regulations, foreign investors may have as much as 95 per cent ownership of an enterprise operating in these areas.

One interpretation of this dramatic decision suggests that the government must be in an enormously powerful position to feel it can afford such a significant policy change. Another interpretation that sounds more tenable is that the government was in a desperate situation economically and politically. This latter interpretation is in fact in line with the admission of the President and his aides in response to criticism from politicians and domestic business communities.[11]

Financially, the regime appeared to be in an urgent need of a huge amount of capital in an increasingly competitive climate to fulfil its ambition of retaining a 6.5 per cent growth rate for GDP. It also had to face its breathtaking foreign debt (approaching US$100,000 million in 1994, or 10 per cent more than the previous year) and the formidable scandals concerning non-performing loans in the state banking sector (see below).[12] The government prefers foreign investors, because they are politically much less threatening than their domestic counterparts.

Immediate opposition to the new regulation came not from anti-capitalist forces as such, but from business communities which have enjoyed government protection, including the press,[13] and from neo-classical economists who subscribe to the rigid notion of separation between public and private economies. Though not intended to do so by those who drafted and ratified it, the new regulation challenged the powerful myth of such a separation.[14]

The new regulation also makes the media bans which followed it three weeks later remarkably ironic. While the government worked hard to attract foreign investment by banning the three publications, it stirred up social unrest which was liable to discourage foreign investment; and the government also demonstrated its heavy-handed inclination to act without due respect for legal procedures which was also of little comfort to foreign investors (see McBeth 1994: 70; Dhakidae 1994: 55). Furthermore, the government was actually sacrificing the same benefits of existing domestic capital investment associated with the drive for foreign investment. When the government banned the three publications in June 1994, *TEMPO* had an annual turnover of Rp. 40,000 million (Utami 1994: 6), and it alone contributed Rp. 5,000 million in tax revenue to the government (Mohamad 1994: 34).

While there is yet no guarantee that the new regulation will eventually yield any benefit to the New Order regime or any other domestic parties in the long run, it had the immediate effect of undermining the regime's political stature in the public eye. It makes the government look ideologically anationalistic; it is legally in contravention of the constitution; socially, it is putting public welfare at the mercy of capitalism.

Bank loan scandals

Following the disclosure in May 1994 of the Indonesian Rp. 1.3 trillion (US$650 million) non-performing bank loan, a big Chinese-Indonesian business man and several top executive managers of the government's Indonesian Development Bank (BAPINDO) were brought to trial. The court found many of the defendants guilty and gave them long prison sentences. Several former state Ministers were implicated. Under strong public pressure from the media and student demonstrations, they were summoned to testify in court. Things seemed to be falling apart.

Corruption may be an inherent part of a system that runs a country for many years. But some corrupt practices and abuses of power are more excessive and do more serious damage to the system than others. The public exposure of major corrupt practices is usually a initiated and further protected by few among country's top elite. Public disclosure of such scandals often, though not invariably, occurs when distribution of the fruits of corruption among the elite has become problematic, leading to bitterness or jealousy.

The Indonesian state banking system had been causing concern among many analysts several months before the BAPINDO case came to light.[15] Already in 1993, one observer estimated that 'at least 20 per cent of state-bank loans [were] non-performing (that is, no interest has been paid on them for three months or more)'; others considered the figure of 20 per cent far too low (Sender 1993: 76). In one bank it could have been as high as 75 per cent (Sender 1993: 75). Less controversial is the view that the figure was increasing from year to year (in 1990, it was estimated at 6 per cent), and the scandal was more rampant in state banks than their private counterparts.[16]

The scale of media interest in the BAPINDO case and its political implications may be the biggest since the mid-1970s scandal of PERTAMINA, the state-owned oil company. The collapse of Bank Summa (in December 1992) and Bank Duta (in 1990) had already astonished the nation. But the BAPINDO affair far surpassed them. And yet there are strong indications that the BAPINDO credit scandal is neither the only nor the worst in operation (Sender 1994). According to Bank Indonesia Governor Soedrajad Djiwandana, the total non-performing bank loans by the end of April 1995 reached Rp. 9.78 billon, of which the notorious BAPINDO's scam constituted Rp. 2.98 billon or 30.5 per cent (*Kompas*, 22 June 1995: 1, 11). Other, and perhaps more serious, cases managed to escape public scrutiny and legal investigation, although their existence were subtly hinted at in the media. The BAPINDO scandal was serious enough to shake up both political and economic institutions in the country, threaten business people and top state bureaucrats, and to destabilise the New Order regime, at least for a time.[17]

Rising labour unrest and demonstrations in North Sumatra

While things go wrong at the highest political and economic levels, new and challenging forces rise up from below. Between 14 and 16 April 1994, the North Sumatran city of Medan and its surrounding areas saw a series of the biggest worker demonstrations since the New Order came to power. Some 30,000 workers took part in the rallies, demanding: (i) an increase in the daily minimum wage from the official figure of Rp. 3,100 (US$1.50) – one of the lowest in Asia – to Rp. 7,000 (US$3.50); (ii) the repeal of the Ministry of Manpower Decree (No. 1/1994) that recognised only the sole government-sanctioned trade union Serikat Pekerja Seluruh Indonesia (SPSI, All Indonesian Union of Workers), and recognition of the alternative union Serikat Buruh Sejahtera Indonesia (SBSI); (iii) an investigation into the death of their fellow worker Rusli; and (iv) the reinstatement of nearly 400 workers who had recently been dismissed following a strike at a local factory.

Unusually, the security forces used minimal violence to disperse the demonstrations. Both civilian state bureaucrats and the military leadership alleged that the mass rallies had turned violent, attacking the local ethnic Chinese, and that NGOs had manipulated the masses to demonstrate in ways typical of the former Indonesian Communist Party. Among these NGOs, the SBSI was accused of being most responsible for the damage. The government arrested and tried over sixty people, including key figures from the SBSI and other NGOs, as well as dozens of the workers themselves.

Despite sufficient conflicting evidence in public reports, nearly all media coverage in Indonesia and overseas, as well as reports from human rights organisations, were pressured to follow the official version. Overlooking the glaring class conflict in this industrial dispute, they diverted the story into a discussion of anti-Chinese issues. Much space was given to the long history of ethnic tension (see Heryanto 1994b), with no regard to the question of labour and capital. Several unpublished reports prepared by NGOs which were involved in the incident commented in passing that anti-Chinese pamphlets had appeared mysteriously towards the end of the first series of demonstrations. Others, like Mochtar Pakpahan, leader of the SBSI, claimed to have evidence that a third party had used thugs and *agents provocateurs* to divert the workers from their original cause and incite anti-Chinese sentiment at the rally. But this point did not receive the attention it deserved.[18]

Labour demonstrations in Medan and the surrounding area had occurred regularly since 1991, leading up to the inevitable climax in mid-April 1994. In most other industrial centres, especially the outskirts of Jakarta and Surabaya (the only Indonesian cities larger than Medan), labour disputes, strikes, and mass rallies were also overwhelming in size and frequency throughout much of the first half of the 1990s.[19] For reasons beyond the immediate issues of labour, some of these events became better known than others.

The death of Marsinah, a 25-year-old female labour activist, in Porong (a small town near Surabaya) in early May 1993 quickly became legendary. Icons, ceremonies, demonstrations, songs, art exhibitions, theatrical performances, posters, scholarly analysis, and rumours honoured her courage in the defence of labour rights and the memory of her heroic death.[20] The Medan labour demonstration took place as the trial for Marsinah's murder was in progress. Urban middle-class activists had been instrumental in the development of the labour movement as a whole and in the public notoriety of cases like the death of Marsinah.[21] Space does not afford a fuller development of the significance of middle- and working-class politics, although is critical to the shape and potential of more substantive opposition movements.

The developments discussed in the three subsections above signal the weakening of the New Order regime. They may have serious repercussions in the long run, but they do not mean the unequivocal defeat of the regime in its public confrontation with social groups supposedly subject to its control and domination. The following three cases are more interesting because they exemplify embarrassing defeats for the government in public disputes with the seemingly powerless masses.

The victory of Megawati

As mentioned earlier, depoliticisation has been thorough and systemic under New Order rule. No political opposition is legitimate, not even as rhetoric or tokenism. Nevertheless, one of the two nominally 'non-government' parties, the PDI, appears recalcitrant from time to time. Though always a loser in general elections, the PDI at least presents the appearance of a threat, and to that extent it compromises the regime's desire for public appearance of totalitarian rule.

Government intervention into PDI affairs has been regular. During the party's congress in 1993, this intervention was unashamedly gross and the press exposed it vividly. Consequently it came as a great embarrassment when all these efforts failed. The government could neither install its supported nominee nor silence the persistent demand from the party's supporters nationwide to elect as party leader Megawati Soekarnoputri, daughter of President Soeharto's predecessor and chief rival in the national myth.[22]

The PDI's miraculous success generated the new catchword *arus bawah*, 'undercurrent', an admiring reference to the politically conscious supporters of Megawati. These people came in their thousands to the party congress in Surabaya despite local intimidation in their many different places of origin. What Megawati and her party realistically could do after the election was questionable, but the dramatic defeat of an old authoritarian regime by the common people in a public contest created the perception that a new phase was approaching. Many observers attribute this to the endorsement of Megawati by certain elements within the military leadership. What may have been less acknowledged is the contribution of bold and partisan journalistic reports during the event. This suggests the need to examine the politics of the middle-class professionals in general, and the threat that the press in particular posed in the months prior to the June 1994 bans.

The closure of the national lottery

The closure of the national lottery on 25 November 1993 was another celebrated success for public confrontation against the otherwise apparently very powerful state apparatus. The state-sponsored lottery has been a major social phenomenon since the 1970s, under different names and through various reorganisations. Regardless of its form or title, the enterprise always generated enormous revenue.

Protests against this legal form of gambling came and went over the years. One reason why the enterprise survived and succeeded was the fact that a great portion of the population, mostly the underprivileged, enthusiastically welcomed it. It absorbed much of their energy, time, and money. The lottery established new social relationships and redefined old ones for millions of Indonesians, and thus assumed a significance well beyond the question of participants' monetary loss and gain.

Two waves of student-led mass demonstrations against the lottery prior to its dissolution are worthy of mention. The first, in late November 1991, was the biggest series of student-led demonstrations since 1978 when the government clamped down violently on all campus-based student politics. Thousands of students in different cities joined separate but equally peaceful protests. These protests were so overwhelming that the international outcry against the notorious killings at the Santa Cruz cemetery (Dili, East Timor) on 12 November 1991 found no immediate echoes in otherwise politically volatile Indonesia. Heavily armed soldiers broke up most of these anti-lottery demonstrations, rescuing Rp. 580,000 million (US$289 million) worth of revenue-generating business.[23]

The second wave of anti-lottery demonstrations that eventually closed down the enterprise took place two years later, by which time lottery earnings had doubled to Rp. 995,000 million (US$460 million) (*Jakarta-Jakarta*, 385, 20–26 November 1993: 18). As before, students appeared in the forefront of these demonstrations. But to a greater extent than in the preceding protests, senior leaders within the Muslim communities took a leading role, and the protests were based on religious and moral values.

The event had four important features relevant to our discussion. First, the closure of the lottery was all the more dramatic in that the government had insisted in public just a few days before that the enterprise would continue despite popular objection. It is thus strikingly similar to the embarrassment over the election of Megawati. Second, the incident underscores the recurring evidence that real politics in Indonesia takes place primarily outside the confines of formal institutions (elections, parliament, or political parties). This suggests a marked contrast to what happened in the Philippines in the first half of 1994, where the dispute between the state-proposed lottery and its critics took place in court (see Tiglao 1994). Third, the mass protest in Jakarta was the first protest rally to reach the Presidential Palace complex. Fourth, to the surprise of many, the military were remarkably soft on the demonstration, again prompting speculation about their deliberate, if passive, endorsement for any move against the President.

Questioning the New Order's genealogy and legitimacy

In discussing issues of ideology in New Order Indonesia, many observers focus on the official state ideology, Pancasila. That is a very tricky endeavour, as the regime's formal propaganda may be a distraction from the real point. In itself Pancasila tells us little about Indonesia. It contains western-derived modern, globally upheld values, formulated in high abstraction. The values of the five principles are not really in dispute. But they also have little bearing on the everyday lives of Indonesians which are, as elsewhere, full of contradictions and ambiguities.[24]

As I discussed on p. 242, the crucial foundation of the New Order's ideology lies in its discourse of a violent genealogy. Officially the abortive coup d'état of 30 September 1965 by the Indonesian Communist Party (PKI), provoked the 'birth' and quick ascendancy of the army-dominated New Order regime. Unlike *Pancasila*, what has officially been termed Pengkhianatan G-30-S/PKI (The Treachery of the 30 September Movement/PKI) is full of historically specific referents. Further, unlike the high-flown *Pancasila*, the narrative on the PKI's treachery has much bearing on the mass killings in 1965–6, among the bloodiest in modern history, where 'in four months, five times as many people died in Indonesia as in Vietnam in twelve years' (Bertrand Russell, as quoted in the Foreword of Caldwell 1975).[25] The killings and intimidation of opponents that ensued in the next twenty-five years laid the foundation of the New Order regime and its impressive economic growth rates. The same events generated a master-narrative of 'Communist threats' that has been a crucially determining principle in the restructuring of social relationships and the redefining of social identities and notions of 'reality'.

The discourse on the threats of Communism and the canonical narrative of Pengkhianatan G-30-S/PKI have not gone without challenge. But criticism is usually voiced outside the formal public domain in anonymous pamphlets, for example, circulated only among urban opponents of the regime. When they enter into the formal public domain, they are too obscure and timid to carry any weight. The following account of an incident involving Wimanjaya K. Liotohe is therefore unprecedented. Ironically, it was brought about by the President and his officials. On 23 January 1994 the President complained that someone had seriously discredited him:

> I was accused of having masterminded the G-30-S/PKI on the pretext that Untung [a lieutenant who led the self-styled 'Revolutionary Council' that kidnapped and killed six generals on the eve of 1 October 1965] was my subordinate. This defamation was presented in the book *Primadosa*.
>
> (*Kompas*, 29 January 1994: 1, 11)

A recurrent event in New Order political ritual has been the prosecution of journalists in the 1970s and students activists in later years for speaking out against the *status quo* and against state bureaucrats. They were tried under a series of colonial-derived Penal Codes that punish anyone for publicly expressing what the regime arbitrarily defines as hatred, insult, or hostility towards the incumbent authorities. Charges of insulting the President have been predominant in recent political trials, although not once has the President himself hinted that he felt insulted, or that he knew or cared that these trials were taking place. Now when for the first time the President has alleged that he has been insulted, no state apparatus has moved to arrest and prosecute the perpetrator. Indeed, the complaint signalled that something had gone seriously wrong.

The President's complaint was more than simply a warning or expression of anger over the book. It was an expression of helplessness, and anger with his state agents for having done nothing to protect him against Wimanjaya K. Liotohe, the author. The next morning the office of the Attorney General issued a decree banning *Primadosa*. Three days later Probosutedjo, a big business person and the President's half-brother, acting as the chairperson of Himpunan Pengusaha Pribumi Indonesia (HIPPI, Association of Indonesian Indigenous Businessmen), more bluntly expressed deep outrage against the President's aides for their failure to protect him. He mournfully described his half-brother's position as a solitary one, abandoned by those responsible for his safety. Probosutedjo demanded that the office of the Attorney General prosecute the author of *Primadosa* (*Kompas*, 29 January 1994: 1, 11). But, again, this call met with no enthusiasm. On the contrary, in April 1994 Wimanjaya K. Liotohe filed a lawsuit against the office of the Attorney General for having banned his book.

The six cases outlined above are far from exhaustive. The list could be tripled to cover the beginning of the 1990s, and to include less significant cases.[26] In yet another significant development, the Jakarta State Administration Court was required to consider whether a lawsuit against the President brought by six NGOs over the reallocation of reforestation funds worth Rp. 400,000 million (US$185 million) had any validity. As it happens, the Court judged that the NGOs did not have the right to bring the case since they were not directly injured parties ('Majelis PTUN: Gugatan Enam LSM Tidak Bisa Diterima', *Kompas*, 13 December 1994: 6; 'Belum Final, Belum Layak', *FORUM Keadilan*, 19, III, 5 January 1995: 86).

TOWARDS COUNTER-HEGEMONIC STRUGGLES

Although none of these cases is dealt with comprehensively, to differing extents each offers evidence in support of the following main points.

The 1990s are witnessing a significant increase in the prominence of opposition movements in Indonesia. The geographical areas involved in the various popular protests have expanded, as have the social backgrounds of those participating in them. There has also been a marked escalation in the frequency and militancy of movements against the New Order regime. Strong moral and religious overtones in several of the protests indicate a continuity with the popular protests of the past. However, opposition in the 1990s features new secular elements.

One outstanding feature of the recent opposition movements is the re-emergence of a conscious attempt to avoid elitism and to take up the cause of the underprivileged. This populist tendency clearly distinguishes recent dissenters from their predecessors since the New Order came to power. Before 1989 student movements found their bases in state universities in the capital city of Jakarta and its close neighbouring city, Bandung. Key figures in these movements reportedly had links, at least informally, with top political elites in Jakarta. Since 1989, centres of the student movements have moved away from Jakarta to various regional cities. Their main partners are predominantly peasants and industrial workers. Not only have state ministers, military or party leaders been excluded from their alliances, in fact those representing the authorities have been the targets of the students' attacks.

As in the past, the new opposition movements are still dominated by university-educated activists and professionals. As well as undergraduate students, they include journalists, artists, lawyers, academics, and NGO activists. This is not surprising. As many have noticed, the urban middle classes include people who have both the resources (material and educational) and the incentives to demand social change. These people certainly benefit from the *status quo* they claim to want to undermine. But a growing proportion of the urban middle classes can no longer accept the *status quo* and their own privileged position in it as morally or politically correct. Even in material terms, these people seem to believe that the majority would benefit more than they would lose from a new social order in the long term.

Obviously, this only applies to limited segments of the urban middle classes, at a particular point of time. Even some of the most radical middle-class activists are more heterogeneous and liable to change than this chapter can describe. Bearing this in mind, we can draw some minimal conclusions about their salient features. Only with some degree of generalisation can we speak of the forms and directions of their opposition movements.

Certain themes predominate in the agenda of the urban middle-class opposition. Daniel Lev (1990) has discussed them most succinctly. The core of these themes comprises 'the separation of society from state', the establishment and reinforcement of the notion of 'rule of law', and social 'equality' (Lev 1990: 31, 35–6, 36). These constitute, I believe, what has lately come to be called *demokratisasi*, 'democratisation'.

A closer scrutiny will undoubtedly reveal ambiguities and differences in meaning in the seemingly unifying and unified word *demokratisasi* as used among activists. The heterogeneous middle class in Indonesia has for some time now appeared to have a significant degree of cohesion. This is not of its own making, but has been made possible by events and forces that lie outside relationships among these diverse middle classes. They virtually all find themselves in a commonly dependent relationship with the New Order state, the central sponsor of political repression and economic development. Antagonism has come to predominate over other elements in their easily changing relationship. If middle-class activists appear to have played a leading role in the struggle for *demokratisasi*, it is partly thanks to specific cultural and political histories. Culturally, middle-class intellectuals in many Third World and former socialist bloc countries enjoy the popular myth of moral superiority. Politically, capitalist industrialisation in countries like Indonesia has not been accompanied by a strong capitalist ideology. Even in the period of highest economic growth and consumerism, the government launched a nationwide campaign for asceticism. This is ostensibly an attempt to fight against the arrival of a hedonist consumer society. The notion of a free market is largely unacceptable and *kapitalisme* (capitalism) is a dirty word.[27]

After this sympathetic account of the middle-class opposition, one still has to gauge the effectiveness of their struggles and their prospects for success. Here I can only briefly review the New Order regime's performance in confronting its domestic opposition as illustrated in the cases above. I will also offer a few preliminary thoughts about middle-class alliances with other social groups. In this way, we can examine Indonesian middle-class opposition in synchronic relationship with – not in isolation from – its political environment.

As suggested earlier, contemporary middle-class opposition is ideologically friendly with the rural peasants and industrial workers. 'Empowering the powerless' has become a common aim of many NGOs, lawyers, human rights activists, journalists, and socially committed artists. Peasant resistance to the Kedong Ombo dam project, protest at the death of Marsinah, and worker protest in Medan are only a few examples of such alliances that have gained impressive success and international fame. They combine grassroots opposition with strategic support from middle-class activists. Peasants in remote areas and urban workers in poverty-stricken neighbourhoods are increasingly aware of the importance of support, however imperfect, from urban middle-class activists in its various forms: journalistic and human rights reports, non-governmental training, litigation in court, academic seminars, and artistic works.

Sustained international support from liberal governments and human rights organisations to enhance such domestic alliances has been useful. Nevertheless, the links between middle-class activists and the less privileged remain *ad hoc*, fragmented, short-lived, and clandestine. State surveillance, periodic prosecutions, and constant intimidation impose severe external pressures. Nor have limited material and educational resources among the oppositional groups – not to mention subjective inter-class divides in lifestyles and values – helped to foster long-term joint strategies and alliances. Where conflicts have not been resolved quickly, the famous 'success stories' of grassroots opposition in alliance with middle-class activists have not ended happily.[28] This leads to the question of alliances between desperate or disillusioned members of the middle classes and those in ruling circles.

Alliances between certain middle-class activists and state agents do sometimes occur, on formal and informal bases. It is never easy to investigate and describe this sensitive area – especially in the limited space available here. Nevertheless, some limited observations are warranted. First, such alliances are in no way systematically orchestrated or controlled by any centre of power. Instead, they develop in a piecemeal fashion, and tend to be open-ended, diffuse, quickly shifting, and mutually suspicious. Second, these various alliances have less and less connection with the 1965–6 violence, or its protracted aftermath. Short-term political and economic interests seem to predominate over the exploration of new alliances. Third, no such alliance seems to have played any significant role in the recent conflicts between the government and its overt opponents. Alliances with the ruling elite may claim to operate quietly behind closed doors for reasons of long-term strategy, but there is no way of assessing their efficacy. This brings us to the final issue to be considered, the question of effective opposition under state hegemony.

Most power relations involve some degree of compromise and trade-off. Even a hegemonic power does not mean 'making a clean sweep of the existing world-view and replacing it with a completely new and already formulated one. Rather, it consists in a process of transformation and of rearticulation of existing ideological elements' (Mouffe 1979: 191–2).

The series of events presented in the preceding sections indicate a steady weakening of the New Order over an extended period; there are no counterbalancing cases favouring the regime. This is more significant if we look back to the past. A decade ago foreign observers described the New Order regime as an omnipotent institution. Ben Anderson described the leitmotiv of New Order governance as the strengthening of the 'state-qua-state' (1983: 488, 1990: 111). More recently, Richard Tanter has asserted that the New Order had the 'capacity to ignore, or at least postpone, cultivation of domestic support and the class compromises which that process requires' (1990: 77, 1991: 13, 204).

In vew of the above, we have grounds to argue that the long-standing hegemonic power of the New Order has encountered a serious crisis in the 1990s. However, the selected cases examined here do not provide evidence for attributing the crisis solely to opposition forces. Neither can we assume that the crisis will necessarily lead to the regime's final dissolution. As things stand, there are chances for the New Order to revitalise itself. Unless the regime makes fatal blunders or sinks into deeper crisis beyond its control, it may have some hope of re-creating its hegemonic position. To do so will require making necessary concessions to, and then appropriating, the opposition's demands. Unless the opposition manages to transcend its present agenda, and go beyond demands for immediate redress in particular cases of abuse of power, or beyond issues of presidential succession, it will not engender substantial consequences for the existing social order.

NOTES

1 The estimates of those massacred vary and it is unlikely the actual figure will ever be known. The figure of one millon is cited by Caldwell (1975: 13), but this is by no means the highest estimate. Southwood and Flanagan (1983: 73) point out, for instance, that Amnesty International's investigations revealed independent estimates of 'many more than a million'. For other estimates, see May (1978: 120) and Crouch (1978: 155).
2 Some of the most important writings on the topic include *Indonesia*, April 1966: 131–204, Notosusanto and Saleh (1968, 1989); Anderson and McVey (1971); Caldwell (1975); Crouch (1978); May (1978); Wertheim (1979); Holtzappel (1979); Southwood and Flanagan (1983); Scott (1986); Bunnell (1990); Cribb (1990); Budiardjo (1991).
3 Pancasila, (Five Principles) is the name of the official state ideology, first formulated by the late President Soekarno in 1945. The five principles are: Belief in the One Supreme God; Just and Civilised Humanity; Unity of Indonesia; Deliberative and Representative Democracy; and Social Justice.
4 For a discussion of the significance of the controversy over the recalling of Bambang Warih, see Arief Budiman (1995).
5 Yayasan Keluaga Bhakti (ed.) (1993) *Tajuk-Tajuk di Bawah Terik Matahari* ('Buds Under the Heat of the Sun'), Jakarta: Gramedia, is probably the best

compilation to date of Indonesians discussing the press. This over-500-page volume gives a good illustration of the wide recognition of the regrettable but unstoppable industrialisation of journalism. The press is portrayed as 'buds' (small, delicate, innocent) that suffer injustice from 'the heat of the sun' (imposition of powerful forces from above). For a view of the general moral outrage following the June 1994 bans, see Utami *et al.* (1994). David Hill (1994) offers an excellent overview of the Indonesian press under the New Order regime for English readers.

6 The joy of discovering a middle-class identity in the aftermath of the June 1994 bans is presented in a reflexive essay by Ayu Utami, a young reporter of *FORUM Keadilan*, and an activist of the Alliance of Independent Journalists (1994: 11). See also Pranowo (1994) for a more detached view.

7 In his defence plea, Atmowiloto described how reporters from other media exaggerated the incident and reinforced the mass demand for *Monitor's* closure. The incident that ostensibly triggered the affair was a readers' poll of their favourite figures that included the Prophet Muhammad and placed him several ranks below other names, including President Soeharto, pop artists, and Atmowiloto himself.

8 In fact, Jakob Oetama handed down not one but two publication licences to the government in response to the angry masses over allegations of offending Islam, leading to the closure of *Monitor* and *Senang*.

9 Interestingly, after losing his previous position in *Jakarta-Jakarta*, Seno Gumira Ajidarma (one of the three editors) managed to publish more than ten short stories in separate but major newspapers. These stories depict more vividly than any journalist reports can possibly do, the horrific violence inflicted upon East Timorese around the time of the Dili killings in 1991. None of these publications provoked anyone. The Jakarta Arts Centre Taman Ismail Marzuki sponsored a public reading of these short stories by eminent literary figures on 19 November 1994 (see *Kompas*, 23 November 1994: 16).

10 I am grateful to Chua Beng-Huat for bringing my attention on many of these events for broader analysis.

11 President Soeharto's statement was made on Sunday, 5 June 1994, in Bogor, to 200 college graduates and former recipients of Supersemar state scholarships (*Kompas*, XIII, 6 June 1994).

12 Although many of the figures in this chapter are shown in US dollars, British usage is retained throughout, rendering 1,000,000,000 as 'a thousand million' and equating 'one billion' with 1,000,000,000,000.

13 Both Jakob Oetama, on behalf of the Association of Newspaper Publishers, and Harmoko, in his capacity as Minister of Information, aired some of the earliest and strongest opposition to the possibility that foreign capital had invaded the media industry. Soon spokespersons of the government amended the earlier official position, assuring that the new regulation would not apply to the media.

14 Conservative economists in Indonesia launched attacks on the new regulation on the basis of a rigid separation between the so-called 'public' and 'private' economies. They appeared to defend and respect the 'public'; but what they actually did – either consciously or not – was (i) defend the rights of 'private' property; (ii) reinforce the notion that the separation was given and/or desirable; and (iii) imply that in practice the private companies have

so far restrained themselves from invading the so-called 'public' interest, space, and economies. I recall Althusser's discussion of Gramsci: 'The distinction between the public and the private is a distinction internal to bourgeois law' (*Ideology and the State*, 1971: 18).

15 See *Far Eastern Economic Review*'s cover story on this (1 April 1993: 72–7).

16 The state banks dominate the total financial assets and bank loans in the country, despite the recent mushrooming of private banks. In 1993 the divide between state banks and private banks in a total of US$ 68.2,000 billion worth of loans was 49 per cent to 41 per cent. The figures in 1989 were 63 per cent to 30 per cent (Habir 1994: 54).

17 The World Bank expressed deep concern about the direct and indirect implications of the case (*Republika*, 9 June 1994: 1).

18 This reference to a 'third party' is generally interpreted as an oblique reference to the military or a faction therein. For details of this matter that run counter to the official version, see Amnesty International's report 'Indonesia; Labour Activists Under Fire' (ASA 21 September 1994, May 1994, pp. 6–7) and a 'White Book' prepared by two local pro-labour NGOs (Yayasan Kelompok Pelita Sejahtera and Yayasan Pondok Rakyat Kreatip), entitled *Tragedi Aksi Akbar Buruh Medan* (*The Tragedy of Medan Labour's Great Action*) (esp. p. 17). Pakpahan's counter-allegations appear in many major news magazines such as *FORUM Keadilan* (3(2), 11 May 1994: esp. 16) and *DëTIK* (18(59), 27 April–3 May 1994: 9). For a preliminary interpretation of the overall event as a class, rather than racial, conflict see Heryanto (1994a, 1994b).

19 See Hadiz (1993, 1994) for more on the phenomenal rise of working-class politics in the 1990s.

20 For a detailed report prepared by an independent fact-finding commission whose conclusion runs counter in almost every respect to the official version, see ILAF (1994).

21 SBSI was one of them. It was established on 25 April 1992 under the leadership of Mochtar Pakpahan, a Ph.D. graduate in State Administration Studies, University of Indonesia. Although the government has repeatedly declared it illegal, no serious legal action has been taken with the specific aim of dismantling it. What the government has done is take a series of minor and *ad hoc* measures to cancel some of the union's activities and arrest the key figures. In 1994 SBSI claimed to have eighty-seven local branches throughout the archipelagic country, embracing an official membership of some 250,000 workers. For more on SBSI see *FORUM Keadilan* (3(2), 11 May 1994: 15), and on Mochtar Pakpahan see *Kompas*, 18 September 1993: 20).

The exact vitality of SBSI and its contribution to the worker movement has been a point of debate among some observers. Apart from the competence of leading individuals within the union, before Pakpahan's prosecution some speculated that the phenomenon was a result of a covert back-up from certain segments of the military. The government's restrained measures must also be related to international pressures, especially from the American human rights organisations. In 1993 the US government threatened to suspend US$600 million worth of benefits enjoyed by Indonesia under the Generalised System of Preferences (GSP), unless it showed a better performance on human rights issues. In early 1994 the New Order hastily repealed the Ministry of Manpower Decree No. 342/1986 that gave the military the power to intervene in labour disputes. Despite the repeal, military intervention reportedly continued (see Amnesty International's report cited in Note 18).

22 For more on the election of Megawati see a report by Gerry van Klinken (1994). It must be noted that the only single significant figure to threaten the incumbent ruler in the New Order ideological battle has been Soekarno, the deceased. Soekarno's picture was virtually the only human face other than President Soeharto's to appear in posters and banners in the campaign period during general elections. Myths about Soekarno apparently became a means of ideological articulation in the urban discontent during the 1987 election. So serious did the government feel this threat that it banned the traditional display of any human representations for campaign purposes in the 1992 general election. It also co-sponsored the publication of books that question, if not undermine, Soekarno's credentials. The effects have been counterproductive.

  In September 1994 the government succeeded in ensuring that a loyalist became the leader of the other 'non-government' party, Partai Persatuan Pembangunan (PPP), but also at high cost. The more popular but defeated nominees opened a hot debate in the media with the object of forming a new party, and thus challenging the government's decision to keep the number of parties to a maximum of three. More seriously, they can be seen to challenge the government's delusion that it rules the country with unanimous consent from its subjects.

23 The estimate came from *Kompas*, 13 September 1991: 1. For reports of the mass rallies and their ugly dispersals see *Kompas*, 20 November 1991: 14; *Bernas*, 23 November 1991; and *TEMPO*, 30 November 1991: 35–6.

24 However, Douglas Ramage (1993) demonstrates how a close examination of competing discourses of Pancasila within specified contexts can be instructive.

25 See Robert Cribb's (1990) edited volume for a recent investigation into the killings themselves, with selected references to relevant literature on the broader perspective.

26 For example, the list can be added to with the cases of: (i) the stubborn insistence of the Medan Church congregation to conduct an independent election of its religious leadership; (ii) the successful demands of some of the thousands of peasants evicted from their villages for the Kedong Ombo dam construction; (iii) the cancellation of a newly drafted Bill against extramarital relationships; (iv) the cancellation of some traffic regulations and the delay of closely related regulations as a direct result of mass demonstrations; (v) the cancellation of privatisation of tax collecting for television licences; (vi) the establishment of the National Human Rights Commission in response to the international pressures after the Dili killings; (vii) the failure of the monopolistic Body for the Protection of Clove Farmers; (viii) the recurrent unrest of city youths at concerts, attacking specifically the rich and security officers; (ix) the ongoing protests against the government's construction of a nuclear plant in Central Java; (x) the acquittals of those previously found guilty in the trials in the murder of Marsinah.

27 This paragraph draws on Hagen Koo's (1991) insightful analysis of the South Korean middle classes. I found many similarities between the two nations' middle-class politics.
28 The fate of the Kedong Ombo peasants remains unclear at the time of writing, after the Supreme Court cancelled its previous decision in their favour. Labour protests subsided dramatically following the arrest and prosecution of Mochtar Pakpahan (leader of the SBSI). The stubborn Indonesian Democratic Party under Megawati's leadership encountered exasperating 'internal' conflicts.

REFERENCES

Anderson, Ben (1983) 'Old State, New Society: Indonesia's New Order in Comparative Historical Perspective', *Journal of Asian Studies*, XLII(3), May: 477–96.
—— (1990) 'Old State, New Society: Indonesia's New Order in Comparative Historical Perspective', in *Language and Power; Exploring Political Cultures in Indonesia*, Ithaca, NY: Cornell University Press, pp. 94–120.
Anderson, Benedict and McVey, Ruth (1971) *A Preliminary Analysis of the October 1, 1965, Coup in Indonesia*, Ithaca, NY: Modern Indonesia Project, SEAP, Cornell University.
Budiardjo, Carmel (1991) 'Indonesia: Mass Extermination and the Consolidation of Authoritarian Power', in Alexander George (ed.) *Western State Terrorism*, New York: Routledge, pp. 180–211.
Budiman, Arief (1995) 'Bambang Warih', *Tiras*, 1(3), 16 February: 30.
Bunnell, Frederick (1990) 'American "Low Posture" Policy Toward Indonesia in the Months Leading up to the 1965 "Coup"', *Indonesia*, 50, October: 29–60.
Caldwell, Malcolm (ed.) (1975) *Ten Years' Military Terror in Indonesia*, Nottingham: Spokesman Books.
Cribb, Robert (1990) 'Problems in the Historiography of the Killings in Indonesia', in *The Indonesian Killings of 1965–1966; Studies from Java and Bali*, Clayton: Centre of Southeast Asian Studies, Monash University, pp. 1–43.
Crouch, Harold (1978) *The Army and Politics in Indonesia*, Ithaca, NY: Cornell University Press.
Dhakidae, Daniel (1994) 'Membunuh Modal, Membunuh Kebudayaan', in Ayu Utami *et al.* (eds) *Bredel 1994*, Jakarta: Aliansi Jurnalis Independen, pp. 48–61.
Habir, Manggi (1994) 'Private Treatment', *Far Eastern Economic Review*, 28 April: 58.
Hadiz, Vedi R. (1993) 'Workers and Working Class Politics in the 1990s', in Chris Manning and Joan Hardjono (eds) *Indonesia Assessment 1993; Labour: Sharing in the Benefits of Growth?*, Canberra: Department of Political and Social Change, pp. 186–200.
—— (1994) 'Challenging State Corporatism on the Labour Front: Working Class Politics in the 1990s', in David Bourchier and John Legge (eds) *Democracy in Indonesia 1950s and 1990s*, Clayton: Centre of Southeast Asian Studies, Monash University, pp. 190–203.

Heryanto, Ariel (1994a) 'A Class Act', *Far Eastern Economic Review*, 16 June: 30.

—— (1994b) 'Chinese Indonesians in Public Culture: Ethnic Identities and Erasure', paper delivered at the conference, Identities, Ethnicities, Nationalities in Asia and Pacific Contexts, La Trobe University, Melbourne, 7–9 July 1994.

Hill, David (1994) *The Press in New Order Indonesia*, Perth: Asia Research Centre, Murdoch University.

Holtzappel, Coen (1979) 'The 30 September Movement: a Political Movement of the Armed Forces or an Intelligence Operation?', *Journal of Contemporary Asia*, IX(2): 216–40.

ILAF (Indonesian Legal Aid Foundation) (1994) *A Preliminary Report on the Murder of Marsinah*, Jakarta: Indonesian Legal Aid Foundation.

Koo, Hagen (1991) 'Middle Classes, Democratization, and Class Formation', *Theory and Society*, 20(4), August: 485–509.

Lev, Daniel (1990) 'Intermediate Classes and Change in Indonesia', in Richard Tanter and Kenneth Young (eds) *The Politics of Middle Class Indonesia*, Clayton: Monash University, pp. 25–43.

McBeth, John (1994) 'The Year of Doing Business', *Far Eastern Economic Review*, 1 September: 70–2.

May, Brian (1978) *The Indonesian Tragedy*, London: Routledge & Kegan Paul.

Mohamad, Goenawan (1994) 'Saya Tidak Percaya Revolusi', an interview with *FORUM Keadilan*, III(7), 21 July: 32–6.

Mouffe, Chantal (1979) 'Hegemony and Ideology in Gramsci', in Chantal Mouffe (ed.) *Gramsci and Marxist Theory*, London: Routledge & Kegan Paul, pp. 168–204.

Notosusanto, Nugroho and Saleh, Ismail (1968) *The Coup Attempt of the September 30 Movement in Indonesia*, Jakarta: Pembimbing Massa.

—— (1989) *Tragedi Nasional Percobaan Kup G30S/PKI di Indonesia*, Jakarta: Intermassa.

Pranowo, Budi L. (1994) 'Kontroversi Peran Kelas Menengah', *Suara Merdeka*, 28 June: 6.

Ramage, Douglas (1993) 'Ideological Discourse in the Indonesian New Order: State Ideology and the Beliefs of an Elite, 1985–1993', doctoral dissertation, South Carolina: International Studies Program, Department of Governmental and International Studies, University of South Carolina.

Scott, James (1986) *Resistance without Protest: Peasant Opposition in the Zakat in Malaysia and to the Tithe in France*, Townsville, Queensland: Asian Studies Association of Australia.

Sender, Henny (1993) 'Unhealthy States', *Far Eastern Economic Review*, 1 April: 75–6.

—— (1994) 'Nor a Lender Be', *Far Eastern Economic Review*, 1 September: 73–4.

Southwood, Julie and Flanagan, Patrick (1983) *Indonesia: Law, Propaganda and Terror*, London: Zed.

Tanter, Richard (1990) 'Oil, IGGI and US Hegemony: The Global Preconditions for Indonesian Rentier-Militarization', in Arief Budiman (ed.) *State and Civil Society in Indonesia*, Clayton: Centre of Southeast Asian Studies, Monash University, pp. 51–98.

—— (1991) 'Intelligence Agencies and Third World Militarization: a Case

Study of Indonesia, 1966–1989', unpublished dissertation, submitted to the Department of Politics, Monash University, February 1991.

Tiglao, Rigoberto (1994) 'And the Winner is . . .', *Far Eastern Economic Review*, 7 April: 76.

Utami, Ayu (1994) 'Surat Seorang Reporter', in Ayu Utami *et al.* (eds) *Bredel 1994*, Jakarta: Aliansi Jurnalis Independen, pp. 1–14.

Utami, Ayu, Santoso, Imran Hasibuan, and Siregar, Liston P. (1994) *Bredel 1994*, Jakarta: Aliansi Jurnalis Independen.

van Klinken, Gerry (1994) 'Soekarno's Daughter Takes Over Indonesia's Democrats', *Inside Indonesia*, 38, March: 2–4.

Wertheim, W. F. (1979) 'Whose Plot? – New Light on the 1965 Events', *Journal of Contemporary Asia*, IX(2): 197–215.

10 New social movements and the changing nature of political opposition in South Korea

*Bronwen Dalton and James Cotton**

INTRODUCTION

Throughout the 1980s, studies on South Korean development often focused upon state direction of economic growth through the promotion of export-oriented industrialisation. To maintain its control over the growth process, the state systematically institutionalised its dominance over society and placed a range of constraints and limitations on social demands. Society-based opposition thus largely nullified, the state presided over a society of depoliticised workers and compliant capitalists committed to the objective of rapid export-oriented industrialisation. However, the dramatic changes in the Republic of Korea since 1987, which include the return to civilian rule and free elections, have led to the need to revise this perspective. Politics has become more pluralised, contending groups (including political parties and movements) now have an independent role, and national policy reflects this growing complexity. In this environment, and especially as a consequence of the reinstatement of the electoral process and subsequent political reforms, there is renewed interest in the role of opposition groups and their relation to economic and social change.

The process of political liberalisation since 1987 has given expression to a wide diversity of social movements, has stimulated changes in the linkages between various social and political groups, and has involved the emergence of new sources of political opposition. This development has been encouraged by the tardiness of the conventional political parties in adapting to this new environment. Despite the decade of change since 1987, successive leadership changes and realignments have demonstrated that political parties are largely still the creatures of their various leadership factions (Yang 1995). Consequently, new social movements (NSMs) have become a major source of opposition and policy critique, advancing environmentalism, feminism, consumer and human rights, and various other consumption and quality-of-life concerns. The most striking political mobilisation in the 1990s is being generated by these movements, involving a variety of community-level non-government organisations (NGOs) addressing one or more aspects of the concerns of these movements. Though these NGOs may have a predominantly middle-class membership base, their agendas promote the interests of diverse and sometimes disadvantaged social elements. Moreover, by virtue of their participatory organisational nature, NSMs have the potential to make a significant contribution to sustaining the process of deepening democratic values, practices, and institutions in South Korea. Yet they also represent a force for political moderation, supplanting the radical worker- and student-based movements of the 1970s and 1980s that played so big a part in bringing the previous authoritarian regime to an end.

This chapter examines the emergence and dynamics of political opposition in South Korea against the backdrop of the country's industrial and political transformation. The central focus, however, is on the role of social movements and the important changes in their nature and role over time. This involves examination of the trade union and student movements, and a case study of one of South Korea's foremost NGOs – the Citizens' Coalition for Economic Justice (CCEJ) – which has recently become a significant avenue through which various NSM concerns are expressed.

LEGACIES OF AUTHORITARIAN RULE

Despite recent political change, there still exists a range of formal rules or legal mechanisms through which the state may obstruct or control organised opposition. During the decades of authoritarianism, the state developed an extensive security and police apparatus and, under such laws as the National Security Law, could legally deploy this apparatus to detect, destabilise, and/or punish elements it identified as challenging state authority. Various agents of control, ranging from riot troops to undercover intelligence agents, were deployed to weaken the organisational ability of existing groups and effectively dissuade others from contemplating revolt.[1] This apparatus protected the position of the state in two ways: it provided the state with the physical means of enforcing compliance, and it acted as a psychological deterrent to groups otherwise inclined to contemplate risks.

A network of informal rules in South Korea has both hindered the organisation of opposition groups and has sometimes generated strong public resentment. Cases of bribery of government officials and tax and real estate scandals have been commonplace. This is not unusual for a developing country but, judging from the nature of the scandals reported since 1990, it seems that those involved are often limited to the most powerful members of a government–industry clique. This has been made possible by the coexistence of South Korea's acutely concentrated economy (the top ten *Chaebol* – industrial groups – accounting for the generation of over 70 per cent of gross national product) with the highly interventionist economic policies of the state (Woo 1991).[2]

Under the export-oriented industrialisation strategy an exclusionary and corporatist political and economic relationship between the state and business was forged which restricted the autonomy of capital. Various state agencies practised 'administrative guidance' based on the implementation of a range of incentives and rewards, as well as some punitive measures, as a means of ensuring the active co-operation of business in realising economic growth. The state's policy levers primarily involved the provision of cheap credit to firms which, through their export success, demonstrated their capacity to lead export-oriented industrialisation. This required large amounts of finance, and increasingly the capacity of the state relied on its ability to mobilise the financial market (Woo 1991). This pattern of government intervention had several negative side-effects, including the emergence of corrupt practices.

Party politics in South Korea is still to be formally institutionalised and exhibits many authoritarian legacies. Opposition parties, though before 1987 they disputed the monopoly of power held by the rulers of the authoritarian state, often did not represent either in their internal organisation or in their commitment to policies and principles an alternative mode of conducting politics. The inability and disinclination of South Korea's political parties to develop coherent policies is partly due to the fact that much of their energy has been spent on waging inter- and intra-party factional struggles. Factional fighting is usually carried out among groups which have differing personal allegiances. Technically, South Korea has had hundreds of opposition parties. However, despite various name changes, for the most part this has involved the same core groups led by the same men. Opposition parties have also tended not to foster broad grassroots support bases, instead relying on the tendency of South Koreans to vote for the representative of their region, regardless of the candidate or policies.

Strict control of the media was a feature of the decades of authoritarian rule in South Korea. From the advent of the Roh Tae-woo administration, freedom of the press has made significant progress, with over 1,494 new local publications launched between 1989 and 1993 (S. H. Lee 1993: 357). But even now the state can still invoke controls under the National Security Law, and information can be withheld on the grounds that it may be sympathetic to North Korea or pose some other threat to national security.[3] Public servants can also be prohibited from releasing information to the press. Such restrictions have created an environment in which deception and dishonesty by politicians and their senior officials sometimes goes undetected, and in which the media can be subject to manipulation.

INDUSTRIALISATION, SOCIAL CHANGE AND RADICAL OPPOSITION

In post-war Korea, extra-parliamentary actors have made a major contribution to political opposition. The emergence and changing character of these extra-parliamentary oppositions has been linked to the social transformations generated by rapid industrialisation.

Prior to the Korean War, the Korean class structure was relatively undeveloped, and the society remained largely agrarian. Having developed in an economy dominated by Japanese interests and the Japanese colonial administration, the Korean bourgeoisie was accustomed to seek state protection and patronage. In addition, agrarian-based interests were eliminated through land reforms. Consequently, class consciousness functional to the development of socialist movements was slow to develop. Furthermore, leftist groups which had been active during the period immediately prior to the Korean War were the target of extensive anti-Communist propaganda disseminated through an intricate security network. As a consequence, initial extra-parliamentary resistance to the new Republic in the South in 1945 took the form of *ad hoc*, populist struggles. However, as the economy grew and became more complex, the class character of Korean society changed, with important implications for organised social and political activity.

In particular, the rise in worker-based opposition was linked to the process of rapid industrialisation. The early period of industrialisation was accompanied by the rapid expansion of labour-intensive light industry. This naturally shaped the structure of the labour force, and between 1959 and 1985 the percentage of the labour force in secondary industry increased from 4.6 to 24.5. By the mid-1980s, industrial wage workers came to constitute the largest occupational grouping, even larger than that of farmers (Koo 1991: 488). However, the most dramatic increase in wage employment followed the shift into heavy industry which the government of Park Chung-hee initiated in 1971. In the period 1970 to 1990 the number of workers in the manufacturing sector increased by a factor of 7.5. These changes in the occupational structure of South Korea are presented in Table 10.1.

Table 10.1 Changes in occupational structure, 1960–90 (in percentages of the population)

	Agriculture, forestry, fisheries	Mining and manufacture	Tertiary industries	Non-wage workers	Wage workers
1960	79.5	5.4	15.1	88.4	11.6
1970	50.4	14.3	35.3	61.2	38.8
1980	34.0	22.5	43.5	52.7	47.3
1990	18.3	27.3	54.4	46.1	53.8

Source: S. J. Lee (1994); original data drawn from South Korean population census

Accompanying the expansion of the working class was the greater physical concentration of workers in large, urban-based manufacturing plants. Import-substitution industrialisation in the early 1960s started the process of mass urban migration as millions of displaced farmers found employment in the new factories. Urban migration intensified during the period of export-oriented industrialisation and again when Korea entered the phase of the construction of heavy industry. According to the 1980 census, 22 per cent of the nation's population lived in Seoul, although only 11 per cent were born there (Steinberg 1989: 198). Many of these migrants found work in *Chaebol* manufacturing plants and by 1985 20 per cent of the workforce was employed in *Chaebol* industrial complexes. By 1980 over half of the nation's manufacturing workforce was located in Seoul and the adjacent Seoul–Inchon corridor (Koo 1990: 673).

Compared with their counterparts under other repressive regimes in East Asia, South Korean workers proved remarkably defiant. The history of the labour movement in the 1970s and 1980s is marked by strikes and violent expressions of labour activism (see Deyo 1987). This collective action was fuelled by both growing workers' consciousness and the harsh realities of working-class life under an authoritarian regime. There was growing dissatisfaction with poor working conditions and the failure of wage increases to match productivity gains, and frustration with the government's corporatist labour strategy.[4] The rapid increase of factory workers and their geographical concentration generated by industrialisation also spurred the development of working-class communities whose social connections extended beyond the workplace, for example into cultural and educational activities. Participation in night schools and small discussion circles organised by students became a major mechanism through which workers regularly met and discussed common concerns (Koo 1993: 152–3).

However, labour activism had to contend with a powerful and ultimately unaccountable state. Indeed, recourse to repression was more frequent in South Korea than in most other authoritarian regimes in East Asia. Hence, protests tended to be short-lived, poorly organised, largely defensive, and easily contained. Successive military governments gave priority to keeping labour organisationally and politically weak in order to sustain an industrialisation strategy based on a low-cost, disciplined labour force. The division of the nation into two hostile states heightened security concerns which were exploited to hold labour in check. If labour activism was not regarded as Communist-instigated, it was portrayed either as destabilising (and thus rendering the country more vulnerable to Communist invasion) or as threatening to the development of national power and defence capability.[5]

The growth of South Korea's middle class was also linked to industrialisation. From 1959 to 1985 employment in the tertiary sector increased from 13.8 to 50.4 per cent of the total workforce. The proportion of white-collar workers increased from 4.8 to 17.1 per cent (Koo 1991: 488–9). In conjunction with the shift from labour-intensive light industry to heavy industry and the consequent industrial development which occurred in the 1970s, demand grew for better-skilled workers, such as technicians and scientists, engineers, and to a lesser extent administrators.[6] This necessarily meant a rise in the demand for university places. Tertiary education, already accorded high prestige as a consequence of Confucian cultural values, began to be perceived as the chief mechanism through which an individual could become upwardly mobile.

South Korea's growing number of students and intellectuals soon began to play a critical role in anti-government movements. Traditionally, intellectuals have been accorded high social status in Korean society, given its Confucian heritage. This was often understood to place upon students a burden of moral responsibility to confront unpopular regimes. Throughout consecutive military governments, students staged a series of violent demonstrations. They played the leading role in the overthrow of the Rhee Syngman regime in the April 1960 uprising. In 1979, student-led protests were significant in the demise of the Park Chung-hee regime (1960–79). By the mid-1980s, they had become a more substantial social force.

In addition to the increase in the growth of the demand for skilled workers there was a rapid expansion in small and medium industry and thus in the number of owners of and workers in such industry. A significant share of the growing new middle class was often self-employed in various small-scale commercial and service activities. Others were absorbed by smaller businesses that formed the intricate network of subcontractors which developed to support the commodity production of the larger conglomerates. Those segments sustained by these subcontracting networks became highly dependent on demand from their main *Chaebol* customer for their income (Amsden 1989: 187–8). Partly due to this dependency, the income for members of this group tended to be quite variable. Moreover, according to Koo (1991: 489), approximately half of the urban self-employed in South Korea earned less than the average household income for blue-collar workers.

Disaffected social forces in South Korea often failed to develop overlapping affiliations or alliances. At particular times some agreement among opposition forces on certain issues emerged. Generally, however, the ability to act in concert was undermined by the numerous logistical obstacles associated with developing networks in a repressive political environment. In the 1960s and 1970s, despite many shared characteristics, linkages between the two groups most likely to fuel opposition to authoritarianism, students and workers, were rare. Until the 1980s, they tended to act independently.

The recognition by these groups of the need to work closer together can be traced to two key events in South Korean political history. One was the suicide of factory worker, Chun Tae-il in November 1970. His widely publicised self-immolation in the name of workers' rights led to him being proclaimed a martyr to the cause of democracy (Dong 1993: 87–8). After this event the *no-hak yondae* (Worker–Student Association) and later organisations such as *Chondaehyop* (National Organisation of Students) emerged to provide formal arrangements under which students entered the workplace and joined the workers' strikes. Such activists became known to the government as 'disguised workers' (Choi 1993: 37). The other event was the Kwangju massacre of 18 May 1980. The military regime under Chun Doo-hwan sent special forces to Kwangju to quell violent anti-government demonstrations. The government claimed that, in the fighting which ensued, around 200 people were killed, but opposition groups maintained the number was well over 2,000. This incident served only to engender greater student militancy, which included the pursuit of enhanced links with factory workers (Koo 1993: 37).

The growing effectiveness of the various student–worker coalitions in turn contributed to the politicisation of the middle class. From the early 1980s, contact and exchange between the middle class and an emerging worker/student alliance increased. One vehicle through which linkages developed was common involvement in the *minjung* movement (Wells 1995). The *minjung* movement refers to broad political, social, and cultural elements embracing populist and nationalist sentiments as well as the ideology of struggle against domination. The literal meaning of the term *minjung* is 'popular masses'. In Koo's (1993: 131) words, it 'implies a broad alliance of "alienated classes", people alienated from the distribution of the fruits of economic growth'.[7] First surfacing in the mid-1970s, *minjung* evolved to incorporate elements from student, labour, and middle-class sections of society, and grew into a pervasive political and cultural movement in the 1980s. It provided the middle class with an outlet for their growing dissatisfaction with the constrictions of authoritarianism, which seemed less and less appropriate given the growing sophistication of Korean society.

The *minjung* movement is no longer a feature of opposition politics in the 1990s but it has left a powerful legacy. It now serves as a model for opposition groups of a strategy by which a movement can strengthen its appeal to the middle class by incorporating the ideal of democracy into a broader social and cultural agenda. Indeed, it was to serve as the prototype of contemporary middle-class movements, the NSMs.

It was, however, the anti-government demonstrations of 1987 that marked the most significant occasion on which the collective action of students, workers, and the middle class altered the course of Korean politics (Cotton 1989). This alliance was precipitated by a tragic incident, resulting from a flagrant abuse of power by police. On 14 January 1987, the torture and death at the hands of police interrogators of the Seoul National University activist, Pak Chong-ch'ol, was reported in the South Korean and foreign daily papers. A critical public reaction to this event preceded an explosion of popular frustration, as members of the middle class joined forces with workers and students in unprecedented mass demonstrations in favour of free and open elections.

However, this middle class–worker alliance, though it defeated Chun Doo-hwan's attempt to perpetuate authoritarian rule, did not survive once democratisation was achieved in the presidential elections of 1987. The notion of a common purpose then dissipated, this development being aided by the extreme radicalism of some of the student groups (some of which – prior to the collapse of European Communism – were committed to the establishment of a North Korean-style *juche* or self-reliance ideology regime on the whole Korean peninsula), and also by the perception that the middle classes had a considerable stake in what had become a relatively prosperous and even affluent country.

Politics in the Sixth Republic became centred upon the manoeuvres of parties and political elites, with radical alternatives pushed to the fringes.

THE POLITICS OF PARLIAMENTARY OPPOSITION IN THE SIXTH REPUBLIC

Political parties, whether as vehicles for policy or as sources of alternative leadership (or 'opposition'), have been poorly institutionalised in Korea (Cotton 1996). From the installation of Park Chung-hee's Yusin constitution in 1972 until party formation and competition was partially liberalised under Chun Doo-hwan in 1985, political party activity was sidelined. Though it was the labour of almost two decades, Park's political machine did not survive him. Chun was more successful, but only a fragment of the party he created (originally the Democratic Justice Party) survived into 1995 as part of the ruling Democratic Liberal Party. The opposition also suffered fragmentation, and the impact of differences between leadership personalities underlined the weakness of party structures and their shallow popular roots. Nevertheless, such figures as Kim Dae-jung and Kim Young-sam kept alive the resistance to authoritarianism. While in the (quasi-competitive) National Assembly elections of 1985 they were able to combine forces in the New Korea Democratic Party, this alignment did not survive their subsequent rivalry, and both leaders went on to compete against each other in the presidential elections of 1987. It is beyond dispute that the history of political parties in Korea in part reflects the deleterious effects of authoritarianism. From the time of the First Republic there have been over 100 Korean political parties, and a relatively small number of leading political figures have been associated with a number of different parties during their careers. Even with the advent of democratisation, parties, rather than being the vehicles for policy or the advocacy of interests, are still largely the creatures of powerful leaders (Ahn 1994).

Despite the social impact of rapid modernisation and the retirement of the military from government, party politics in democratised Korea continues to be dominated by personal ties and regional loyalties. This proposition is reflected in the career of the best-known 'opposition' figure, Kim Dae-jung. Kim was a candidate in both the 1987 and 1992 presidential elections (and may yet run in 1997 under the banner of the party he formed in 1995, the National Congress for New Politics). From 1990, his party (the Democratic Party, DP) was also the chief 'opposition' party in the National Assembly. The Kim Dae-jung vote has been remarkably consistent. Over 80 per cent of the voters who supported him in the 1987 presidential elections also voted for him in the 1992 contest. This consistency has not, however, yielded Kim office. In the latter contest, Kim stood against Kim Young-sam, a long-standing opposition figure and also an unsuccessful candidate in the 1987 elections. In the meantime, Kim Young-sam had shifted his position in the party re-alignment of 1990 in which he brought his erstwhile opposition grouping into the government. Hyundai company Honorary Chairman Chung Ju-yung of the Unification National Party was the third candidate. As Kim Young-sam was perceived by many to have changed sides, it was expected that he would lose some votes to the other candidates. With Chung not likely to amass enough of a following to win office, Kim Dae-jung had to pick up most of these defectors to win. In the event, the defectors favoured Chung, denying Kim Dae-jung victory. Kim Dae-jung kept his loyal followers, but did not broaden his support base. This pattern has continued and in the general elections on 11 April, 1996, Kim Dae Jung's party received little support from outside his home province. Kim had calculated on an increase in support from Seoul voters, but the reverse eventuated with the ruling party gaining the majority of the seats in the capital and the surrounding Kyonggi province (*Far Eastern Economic Review.* 25 April 1996: 22–3).

The explanation for this electoral outcome lies in the regional nature of political support in South Korea. In the Honam/Kwangju area of the southwest, Kim has consistently succeeded in capturing between 80 per cent and 90 per cent of the vote; in Seoul (which accounts for around 25 per cent of the electorate), he has managed to capture about 30 per cent (many of whom may actually regard themselves as affiliated with Honam). In other regions he has performed poorly (Bae 1995; Bae and Cotton 1993). This hypothesis is supported by the fact that those deserting Kim Young-sam in 1992 were more often than not from areas other than his regional base in Yongnam. Korean electoral behaviour is further complicated by the existence of an educational variable, but regional affiliation appeared to be the strongest factor in the 1987 and 1992 results. The outcome of the June 1995 local elections are completely consistent with the pattern established in 1987 and 1992. Kim Dae-jung's DP (with Kim himself campaigning strongly despite his 'retirement') secured a plurality in Seoul, but elsewhere won only in the contests in Honam/Kwangju. The ruling Democratic Liberal Party won elsewhere, except where the defection of faction leader Kim Jong-pil led to the loss to his new party of his home region (*Korea Newsreview*, 1 July 1995: 4–7). Kim Dae-jung subsequently returned to active politics, and when the leadership of the DP (which Kim had himself chosen) criticised him for breaking his solemn vow to retire, Kim founded a new party which then attracted the bulk of the Assembly men and party branches formerly in the DP.

Political leadership manoeuvres and the predominance of regional loyalties prevented the emergence of issue-oriented politics in the Sixth Republic. Even during the Roh Tae-woo era, though the President was a former general (and, moreover, Chun Doo-hwan's chosen successor) and the opposition parties before the realignment of 1990 had a majority in the National Assembly, the thorough scrutiny of the former Chun regime which some anticipated did not eventuate. Though Chun himself was obliged to apologise for his past conduct, and then spend over a year in retreat in a mountain temple, those responsible for the Kwangju incident were not brought to account, nor was there a thoroughgoing reform of the laws and institutions inherited from the past. Once in charge as President from 1993, Kim Young-sam instituted a number of potentially far-reaching political reforms, and was careful to distance himself from personnel associated with his two predecessors, but he resisted a retrospective review of their administrations until evidence of Roh Tae-woo's financial malfeasance became overwhelming. At the same time, the political system was slow to take up many of the issues which had emerged in a society that was both post-authoritarian and also by this stage comprehensively industrialised. In the absence of issue-based politics emerging in the legislature, and with the parties slow to seek affiliation with interest groups, a number of new social movements emerged to occupy parts of this political space.

THE RISE OF NEW SOCIAL MOVEMENTS

In the late 1980s, trade unions were able to extract considerable concessions from employers. Between 1987 and 1991, real wages rose by around 11 per cent. Hours worked per week were reduced from sixty to forty-four between the middle and end of the 1980s. The 1987 'spring offensive' of action by unions proved to be an industrial watershed. In this year there were over 3,300 strikes across the country. Against the backdrop of frustration with low wages and poor working conditions, and in the context of rapid political liberalisation, there emerged a strain of politically tinged activism which questioned the whole capitalist development process. The Ministry of Labour claimed that in 1987, 70 per cent of labour strikes were concerned solely with wage demands and that this figure dropped to 50 per cent and 49 per cent respectively in 1988 and 1989. Also during this period, the Ministry expressed concern that a considerable number of union campaigns had leftist overtones of class struggle.[8]

However, both the material gains and the demonstration of organisational power by unions soon precipitated a cautious reaction from the middle class. While initially supportive of the improvements for workers, the middle class became concerned that the overall growth of the economy would be threatened by further worker demands. Toleration of financial loss or inconvenience caused by industrial action appears to have evaporated. As early as 1989, public surveys indicated that a majority of middle-class respondents wanted to see government intervention to control labour unrest (Donga-A Research Institute 1990). The alliance that was formed between workers and elements of the middle class thus proved a temporary one, no longer held together by the shared objective of ending authoritarian military rule. The growing middle-class antipathy towards worker activism in the 1990s was encouraged by conservative forces in the media (see Shim 1994a: 69; *Seoul Kyongje Shinmun*, 5 July 1994: editorial).

Consequently, in the 1990s the South Korean labour movement entered a new, deradicalised phase, in acknowledgement that the support for its traditional agenda had eroded. Labour disputes declined from 322 in 1990 to 144 in 1993. The combined work days lost due to labour disputes amounted to ninety-three in 1991, eighty-four in 1992, and thirty-four in 1993. On average, strikes in 1994 lasted only two days, and wage increases were considerably lower than in earlier years.[9] Significantly, labour activism has receded at South Korea's large heavy-industrial plants and among traditionally militant white-collar worker groups such as the National Teachers' and Education Workers' Union (Shim 1994a: 69; *Korea Newsreview*, 29 April 1995: 34; Shim 1994b: 22).[10]

Student demonstrations remain a feature of the South Korean political landscape, although the style and extent of the confrontations are changing. There was a rapid decrease in the use of Molotov cocktails and tear gas by the early 1990s (*Korea Newsreview*, 19 October 1991: 9–10).[11] Home Affairs Minister Lee Dong-ho reported in 1992 to a cabinet meeting that the number of rallies held by students to mark the 19 April 1960 student uprising fell 83 per cent from the 1991 figure. The number of illegal assemblies also dropped 73 per cent from the previous year (*Korea Newsreview*, 2 May 1992: 11).[12] There has also been a decline in 'alternative curricula' or leftist book sales among students, down from 94,000 in 1990 to 40,000 in 1991 (*Korea Newsreview*, 19 October 1991: 9), as students have shifted their attention away from political campaigns to career prospects.[13]

Although the traditional forms of radical opposition led by trade unions and students are on the wane, the perception that capitalist development generates inequities and environmentally damaging consequences is being heightened, ensuring that there will be popular demands for these issues to be addressed in government policy. Emerging for the first time is an acute awareness of the huge social costs associated with rapid but largely unregulated economic growth. A number of instances of violent and amoral crime have led to the realisation that the traditional cohesion of Korean society is at risk. Through its failure to address these concerns, the government and some sections of South Korean capital have become the target of vigorous society-based opposition.[14] The focus of opposition groups has changed from ideologically charged struggle for economic equity and democracy to the promotion of diverse agendas which extend beyond strictly economic and political objectives. They include social and quality-of-life considerations that have not previously enjoyed such priority in public debate. It is in this climate that new social movements have surfaced, many of which address relatively discrete aspects of public policy. But before taking a closer look at these movements, let us specify in greater detail some of the issues that have generated public concern in contemporary South Korea.

First, the state has been slow to undermine the privileged position of the major conglomerates and the financial and taxation benefits which they enjoy. Second, there is widespread concern over the government's failure to provide policies aimed at achieving environmentally sustainable growth and also a socially acceptable level of community infrastructure. Third, the issue of citizenship has stimulated more marginalised sections of the community to pursue more equal status. Finally, a perceived failure of the state to deal more constructively with the question of reunification with North Korea has also generated strong criticism.[15]

Though the state now pursues a less comprehensive economic agenda, intervention in the market sometimes still favours particular business interests. This is a source of irritation to competitors, as well as to those more generally interested in curbing possible abuses of public power. The payment of large 'political contributions' by big business to the ruling party in exchange for special concessions, and more generally the provision of cheap credit or 'policy loans', were not uncommon practices in the Roh Tae-woo administration (Woo 1991), and many Koreans remain convinced that these practices continue.[16]

In addition, the financial and tax systems continue to discriminate against both small companies and individual consumers, and so exacerbate the disproportionate distribution of wealth in South Korean society. Much of the available capital continues to be channelled to the larger conglomerates, while small business and private individuals are forced to borrow from the (illegal but tolerated) curb market where interest rates are much higher. In 1983, the thirty largest conglomerates had 48 per cent of total bank credit, the top five holding 24.2 per cent (*Donga Ilbo*, 22 August 1984: 3). Much of the cheap credit made available to big business has been channelled into high-performing, although non-productive, investments in real estate (Kwon 1993: 126–7).[17] Government campaigns to induce the conglomerates to divest themselves of their excess holdings of property have been less than fully successful.

Of the array of changing popular perceptions, one of the most profound is a growing awareness of the environmental costs of rapid economic growth. The impact of environmental pollution on South Korea's air, rivers, and sea shores caused by the indiscriminate discharge of wastes from plants and factories has been widespread. In Seoul the pollution problem is particularly serious. According to one report, it is the world's second most polluted city, beaten only by Mexico City (*Korea Newsreview*, 27 November 1993: 9). Seoul air contains one of the world's highest concentrations of sulphur dioxide and, according to a Seoul National University study, 67 per cent of the rain falling on that city contains enough acid to pose a hazard to human beings (Hepenstall 1985: 70). The community is becoming increasingly alarmed by this situation, as is reflected in a recent survey which reported that six in ten Seoul residents believed that the city's water is not fit to drink (*Korea Newsreview*, 16 October 1993: 11). Although legislation exists to deal with these problems, consecutive governments have failed to devote sufficient resources to ensure that the limited environmental protection and safety laws in South Korea are properly enforced.[18]

The state has also invested too little in basic social services such as housing, recreational facilities, public transport, health, and education. The quantity and quality of housing in urban areas is a serious problem. The greatest obstacle to the expansion of the housing supply lies in the high price of urban land. Renaud (1992) argues that the South Korean housing market is perhaps the most distorted among market economies.[19] One consequence of high land prices has been the rapid expansion of what the government terms 'illegal housing' or what are more generally know as 'moon villages', sprawling shantytowns on the outskirts of Seoul and other major urban areas.

Economic growth has translated into more leisure time for many South Koreans, but there have been many cases of recreational spaces, parks, and sports facilities being appropriated for further high-rise complexes. In November 1993 the Seoul city government announced plans to transform one of the largest undeveloped spaces in the capital, zoned as part of the green belt, into an international centre for trade information. This proposal has generated fierce resistance from environmental groups, and the issue remains unresolved (Kwak 1993: 9).

Transportation infrastructure in South Korea also remains underdeveloped. The construction of roads has not kept pace with the rise of passenger car ownership, and the major cities experience constant traffic jams. In 1988 the South Korean road toll was the second highest (per capita) in the world after India. In 1980 deaths on South Korean roads amounted to 5,608, and by 1990 the figure stood at 12,325 (Kwon 1993: 78). The Kim Young-sam government (1993–) has been plagued by a spate of transport- and infrastructure-related disasters which has generated a public outcry (*Korea Herald*, 29 April 1995: 3). Such disasters include the collapse of the Song Su bridge in Seoul in October 1994, resulting in thirty-two deaths, a fire on a ferry at Chungju lake later that month, resulting in twenty-one deaths, train derailments, plane crashes, a gas explosion in Seoul in December 1994, and a gas explosion in Taegu resulting in ninety-seven deaths in April 1995.[20] The collapse of the Sampoong department store building in July 1995 in Seoul, with the loss of 200 lives, demonstrated the urgency of the need to upgrade the nation's often shoddy infrastructure.

The budget for education and other community services is still much smaller proportionally than in developed countries, and social security-related expenditure currently accounts for only 1.4 per cent of GNP (Lee 1994). Despite the fact that the majority of the population now lives in nuclear families, state social security policies still reflect Confucian values which view the welfare of individuals as the responsibility of the family. The education system, in particular, is the subject of increasing public criticism. Issues causing concern include high student–teacher ratios, the need to reform the intensely competitive university entrance examination system, and the proliferation of private institutes or cram schools. Cram schools (usually designed to prepare students for college entrance) have become a booming industry in South Korea and their expense has imposed real financial strain on middle-and lower-income parents. One researcher estimates that education-related expenses account for up to 50 per cent of middle-income household expenditure (Lee 1994).

The social position of women has also become an important public issue. Amsden (1989: 203) cites data collated by the International Labour Office indicating that South Korea holds the world record for the greatest wage gap between male and female workers in manufacturing. Considerable social stigma is attached to divorced, childless, or older single women, and the preference for male children has led to the spread of illegal sex determination tests followed by abortions of unwanted females (*Korea Newsreview*, 19 October 1994: 11).

Another area of public concern is the Kim Young-sam adminis- tration's lack of positive policy measures to promote North–South Korean dialogue. Around the time of Kim Il-sung's death in July 1994, and shortly after Seoul had agreed to engage in the first direct meeting of the two Korean heads of state, the authorities mobilised 28,000 police to prevent students from staging mourning ceremonies. In the same month, the South Korean Foreign Ministry released Soviet documents which appeared to show that the North had masterminded the Korean War. Claims by the Sogang University president that '15,000 *jusapa*' (those favouring the *juche* or self-reliance ideology of Kim Il-sung) have infiltrated political circles, mass communication media and uni- versities also led to the detention of over 2,000 people. This included nine Kyongsang University professors who were held on suspicion of 'benefiting the enemy' (as defined by the National Security Law).

In the formative years of South Korean economic development, those opposition elements that did emerge focused primarily on the struggle against authoritarianism and for a greater degree of economic justice.[21] However, the political system itself is now no longer a matter of fundamental dispute, and rapid economic growth has generated the preconditions to resolve problems associated with obtaining basic needs. Moreover, the new regime's greater tolerance for collective action has fostered among South Korea's citizenry the development of new expectations and aspirations. As the issues listed above suggest, the equity issue has been displaced by the question of relative poverty. In addition, quality-of-life considerations now figure prominently in public contestation over government policy. Rather than political parties or the established social movements adapting to strengthen or consolidate their popular appeal, the tendency has been for new organisations to emerge. Thus the impetus has been provided for new social movements.

There is now a considerable volume of theoretical literature on NSMs, most of which is centred on developments in the industrialised, liberal democratic societies. NSMs are often depicted as inherently radical, and this perspective is echoed in terms sometimes applied in the literature on South Korea such as 'anti-systemic movements' (Lee and Smith 1991) and 'critical social movements' (Lee 1993). Here the term is employed more cautiously, not necessarily ascribing an anti- systemic character to NSMs. Generally the organisational expression of South Korean NSMs is in the form of a non-government organisation. Typically voluntary, non-profit associations, they tend to advance a generalised public-interest agenda, and are concerned with such issues as environmentalism, feminism, consumer rights, and other quality-of-life or consumption issues.

Since the pro-democracy struggles of 1987 there has been a mushrooming of NSMs with hundreds of organisations nationwide formed between 1990 and 1995. Currently there are over twenty environmental movements alone.[22] It is outside the scope of this discussion to examine the full range of such organisations.[23] Rather, we will focus on the Citizens' Coalition for Economic Justice in order to provide a case study of the reorientation that has been occurring in oppositional politics. Apart from being one of the largest and best-known NGOs in South Korea, this organisation is broadly representative of the NSMs of the 1990s. Along with many other groups active in the 1990s, the CCEJ has adopted a social justice agenda, draws its membership overwhelmingly from the middle-class population of Seoul, has formed various linkages with other NSMs while remaining relatively independent from organised labour and political parties, and has explicitly adopted non-violent and peaceful tactics which centre on the development and mobilisation of organised popular opinion.

THE CITIZENS' COALITION FOR ECONOMIC JUSTICE

Founded in July 1989, the CCEJ describes itself as a 'grassroots citizens' organisation working for a more just, sustainable, and equitable society in Korea' (CCEJ 1994: 2). However, its version of economic justice is somewhat different from that advanced by labour and student groups in the 1970s and 1980s, with more emphasis on assorted social and consumption-related issues not immediately arising out of disputes in the workplace. The membership, organisational structure, and linkages with other groups also differ from earlier social movements in South Korea.

The CCEJ is one of the largest NGOs in South Korea and is comprised of twenty regional chapters with nearly 10,000 members. It is a nationwide organisation, but according to a 1993 survey, 59.7 per cent of its members were from Seoul and a further 13.3 per cent from the surrounding Kyonggi Do area.[24] The CCEJ has seventeen main departments, all of which are co-ordinated from the head office in Seoul.

The movement was founded by around 500 people from various professions including professors, labourers, housewives, students, young adults, and businessmen (CCEJ 1994: 3). However, data on the occupational background of members, as shown in Figure 10.1, clearly indicate that the vast majority of members are middle-class. Politicians, academics, medical workers, media workers, arts and culture workers, legal workers, small business owners, office workers, and government workers together account for 59.7 per cent of total membership. Other occupational groups such as ministers of religion, members of social organisations, students, and housewives may also be considered within this middle-class grouping. With these groups included, the percentage totals 84.3 per cent of members. As can be gleaned from the representation of professional categories in Figure 10.1, educational levels of members are very high. Of the membership in 1991, 63 per cent were university graduates, with a further 21 per cent having undergone some sort of graduate training. The average age of membership is also notably young, 68.5 per cent being under the age of 40 and 28.7 per cent under the age of 30 (CCEJ 1994: 327).

Despite the predominantly middle-class membership of the CCEJ, its causes and campaigns transcend this base, often involving attempts to represent the interests of some of the most marginalised groups in South Korean society. Examples include the opening of 'Mercy's House for

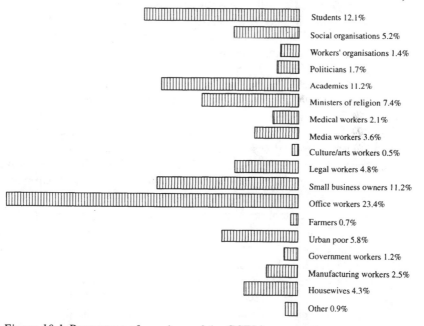

(9,229 members as of 30 December 1993)

Students 12.1%
Social organisations 5.2%
Workers' organisations 1.4%
Politicians 1.7%
Academics 11.2%
Ministers of religion 7.4%
Medical workers 2.1%
Media workers 3.6%
Culture/arts workers 0.5%
Legal workers 4.8%
Small business owners 11.2%
Office workers 23.4%
Farmers 0.7%
Urban poor 5.8%
Government workers 1.2%
Manufacturing workers 2.5%
Housewives 4.3%
Other 0.9%

Figure 10.1 Percentage of members of the CCEJ by occupation

Source: CCEJ (1994a: 327)

the Poor', the Anti-Urban Renewal Campaign (to protect low-income housing), and a campaign directed against exploitation of foreign workers. Other campaigns have promoted causes pursued by other groups: the 'Response to the Uruguay Round Campaign', for example, has taken up a cause pursued by farmers, and the 'Alleviation of Economic Concentration by the *Chaebol* Campaign' has articulated many of the concerns of small businesses. The CCEJ also provides a forum for many dissidents, thus improving their access to the established media. Other campaigns have focused on the protection of the environment and on consumer rights, as well as on giving additional emphasis to the rights of women and the aged.

The CCEJ shows some ambiguity in its orientation: many of the activities promote the interests of marginalised groups while others attempt to advance the interests of the more privileged. But many of the issues taken up by the CCEJ, such as the environment, transcend sectional interests (Lee 1994; S. H. Lee 1993). Petrochemical smog, traffic congestion, or the chemical contamination of domestically grown cabbages for *kimchi* (an essential element in the Korean diet) are likely to affect the lifestyles of both the rich and the not-so-rich. In any case, during the period of rapid economic growth, income differentials have dramatically narrowed, which tends to equalise susceptibility to the costs of industrialism (Kwon 1993: 117–18).[25] With this observation in mind, some authors maintain that such groups are not class-based (S. H. Lee 1993; S. J. Lee 1993).

The CCEJ eschews revolutionary posturing, and tends to avoid directly characterising problems as inherently systemic. In its own words, it aims 'to cure the deep-rooted economic injustices through workable and rational alternatives' (Shin 1994). Little if any discussion of an alternative social order enters its discourse. Rather, its focus is on more general consumption issues. This reflects both the conservative character of many of its middle-class members and a fear of Communism the persistence of which derives from the ideological residue of the state's early anti-Communist campaigns. The July–August 1994 edition of the CCEJ's magazine *Civil Society* covered the *jusapa* controversy. The coverage was highly critical of the government's handling of the affair, but it made it clear that the CCEJ did not side with such views. The subtitle of one article read: 'No matter how important it is to warn against a wrong ideological trend, academic freedom should not be suffocated as a result' (*Civil Society*, 4, July–August 1994: 3).

While the need to protect certain workers' rights enters the members' discourse, their commitment is certainly not unqualified. The CCEJ has become involved in some industrial issues, but not always as a union sympathiser. In June 1994, for example, the CCEJ adopted the role of mediator in the train and subway workers' strike. According to *Civil Society* (August 1994: 18), 'mediation efforts by six respected elders [from CCEJ] on June 30 were successful in getting all the striking train and subway workers back on the job'. Despite the absence of formal linkages, dissociation from organised labour is not CCEJ policy and linkages with labour groups can and have been temporarily forged. But whether any joint activity is engaged in depends on the issues involved (Shin 1994), and co-operation with labour organisations is not especially pursued. Generally, the CCEJ tends to avoid formal, institutionalised relationships with other organisations, especially political parties.

However, the building of 'alliances' with other civic groups appears to be an important objective for CCEJ leaders. The CCEJ has developed extensive linkages with a variety of groups, including Buddhist and Christian societies as well as the academic community, farmers, students, and other civic groups. In September 1994 thirty-six other NGOs joined with the CCEJ to inaugurate an umbrella organisation called *Shinminhyop* (Korean Council of Citizens' Organisation), with the aim of creating a 'permanent structure for solidarity' (*Civil Society*, 5, September–October 1994: 11).[26] Emphasis has also been placed on the need to develop international links. In October 1994, in Los Angeles, the CCEJ launched the idea of a 'Korea Global Network' to link the CCEJ with Korean communities overseas (*Civil Society*, 5, September–October 1994: 14). In March 1995 representatives attended the World Summit for Social Development NGO Forum '95 in Copenhagen (*Civil Society*, 5, September–October 1994: 14).

The CCEJ has also developed extensive links with sections of the South Korean media. In 1994 over ninety articles on CCEJ activities appeared in the South Korean press, the vast majority of which were sympathetic to the movement and its causes. Some of the headlines on these articles read 'CCEJ leads fight against rice market liberalisation' (*Hankyoreh Shinmun*, 2 April 1993), 'The age of the citizens' movement is coming' (*Hankyoreh Shinmun*, 2 January 1993), and 'Financial real name accounts: victory for citizens' movement' (*Kookmin Ilbo*, 13 August 1993).[27]

The politically moderate character of the CCEJ is evident in its preference for negotiation and the seeking of consensus. In addition to sponsoring peaceful demonstrations, much energy is directed at lobbying the central government or relevant local authorities as well as attempting to bring issues to the attention of the media. CCEJ strategists

292 *Bronwen Dalton and James Cotton*

openly profess a commitment to the current political system and the orderly conduct of legislative deliberation and review. The organisation's reluctance to become involved in direct political action was illustrated during the train and subway workers' strike in June 1994. The CCEJ called for both sides to 'immediately show a mature attitude and return to dialogue' (*Civil Society*, August 1994: 18).

Despite the CCEJ's attitude to strike action, it generally emphasises grassroots activities. In its effort to expand its appeal and seek members, the CCEJ has instigated the establishment of various citizens' discussion groups. The CCEJ has also established and made widely available a range of citizens' services which have become very popular. In 1990, for instance, it opened the Economic Injustice Complaint Centre (EICC). In 1994 alone, the EICC assisted in filing over 10,000 individual grievances cases.[28]

This examination of the activities, strategies, and goals of the Coalition demonstrates that the CCEJ has become an important new mechanism for the articulation of a variety of social interests. However, this examination also suggests that despite its commitment to altering a range of government policies as well as lobbying for an extension of citizens' rights, the CCEJ has set distinct ideological boundaries on the extent of change it is prepared to advocate.

CONCLUSION

For years, successive authoritarian regimes in South Korea successfully contained the expression of political opposition. However, in the transition to democracy in 1987, labour and student groups often dominated by left-wing leaderships committed to confrontational tactics played a crucial role in mobilising popular protest against the continuation of military authoritarianism. At that time, the democratic goals championed by these movements earned them widespread public respect and sympathy. Despite this contribution, in the post-authoritarian era their broader socialist goals and confrontational strategies rapidly undermined the public support they had enjoyed. So far, however, conventional political parties have been fixated upon leadership issues, and thus have been slow to seek affiliations with grassroots interests or mobilise support for new policy approaches. To occupy the newly opened political space, there have emerged a number of middle-class-based social movements pursuing a more limited agenda. Rather than dispute the legitimacy of the political system, they have taken as their focus the government's failure to meet popular aspirations for a more balanced approach to industrial growth, social welfare, and the environment.

To be sure, the capacity of these NSMs to reconcile the objectives of their constituents with the powerful interests which have developed in modern Korean society will be tested. Their predominantly middle-class membership may undermine their willingness to challenge these interests and render the organisations susceptible to co-optation.[29] Nevertheless, these NSMs have the potential to play a prominent role in institutionalising South Korea's fledgling democracy. Thus, some writers have argued that problem-oriented, citizen-centred politics has a future in South Korea, and that NSMs and other political interventions of the middle class will exert a powerful democratising force (Han 1988; Koo 1991). Certainly a number of features of these NSMs suggest their continued importance is assured.

Their close relationship with grassroots support has contributed to the ability of these groups to make their agenda relevant to their constituencies. Independence from obligations to entrenched interests can also promote adaptability. Untainted and unfettered by the conventions, preferences, commitments, and values that are characteristic of political parties or organised labour groups, their leadership can be more flexible and democratic. This flexibility should serve them well through the current transition from industrial to post-industrial society. The middle-class character of these movements may also be a factor in their durability, given the continued growth in size and influence of this section of Korean society. Korean post-war history has been marked by an episodic struggle between a strong state and a contentious civil society. However, for the first time non-state occupants of the political space may be sufficiently resilient to assert a legitimate role. Indeed, there are some indications that the need for such a role has been recognised by other political actors.

In the current context, the direction of Korea's new democracy will be closely related to the dynamism of non-conventional forms of opposition and their relationship to the state and to the political parties. In particular, whether Korea's democracy will allow for more popular participation and address the current injustices and problems existent in the society will largely depend upon the strength and effectiveness of the country's new middle-class movements. These represent a vast array of interests, goals, and strategies which must be taken into account in the contemporary political climate.

NOTES

* We wish to acknowledge the considerable efforts of Garry Rodan in the revision of this chapter.

1 The role of the Korean Central Intelligence Agency (KCIA) in the selection of Korean Federation of Trade Unions (FKTU) leaders, for example, is well documented (see Choi 1989).

2 According to a study by Schroders Securities, at the beginning of the 1990s, sales receipts for the top ten *Chaebol* totalled more than 77 per cent of Korea's gross national product. See Schroders Securities Asia Research Korea, December 1991.

3 In October 1994 Kim Jong-pil, then chairman of the ruling Democratic Liberal Party, reaffirmed his party's decision not to abolish the controversial National Security Law, which bans pro-North Korean activities.

4 During the period of the Chun Doo-hwan administration (1980–7), government co-optation of union leadership was extensive.

5 The establishment of anti-Communist hegemony was carried out with the collusion of Korean business and was dependent as much on the policies of business as on the capacity of the state. Conglomerates pushed the family-oriented managerial philosophy which became mixed with the prevailing anti-Communist or 'national security' ideology. Significant moral pressure was applied to workers from both the state and the corporate sector to be obedient and hardworking for the sake of both protecting and building the nation (Choi 1983: 231–90). Business supported the establishment of state-sponsored welfare and youth organisations and movements for this purpose. The Factory *Saemaul* (New Community) Movement, for example, aimed to put labour on an ideological war footing against the Communist enemy to achieve production objectives set both by the technocrats and by business owners.

6 Koo notes that the rise of the proportion of the population in the bureaucracy was modest, from 0.5 to 1.7 per cent. He claims that this supports the argument that the growth in the middle class was most directly linked to the industrialisation process (Koo 1991: 488–9).

7 For further elaboration on the meaning of *minjung*, see Choi (1993: 17).

8 Examples of slogans used by unionists included: 'Go away capitalist society: we want labour liberation'; 'We Koreans are like those who became slave tenants after giving away our precious land, comrade workers! It is an armed revolt that will give us victory in our revolution!' (*Business Korea*, December 1989: 14).

9 In 1994 the Korean Federation of Trade Unions and the Korean Employers' Federation reached an agreement to limit wage rises to between 5 and 8.7 per cent (Shim 1994a: 69).Transport strikes in late June 1994 lasted only seven days and the unions accepted a small 3 per cent wage rise, a fraction of their original demand (Shim 1994a: 69).

10 In July 1994 Hyundai Motor Company workers voted to continue to negotiate a pay rise rather than strike, and traditionally militant workers at Daewoo Shipbuilding and Heavy Machinery refused union leaders' demands to strike in July. Later in 1994 the National Teachers' Union advised teachers not to strike (Shim 1994b: 22).

11 The article 'Drastic decrease in use of firebombs' also mentioned that the leader of the largest student organisation, *Chondaehyop*, Lee Sang-chol, appealed to student activists not to use firebombs and that two major student demonstrations had ended with students retreating to subway exits to hand out leaflets. It also referred to a tacit agreement between students and riot

police that if the former refrained from fire-bomb throwing the latter would not use tear gas (*Korea Newsreview*, 19 October 1991: 10).

12 This figure is perhaps questionable as it was reported by the Home Affairs Minister. The Ministry often only records student demonstrations deemed to be 'legal', thus other demonstrations may have gone unrecorded.

13 In the words of one student from Sangmyon Women's University: 'There are not so many students who are reading political and social science books these days, [they prefer] light novels or poems or they would rather spend time studying for entrance examinations for big business corporations' (*Korea Newsreview*, 19 October 1991: 18).

14 This statement refers primarily to big business or the *Chaebol*. The relationship between the state and *Chaebol* is complex and problematic, since big business is at once part of and outside the state.

15 Although these issues are discussed separately, it is important to note that many are interrelated and it can be difficult to distinguish where one issue may end and another begin. Issues which focus around environmental law violations, for example, may also be related to allegations of corruption linking senior bureaucrats and business figures.

16 The 'contributions' made to the state by firms listed on the Seoul Stock Exchange were equivalent to 22 per cent of their net profit in 1985. Hyundai Group Honorary Chairman Chung Ju-yung admitted to donating US$2.5 million to former President Chun Doo-hwan's 'think tank-retirement fund', the Ilhae Foundation (Woo 1991: 199).

17 The thirty largest corporations control about 42,000 hectares, much of it unused. Its book value, estimated in 1986 at around US $15 billion, has since risen by approximately 70 per cent. Real-estate speculation has fuelled the escalation of land prices in urban areas (Kwon 1993: 126–7).

18 One well-known case was the failure of the Taegu District Environmental Authority to detect the discharge of the chemical phenol by a Doosan-owned factory into the Taegu water supply. The Authority inspected the Doosan plant responsible for the discharge five times before the company was eventually fined 100,000 *won* (around US$125) for violation of environmental regulations. The contamination had continued for five months until the stench of the chemical eventually alerted consumers (*Korea Newsreview*, March 1991: 9).

19 The ratios of rental payments (and rental payments excluding utilities) to household income in Seoul as of 1991 were 9.25 and 0.322 respectively – the highest among the fifty-two largest world cities (Kwon 1993: 93–4).

20 Following the Song Su bridge tragedy, several other major bridges in Seoul were identified as being near collapse (*Korea Newsreview*, October 1994: 4).

21 Environmental groups have existed in Korea since the 1970s but for the most part these groups were small and connected with churches or based in universities (Bello and Rosenfeld 1992: 111).

22 The 'green' movements encompass a range of groups including anti-pollution, environmental protection, anti-nuclear, and peace movements. Such groups include the Korea Anti-Pollution Movement Association, Korean Federation for a United Environmental Movement, Anti-Nuclear Movement and several departments of larger NSMs, including the YMCA,

YWCA, CCEJ and Citizens' Research Council on Consumer Protection, created specifically to address environmental concerns.

23 An extensive review of the activities of a cross-section of Korean NSMs is beyond the scope of this chapter. As these movements are diverse and often fragmented, data are sometimes difficult to obtain.

24 Most of Korea's middle class live in Seoul. This can be seen from the fact that in 1998,

> Seoul had 40 per cent of all registered cars; 43 per cent of all firms employing more than five persons; 62 per cent of all bank loans; 53 per cent of all domestic tax collections; 36 per cent of all telephones; 37 per cent of all college and university enrolment; 44 per cent of all medical doctors – but only 22.3 per cent of the population.
>
> (Steinberg 1989: 198)

25 According to Economic Planning Board data cited by Kwon (1993: 117), income distribution improved markedly during the period 1980–8 with the decile distribution ratio increasing from 35 per cent in 1980 to 47 per cent in 1988. Other measures of inequality such as the Gini coefficient and Theil index also showed significant improvement during the same period. An example of how a narrowing of the income gap can lead to an equalisation of the effects of industrialism would be the effect of a rise in inflation. Thus, a larger cross-section of Koreans would be affected to a similar degree.

26 The members include the CCEJ, YMCA, YWCA, Korean Federation for a United Environmental Movement, Korean Women's Associations United, Movement for the Practice of Christian Ethics, Korea Women's Council for National Reunification, Citizens' Union for Good Media, Citizens' Research Council on Consumer Protection, and Parents for a Humane Education.

27 The last headline refers to a campaign calling on the government to ban the practice of concealing assets in false-name bank accounts. This was accomplished in legislation introduced by the Kim Young-sam administration in 1994.

28 These cases were highly diverse, ranging from complaints made against local tax offices and employers, as well as against other local and national government authorities. The cost of running this service accounts for about 30 per cent of the CCEJ's total expenditure (Shin 1994).

29 The Kim Young-sam administration adopted a high-profile campaign against corruption, as well as increasing the focus of the government on the environment. Kim's 'real-name' financial reforms undoubtedly made possible the discovery in October 1995 of former president Roh Tae-woo's illicitly accumulated political funds.

REFERENCES

Ahn, Chung-Si (1994) 'Democratization and Political Reform in Korea: Development, Culture, Leadership and Institutional Change', in Shin Doh Chull, Myeong-han Zoh and Myung Chey (eds) *Korea in the Global Wave of Democratization*, Seoul: Seoul National University Press, pp. 161–78

Amsden, Alice (1989) *Asia's Next Giant: South Korea and Late Industrialisation*, Oxford and New York: Oxford University Press.

Ash, Timothy Garton (1990) 'Eastern Europe: Après le Déluge, Nous', *New York Review of Books*, 16 August: 51–7.

Bae, Sun-kwang (1995) 'Continuity or Change: the Voter's Choice in the 1992 Presidential Election', in James Cotton (ed.) *Politics and Policy in the New Korean State: from Roh Tae-woo to Kim Young-sam*, New York: St Martin's Press, pp. 66–82.

Bae Sun-kwang and Cotton, James (1993) 'Regionalism in Electoral Politics', in James Cotton (ed.) *Korea under Roh Tae-woo. Democratisation, Northern Policy and Inter-Korean Relations*, Sydney: Allen & Unwin, pp. 170–84.

Bello, Walden and Rosenfeld, Stephanie (1992) *Dragons in Distress: Asia's Economies in Crisis*, London: Penguin Books.

Choi, Jang Jip (1983) 'Interest Control and Political Control in South Korea: a Study of Labor Unions in Manufacturing Industries, 1961–1980', Ph.D. dissertation, Department of Political Science, University of Chicago, August.

—— (1989) *Labour and the Authoritarian State: Labour Unions in South Korean Manufacturing Industries, 1961–1980*, Seoul: Korea University Press.

—— (1993) 'Political Cleavages in South Korea', in H. Koo (ed.) *State and Society in Korea*, Ithaca, NY: Cornell University Press, pp. 13–50.

CCEJ (1994a) *A Compendium in Commemoration of the Fourth Anniversary of the CCEJ* (in Korean), Seoul: CCEJ.

—— (1994b) *Of the Citizens, By the Citizens, For the Citizens*, Seoul: CCEJ.

Chong, Chuyong (1986) *I Achimi do solleim ul an'go* ('Feeling the Thrill Again This Morning'), Seoul: Samsung Ch'ulpansa.

Cotton, James (1989) 'From Authoritarianism to Democracy in South Korea', *Political Studies* 37(2): 244–59.

—— (1996) 'Opposition in Asian Constitutional Systems: Characteristics and Democratic Potential', *Government and Opposition*, 31(2): 175–92.

Dahl, Robert A. (1971) *Polyarchy: Participation and Opposition*, New Haven, Conn.: Yale University Press.

Deyo, Fred C. (1987) 'State and Labour: Modes of Political Exclusion in East Asian Development', in Fred Deyo (ed.) *The Political Economy of New Asian Industrialism*, Ithaca, NY: Cornell University Press, pp. 182–202.

Dong, Won-mo (1993) 'The Democratisation of South Korea: What Role Does the Middle Class Play?', in James Cotton (ed.) *Korea under Roh Tae-woo*, Sydney: Allen & Unwin, pp. 74–91.

Dong-A Research Institute (1990) 'Current Political Attitudes of the Koreans', *Monthly Diary*, February: 272–98.

Eckert, Carter J. (1993) 'The Korean Bourgeoisie', in Hagen Koo (ed.) *State and Society in Contemporary Korea*, Ithaca, NY: Cornell University Press, pp. 95–130.

Han, Sang-jin (1988) 'Are the Korean Middle Classes Conservative?' (in Korean), *Sasang kwa Chungchaek*, 3, Summer: 114–32.

Han, Wan-Sang, Kwon, Tae-Hwan, and Hong, Doo-Seung (1987) *Korean Middle Classes: Research Data Book II on Korean Society in Transition* (in Korean), Seoul: Hankook Ilbo.

Hepenstall, Sonya (1985) 'A Smell of Success in the Battle Against Pollution', *Far Eastern Economic Review*, 18 July: 70.

Kim Seung-Kuk (1987) 'Class Formation and Labor Process in Korea: With

Special Reference to Working Class Consciousness', in Kim Kyong-Dong (ed.) *Dependency Issues on Korean Development*, Seoul: Seoul National University Press.

Koo, Hagen (1990) 'From Farm to Factory: Proletarianization in Korea', *American Sociological Review*, 55, October: 669–81.

—— (1991) 'Middle Classes, Democratisation, and Class Formation: the Case of South Korea', *Theory and Society*, 20: 485–509.

—— (1993) 'The State, Minjung, and the Working Class in South Korea', in Hagen Koo (ed.) *State and Society in Contemporary Korea*, Ithaca, NY: Cornell University Press, pp. 152–3.

Korean Institute of Labour Studies (1990) *A Study of Workers' Attitudes about Labour Problems and Labour Relations*, Seoul: Korean Institute of Labour Studies.

Kwak, Young-sup (1993) 'Seoul to Develop Nanjido', *Korea Newsreview*, 20 February: 9.

Kwon, Soonwon (1993) *Economic Advances and Quality of Life in Social Policy in Korea: Challenges and Responses*, Seoul: Korea Development Institute.

Lee, See-Jae (1993) 'Tasks and Movements of the Social Movements in Korea in the 1990s', *Korea Journal*, 33(2), Summer: 17–36.

Lee, Sook-Jong (1994) 'Contemporary Korean Society', Sejong Institute, paper presented at Yonsei University, December.

Lee, Su-Hoon (1993) 'Transitional Politics of Korea, 1987–1992: Activation of Civil Society', *Pacific Affairs*, 66(3): 351–67.

Lee, Su-Hoon and Smith, David A. (1991) 'Antisystemic Movements in South Korea: the Rise of Environmental Activism', Section III paper presented at the Fifteenth Annual Meeting of PEWS, University of Hawaii, 28–30 March.

Office of Police (1993) *White Paper on Road Traffic 1991*, cited in Kwon, Soonwon, *Economic and Advances and Quality of Life in Social Policy in Korea: Challenges and Responses*, Seoul: Korea Development Institute.

Renaud, Bertrand (1992) 'Confronting a Distorted Housing Market: Can Korean Policies Make a Break with the Past?', paper presented at the Symposium on Social Issues in Korea at USCD, June.

Rodan, Garry and Hewison, Kevin (1994) 'Whatever Happened to the Revolution: the Decline of the Left in Southeast Asia', in Ralph Miliband and Leo Panitch (eds) *The Socialist Register 1994*, London: Merlin Press, pp. 235–62.

Schroders Securities Asia Research Korea (1990) December.

Shim Jae Hoon (1994a) 'End of the Line Union Tempers Cool in South Korea', *Far Eastern Economic Review*, 14 July: 69.

—— (1994b) 'Union Blues: Organised Teachers Retreat in Clash with Government', *Far Eastern Economic Review*, 4 November: 22.

Shin, Dae Kyun (1994) Interview, December, Seoul: CCEJ Offices.

Steinberg, David (1989) *The Republic of Korea: Economic Transformation and Social Change*, Boulder, Colo.: Westview Press.

Tsurutani, Taketsugu (1977) *Political Change in Japan: Response to Postindustrialism*, New York: David McKay Company Inc.

Wells, Kenneth M. (ed.) (1995), *Korea's Minjung Movement*, Honolulu: University of Hawaii Press.

Woo, Jung-en (1991) *Race to the Swift: State and Finance in Korea Industrialisation*, New York: Columbia Press.

Yang, Sung Chul (1994) 'South Korea's Top Bureaucratic Elites 1948–1993', *Korea Journal*, 34(3), Autumn: 5–19.
—— (1995) 'An Analysis of South Korea's Political Process and Party Politics', in James Cotton (ed.) *Politics and Policy in the New Korean State. From Roh Tae-woo to Kim Young-sam*, New York: St Martin's Press, pp. 6–34.
Yoo, Hi-Jung (1988) 'A Study of the Social Consciousness of the Middle Classes in Korea' (in Korean), unpublished Ph.D. dissertation, Ewha Women's University, Seoul.

11 Mobilisational authoritarianism and political opposition in Taiwan

Shelley Rigger

Despite its 'Free China' sobriquet, the Republic of China on Taiwan did not have much of a political opposition before 1975. Twenty years later, however, Taiwan had one of the most vibrant oppositions in East Asia, including an electoral wing dominated by the Democratic Progressive Party (DPP, founded in 1986), and the Chinese New Party (CNP, founded in 1993), as well as a broad variety of protest movements, ranging from anti-nuclear activists to students fighting ideological indoctrination in schools. Taiwan's political opposition has much in common with other oppositions described in this volume; as in other countries, social forces that emerged in the course of industrialisation played an important role in its development. But in other ways, Taiwan's political opposition is unique. Ethnic cleavages played a far more important role in its development than economic ones, for example, and the fundamental question of Taiwan's national identity haunted its every move. As a result, the opposition's capacity to respond to economic issues is constrained. Fortunately for the opposition, its principal antagonist, the Nationalist Party, or Kuomintang (KMT), suffers from the same handicap.

Most scholars classified the Republic of China (ROC) as an authoritarian state from the 1950s to the mid-1980s, not least because the island was under martial law until 1987. Clearly, the Kuomintang was determined to control the island's political and economic life, although the debate over its motivations remains unresolved. Where some observers see a simple lust for power, others see a sincere commitment to the historical mission of re-establishing Nationalist government over all China. In either case, the interests of Taiwan and its native-born population were to play only a supporting role in the ROC drama. Moreover, there was no room on the stage for actors hoping to challenge the KMT's dominant position.

Characterising Taiwan under martial law as an authoritarian state is valid but not especially informative. While the KMT made ample use of such conventional tools of authoritarian government as ideological indoctrination, censorship, and repression of dissent, its success rested in large part on winning popular legitimacy. The Nationalist leadership was not satisfied with the Taiwanese people's passive compliance. Instead, the KMT expected – and to an impressive extent received – the active participation and support of its citizens. By drawing the population into the public realm through channels established, legitimated, and maintained by the state, the ruling party was able to stunt the growth of a civil society in Taiwan. The result was a state and society fused in what we shall call 'mobilisational authoritarianism'.

Mobilisational authoritarianism was based on the idea that obedience rendered under coercion is a less reliable foundation for a state (especially a state at war, which the ROC considered itself to be until 1991) than voluntary co-operation. Both Sun Yat-sen and Chiang K'ai-shek emphasised the importance of enmeshing citizens in public life by involving them in a vanguard party and its subsidiary organisations. The notion that citizens needed to be mobilised behind a revolutionary party was central to Sun's theory of political tutelage and development. In 1952, following Sun's ideological model, the KMT called for the establishment of farmers' and workers' organisations to improve living standards, build a foundation for democracy, and promote co-operation between labour and capital (*KMT Manifesto* 1952: 33). As Chiang K'ai-shek put it:

> Every citizen should belong to an Organization so that he can discharge his share of responsibility to the best of his ability. An organised citizenry can, on the negative side, prevent Communist infiltration and, on the positive side, lay the ground work for national mobilisation.
>
> (quoted in Chang 1955: 34)

Attaining a state of mobilisation required the ROC government to rely less on repression than on indoctrinating the population ideologically and co-opting social forces as they appeared. On Taiwan, the KMT evolved two main strategies for achieving this co-optation. On the one hand, the party channelled emerging socio-economic interests into state-sponsored organisations. On the other hand, it reinforced this essentially corporatist strategy by sponsoring local elections, which were designed to draw ambitious local elites and citizens – including those who fell outside the boundaries of corporatist organisations – into the ruling party fold.

PARTY-STATE CORPORATISM

According to the pluralist theory of interest-group formation, groups of citizens organise themselves independently to pursue common interests; the state is merely a referee among these independent groups. In contrast, the corporatist model of interest aggregation envisions a society in which the state itself sponsors and supervises groups. Ruth B. Collier and David Collier define corporatism in terms of three types of state action: '(1) state structuring of groups that produces a system of *officially sanctioned*, non-competitive, compulsory interest associations, (2) *state subsidy* of these groups, and (3) *state-imposed constraints* on demand-making, leadership, and internal governance' (Collier and Collier 1979: 968; their italics).

Corporatism's defining characteristics – state structuring, state subsidy, and state control – describe Taiwan's interest-group system well.[1] Most politically active groups originated within the ROC party-state and are sustained by it. To realise its goal of involving every citizen in one or another organisation, the KMT government gave its blessing to a wide range of associations, including the farmers' associations, water conservancy (irrigation) associations, labour unions, chambers of commerce, women's associations, and industrial and professional groups. With the party-state's blessing came the exclusive right to organise a profession or group. Some groups – including farmers, women, labour, and industrialists – even enjoyed reserved seats in legislative bodies. The regime made no secret of its intention to control these organisations. In the 1970s, Lerman examined a number of ROC government publications and found in them 'a paternalistic attitude' and ample evidence of 'the elite's intention to control the associations closely and to ensure their primary orientation toward approved goals' (Lerman 1979: 212). With the dawn of political reform in the 1980s, groups independent of the party and state have emerged. But these organisations lag far behind their state-sponsored counterparts in resources and influence.

In exchange for their privileged position, the quasi-governmental organisations relinquished the possibility of autonomous political action. Agents of the ruling party or government scrutinised their personnel decisions, budgets, and policies. As a result, the associations are far more effective as channels for communicating the state's policies to their members than for articulating or promoting the members' interests *vis-à-vis* the state. Sociologist Hsin-huang Michael Hsiao's description of the role of labour unions applies equally well to other quasi-governmental organisations: all the unions were completely demobilised and coerced and thus became at best the administrative or even party arms of the KMT state. Dependent 'productionist' labour unions were actively and widely established, on the one hand, yet autonomous 'consumptionist' unions were largely pre-empted and prohibited, on the other (Hsiao 1992: 156). Indeed, a 1984 survey found that 66 per cent of unionised workers believed labour unions to be 'useless in promoting their economic interests' (Tien 1989: 50).[2]

Corporatist organisations also play a role in elections. Their large grassroots memberships make them an important source of votes for KMT candidates. Mobilising unattached (or 'floating') voters is risky, so the corporatist organisations – with their up-to-date membership lists and carefully cultivated *esprit de corps* – are especially valuable to the party. As Table 11.1 illustrates, voters in special constituency elections – that were reserved for members of the appropriate corporatist organisations – supported the KMT by extraordinarily wide margins. Unlike floating votes, group members' ballots can be targeted to the candidates who need them most. Ideally, association votes should be able to be transferred from one candidate to another late in a campaign. In reality, many group members have their own preferences, and telling rank-and-file members how to vote is a touchy business. Still, the party's access to, and information about, group members is much greater than it is for unaffiliated voters.

Table 11.1 Performance in special constituency elections (occupational and aboriginal categories, Legislative Yuan)

	1980		1983		1986		1989	
	Votes (%)	Seats	Votes (%)	Seats	Votes (%)	Seats	Votes (%)	Seats
KMT	82.4	16	87.5	18	84.7	17	65.5	13
TW/DPP	1.3	0	3.1	0	6.9	0	19.9	3
Independent	16.3	2	9.4	0	8.4	0	14.6	2

Source: Hu Fo and Chu Yun-han in T. J. Cheng and Stephan Haggard (eds) (1992) *Political Change in Taiwan*, Boulder, Colo.: Lynne Reinner Publishers: 183–4.
Note: TW refers to Tangwai.

The ROC government's corporatist style of interest-group management enhanced its control over Taiwanese society and politics. And by reducing the economic and political space available for an independent civil society, corporatism retarded the development of political opposition. The overwhelming social, economic, and political predominance of party-state sponsored organisations, combined with repressive measures, prevented the development of autonomous interest groups. At the same time, clientelistic networks oriented towards electoral competition colonised many corporatist organisations at the local level and appropriated their resources and power.

ELECTORAL MOBILISATION

The second pillar of mobilisational authoritarianism, which complemented the KMT's corporatist institutions, was local elections. Competing for electoral office, which offered both status and material rewards, gave local elites a role and an interest in the ROC state and the Nationalist Party. Local politicians, in turn, brought ordinary citizens into the system as their supporters and as recipients of patronage. Although the ROC regime was imposed in the face of strong resistance in the 1940s, within a few years its strategy of rewarding local leaders who were willing to co-operate (while relentlessly suppressing those who were not) succeeded in creating a large class of local notables who saw their personal interests as congruent with those of the regime. These local politicians extended the state's reach to the grassroots by mobilising personal networks to assist their electoral bids. The networks they built are called local factions (*difang paixi*).[3]

Taiwan's local factions are local in that they exist only within individual counties; each one's influence ends at the county line. Because a candidate can win any ROC election merely by capturing a majority of votes in his or her home county (thanks to Taiwan's multi-member districts and single, non-transferable vote electoral formula), this is the most efficient size for a local faction.[4] Local factions are based on the exchange of political support and co-operation for political and material benefits. Faction leaders string together chains of supporters in local government (including township (*xiang*), village (*cun*), ward (*li*) and neighbourhood (*lin*) heads), corporatist organisations (farmers', women's, and irrigation associations, etc.), and society (religious, business, and community leaders). These local bosses, known in Taiwanese as *tiau-a-ka*, use their influence over others to mobilise support for the factions' chosen candidates. In exchange, the factions dole out status, political assistance, and material rewards (licences, public works contracts, government jobs, and money). In order to maintain their clientelistic networks, factions need access to political and material benefits. Electing members to public office accomplishes both aims: the prestige of holding office is itself a political benefit, while the power of office allows factions to turn public resources to their own ends.

As clientelistic organisations, local factions have taken on political, economic, and social functions that put them in direct competition with one another for resources of all kinds, leading to passionate rivalries. Compounding this antagonism is the strong emotional identification many politicians and *tiau-a-ka* feel with their factions. It is not surprising, then, that many politicians speak of rival factions as the 'enemy'. As a KMT official in Tainan County said in 1991, 'The most important thing, as far as factions are concerned, is to defeat your enemy. And the enemy is the other faction, not the DPP [the opposition party]' (Rigger 1994a: 28).

By creating opportunities for local elites to participate in the system through electoral politics, the ROC government captured yet another potential source of resistance and opposition. Political energy that might otherwise have been directed at competing for power against the regime was directed instead at local political rivals. At the same time, elections facilitated the ruling party's recruitment of authentic local leadership; as Linda Gail Arrigo has pointed out, the KMT even won over independent politicians whose campaign rhetoric criticised the ruling party once those individuals took office (Arrigo 1994: 148). Moreover, economic grievances that might have given rise to class-based social movements were defused when local factions distributed particularistic benefits to their supporters, a practice the ruling party encouraged. In sum, by cultivating competitive clientelistic networks that cut across class lines, the KMT derailed class-based mobilisation. And because local factions were concerned with particularistic goals, local elections were incapable of providing meaningful representation for socio-economic groups. Paradoxically, then, competitive local elections actually retarded the development of a civil society. Instead of creating autonomous organisations to represent competing interests, local elections limited group development to corporatist associations and patronage networks established, maintained, and ultimately controlled by the state.

THE POLITICAL OPPOSITION

In February 1947, a Taiwanese rebellion against KMT rule nearly drove the Nationalists off the island. During the ensuing months of reprisals and years of repression, thousands of politically active Taiwanese were executed or imprisoned, including much of the island's pre-war intelligentsia and social elite. Political repression was intense throughout the 1950s, and it was not until the late 1980s that the last political prisoners were released. These measures, combined with a vigorous programme of ideological indoctrination and the co-optation mechanisms described in the previous section, dissuaded most Taiwanese from challenging the ROC government. From 1947 until the mid-1970s, Taiwan's political opposition was limited to a few small groups: mainlander intellectuals committed to Nationalist ideology but unhappy with the KMT's ruling style (such as Lei Chen), independent local politicians (such as Kao Yu-shu and Wu San-lien), and Taiwan independence activists living overseas. None of these groups was able to alter ROC policy or attract a national grassroots following.

It is a truism of political science that economic development tends to create or unleash social forces that resist authoritarian control. A swelling middle class of educated, white-collar workers requires more of the state than law and order. These independent professionals and entrepreneurs demand a say in political decision making. Yet in Taiwan, many of the people political scientists would expect to join this movement (teachers and small business owners, for example) remained loyal to the ruling party. Mobilisational authoritarianism proved far more resilient than many social scientists would have predicted. Thanks to its corporatist arrangements, the ROC government retained the support of large sectors of the workforce, while local factions maintained their hold on workers, farmers, and small business owners in most areas. Nonetheless, by the mid-1970s, a significant number of middle-class Taiwanese lived beyond the reach of the KMT's mobilisational apparatus. Among those most likely to be alienated from the ROC state were independent professionals, small-scale entrepreneurs dissatisfied with the patronage supplied by local factions, and local politicians whose ambitions were stymied by KMT bureaucrats. These groups formed the core of Taiwan's political opposition in the 1970s and 1980s.

Leadership for the budding opposition movement came from two elite groups: urban professionals (lawyers, physicians, and intellectuals) and local politicians.[5] In the 1970s, Taiwan's economic and political fortunes showed signs of ebbing. The decade brought a long string of international defeats (including the loss of the ROC's United Nations seat and the severance of diplomatic relations with most of the world), and the oil shock-induced world recession hit the economy hard. Taiwanese who were educated overseas found the setbacks especially galling. Not only had they been exposed to liberal western ideologies; more concretely, their host countries no longer honoured their ROC passports. The loss of the international stature and performance legitimacy that had sustained the KMT party-state in the boom years 'awakened the political awareness of some segments of the emerging middle class

[who] began to evaluate from their own perspective Taiwan's international and political environment and contemplate possible reforms' (Chu 1992: 34). To its small – but growing – ranks the opposition added lawyers disillusioned with the arbitrariness of the ROC's authoritarian legal system and journalists disgusted with press censorship.[6]

From the beginning, Taiwan's political opposition fought its most decisive battles in the electoral arena. Elections offered the opposition a chance to demonstrate its commitment to peaceful reform, build a grassroots following, and beat the KMT at its own game. To do so, urban elites made common cause with disgruntled local politicians, many of whom were genuinely fed up with the ROC regime (others would prove later to be opportunists). Even though elected officials wielded almost no influence over national policy, local power, economic privilege, and social status were at stake in elections, and local factions fought fiercely for the spoils of victory. The KMT had learned to take advantage of this competition by balancing the power of local factions and confining it to the local electoral arena. In some municipalities, for example, the ruling party alternated executive nominations between factions, ensuring that no faction would get the upper hand. The party also manipulated financial and organisational resources to maintain a balance of power. Faction leaders were well aware of these interventions, and many resented them bitterly. A few eventually became so frustrated that they left the KMT, taking entire factions with them. The most famous example of this is Yu Teng-fa, a Kaohsiung County political boss who led his Black Faction in a mass defection. Yu became a highly vocal critic of the regime; the list of his assistants in the late 1970s is a Who's Who of southern Taiwan's opposition leaders today.[7]

The alliance of urban professionals and local politicians provided leadership for the budding opposition, but to thrive, the movement also needed financial support and grassroots organisation. Fortunately for the opposition, the ROC's economic development strategy had nurtured a constituency for political change within the affluent entrepreneurial sector. From 1953 to 1963, the ROC followed a strategy of import substitution industrialisation (ISI). Under this economic model, the state promoted large companies (many of them publicly owned) and heavy industry to reduce Taiwan's dependence on imported goods. It provided financial assistance, subsidies, tariff protection, and price supports to encourage rapid industrial growth. A number of key industries were either nationalised or brought under joint public-private ownership (cement, petroleum refining, steel); multi-national corporations set up shop in mid-stream manufacturing. This strategy gave birth to a class of mainlander and Taiwanese capitalists involved in large-scale consumer manufacturing, but this new bourgeoisie lacked political influence. As Thomas Gold writes, 'the state bureaucracy, not tied to the bourgeoisie but increasingly committed to capitalist development, retained its hegemonic position and acted in the bourgeoisie's interests without allowing itself to become its instrument' (Gold 1988: 184). In this phase, the state's favouritism towards elite firms was not yet a source of resentment, since wages and living standards were rising.

Beginning in the early 1960s, ROC economic planners added export-oriented industrialisation to their ISI strategy. The new policy sparked an explosion in the number of small manufacturing firms – such, in fact, that the value of goods produced in the private sector consistently surpassed public sector production. These small and medium-sized enterprises (SMEs) received few of the benefits afforded to firms in the economic elite. One of the greatest disadvantages they faced was a severe shortage of capital for new ventures. The financial sector was entirely state-controlled, and took a dim view of small, family-owned businesses. As a result, SMEs were cut off from conventional credit sources; they had no choice but to go to underground financial markets and lending clubs for loans. State banks subsidised elite firms with loans at below-market interest rates while denying SMEs credit at any price (Winn and Yeh 1994: 200). Nor were the conflicts between SMEs and the state limited to banking. According to Susan Greenhalgh, relations between the state and family firms sometimes resembled:

> an outright struggle, in which the state has attempted to encourage mergers and eliminate unprofitable firms . . . while family enterprises have sought to retain their independence by refusing to merge, employing illegal means to maintain profits (going underground, evading taxes, using loans to speculate in the real estate market) and moving transactions through informal channels to avoid government scrutiny.
>
> (Greenhalgh 1988: 242)

The effects of the ROC government's disadvantageous policies towards SMEs were mitigated somewhat by its willingness to tolerate informal credit markets and by the availability of local government patronage. Many SMEs enjoyed close ties with local factions, which supplied their friends with valuable benefits. Local governments awarded juicy public works contracts to friendly construction companies and assigned such local monopolies as inter-city bus routes to their political supporters. In Hsinchu City, for example, supporters of one local faction controlled the passenger transport service, while its competitor's minions ran the cargo lines. But not all entrepreneurs were content with their second-tier status. Even some who benefited from factional politics grew dissatisfied with the treatment they received, compared to the state's generosity towards large corporations. These disgruntled business people became an important (if surreptitious) source of financial support for the opposition (Shiau 1994: 14).[8]

As economic development progressed in the 1970s, Taiwan's workforce shifted from farming to white-collar work and SME manufacturing. These jobs released workers from the network of corporatist organisations the KMT had established to channel their participation in system-supporting directions. While farmers were 'captured' by the farmers' associations, and workers in large factories were organised in state-supported company unions, independent professionals, entrepreneurs, and employees of SMEs all were beyond the reach of corporatist groups. Prosperity and modernisation brought difficult choices; some economic sectors were left behind. However, the political opposition was slow to win over these budding social forces. Undoubtedly, decades of political repression intimidated some potential supporters. However, elections were at least as important a mitigating force preventing the disintegration of mobilisational authoritarianism. But for their relationship with local factions, many more of the workers and farmers who saw their relative economic positions deteriorating during the recession of the early 1970s and real estate and stock market booms of the 1980s might have joined the opposition. As it was, however, local factions were able to use social incentives and patronage to keep these voters tied to the ruling party. Indeed, prosperity brought with it increased government revenues, which in turn enriched the local factions, giving them more resources for recruiting and maintaining support networks. As Chu Yun-han wrote:

> the election has become the major institution to assimilate emerging economic and social forces into the political system. Facing recurring electoral challenges, the party-sanctioned local factional networks are more adaptive than the formal party apparatus to socioeconomic changes. . . . When traditional clientelist networks could no longer deliver votes as effectively as they once did, faction-centered or candidate-centered clientelism was expanded to incorporate more secondary associations and regional business concerns, especially in rapidly urbanizing areas. Also, more and more new contenders were drawn into the electoral process to seek political access and economic privilege, since electoral success could be readily translated into

instant social prestige and handsome economic gain. With an ever-expanding economy, both the cost and the stakes of elections became ever greater for the established factions.

(Chu 1994a: 102)

Mobilisational authoritarianism combined with the ROC's strong economic performance and the fear of Communist aggression to shortcircuit any hope for a political opposition based on economic grievances or class solidarity (Gold 1988: 203). Instead, the issues that resonated with Taiwan's budding opposition movement were political ones, namely political reform and ethnic justice. These two issues (and the national identity issue, which emerged later) were inseparable. In a nutshell, the ROC's authoritarian, KMT-dominated political structure allowed the 15 per cent of Taiwan residents identified as 'mainlanders' to exercise political authority over the 85 per cent identified as 'Taiwanese'. Thus, for many ROC citizens, loosening the ruling party's political control meant self-determination for the majority ethnic group; 'democratisation' was defined as a Taiwan governed by and for the Taiwanese majority.[9] In short, ethnic justice and political reform were inextricably connected, and together they formed the opposition party's ideological foundation.

The tension between those who came to Taiwan with the Nationalist government between 1945 and 1949 (the group known as mainlanders) and the native-born Taiwanese has many sources. Fifty years of Japanese colonial rule altered Taiwan's political, economic, and social patterns, producing cultural and material gaps between the Taiwanese and the newly arrived mainlanders. These differences were largely to blame for the 28 February Incident of 1947, which further exacerbated the tensions between the two groups. Perhaps these conflicts might have been overcome had the KMT not imposed an ethnic division of labour on the island that constrained the Taiwanese population's opportunities and devalued their contributions. But the Nationalists did impose such a division, and as Marshall Johnson put it, 'Once this correlation of social position and provincial origin was established in practice, ethnicity became part of the sense of the possible and the sense of limits for persons in both groups' (Johnson 1992: 76).[10]

The ethnic division of labour gave the mainlanders control over the island's political and economic life, and enforced a Chinese cultural identity that denigrated Taiwan and its people. Mainlanders were vastly over-represented in the central government, the management of state-owned businesses, academia, and cultural life. Mainland-born Presidents Chiang K'ai-shek (1949–75) and Chiang Ching-kuo (1978–88) dominated the ROC government with their 'strong-man' ruling style. It was only after the younger Chiang's death in 1988 that a native Taiwanese, Lee Teng-hui, acceded to the island's highest office.[11] Members of the ROC's two legislative bodies (the Legislative Yuan and National Assembly) were elected on mainland China in 1947 and frozen in office until after 1990, ostensibly because it was impossible to hold elections in the mainland provinces they represented.

Central government bureaucrats also were drawn overwhelmingly from the mainlander community, as were military leaders and ruling party members. For more than two decades, a glass ceiling prevented all but a handful of local politicians from moving into the national political arena. In the late 1970s, the ROC party-state launched a 'Taiwanisation' campaign to recruit native Taiwanese for government and party posts. The Taiwanese representation in those bureaucracies increased, but mainlanders still hold a disproportionate share of positions. For example, the KMT's Taiwanisation campaign yielded a party that was about 70 per cent Taiwanese in the late 1980s, at a time when the Taiwanese population was between 85 and 90 per cent (Tien 1989: 85).

In Taiwan, ethnic and political domination reinforced one another, so those outside the favoured community found themselves consistently relegated to second-class status. For many Taiwanese, this state of affairs was not enough to propel them into the political opposition. They were satisfied with the niches permitted to Taiwanese – agriculture, business, local politics. But the opposition did attract those Taiwanese who could not ignore the denial in practice of political rights guaranteed by the ROC constitution or who felt acutely the sensation of permanent ethnic disadvantage. Thus, the opposition's emphasis on ethnic cleavages reinforced the effects of mobilisational authoritarianism to create an opposition movement with little discernible class character. As Wang Fu-ch'ang put it,

> the ethnic division in Taiwan's politics is greater than the class division [because] . . . the inequality in the distribution of political power along ethnic lines is more evident than the power inequality among classes, and for this reason more easily became a foundation for political mobilisation.
>
> (Wang 1990: 45)

Taiwan's political opposition includes two very different strands. One is elite-led and devoted to winning political power through elections; the other is comprised of several broad-based protest movements. The electoral opposition began in the 1970s as a congeries of disgruntled local politicians, reform-minded professionals and full-time activists. Throughout the decade, individual candidates challenged the KMT in local elections. Unlike the local factions (which competed within the ruling party for status and patronage opportunities) and the old independents (who often used their personal electoral machines as leverage to persuade the KMT to cut them in on patronage benefits), candidates from the new electoral opposition represented an authentic alternative to the ruling party. In their campaigns they attacked the KMT's policies and record openly.

In 1975, the opposition activist Kang Ning-hsiang published the *Taiwan Political Review*, which the government promptly banned. Two years later, Kang and fellow opposition candidate Huang Hsin-chieh defied KMT rules and held a series of rallies throughout the island. Non-KMT candidates stunned the ruling party by capturing twenty-one of seventy-seven seats in the Taiwan Provincial Assembly that year. After the election, voters suspecting fraud fought with police in the city of Chungli, calling even more attention to the growing movement. In 1979, opposition activists calling themselves the *tangwai* ('outside the party') helped to launch *Formosa Magazine (Meilitao)*; in December, they sponsored a rally in Kaohsiung which erupted into violence. Forty-one opposition activists were tried in connection with the incident, eight of them in a military court. Among those receiving long sentences were the magazine's publisher, Huang Hsin-chieh, and its editor, Shih Ming-teh. Shih had just finished serving a fifteen-year term for another political offence when he attended the December demonstration. He was sentenced to life in prison.[12] Others incarcerated for involvement in the 'Kaohsiung Incident' included followers of Yu Teng-fa, the Kaohsiung County faction boss, and Taiwan provincial assembly member Lin Yi-hsiung.

Throughout the 1970s, the electoral opposition emphasised political reform and ethnic justice. In particular, the *tangwai* demanded that martial law be lifted and basic human and civil rights respected. The movement also pressed the ruling party to increase the number of elected positions in the national government and put an end to such widespread electoral violations as vote buying and fraud. Since 1969, the ROC had been holding supplementary elections to fill legislative and National Assembly seats left vacant by the ageing incumbents brought from mainland China in 1949. The *tangwai* argued that the time had come to replace those incumbents with legislators elected on Taiwan, a goal which finally was attained in 1992. In the 1980s, the *tangwai* continued its campaign for political reform, while its candidates captured an increasing share of electoral positions. In 1986, the movement defied martial law and formed a political party, the Democratic Progressive Party (DPP). After President Chiang Ching-kuo lifted martial law in 1987, dozens of new parties sprang up, but none has been able to challenge the DPP's status as the island's leading opposition party.

Since the beginning, then, the *tangwai*/DPP strand of Taiwan's political opposition has been devoted to increasing contestation, participation, and accountability in ROC politics. They also expect the political influence of native Taiwanese to increase until it is proportional to their share of the population, and many of them believe that in the process, Taiwan will become an independent country. Oppositionists in this camp are also committed to using electoral politics to achieve their goals. According to Chu, elections were bound to play a critical role in Taiwan's political change because:

> First, when a society has no previous experience of competitive democracy, democratic legitimacy takes root mainly through electoral processes. Second, when the range of confrontational and mobilizational strategies available to the opposition is highly restricted by the prevailing socio-economic structures, elections are likely to become the only mobilization mechanism available to the opposition to exert popular pressures on [the] incumbent regime over the issues of democratic reform. In Taiwan, both conditions exist. Elections have turned out to be the principal mechanism through which changes in the social structure brought about by rapid industrialisation were translated into a political force for weakening the entrenched authoritarian order.
>
> (Chu 1992: 48)

Electoral politics was the major – but not the only – channel oppositionists used to challenge the ROC's authoritarian regime. For some, protest movements were the preferred method of social and political change. According to Hsin-huang Michael Hsiao:

> by the end of 1989, eighteen social movements had already taken shape ... including the consumers [sic] movement (1980), the anti pollution local protest movement (1980), the natural conservation movement (1982), the women's movement (1982), the aborigines human rights movement (1983), the students' movement (1986) ... the new testament church protests (1986), the labor movement, the farmers' movement, the teachers' rights movement, the handicapped and disadvantaged welfare group protests, the veterans' welfare protests, the political victims human rights move-

ment, and the mainlanders home-visiting movement [all in 1987] . . .
the Taiwanese home-visiting movement (1988), the antinuclear
power movement (1988), the Hakka rights movement (1988), and the
nonhomeowners 'snail' movement (1989).

(Hsiao 1992: 154)

Many of the early protest movements sprang up in reaction to
particular incidents that affected small, well-defined communities.
These movements rarely survived the resolution of the specific problem
at issue in their case. For example, victims of environmental pollution
were more interested in expelling the polluter or winning compensation
for their suffering than in passing legislation to prevent future environmental destruction. Independent labour actions rarely had economic objectives; between 1983 and 1987, a majority of industrial
actions were protests against violations of workers' legal rights (Hsiao
1992: 159). Even so, labour protesters' targets were specific grievances; very few envisioned a unified labour movement with political
ambitions.

Protest movements benefited greatly from the electoral opposition's
achievements. After martial law was lifted, for example, the number
and size of these movements expanded rapidly to fill the newly opened
political space. They employed tactics they could not have considered
before, including mass protests and publications. As Chu Yun-han has
explained, social movements grew rapidly in the 1980s because the
ROC state was no longer capable of assimilating demanding new social
forces into the structures provided by mobilisational authoritarianism.
In addition, through a fearful process of trial and error, the political
opposition had identified the limits of the regime's willingness to
repress dissent (Chu 1994a: 106–7). Yet despite their affinities, most
protest movements avoided associating too closely with the electoral
opposition. Even though the DPP's positions were far more favourable
to protest movements than those of the ruling party, non-partisanship
remained a goal of many protest groups. Those that became identified
with the opposition party found their sincerity questioned and their
effectiveness blunted. Association with politicians, whose motives
many Taiwanese question, hurt protest movements, while too tight a
link with opposition ideologies, especially Taiwan independence,
confused their missions and chased away potential supporters (Hsiao
1992: 165).

The existence of a strong electoral opposition and a variety of protest
movements testifies to the expansion of Taiwan's civil society. Until
the 1980s, the structures of mobilisational authoritarianism gobbled up

emerging social forces and incorporated them into the state. But as soon as President Chiang lifted martial law in 1987, the tentative stirrings that began in the 1970s bloomed into a full-scale civil society, beyond the ROC state's capacity to control (see Chu 1994a: 106; Pang 1992: 26–7). Even social forces traditionally captive to the party-state have grown more autonomous. In elections since 1989, for example, local factions have demanded more and more of a voice in the selection of candidates. When their representatives were not nominated, some factions threw their votes to the opposition party (see Rigger 1993: *passim*). In the early 1990s, the KMT came under intense criticism for nominating too many 'golden oxen' (*jinniu*) – wealthy candidates who could pay for their own campaigns, but had little else to recommend them. Even the suspicion that the tail might be wagging the dog indicated a sea change in Taiwan's politics.

Despite its difficulties, the KMT is still the majority party in Taiwan. It clung to a narrow majority in the 1995 legislative election, winning eighty-five out of 164 seats. Nonetheless, with the opposition divided between the DPP's fifty-four seats and the New Party's twenty-one, the KMT still dominates the legislature. The President is a KMT member, as are his cabinet ministers. While the DPP's best hope for seizing power soon would be to win the presidency in 1996, few DPP members hold out much hope of doing so. And national politics is the DPP's strongest suit; when it comes to local politics (below the county level), the opposition party has made even less progress. The New Party, for its part, still appeals mainly to mainlanders and middle-class voters in metropolitan Taipei.

How has the KMT maintained its position in the face of the strong challenges mounted by the electoral opposition and protest movements? Perhaps the KMT's greatest advantage is its flexibility on policy matters. A combination of pragmatic ideology, strong central leadership and crafty manoeuvring has allowed President Lee to co-opt many of the most popular planks in the DPP platform. For example, with martial law out of the way and direct, competitive, fair elections in place for nearly every political office in the land, the DPP's calls for 'democrat-isation' seem outmoded. Likewise, Taiwanisation of the party and state apparatus has undermined the appeal of the ethnic justice issue. While few would deny that there is more to be done, surveys show the Taiwanese to be more concerned about other issues, especially crime, corruption, and pollution.

The one DPP position the KMT will not take over is the opposition's advocacy of Taiwan independence. This issue gives the DPP a strong identity; unfortunately, it is not popular enough to bring the opposition party to power (Chu 1992: 97). For a time, the opposition seemed to have found a more appealing way to market the issue. Instead of seeking independence outright, the party advocated a return to the United Nations. (Taiwan withdrew from the UN in 1972 when the People's Republic of China was seated.) The 'return to the UN' campaign turned out to be immensely popular. After a bit of dickering between reformist and conservative factions within the ruling party, however, the KMT came out in support of UN participation, and the KMT-led Foreign Ministry stepped neatly into the vanguard. The DPP was left with no choice but to demonstrate its co-operative spirit by getting behind the KMT-led UN campaign.

Political reform, ethnic justice, and national identity are fundamental issues. The first two have resolved into a consensus, while the third appears stalemated for the time being. As a result, the opposition is forced to look for new issues with which to attract supporters away from the majority party. This new stage of Taiwan's political development poses profound challenges for both parties. Because of the over-whelming emphasis on elections in the ROC, the logic of Taiwanese politics forces any party that hopes to form a government to embrace a diverse collection of voters. Precisely because it is a cross-class coalition of white-collar professionals, intellectuals, workers, farmers, small business men, and local political bosses, the DPP will find it especially difficult to identify issues that can unify that coalition, once the fundamental issues (political reform, ethnic justice, and national identity) lose their potency. According to Chu Yun-han, this already is the case (Chu 1994b: 9).

For its part, the KMT still faces dissatisfaction on a number of important issues. Above all, the ruling party is under pressure to do something about corruption and the abuse of money in politics. Not even an island-wide crackdown led by Justice Minister Ma Ying-jeou himself was enough to quell the outcry against vote buying; in early 1994, the ROC government unveiled a plan to create a government bureau devoted solely to fighting corruption. As political reform increased the national legislature's policy-making role, well-heeled special-interest groups made an appearance, intensifying worries about legislative corruption. Corruption also is a factor in the poor quality of public services provided by KMT-dominated local governments. In 1994, the ruling party incumbent lost the Taipei City mayoral race. His defeat was due primarily to his administration's wretched record on public construction and services. The mayor's administration reached its nadir when the desperately needed mass rapid transit system failed to open after years of unpardonable delays, cost over-runs, and other disasters.

Besides the problems of money politics and government inefficiency, urban Taiwanese face economic difficulties as well. Astronomical increases in the price of land and housing that accompanied the rapid urbanisation and real-estate boom of the 1980s threatened urban professionals' standard of living, exacerbating their political discontent. At the same time, group demands for social welfare provisions increased, forcing the KMT to embrace such programmes as health insurance for farmers and social security for the elderly. The KMT also faces discord over the growing gap between rich and poor in Taiwan, which has long celebrated its record of 'growth with equality'. The ruling party's inability to solve Taiwan's profound environmental problems, to ensure fairness in the educational system without destroying students' creativity and health, to control Taiwan's business ties with mainland China and to improve the island's international status – all of these contribute to political discontent.

Economic change even threatens to undermine the long-standing relationship between the ruling party and farmers. Despite the iron grip of the Farmers' Associations and local factions in the countryside, falling agricultural incomes have convinced some farmers that the government no longer has their interests at heart. ROC policy makers admit that agriculture's share of the economy will continue to decline in the face of growing international pressure to increase agricultural imports. Farmers will be sacrificed to narrow Taiwan's trade gap with the US and other countries. Only the relentless efforts of entrenched local factions and corporatist organisations permit KMT candidates to win rural elections. The election of DPP county executives in rural Tainan and Penghu counties in the early 1990s was thus an ominous sign for the ruling party.

POLITICAL TRAJECTORIES IN THE 1990S

In short, neither of Taiwan's leading parties can capitalise easily on the issues that voters find most salient. What, then, is the nature of political opposition and contestation in Taiwan in the 1990s? Within the political elite, the competition is intense. KMT and DPP candidates contest every election vigorously. In 1993, the Chinese New Party broke away from the KMT and joined the electoral fray. In its first two contests, the 1993 municipal executive elections and the 1994 races for Taipei and Kaohsiung mayor and Taiwan provincial governor, the CNP's vote share was limited outside its stronghold in the Taipei metropolitan region. The party improved its performance in the 1995 legislative elections, capturing twenty-one seats with 13 per cent of the popular vote. The CNP benefited from the KMT's factional battles, pulling away mainlander votes linked to the conservative non-mainstream faction. In 1996, non-mainstream stalwarts Lin Yang-kang and Hao Pei-tsun challenged the KMT's presidential ticket. Although technically independent, the Lin Hao state enjoyed the New Party's support, and it captured the 15 per cent vote share CNP candidates won in other contest. The DPP, too, is riven by factionalism. Relations between the pragmatic, centrist Formosa faction and the more ideological New Tide faction are strained.

The political reform process opened numerous channels for political contestation; electoral competition is only one of these, albeit an important one. Another is the growing influence of legislative politics in the policy-making process. KMT bills are still virtually assured of passage in the legislature, thanks to the party's substantial majority, but elected representatives are much more likely to leave their mark on legislation than ever before. In fact, opposition legislators have forced the KMT to revise a handful of proposals. For example, their protests compelled the KMT to submit three controversial national security Bills to the Council of Grand Justices for review. In another case, legislators of the KMT, DPP, and CNP negotiated a proposal to change interpellation procedures, only to have the agreement rejected by the cabinet. Legislators have also pressed for – and received – reductions in defence expenditures. Elected officials at other levels of government also enjoy increased influence on policy outcomes in the post-reforms era.

Protest movements, too, sometimes win their fights. The most impressive victories have occurred in the environmental realm. In 1991, a coalition of environmentalists, grassroots activists, and local politicians in Ilan County forced the powerful Formosa Plastics corporation to relocate a planned oil refinery outside the county. Anti-nuclear activists in Taipei County fended off construction of a second nuclear power plant in Kungliao township, on the island's northeastern coast, well into the 1990s. The anti-nuclear movement brought together aggrieved citizens, conservationists, DPP leaders, and taxi drivers in a chaotic, but effective, alliance. Grassroots activists littered the northeastern countryside with anti-nuclear posters while activists protested around the clock in front of the Legislative Yuan. Underground radio stations sympathetic to the opposition notified taxi drivers when votes or other legislative actions were imminent; at a moment's notice hundreds of drivers raced to the legislature and jammed the streets with their distinctive yellow cabs. Taipei County's DPP executive Yu Ching campaigned on a resolutely anti-nuclear platform. He promised to withhold county construction permits for the power plant, although central authorities overruled his decision. Yu's position was extremely popular. In 1989 he captured 62 per cent of the vote in Kungliao. Four years earlier the township had supported Yu's KMT opponent by the same percentage. In 1994, Taipei County citizens attempted to recall county council members who had voted for the nuclear project.

Taiwan's political opposition is still divided into two main strands: the electoral opposition, in which the Democratic Progressive Party is the leading force, followed at some distance by the Chinese New Party, and the protest movements. The latter have appeared in response to particular events and issues affecting large numbers of Taiwanese – environmental degradation, inflated housing prices, inadequate consumer safeguards. Much as they would like to, none of the political parties has been able to capitalise on the discontent motivating the protest movements. Because Taiwan's political parties place overwhelming importance on electoral performance, they are handicapped in their efforts to respond to new issues. Under mobilisational authoritarianism the KMT developed into a cross-class coalition of farmers, workers, entrepreneurs, soldiers, and civil servants. In the absence of easily exploited socio-economic cleavages, ethnicity proved to be the opposition's most potent organising tool. Taiwan's progress toward new issues and cleavages has been halting at best. In the important gubernatorial and mayoral races of 1994, such policy considerations as local construction and the quality of public services dominated the campaign. But issues of identity and national security returned to centre stage in 1996 when the People's Republic of China tried to use military exercises and missile tests off the the Taiwanese coast to influence Taiwan's first direct presidential election. In response, Taiwan's voters gave the target of Beijing's irritations, incumbent president Lee Teng-hui, a resounding endorsement: 54 per cent of the vote in a four-way race.

Both leading parties' cross-class constituencies remained coherent as long as the key issues under debate were such fundamental questions as national identity, ethnic justice, or the pace of political reform. Once these issues were exhausted, however, the new concerns that appeared in their place threatened the parties' internal cohesion. Environmental demands drove wedges between entrepreneurs and conservationists. Anti-corruption drives were popular with voters, but offended local faction bosses. Farmers demanded subsidies and tariffs while business fretted about export markets. Since the DPP and the KMT both rely on all these groups to win Taiwan's competitive elections, the problem is severe. The result is not a straightforward shift of support from the majority party to the opposition, but a growing three-way party split and an increasingly unpredictable electorate whose preferences neither major party can accommodate.

NOTES

1 For an extended discussion of the ROC's corporatist system, see Tien (1989: 43–63).

2 Independent organisations have found more fertile ground in labour than in farming or other sectors. The government, too, has given labour unions somewhat more leeway than other groups. This probably is a response to an embarrassing defeat workers dealt the corporatist labour movement by rejecting party-backed 'labour' candidates in elections since 1989.

3 Recently, a number of ROC scholars and journalists have published studies of Taiwan's local factions; thus, their overall character is well understood (see Tien 1989: 164–71; Wu 1987; Chao 1978a, 1978b, 1989; Huang 1990a, 1990b). Until 1987, the ban on new parties forced most political aspirants to channel their ambitions through the ruling party. Even in the 1990s, however, most faction-based candidates still ran for office under the banner of the KMT, and factions consulted with the ruling party on key decisions.

4 After 1994 there were two exceptions to this rule, the Taiwan Provincial Governorship and the ROC presidency.

5 Many of these figures were disgruntled KMT members who broke away from the party because they were convinced that there was no hope of reforming it from within. They include Yu Teng-fa, Chang Chun-hong and Hsu Hsin-liang.

6 According to Taiwan media expert Chin-chuan Lee, a few liberal journalists schooled in US media values and methods regularly passed on censored material to opposition publications (Lee 1994: 12).

7 In 1986 Yu Teng-fa's successor, daughter-in-law Yu Chen Yueh-ying, merged the Black Faction with the newly formed opposition Democratic Progressive Party.

8 Businesses are careful to avoid too close an association with the opposition party; rumours abound in Taiwan about entrepreneurs who suffered mysterious setbacks when they revealed their political loyalties. The string of highly publicised misfortunes that befell the DPP-linked Hai Pa Wang restaurant chain in the early 1990s is a particularly famous case. In interviews, opposition sympathisers often tell me they live in fear of a tax audit.

9 Initially, the political opposition shied away from the issue of national identity (that is, whether Taiwan should seek independence from China), both because independence advocacy was considered subversive and carried harsh penalties and because not all opposition leaders supported independence (e.g. Yu Teng-fa). But by the late 1980s, as the ROC relaxed its laws against independence advocacy, Taiwan independence had become the standard by which many oppositionists measured progress towards ethnic justice and democracy. The logic of this position is that as long as Taiwan is governed by a state whose goal is unification with mainland China, the question of national identity will never be subject to democratic

resolution; thus, until the national identity issue is resolved, Taiwan cannot be fully democratic. Moreover, because the idea of unification makes Taiwan subordinate to China, until the unification goal is abandoned, the Taiwanese people will be subordinate to the mainlanders in Taiwan, undermining ethnic justice.

10 Taiwanese social scientists, journalists, and activists have produced vast amounts of material on Taiwan's ethnic problem. For a recent, full-length study in English, see Alan Wachman, *Taiwan: National Identity and Democratization*, Armonk, NY: M. E. Sharpe, 1994.

11 The people of Taiwan directly elected their President for the first time in 1996.

12 The last of the Kaohsiung prisoners to be released was Shih Ming-teh. He left prison in 1990.

REFERENCES

Arrigo, Linda Gail (1994) 'From Democratic Movement to Bourgeois Democracy: the Internal Politics of the Taiwan Democratic Progressive Party in 1991' in Murray A. Rubenstein (ed.) *The Other Taiwan*, Armonk, NY: M. E. Sharpe, pp. 145–80.

Chang Chi-yun (circa 1955) *The Rebirth of the Kuomintang, the Seventh National Congress*, trans. Nee Yuan-ching, Taipei: China Cultural Service.

Chao Yung-mao (1978a) *Taiwan difang paixi yu difang jianshe zhi guanxi* ('The Relationship between Local Factions and Local Construction in Taiwan'), Taipei: Te-hsin-shih Publishers.

—— (1978b) *Taiwan difang zhengzhi yu difang jianshe zhi zhanwang* ('A Survey of Taiwan's Local Politics and Local Construction'), Taipei: Te-hsin-shih Publishers.

—— (1989) 'Difang paixi yu xuanju guanxi-Yi ge gainian jiagou de fenxi' ('The Relationship Between Local Factions and Elections: an Attitude Structure Analysis'), *Zhongshan Shehui Kexue Jikan*, 4(3): 58–70.

Chu Yun-han (1992) *Crafting Democracy in Taiwan*, Taipei: Institute for National Policy Research.

—— (1994a) 'Social Protests and Political Democratization in Taiwan', in Murray A. Rubenstein (ed.) *The Other Taiwan*, Armonk, NY: M. E. Sharpe, pp. 99–113.

—— (1994b) 'Electoral Competition, Social Cleavages, and the Evolving Party System', paper delivered at a conference sponsored by the Gaston Sigur Center, George Washington University, and the Institute for National Policy Research, Washington, DC, 8–9 April.

Collier, Ruth Berins and Collier, David (1979) 'Inducements versus Constraints: Disaggregating "Corporatism"', *American Political Science Review*, 73: 967–86.

Gold, Thomas (1988) 'Entrepreneurs, Multinationals, and the State', in Edwin A. Winckler and Susan Greenhalgh (eds) *Contending Approaches to the Political Economy of Taiwan*, Armonk, NY: M. E. Sharpe, pp. 175–205.

Greenhalgh, Susan (1988) 'Families and Networks in Taiwan's Economic Development', in Edwin A. Winckler and Susan Greenhalgh (eds) *Contending Approaches to the Political Economy of Taiwan*, Armonk, NY: M. E. Sharpe, pp. 224–45.

Hsiao, Hsin-huang Michael (1992) 'The Labor Movement in Taiwan: a Retrospective and Prospective Look', in Denis Fred Simon and Michael Y. M. Kau (eds) *Taiwan: Beyond the Economic Miracle*, Armonk, NY: M. E. Sharpe, pp. 151–67.

Huang Teh-fu (1990a) 'Xuanju, difang paixi yu zhengzhi zhuanxing: qishiba niandi sanxiang gongzhirenyuan xuanju zhi xingsi' ('Elections, Local Factions and Political Transition: Reflections on the 1989 Elections'), *The Journal of Sunology: A Social Science Quarterly*, 5(1), 84–96.

—— (1990b) 'Local Factions, Party Competition and Political Democratization in Taiwan', *Guoli zhengzhi daxue xuebao*, 61: 723–45.

Johnson, Marshall (1992) 'Classification, Power and Markets: Waning of the Ethnic Division of Labor', in Denis Fred Simon and Michael Y. M. Kau (eds) *Taiwan: Beyond the Economic Miracle*, Armonk, NY: M. E. Sharpe, pp. 69–97.

Kuomintang Manifesto and Platform Adopted by the Seventh National Convention, October 1952 (1954) Taiwan: China Cultural Service.

Lee Chin-chuan (1994) 'Sparking a Fire: the Press and the Ferment of Democratic Change in Taiwan', paper delivered at a conference sponsored by the Gaston Sigur Center, George Washington University, and the Institute for National Policy Research, Washington, DC, 8–9 April.

Lerman, Arthur (1979) *Taiwan's Politics: the Provincial Assemblyman's World*, Washington, DC: University Press of America.

Pang Chien-Kuo (1992) 'The Changing Relationship Between the State and Society in Taiwan During the 1980s', *National Taiwan University Journal of Sociology*, 21, June: 1–34.

Rigger, Shelley (1993) 'The Risk of Reform: Factional Conflict in Taiwan's 1989 Municipal Elections', *American Journal of Chinese Studies*, October: 201–32.

—— (1994a) 'Machine Politics in the New Taiwan', unpublished dissertation.

—— (1994b) 'Trends in Taiwan: A Political Perspective' *Issues and Studies*, 30(11), November: 1–22.

Shiau Chyuan-Jenq (1994) 'Election and the Changing State–Business Relationships', paper delivered at a conference sponsored by the Gaston Sigur Center, George Washington University, and the Institute for National Policy Research, Washington, DC, 8–9 April.

Tien Hung-mao (1989) *The Great Transition: Political and Social Change in the Republic of China*, Stanford, Calif.: Hoover Institution Press.

Wang Fu-ch'ang (1990) 'Zuqun dongyuan yu Taiwan fandui yundong de zhichi zhuanyi' ('Ethnic Mobilisation and the Shifting Support of Taiwan's Opposition Movement'), *Zhongguo Luntan*, 360, September: 42–52.

Winn, Jane Kaufman and Yeh, Tang-Chi (1994) 'Relational Practices and the Marginalization of Law: Informal Financial Practices of Small Businesses in Taiwan', *Law and Society Review*, 28(2): 193–232.

Wu Nai-teh (1987) 'The Politics of a Regime Patronage System: Mobilization and Control Within an Authoritarian Regime', unpublished Ph.D. dissertation, University of Chicago.

Index

Printed in the United States
by Baker & Taylor Publisher Services